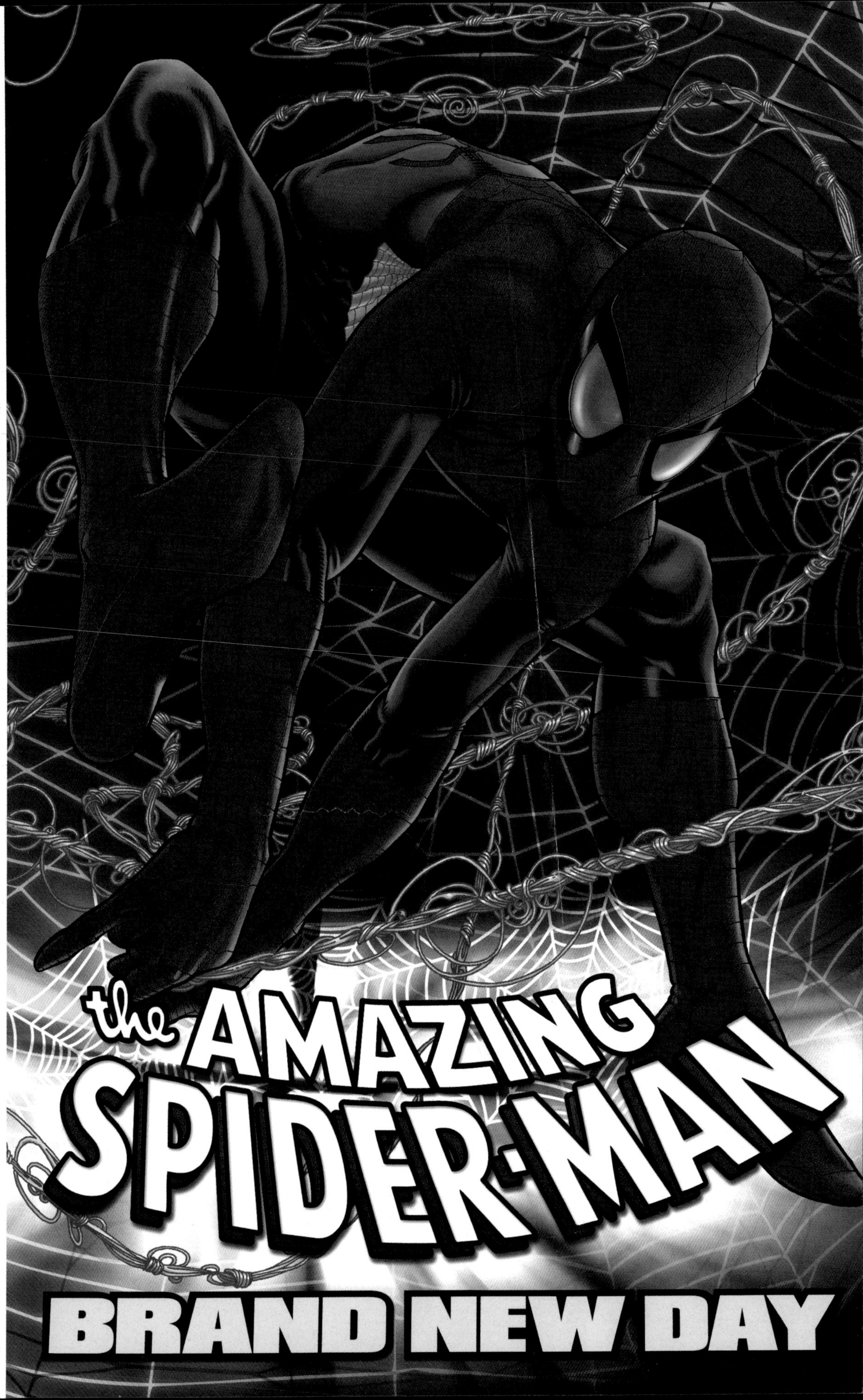
the AMAZING SPIDER-MAN
BRAND NEW DAY

the AMAZING SPIDER-MAN
BRAND NEW DAY

SPIDER-MAN: SWING SHIFT
Writer: **DAN SLOTT** · Penciler: **PHIL JIMENEZ**
Inkers: **ANDY LANNING** with **JOHN DELL** · Colorist: **JEROMY COX**

AMAZING SPIDER-MAN #546-548
Writer: **DAN SLOTT** · Penciler: **STEVE MCNIVEN**
Inker: **DEXTER VINES** · Colorists: **MORRY HOLLOWELL** & **DAVE STEWART**

"PARK AVENUE INTERLUDE"
Writer: **MARC GUGGENHEIM** · Penciler: **GREG LAND**
Inker: **JAY LEISTEN** · Colorist: **JUSTIN PONSOR**

"THE ASTONISHING AUNT MAY!"
Writer: **BOB GALE** · Artist: **PHIL WINSLADE**
Colorist: **CHRIS CHUCKRY**

"HARRY AND THE HOLLISTERS"
Writer: **ZEB WELLS** · Artist: **MIKE DEODATO**
Colorist: **RAINIER BEREDO**

AMAZING SPIDER-MAN #549-551
Writer: **MARC GUGGENHEIM** · Artist: **SALVADOR LARROCA**
Colorists: **JASON KEITH** & **STEPHANE PERU**

SPIDER-MAN: BRAND NEW DAY VOL. 1. Contains material originally published in magazine form as AMAZING SPIDER-MAN #546-551, SPIDER-MAN: SWING SHIFT and VENOM SUPER-SPECIAL. First printing 2008. Hardcover ISBN# 978-0-7851-2843-4. Softcover ISBN# 978-0-7851-2845-8. Published by MARVEL PUBLISHING, INC., a subsidiary of MARVEL ENTERTAINMENT, INC. OFFICE OF PUBLICATION: 417 5th Avenue, New York, NY 10016. Copyright © 1995 and 2008 Marvel Characters, Inc. All rights reserved. Hardcover: $24.99 per copy in the U.S. and $26.50 in Canada (GST #R127032852). Softcover: $15.99 per copy in the U.S. and $16.75 in Canada (GST #R127032852). Canadian Agreement #40668537. All characters featured in this issue and the distinctive names and likenesses thereof, and all related indicia are trademarks of Marvel Characters, Inc. No similarity between any of the names, characters, persons, and/or institutions in this magazine with those of any living or dead person or institution is intended, and any such similarity which may exist is purely coincidental. **Printed in the U.S.A.** ALAN FINE, CEO Marvel Toys & Publishing Divisions and CMO Marvel Entertainment, Inc.; DAVID GABRIEL, SVP of Publishing Sales & Circulation; DAVID BOGART, SVP of Business Affairs & Talent Management; MICHAEL PASCIULLO, VP of Merchandising & Communications; JIM O'KEEFE, VP of Operations & Logistics; DAN CARR, Executive Director of Publishing Technology; JUSTIN F. GABRIE, Director of Editorial Operations; SUSAN CRESPI, Editorial Operations Manager; OMAR OTIEKU, Production Manager; STAN LEE, Chairman Emeritus. For information regarding advertising in Marvel Comics or on Marvel.com, please contact Mitch Dane, Advertising Director, at mdane@marvel.com. For Marvel subscription inquiries, please call 800-217-9158.

10 9 8 7 6 5 4 3 2 1

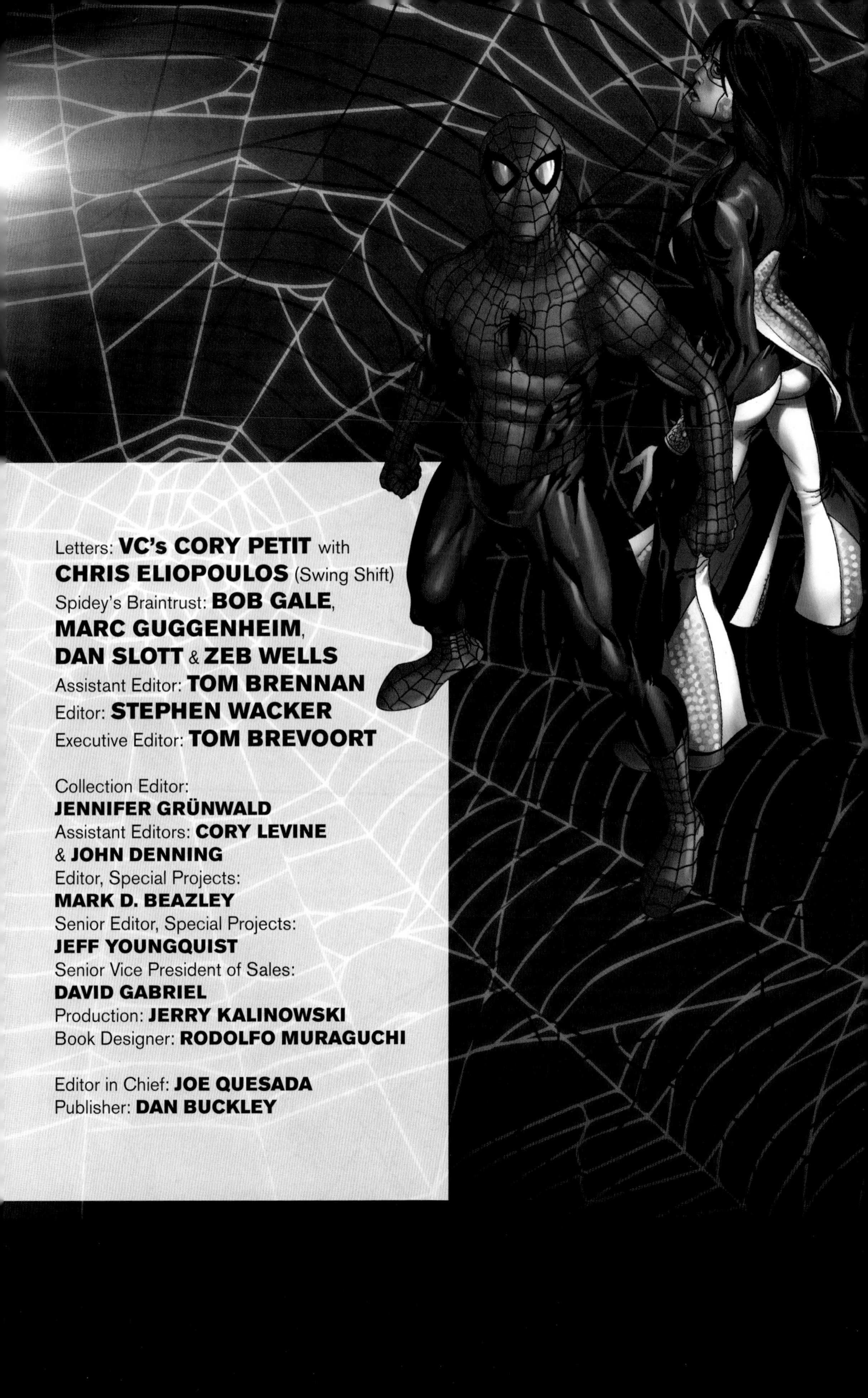

Letters: **VC's CORY PETIT** with
CHRIS ELIOPOULOS (Swing Shift)
Spidey's Braintrust: **BOB GALE**,
MARC GUGGENHEIM,
DAN SLOTT & **ZEB WELLS**
Assistant Editor: **TOM BRENNAN**
Editor: **STEPHEN WACKER**
Executive Editor: **TOM BREVOORT**

Collection Editor:
JENNIFER GRÜNWALD
Assistant Editors: **CORY LEVINE**
& **JOHN DENNING**
Editor, Special Projects:
MARK D. BEAZLEY
Senior Editor, Special Projects:
JEFF YOUNGQUIST
Senior Vice President of Sales:
DAVID GABRIEL
Production: **JERRY KALINOWSKI**
Book Designer: **RODOLFO MURAGUCHI**

Editor in Chief: **JOE QUESADA**
Publisher: **DAN BUCKLEY**

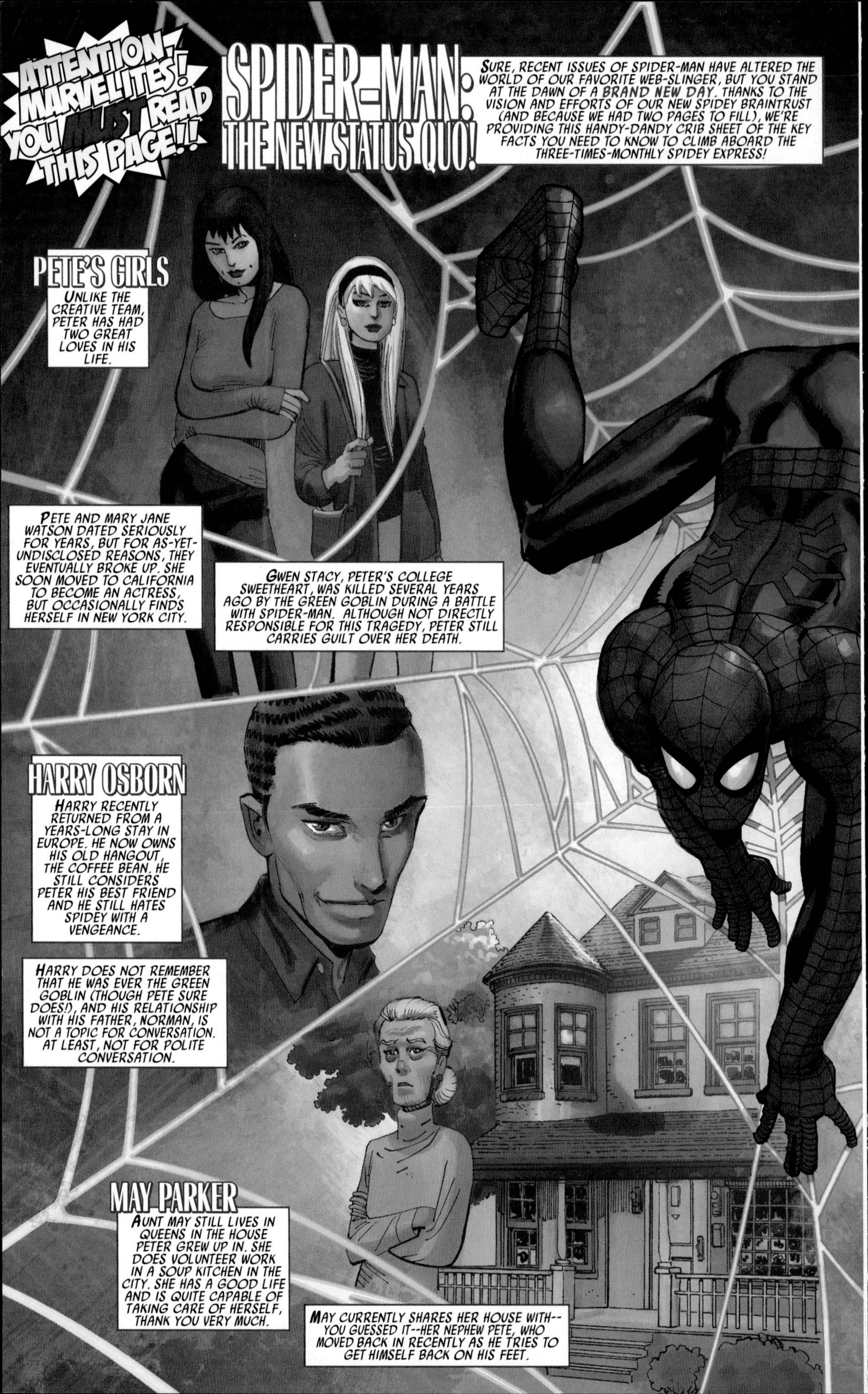
ATTENTION, MARVELITES! YOU MUST READ THIS PAGE!!
SPIDER-MAN: THE NEW STATUS QUO!
SURE, RECENT ISSUES OF SPIDER-MAN HAVE ALTERED THE WORLD OF OUR FAVORITE WEB-SLINGER, BUT YOU STAND AT THE DAWN OF A BRAND NEW DAY. THANKS TO THE VISION AND EFFORTS OF OUR NEW SPIDEY BRAINTRUST (AND BECAUSE WE HAD TWO PAGES TO FILL), WE'RE PROVIDING THIS HANDY-DANDY CRIB SHEET OF THE KEY FACTS YOU NEED TO KNOW TO CLIMB ABOARD THE THREE-TIMES-MONTHLY SPIDEY EXPRESS!
PETE'S GIRLS
UNLIKE THE CREATIVE TEAM, PETER HAS HAD TWO GREAT LOVES IN HIS LIFE.
PETE AND MARY JANE WATSON DATED SERIOUSLY FOR YEARS, BUT FOR AS-YET-UNDISCLOSED REASONS, THEY EVENTUALLY BROKE UP. SHE SOON MOVED TO CALIFORNIA TO BECOME AN ACTRESS, BUT OCCASIONALLY FINDS HERSELF IN NEW YORK CITY.
GWEN STACY, PETER'S COLLEGE SWEETHEART, WAS KILLED SEVERAL YEARS AGO BY THE GREEN GOBLIN DURING A BATTLE WITH SPIDER-MAN. ALTHOUGH NOT DIRECTLY RESPONSIBLE FOR THIS TRAGEDY, PETER STILL CARRIES GUILT OVER HER DEATH.
HARRY OSBORN
HARRY RECENTLY RETURNED FROM A YEARS-LONG STAY IN EUROPE. HE NOW OWNS HIS OLD HANGOUT, THE COFFEE BEAN. HE STILL CONSIDERS PETER HIS BEST FRIEND AND HE STILL HATES SPIDEY WITH A VENGEANCE.
HARRY DOES NOT REMEMBER THAT HE WAS EVER THE GREEN GOBLIN (THOUGH PETE SURE DOES!), AND HIS RELATIONSHIP WITH HIS FATHER, NORMAN, IS NOT A TOPIC FOR CONVERSATION. AT LEAST, NOT FOR POLITE CONVERSATION.
MAY PARKER
AUNT MAY STILL LIVES IN QUEENS IN THE HOUSE PETER GREW UP IN. SHE DOES VOLUNTEER WORK IN A SOUP KITCHEN IN THE CITY. SHE HAS A GOOD LIFE AND IS QUITE CAPABLE OF TAKING CARE OF HERSELF, THANK YOU VERY MUCH.
MAY CURRENTLY SHARES HER HOUSE WITH--YOU GUESSED IT--HER NEPHEW PETE, WHO MOVED BACK IN RECENTLY AS HE TRIES TO GET HIMSELF BACK ON HIS FEET.

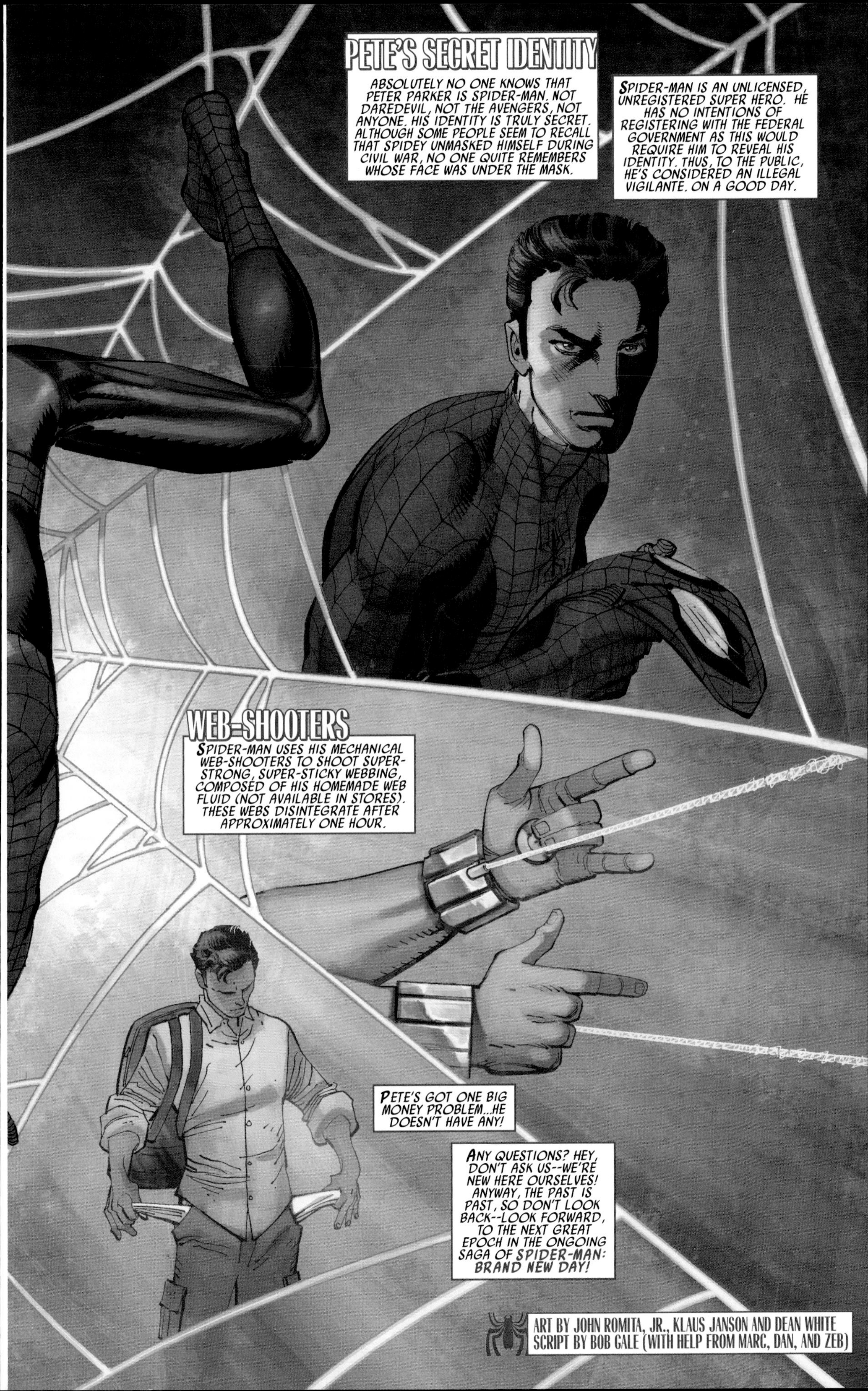
PETE'S SECRET IDENTITY
ABSOLUTELY NO ONE KNOWS THAT PETER PARKER IS SPIDER-MAN. NOT DAREDEVIL, NOT THE AVENGERS, NOT ANYONE. HIS IDENTITY IS TRULY SECRET. ALTHOUGH SOME PEOPLE SEEM TO RECALL THAT SPIDEY UNMASKED HIMSELF DURING CIVIL WAR, NO ONE QUITE REMEMBERS WHOSE FACE WAS UNDER THE MASK.
SPIDER-MAN IS AN UNLICENSED, UNREGISTERED SUPER HERO. HE HAS NO INTENTIONS OF REGISTERING WITH THE FEDERAL GOVERNMENT AS THIS WOULD REQUIRE HIM TO REVEAL HIS IDENTITY. THUS, TO THE PUBLIC, HE'S CONSIDERED AN ILLEGAL VIGILANTE. ON A GOOD DAY.
WEB-SHOOTERS
SPIDER-MAN USES HIS MECHANICAL WEB-SHOOTERS TO SHOOT SUPER-STRONG, SUPER-STICKY WEBBING, COMPOSED OF HIS HOMEMADE WEB FLUID (NOT AVAILABLE IN STORES). THESE WEBS DISINTEGRATE AFTER APPROXIMATELY ONE HOUR.
PETE'S GOT ONE BIG MONEY PROBLEM...HE DOESN'T HAVE ANY!
ANY QUESTIONS? HEY, DON'T ASK US--WE'RE NEW HERE OURSELVES! ANYWAY, THE PAST IS PAST, SO DON'T LOOK BACK--LOOK FORWARD, TO THE NEXT GREAT EPOCH IN THE ONGOING SAGA OF SPIDER-MAN: BRAND NEW DAY!
ART BY JOHN ROMITA, JR., KLAUS JANSON AND DEAN WHITE
SCRIPT BY BOB GALE (WITH HELP FROM MARC, DAN, AND ZEB)

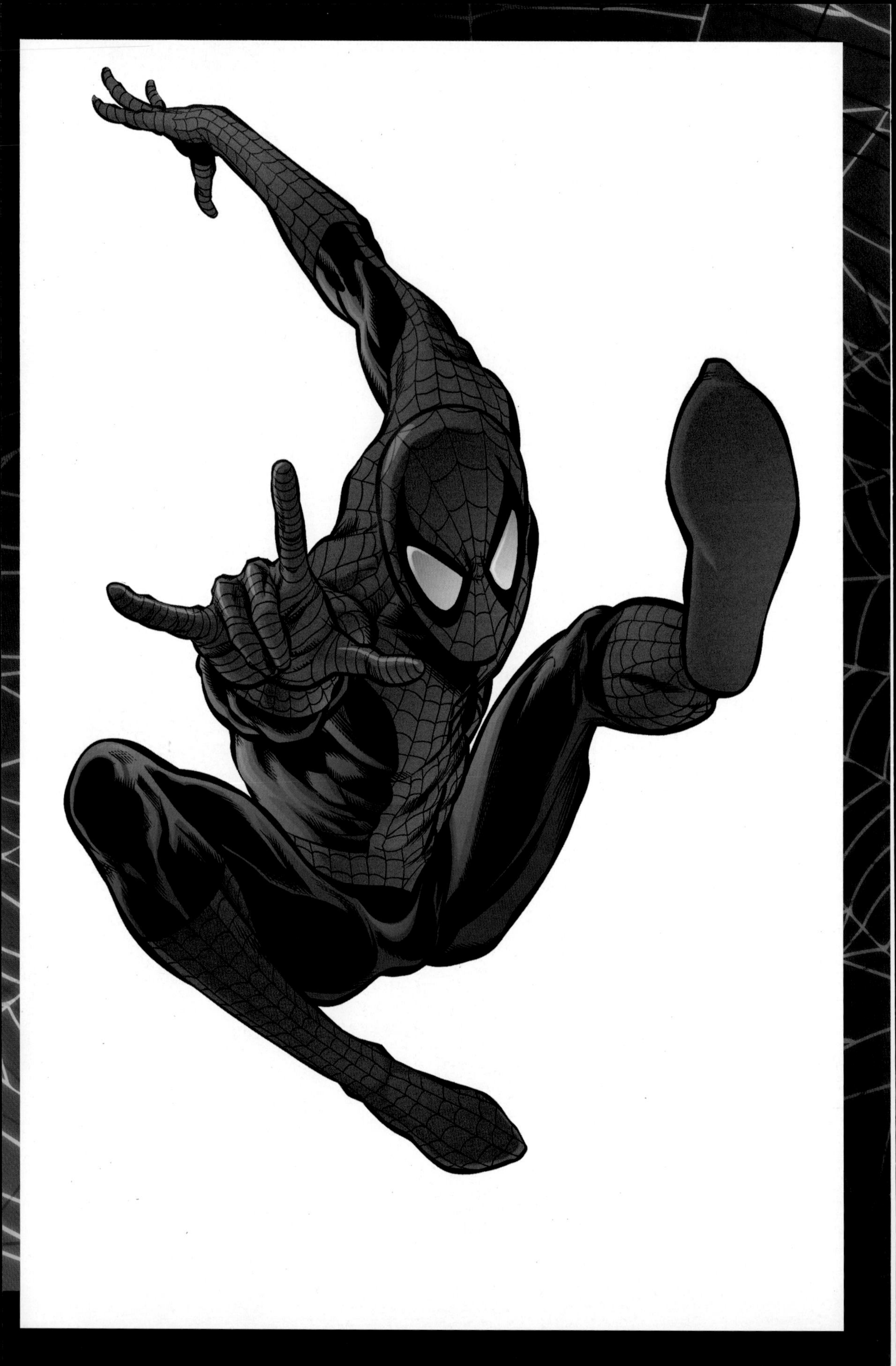

SPIDER-MAN: FREE COMIC BOOK DAY 2007

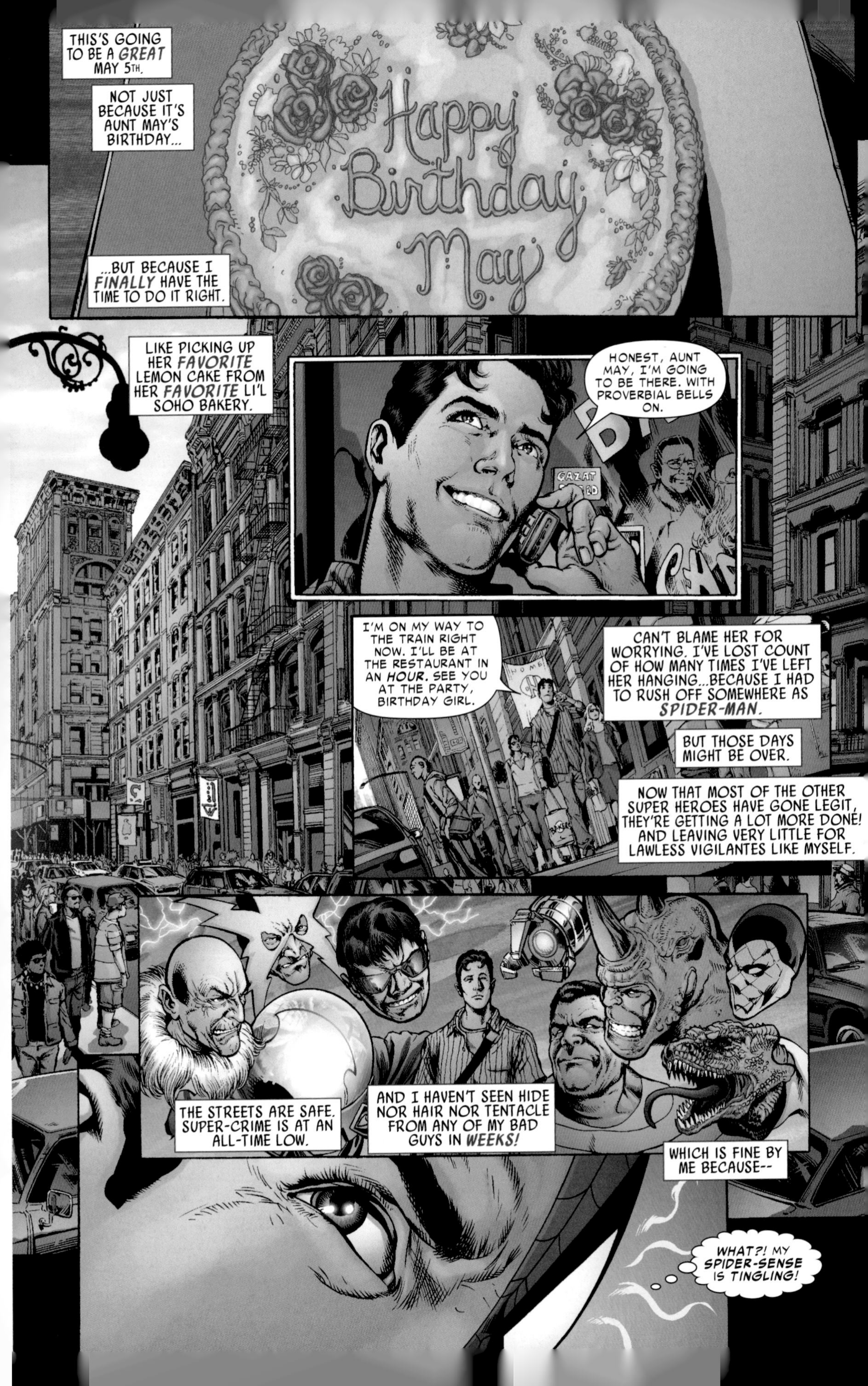
THIS'S GOING TO BE A GREAT MAY 5TH.
NOT JUST BECAUSE IT'S AUNT MAY'S BIRTHDAY...
Happy Birthday May
...BUT BECAUSE I FINALLY HAVE THE TIME TO DO IT RIGHT.
LIKE PICKING UP HER FAVORITE LEMON CAKE FROM HER FAVORITE LI'L SOHO BAKERY.
HONEST, AUNT MAY, I'M GOING TO BE THERE. WITH PROVERBIAL BELLS ON.
I'M ON MY WAY TO THE TRAIN RIGHT NOW. I'LL BE AT THE RESTAURANT IN AN HOUR. SEE YOU AT THE PARTY, BIRTHDAY GIRL.
CAN'T BLAME HER FOR WORRYING. I'VE LOST COUNT OF HOW MANY TIMES I'VE LEFT HER HANGING...BECAUSE I HAD TO RUSH OFF SOMEWHERE AS SPIDER-MAN.
BUT THOSE DAYS MIGHT BE OVER.
NOW THAT MOST OF THE OTHER SUPER HEROES HAVE GONE LEGIT, THEY'RE GETTING A LOT MORE DONE! AND LEAVING VERY LITTLE FOR LAWLESS VIGILANTES LIKE MYSELF.
THE STREETS ARE SAFE. SUPER-CRIME IS AT AN ALL-TIME LOW.
AND I HAVEN'T SEEN HIDE NOR HAIR NOR TENTACLE FROM ANY OF MY BAD GUYS IN WEEKS!
WHICH IS FINE BY ME BECAUSE--
WHAT?! MY SPIDER-SENSE IS TINGLING!

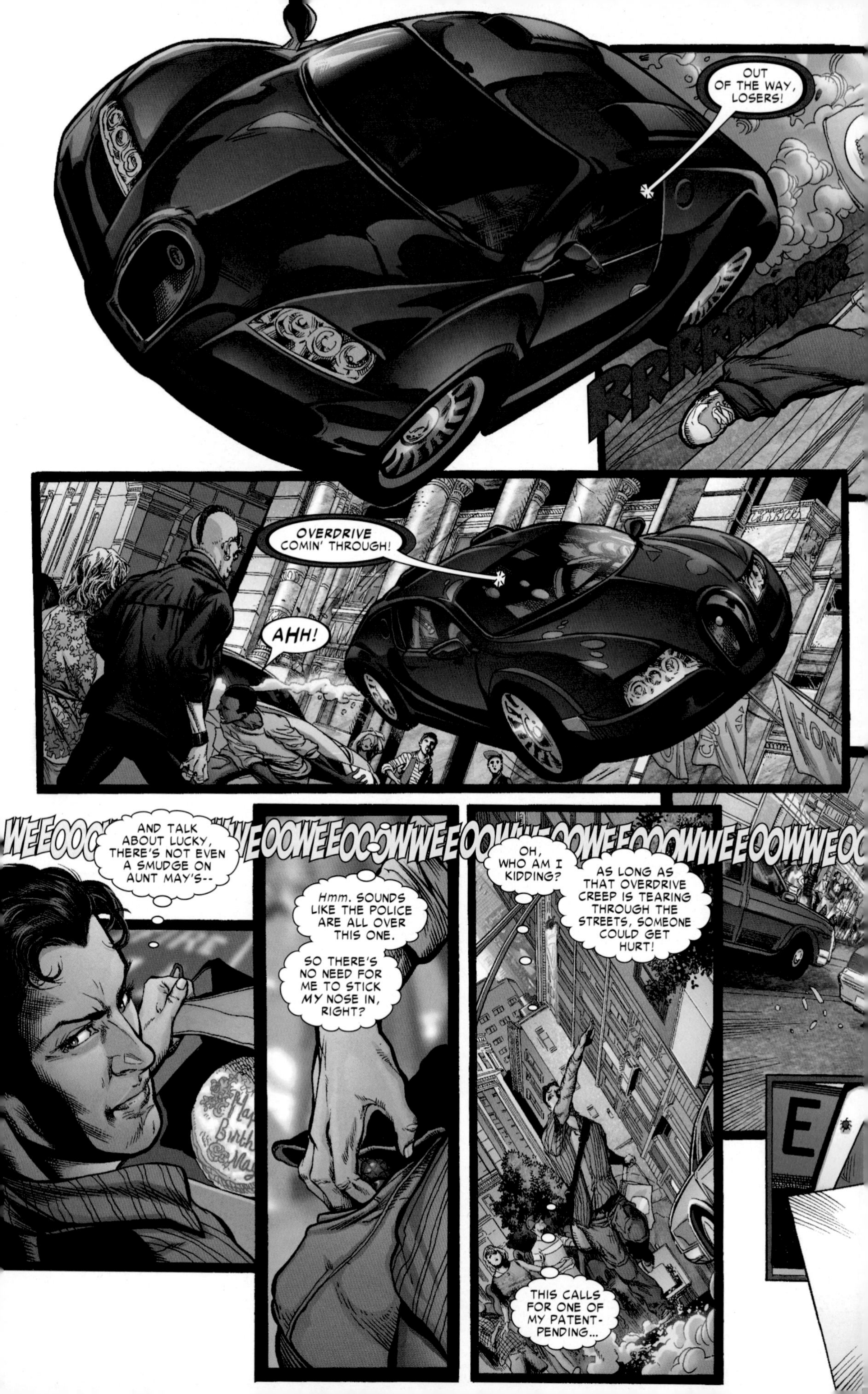
OUT OF THE WAY, LOSERS!
RRRRRRRRRRRR
OVERDRIVE COMIN' THROUGH!
AHH!
WEE OOOWEE OOWE EOOOWWE EOOWWEEOOOWE EOOOWWE EOOWWE EO
AND TALK ABOUT LUCKY, THERE'S NOT EVEN A SMUDGE ON AUNT MAY'S--
Hmm. SOUNDS LIKE THE POLICE ARE ALL OVER THIS ONE.
SO THERE'S NO NEED FOR ME TO STICK MY NOSE IN, RIGHT?
OH, WHO AM I KIDDING?
AS LONG AS THAT OVERDRIVE CREEP IS TEARING THROUGH THE STREETS, SOMEONE COULD GET HURT!
THIS CALLS FOR ONE OF MY PATENT-PENDING...

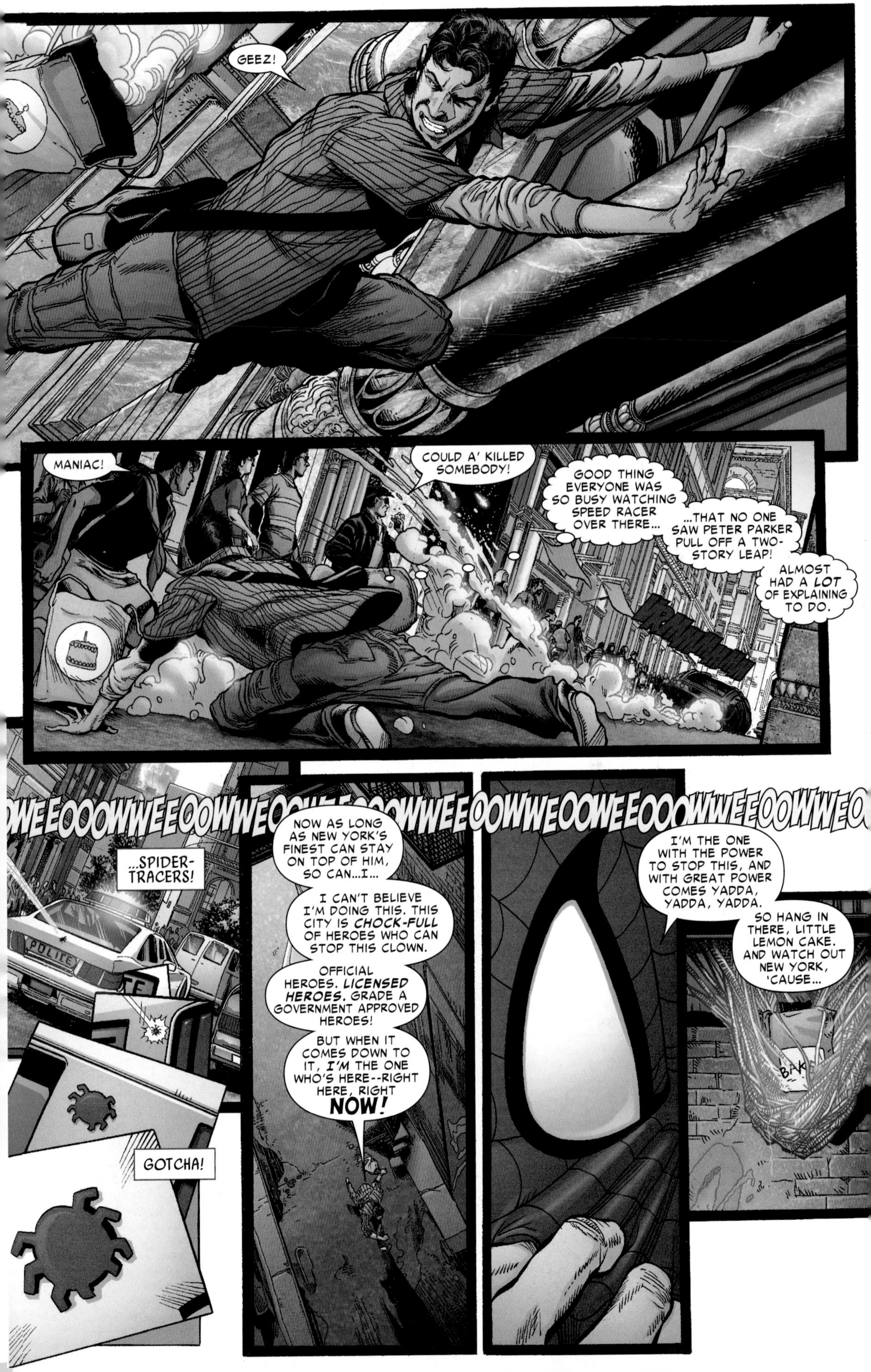
GEEZ!
MANIAC!
COULD A' KILLED SOMEBODY!
GOOD THING EVERYONE WAS SO BUSY WATCHING SPEED RACER OVER THERE...
...THAT NO ONE SAW PETER PARKER PULL OFF A TWO-STORY LEAP!
ALMOST HAD A LOT OF EXPLAINING TO DO.
...SPIDER-TRACERS!
GOTCHA!
NOW AS LONG AS NEW YORK'S FINEST CAN STAY ON TOP OF HIM, SO CAN...I...
I CAN'T BELIEVE I'M DOING THIS. THIS CITY IS CHOCK-FULL OF HEROES WHO CAN STOP THIS CLOWN.
OFFICIAL HEROES. LICENSED HEROES. GRADE A GOVERNMENT APPROVED HEROES!
BUT WHEN IT COMES DOWN TO IT, I'M THE ONE WHO'S HERE--RIGHT HERE, RIGHT NOW!
I'M THE ONE WITH THE POWER TO STOP THIS, AND WITH GREAT POWER COMES YADDA, YADDA, YADDA.
SO HANG IN THERE, LITTLE LEMON CAKE. AND WATCH OUT NEW YORK, 'CAUSE...

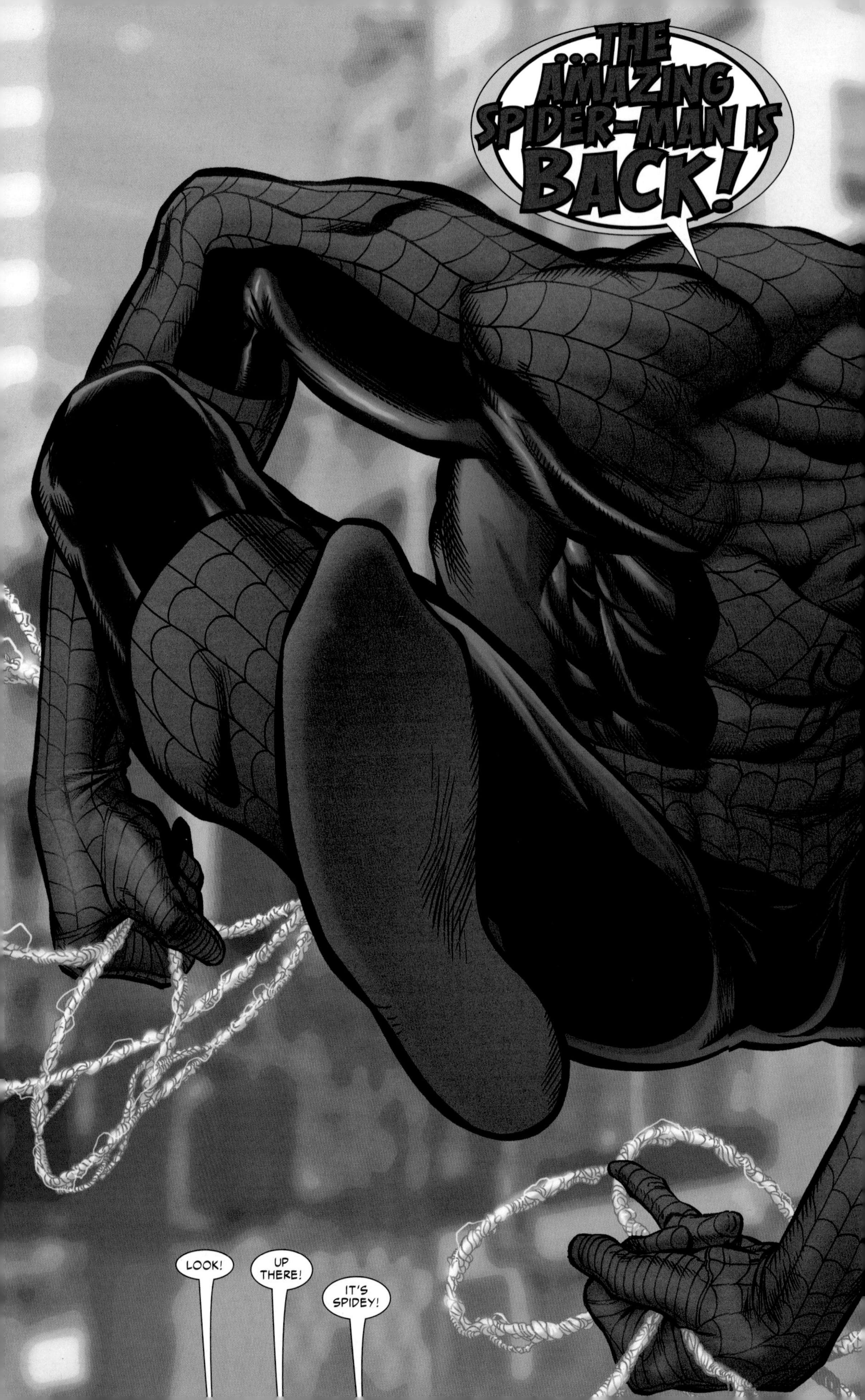
...THE AMAZING SPIDER-MAN IS BACK!
LOOK!
UP THERE!
IT'S SPIDEY!

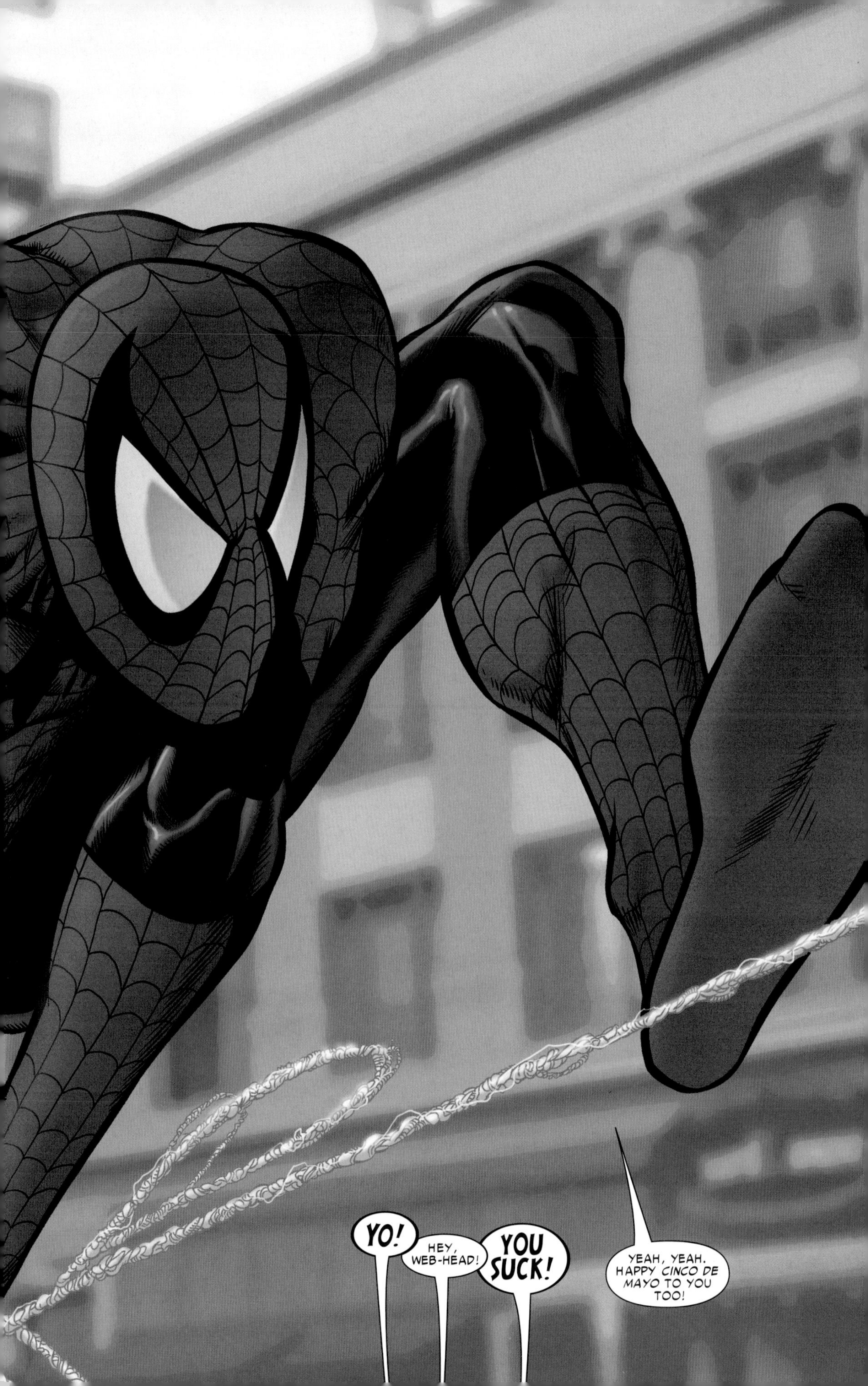
YO!
HEY, WEB-HEAD!
YOU SUCK!
YEAH, YEAH. HAPPY CINCO DE MAYO TO YOU TOO!

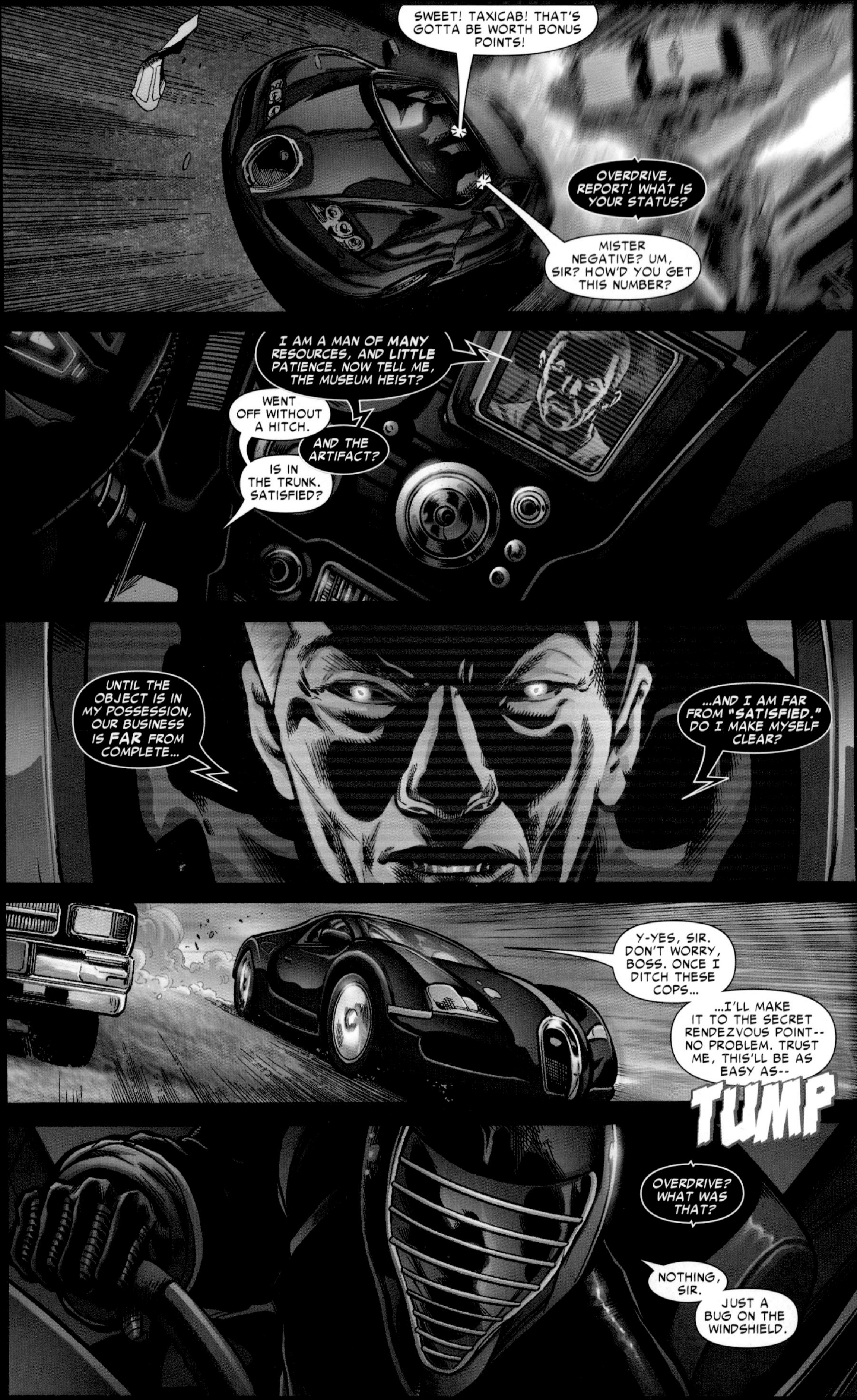
SWEET! TAXICAB! THAT'S GOTTA BE WORTH BONUS POINTS!
OVERDRIVE, REPORT! WHAT IS YOUR STATUS?
MISTER NEGATIVE? UM, SIR? HOW'D YOU GET THIS NUMBER?
I AM A MAN OF MANY RESOURCES, AND LITTLE PATIENCE. NOW TELL ME, THE MUSEUM HEIST?
WENT OFF WITHOUT A HITCH.
AND THE ARTIFACT?
IS IN THE TRUNK. SATISFIED?
UNTIL THE OBJECT IS IN MY POSSESSION, OUR BUSINESS IS FAR FROM COMPLETE...
...AND I AM FAR FROM "SATISFIED." DO I MAKE MYSELF CLEAR?
Y-YES, SIR. DON'T WORRY, BOSS. ONCE I DITCH THESE COPS...
...I'LL MAKE IT TO THE SECRET RENDEZVOUS POINT-- NO PROBLEM. TRUST ME, THIS'LL BE AS EASY AS--
TUMP
OVERDRIVE? WHAT WAS THAT?
NOTHING, SIR.
JUST A BUG ON THE WINDSHIELD.

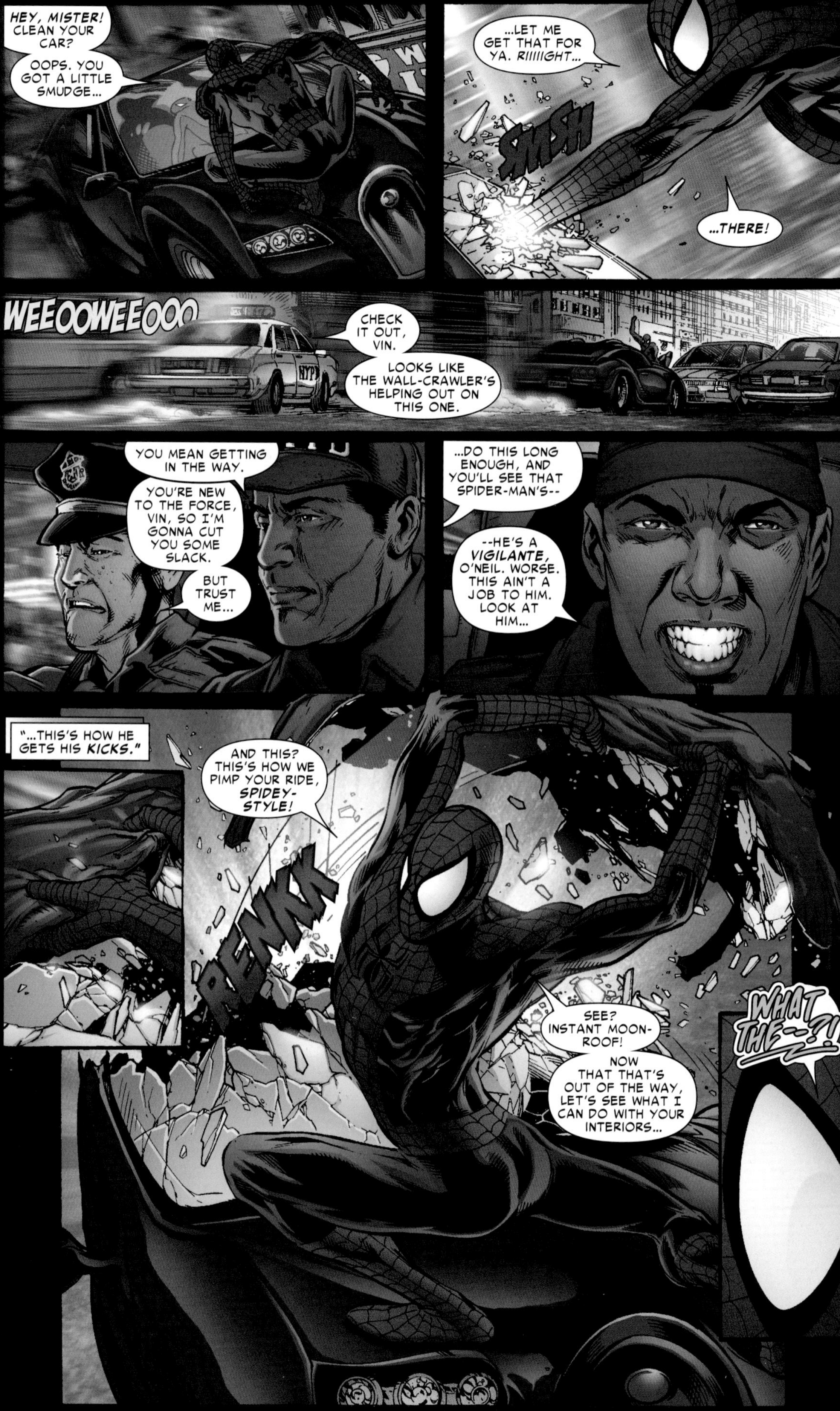
HEY, MISTER! CLEAN YOUR CAR?
OOPS. YOU GOT A LITTLE SMUDGE...
...LET ME GET THAT FOR YA. RIIIIIGHT...
SMSH
...THERE!
WEEOOWEEOOO
CHECK IT OUT, VIN.
LOOKS LIKE THE WALL-CRAWLER'S HELPING OUT ON THIS ONE.
YOU MEAN GETTING IN THE WAY.
YOU'RE NEW TO THE FORCE, VIN, SO I'M GONNA CUT YOU SOME SLACK.
BUT TRUST ME...
...DO THIS LONG ENOUGH, AND YOU'LL SEE THAT SPIDER-MAN'S--
--HE'S A VIGILANTE, O'NEIL. WORSE. THIS AIN'T A JOB TO HIM. LOOK AT HIM...
"...THIS'S HOW HE GETS HIS KICKS."
AND THIS? THIS'S HOW WE PIMP YOUR RIDE, SPIDEY-STYLE!
RENKK
SEE? INSTANT MOON-ROOF!
NOW THAT THAT'S OUT OF THE WAY, LET'S SEE WHAT I CAN DO WITH YOUR INTERIORS...
WHAT THE--?!

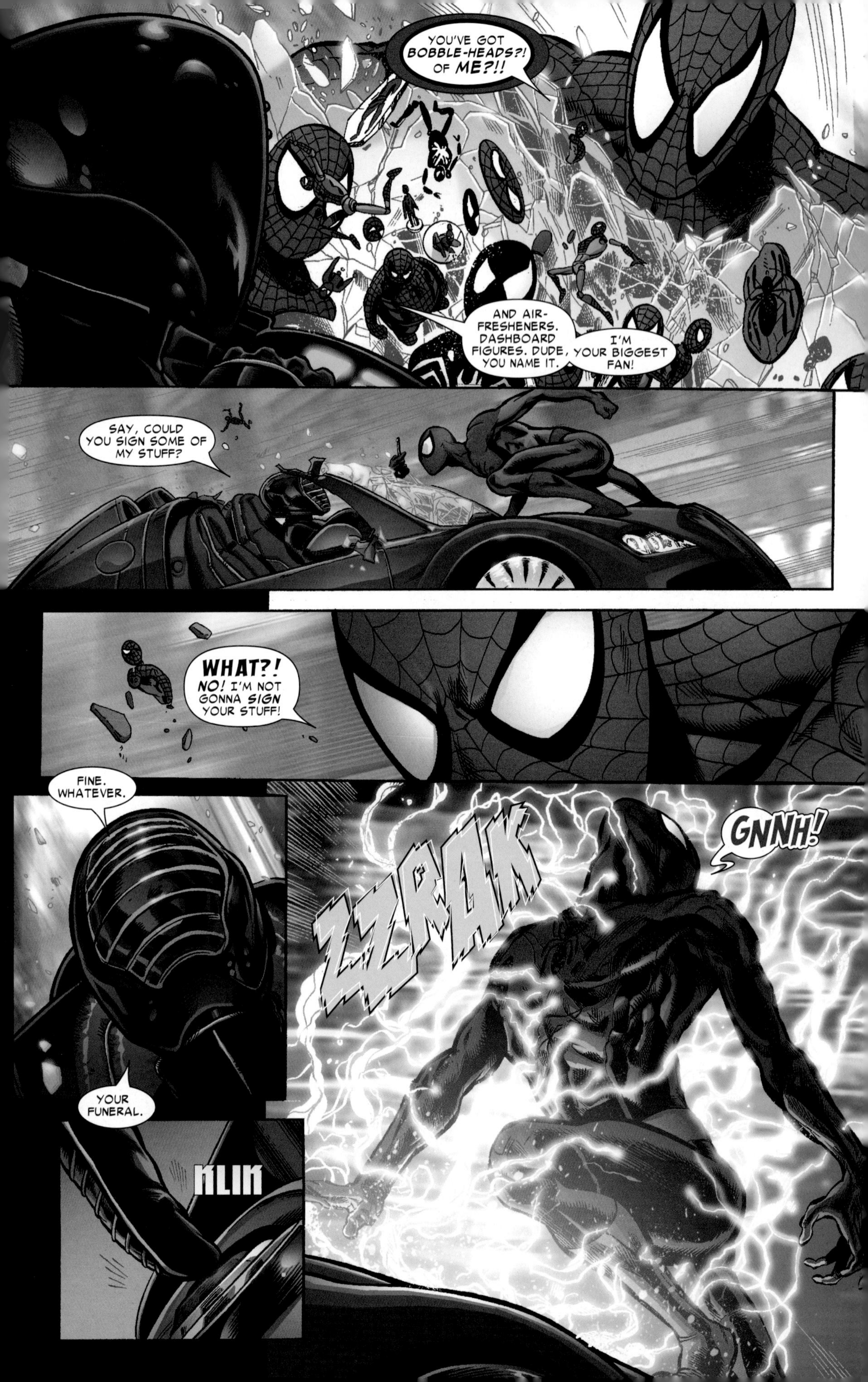
YOU'VE GOT BOBBLE-HEADS?! OF ME?!!
AND AIR-FRESHENERS. DASHBOARD FIGURES. DUDE, YOU NAME IT.
I'M YOUR BIGGEST FAN!
SAY, COULD YOU SIGN SOME OF MY STUFF?
WHAT?! NO! I'M NOT GONNA SIGN YOUR STUFF!
FINE. WHATEVER.
YOUR FUNERAL.
KLIK
ZZRAK
GNNH!

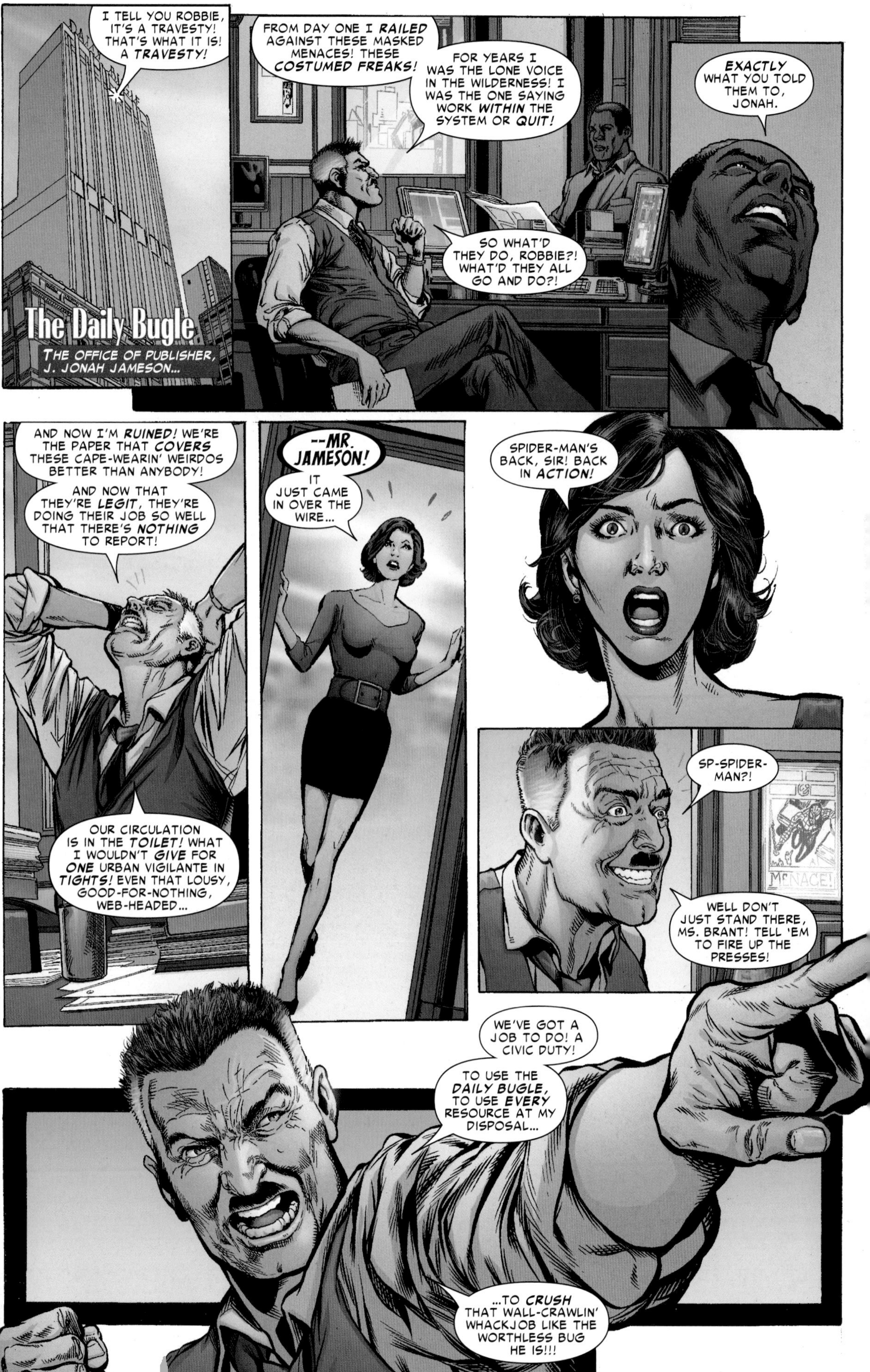
I TELL YOU ROBBIE, IT'S A TRAVESTY! THAT'S WHAT IT IS! A TRAVESTY!
The Daily Bugle
THE OFFICE OF PUBLISHER, J. JONAH JAMESON...
FROM DAY ONE I RAILED AGAINST THESE MASKED MENACES! THESE COSTUMED FREAKS!
FOR YEARS I WAS THE LONE VOICE IN THE WILDERNESS! I WAS THE ONE SAYING WORK WITHIN THE SYSTEM OR QUIT!
SO WHAT'D THEY DO, ROBBIE?! WHAT'D THEY ALL GO AND DO?!
EXACTLY WHAT YOU TOLD THEM TO, JONAH.
AND NOW I'M RUINED! WE'RE THE PAPER THAT COVERS THESE CAPE-WEARIN' WEIRDOS BETTER THAN ANYBODY!
AND NOW THAT THEY'RE LEGIT, THEY'RE DOING THEIR JOB SO WELL THAT THERE'S NOTHING TO REPORT!
OUR CIRCULATION IS IN THE TOILET! WHAT I WOULDN'T GIVE FOR ONE URBAN VIGILANTE IN TIGHTS! EVEN THAT LOUSY, GOOD-FOR-NOTHING, WEB-HEADED...
--MR. JAMESON!
IT JUST CAME IN OVER THE WIRE...
SPIDER-MAN'S BACK, SIR! BACK IN ACTION!
SP-SPIDER-MAN?!
MENACE!
WELL DON'T JUST STAND THERE, MS. BRANT! TELL 'EM TO FIRE UP THE PRESSES!
WE'VE GOT A JOB TO DO! A CIVIC DUTY!
TO USE THE DAILY BUGLE, TO USE EVERY RESOURCE AT MY DISPOSAL...
...TO CRUSH THAT WALL-CRAWLIN' WHACKJOB LIKE THE WORTHLESS BUG HE IS!!!

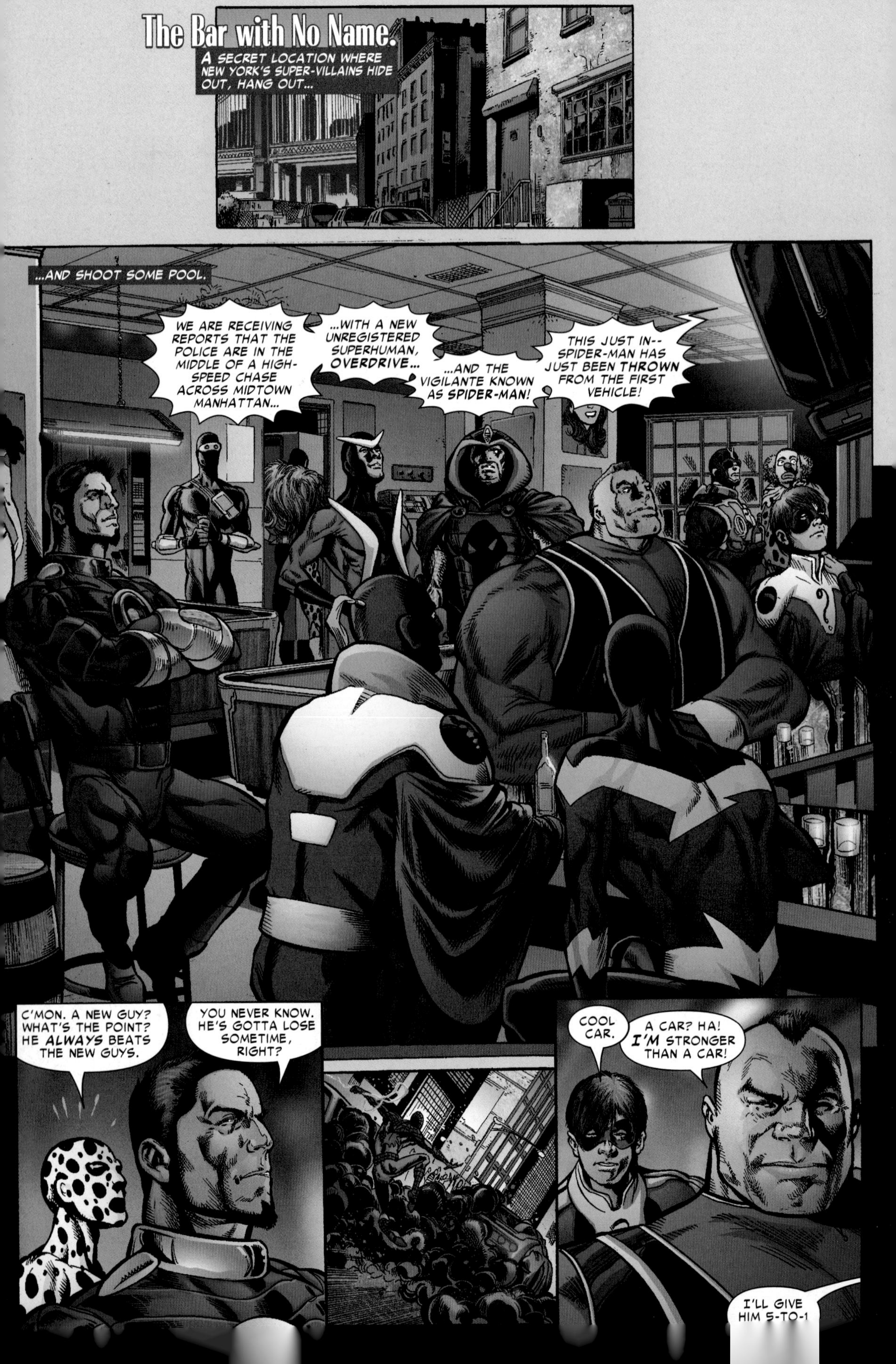
The Bar with No Name.
A SECRET LOCATION WHERE NEW YORK'S SUPER-VILLAINS HIDE OUT, HANG OUT...
...AND SHOOT SOME POOL.
WE ARE RECEIVING REPORTS THAT THE POLICE ARE IN THE MIDDLE OF A HIGH-SPEED CHASE ACROSS MIDTOWN MANHATTAN...
...WITH A NEW UNREGISTERED SUPERHUMAN, OVERDRIVE...
...AND THE VIGILANTE KNOWN AS SPIDER-MAN!
THIS JUST IN-- SPIDER-MAN HAS JUST BEEN THROWN FROM THE FIRST VEHICLE!
C'MON. A NEW GUY? WHAT'S THE POINT? HE ALWAYS BEATS THE NEW GUYS.
YOU NEVER KNOW. HE'S GOTTA LOSE SOMETIME, RIGHT?
COOL CAR.
A CAR? HA! I'M STRONGER THAN A CAR!
I'LL GIVE HIM 5-TO-1

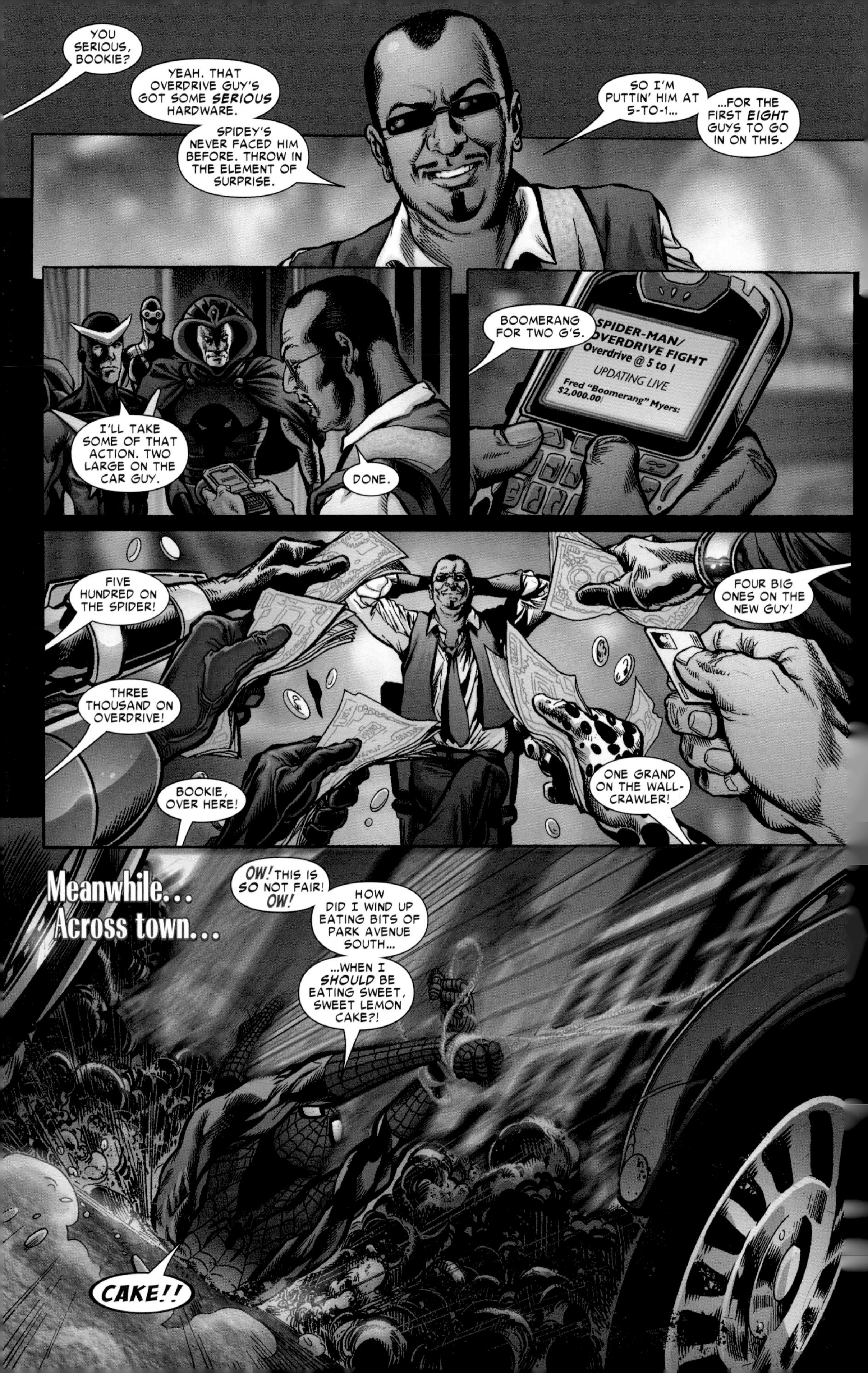
YOU SERIOUS, BOOKIE?
YEAH. THAT OVERDRIVE GUY'S GOT SOME SERIOUS HARDWARE.
SPIDEY'S NEVER FACED HIM BEFORE. THROW IN THE ELEMENT OF SURPRISE.
SO I'M PUTTIN' HIM AT 5-TO-1...
...FOR THE FIRST EIGHT GUYS TO GO IN ON THIS.
I'LL TAKE SOME OF THAT ACTION. TWO LARGE ON THE CAR GUY.
DONE.
BOOMERANG FOR TWO G'S.
SPIDER-MAN/ OVERDRIVE FIGHT
Overdrive @ 5 to 1
UPDATING LIVE
Fred "Boomerang" Myers: $2,000.00
FIVE HUNDRED ON THE SPIDER!
FOUR BIG ONES ON THE NEW GUY!
THREE THOUSAND ON OVERDRIVE!
BOOKIE, OVER HERE!
ONE GRAND ON THE WALL-CRAWLER!
Meanwhile... Across town...
OW! THIS IS SO NOT FAIR! OW!
HOW DID I WIND UP EATING BITS OF PARK AVENUE SOUTH...
...WHEN I SHOULD BE EATING SWEET, SWEET LEMON CAKE?!
CAKE!!

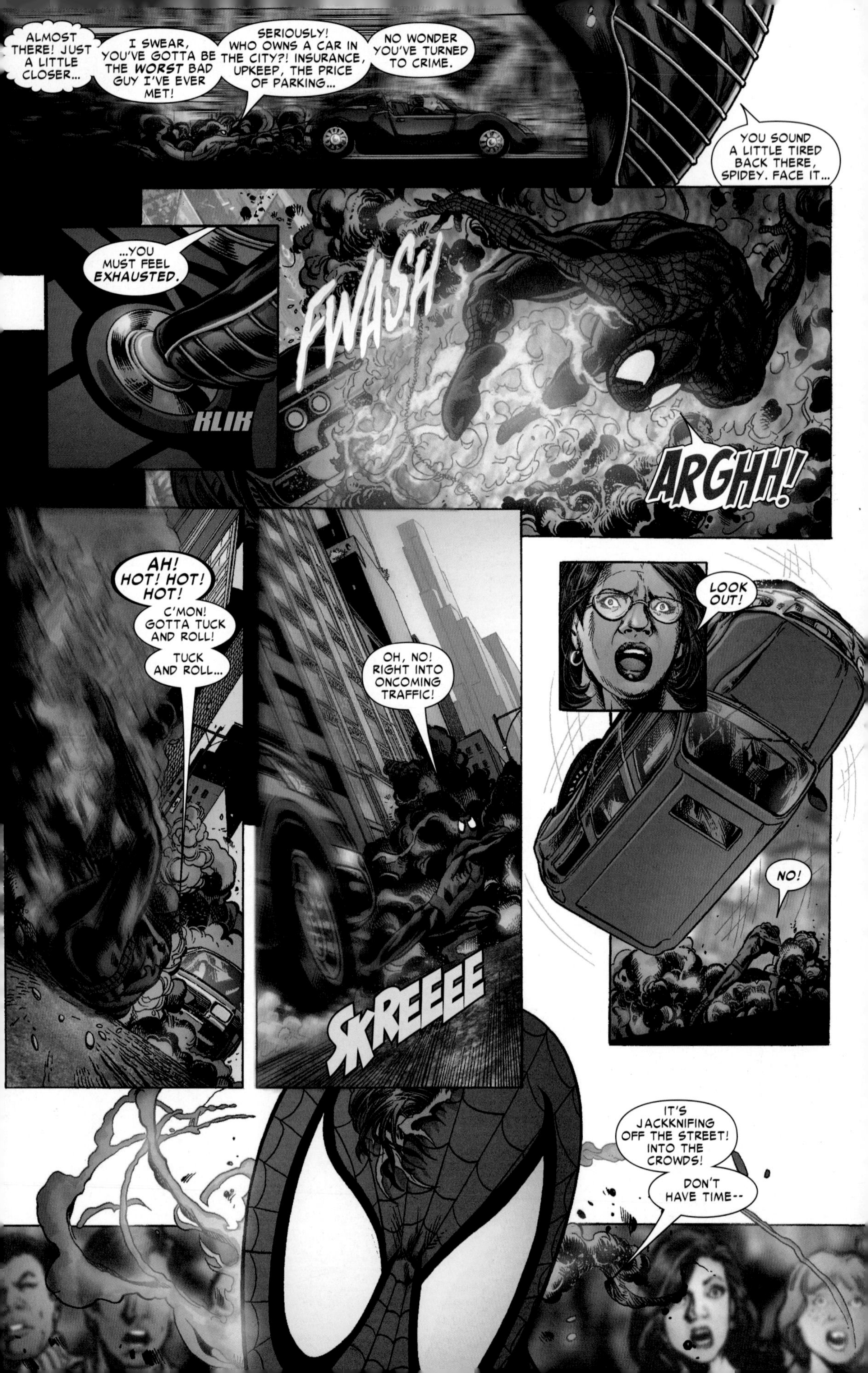
ALMOST THERE! JUST A LITTLE CLOSER...
I SWEAR, YOU'VE GOTTA BE THE WORST BAD GUY I'VE EVER MET!
SERIOUSLY! WHO OWNS A CAR IN THE CITY?! INSURANCE, UPKEEP, THE PRICE OF PARKING...
NO WONDER YOU'VE TURNED TO CRIME.
YOU SOUND A LITTLE TIRED BACK THERE, SPIDEY. FACE IT...
...YOU MUST FEEL EXHAUSTED.
KLIK
FWASH
ARGHH!
AH! HOT! HOT! HOT!
C'MON! GOTTA TUCK AND ROLL!
TUCK AND ROLL...
OH, NO! RIGHT INTO ONCOMING TRAFFIC!
SKREEEE
LOOK OUT!
NO!
IT'S JACKKNIFING OFF THE STREET! INTO THE CROWDS!
DON'T HAVE TIME--

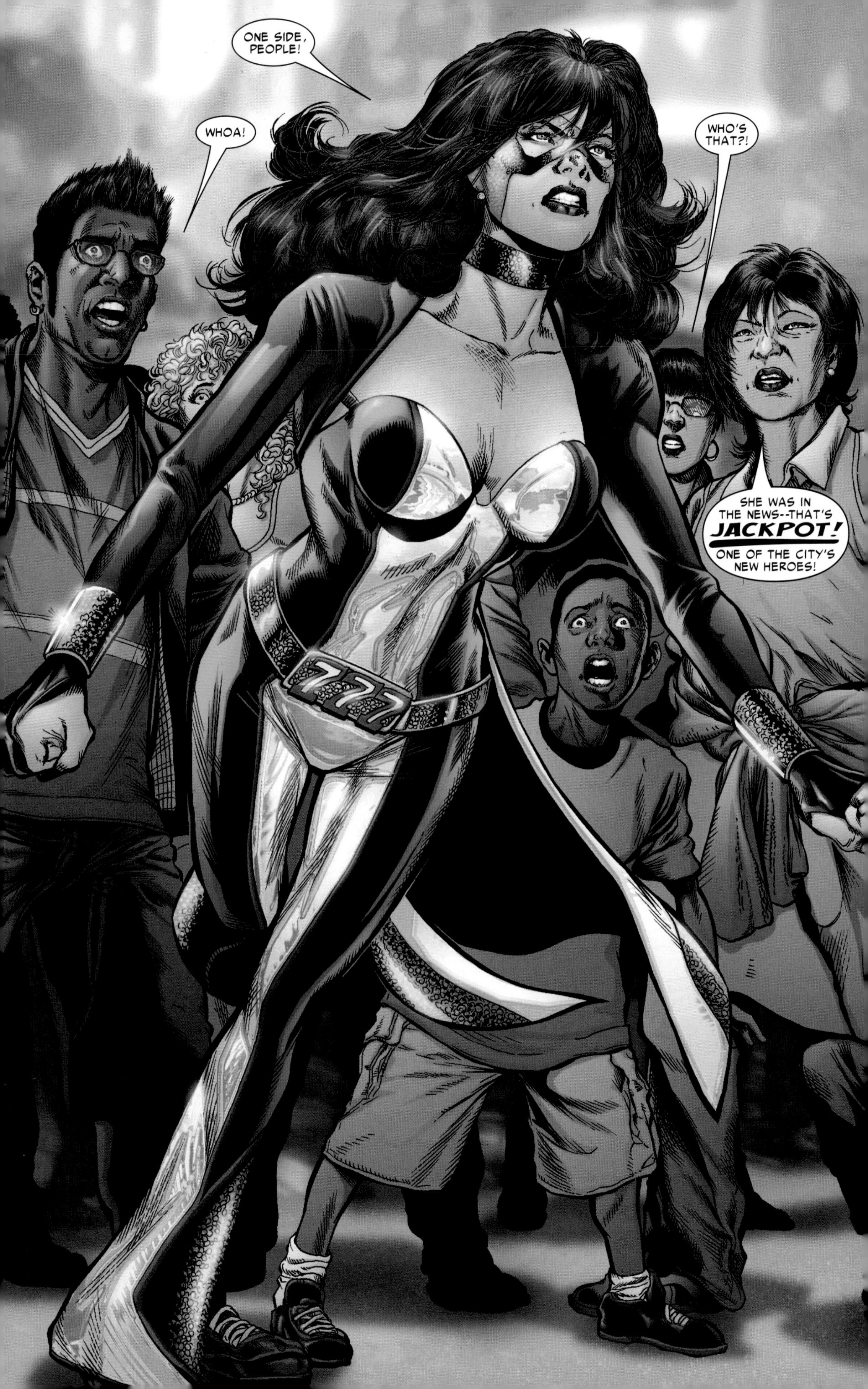
ONE SIDE, PEOPLE!
WHOA!
WHO'S THAT?!
SHE WAS IN THE NEWS--THAT'S JACKPOT! ONE OF THE CITY'S NEW HEROES!

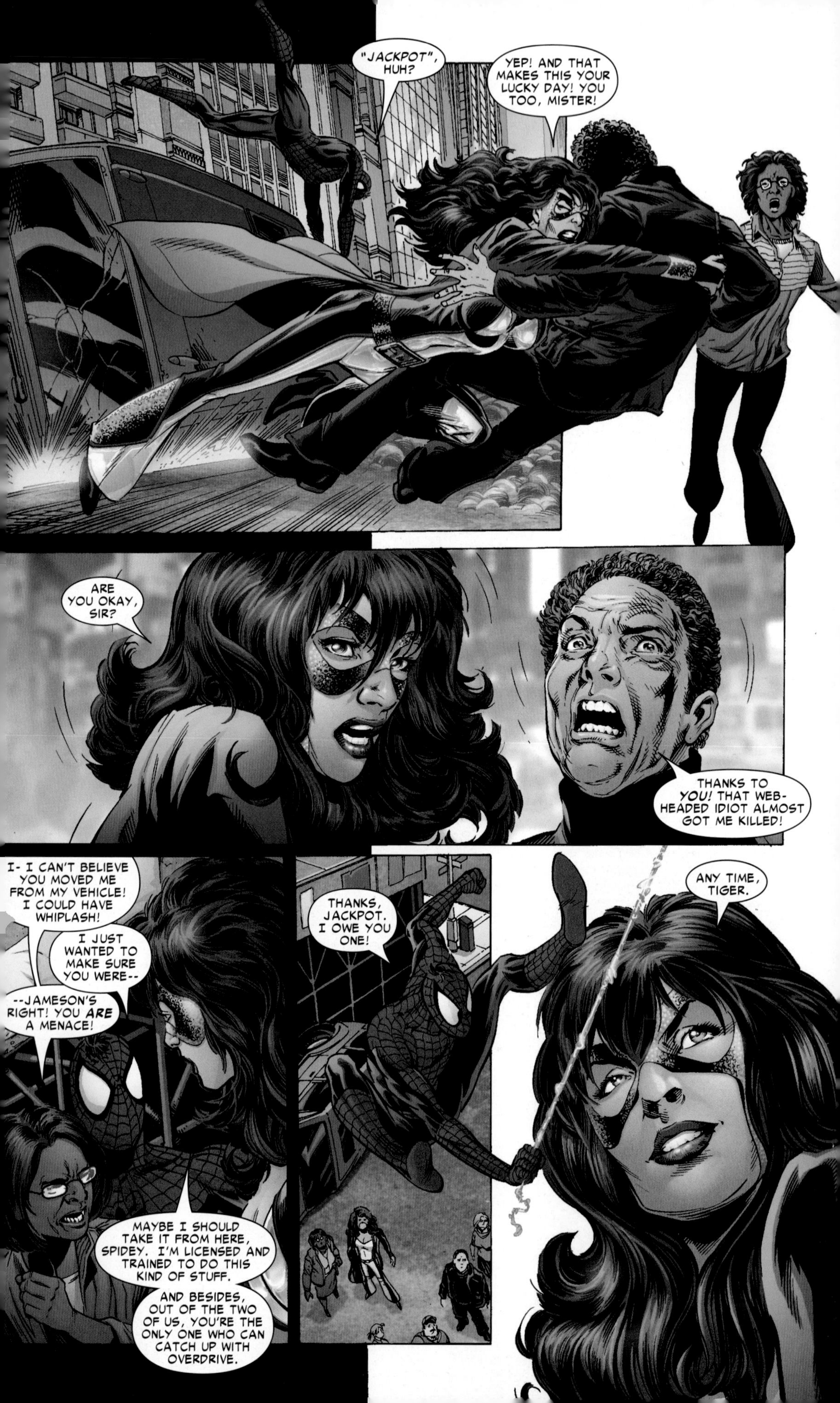
"JACKPOT", HUH?
YEP! AND THAT MAKES THIS YOUR LUCKY DAY! YOU TOO, MISTER!
ARE YOU OKAY, SIR?
THANKS TO *YOU!* THAT WEB-HEADED IDIOT ALMOST GOT ME KILLED!
I- I CAN'T BELIEVE YOU MOVED ME FROM MY VEHICLE! I COULD HAVE WHIPLASH!
I JUST WANTED TO MAKE SURE YOU WERE--
--JAMESON'S RIGHT! YOU *ARE* A MENACE!
MAYBE I SHOULD TAKE IT FROM HERE, SPIDEY. I'M LICENSED AND TRAINED TO DO THIS KIND OF STUFF.
AND BESIDES, OUT OF THE TWO OF US, YOU'RE THE ONLY ONE WHO CAN CATCH UP WITH OVERDRIVE.
THANKS, JACKPOT. I OWE YOU ONE!
ANY TIME, TIGER.

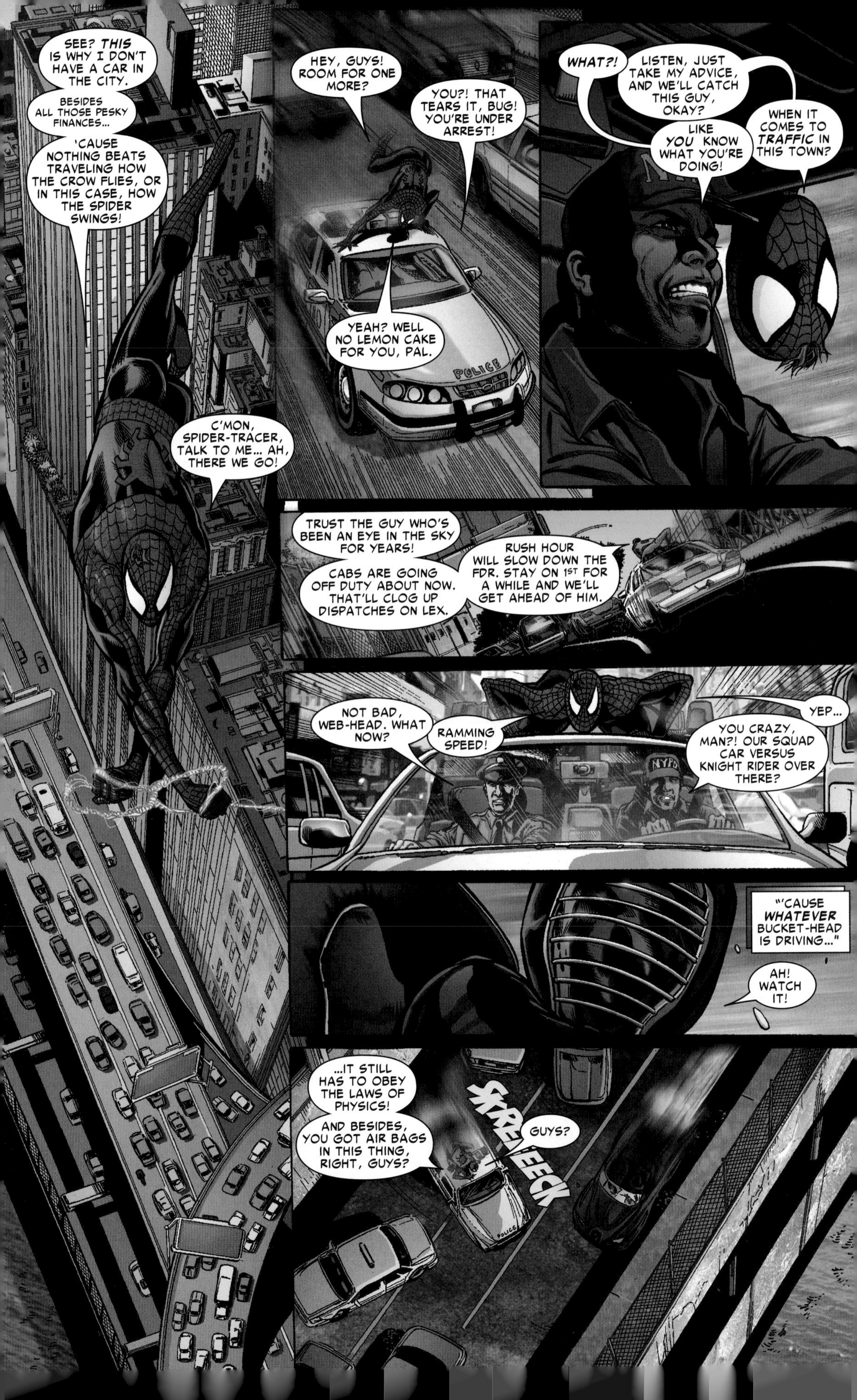

SEE? THIS IS WHY I DON'T HAVE A CAR IN THE CITY.
BESIDES ALL THOSE PESKY FINANCES...
'CAUSE NOTHING BEATS TRAVELING HOW THE CROW FLIES, OR IN THIS CASE, HOW THE SPIDER SWINGS!
C'MON, SPIDER-TRACER, TALK TO ME... AH, THERE WE GO!
HEY, GUYS! ROOM FOR ONE MORE?
YOU?! THAT TEARS IT, BUG! YOU'RE UNDER ARREST!
YEAH? WELL NO LEMON CAKE FOR YOU, PAL.
POLICE
WHAT?!
LISTEN, JUST TAKE MY ADVICE, AND WE'LL CATCH THIS GUY, OKAY?
LIKE YOU KNOW WHAT YOU'RE DOING!
WHEN IT COMES TO TRAFFIC IN THIS TOWN?
TRUST THE GUY WHO'S BEEN AN EYE IN THE SKY FOR YEARS!
CABS ARE GOING OFF DUTY ABOUT NOW. THAT'LL CLOG UP DISPATCHES ON LEX.
RUSH HOUR WILL SLOW DOWN THE FDR. STAY ON 1ST FOR A WHILE AND WE'LL GET AHEAD OF HIM.
NOT BAD, WEB-HEAD. WHAT NOW?
RAMMING SPEED!
YEP...
YOU CRAZY, MAN?! OUR SQUAD CAR VERSUS KNIGHT RIDER OVER THERE?
"'CAUSE WHATEVER BUCKET-HEAD IS DRIVING..."
AH! WATCH IT!
...IT STILL HAS TO OBEY THE LAWS OF PHYSICS!
AND BESIDES, YOU GOT AIR BAGS IN THIS THING, RIGHT, GUYS?
SKREEEEECK
GUYS?

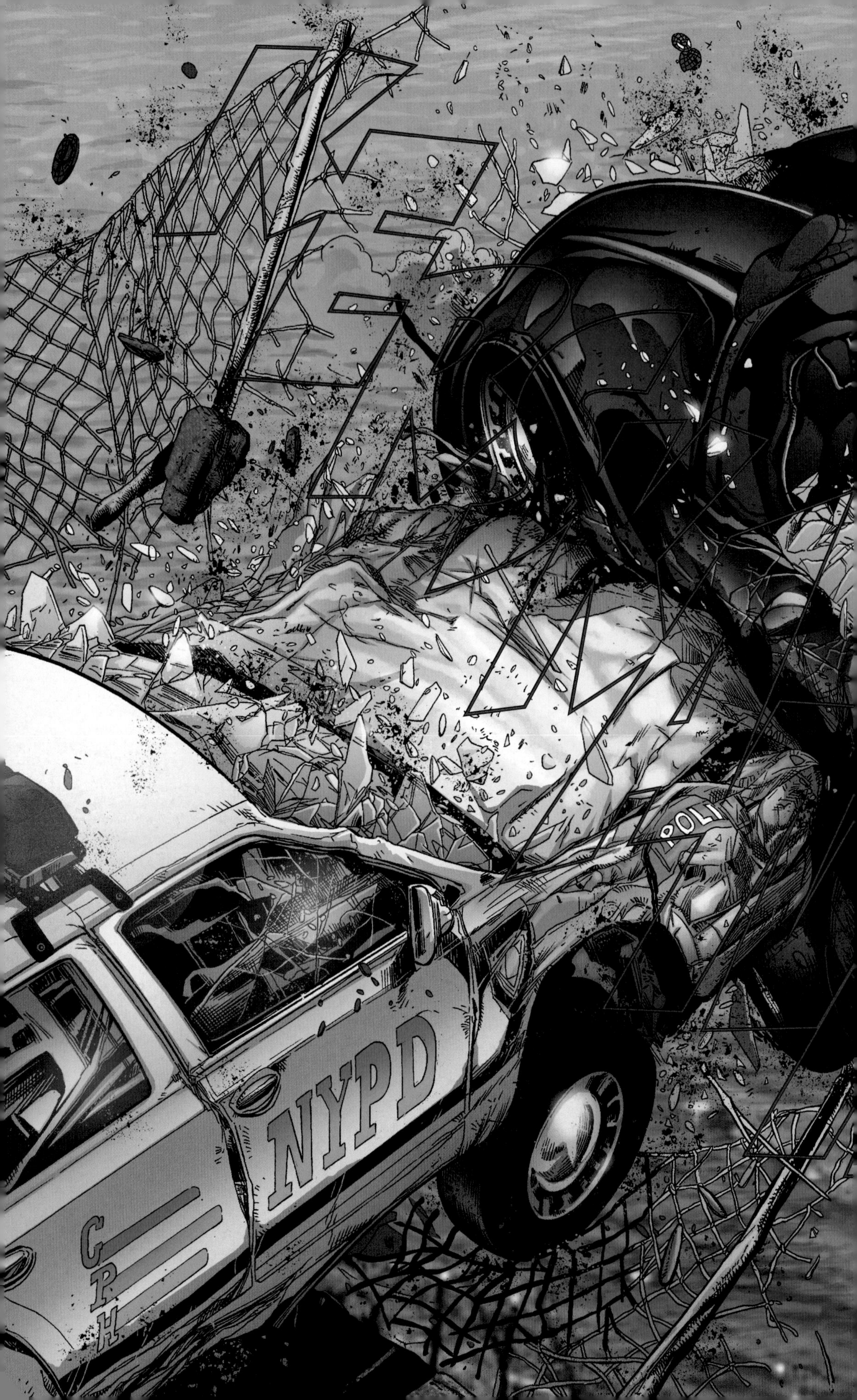
POLI
NYPD
CPH

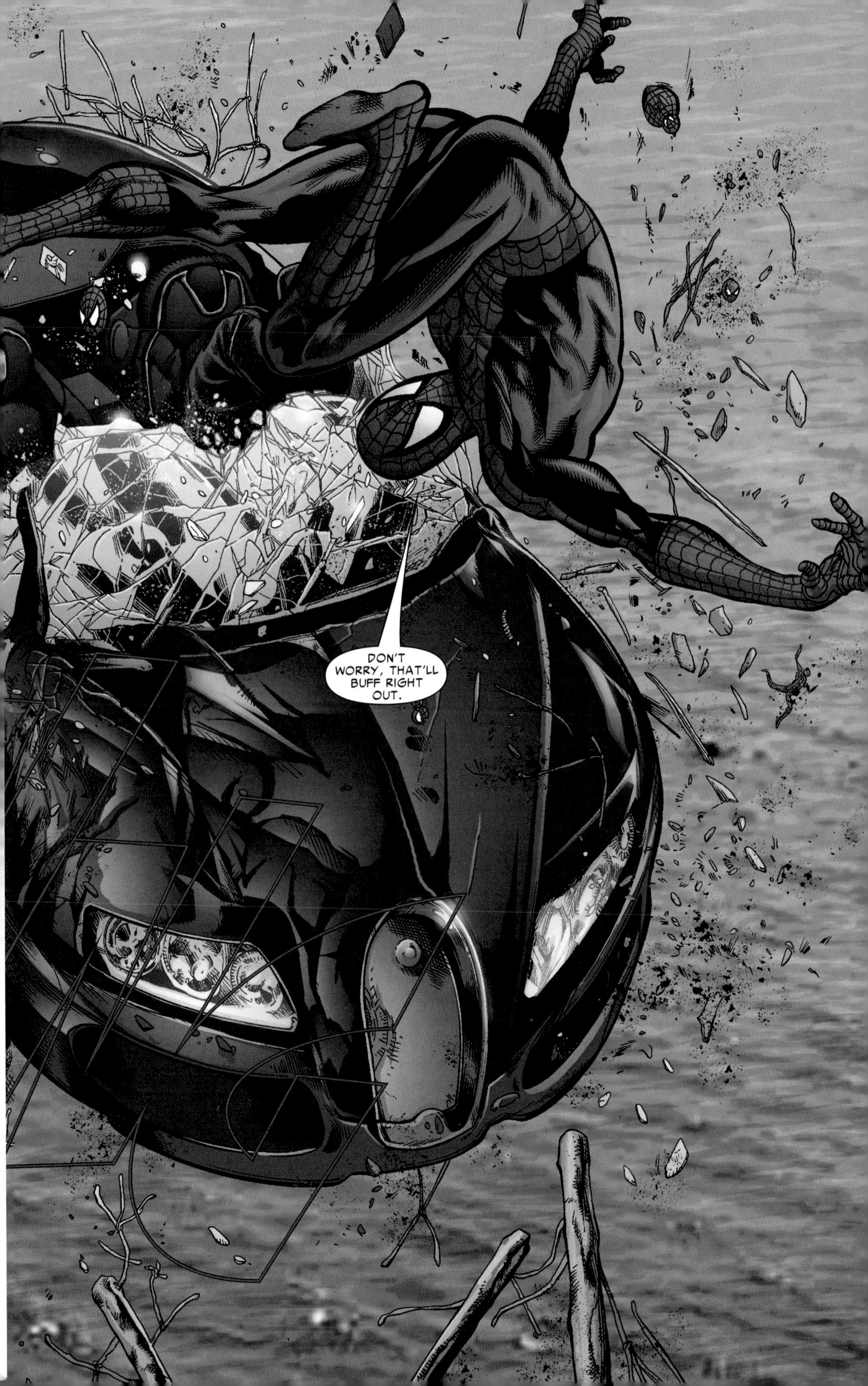
DON'T WORRY, THAT'LL BUFF RIGHT OUT.

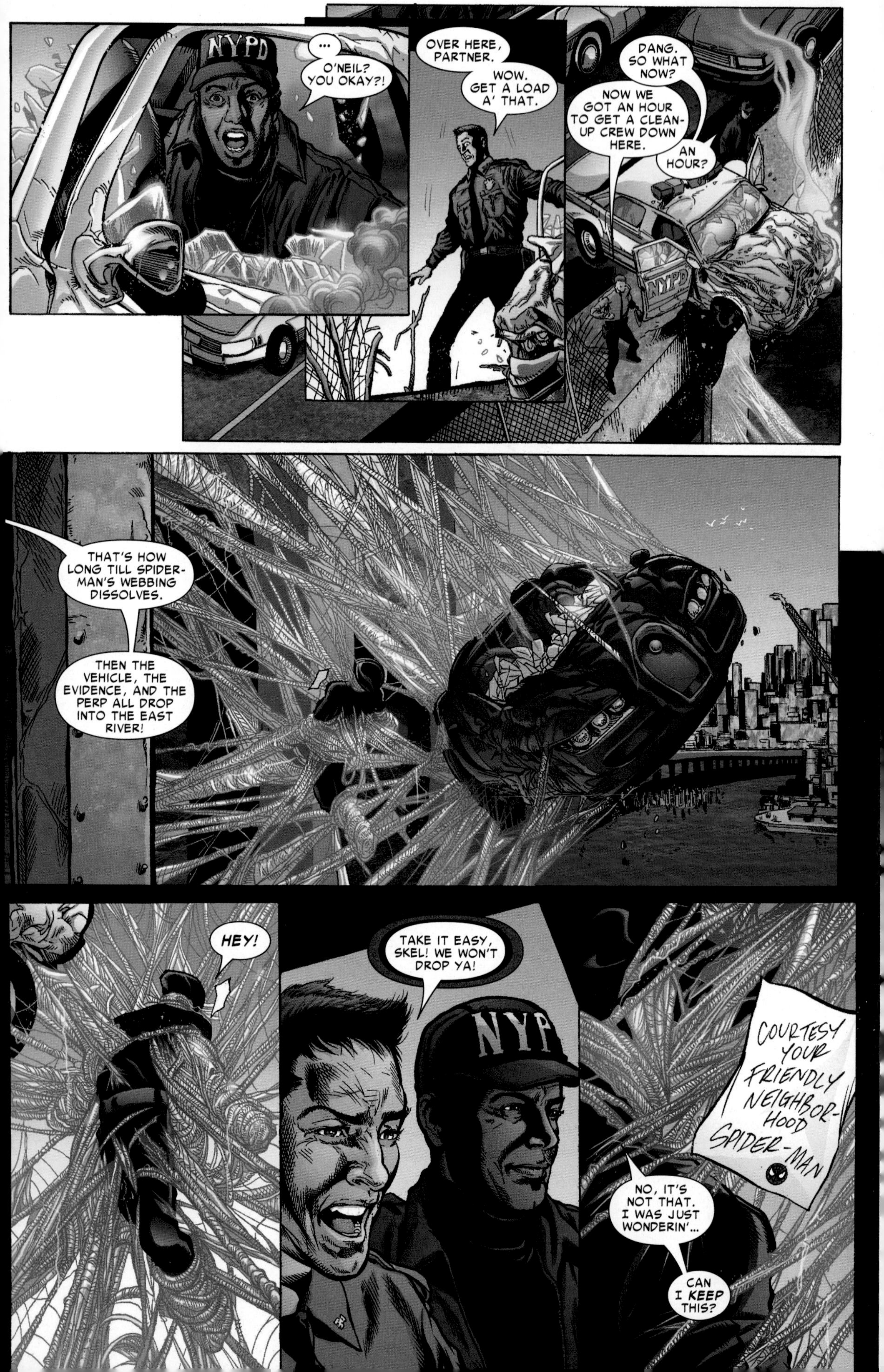
...
O'NEIL? YOU OKAY?!
OVER HERE, PARTNER.
WOW. GET A LOAD A' THAT.
DANG. SO WHAT NOW?
NOW WE GOT AN HOUR TO GET A CLEAN-UP CREW DOWN HERE.
AN HOUR?
THAT'S HOW LONG TILL SPIDER-MAN'S WEBBING DISSOLVES.
THEN THE VEHICLE, THE EVIDENCE, AND THE PERP ALL DROP INTO THE EAST RIVER!
HEY!
TAKE IT EASY, SKEL! WE WON'T DROP YA!
COURTESY YOUR FRIENDLY NEIGHBOR-HOOD SPIDER-MAN
NO, IT'S NOT THAT. I WAS JUST WONDERIN'...
CAN I KEEP THIS?

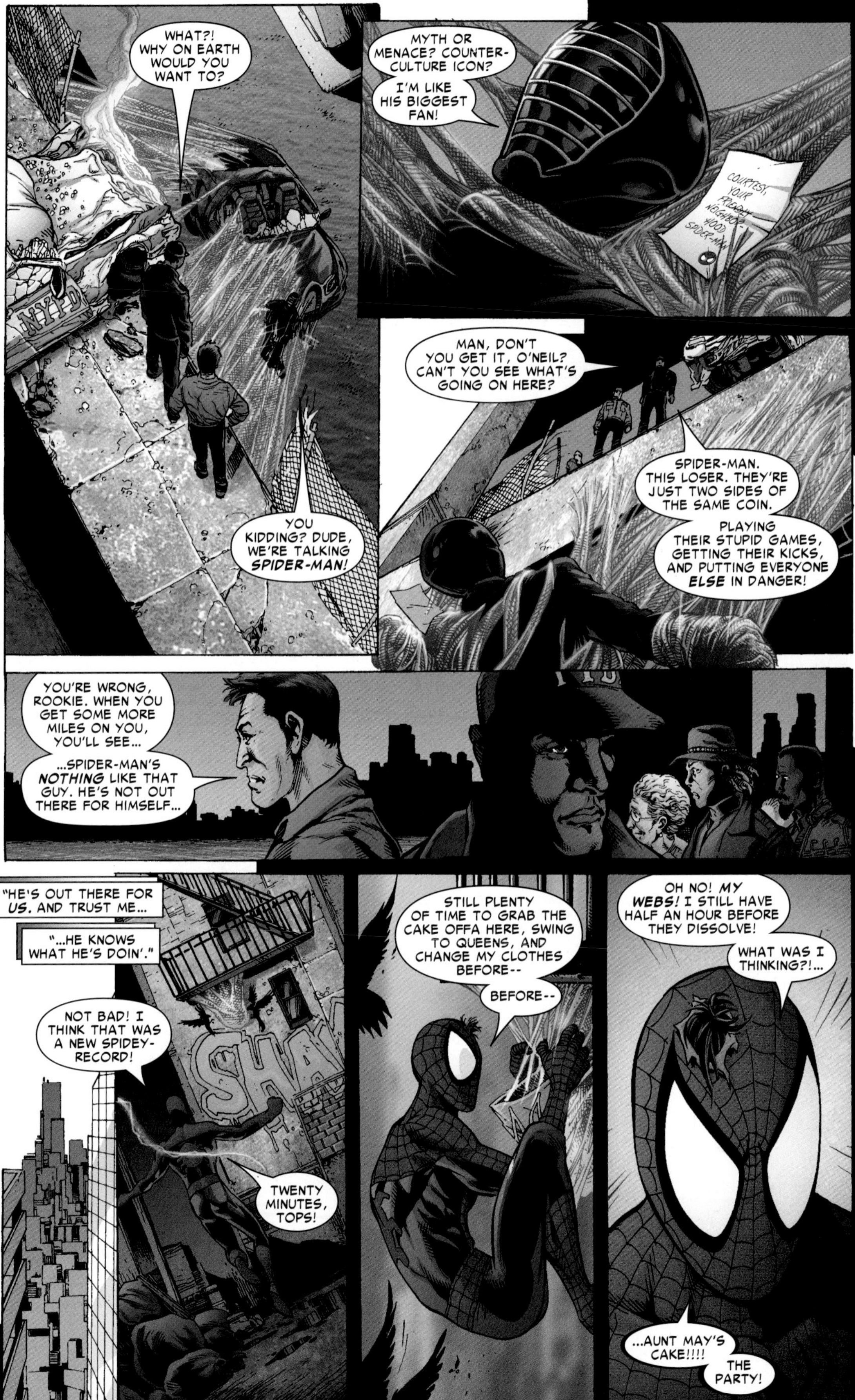
WHAT?! WHY ON EARTH WOULD YOU WANT TO?
YOU KIDDING? DUDE, WE'RE TALKING SPIDER-MAN!
MYTH OR MENACE? COUNTER-CULTURE ICON?
I'M LIKE HIS BIGGEST FAN!
COURTESY, YOUR FRIENDLY NEIGHBOR-HOOD SPIDER-MAN
MAN, DON'T YOU GET IT, O'NEIL? CAN'T YOU SEE WHAT'S GOING ON HERE?
SPIDER-MAN. THIS LOSER. THEY'RE JUST TWO SIDES OF THE SAME COIN.
PLAYING THEIR STUPID GAMES, GETTING THEIR KICKS, AND PUTTING EVERYONE ELSE IN DANGER!
YOU'RE WRONG, ROOKIE. WHEN YOU GET SOME MORE MILES ON YOU, YOU'LL SEE...
...SPIDER-MAN'S NOTHING LIKE THAT GUY. HE'S NOT OUT THERE FOR HIMSELF...
"HE'S OUT THERE FOR US. AND TRUST ME...
"...HE KNOWS WHAT HE'S DOIN'."
NOT BAD! I THINK THAT WAS A NEW SPIDEY-RECORD!
TWENTY MINUTES, TOPS!
STILL PLENTY OF TIME TO GRAB THE CAKE OFFA HERE, SWING TO QUEENS, AND CHANGE MY CLOTHES BEFORE--
BEFORE--
OH NO! MY WEBS! I STILL HAVE HALF AN HOUR BEFORE THEY DISSOLVE!
WHAT WAS I THINKING?!...
...AUNT MAY'S CAKE!!!!
THE PARTY!

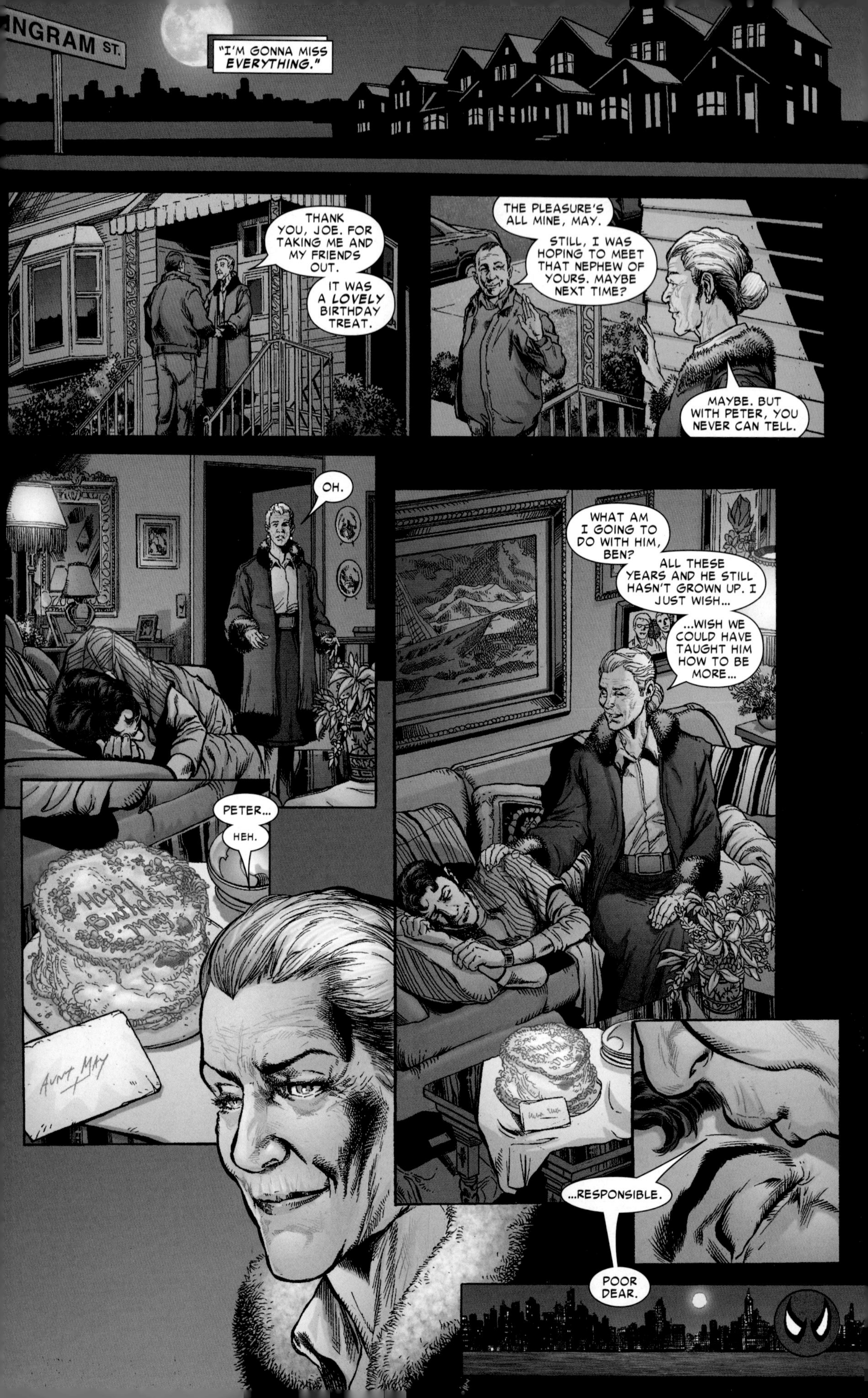
INGRAM ST.
"I'M GONNA MISS EVERYTHING."
THANK YOU, JOE. FOR TAKING ME AND MY FRIENDS OUT.
IT WAS A LOVELY BIRTHDAY TREAT.
THE PLEASURE'S ALL MINE, MAY.
STILL, I WAS HOPING TO MEET THAT NEPHEW OF YOURS. MAYBE NEXT TIME?
MAYBE. BUT WITH PETER, YOU NEVER CAN TELL.
OH.
PETER...
HEH.
Happy Birthday May
AUNT MAY
WHAT AM I GOING TO DO WITH HIM, BEN?
ALL THESE YEARS AND HE STILL HASN'T GROWN UP. I JUST WISH...
...WISH WE COULD HAVE TAUGHT HIM HOW TO BE MORE...
...RESPONSIBLE.
POOR DEAR.

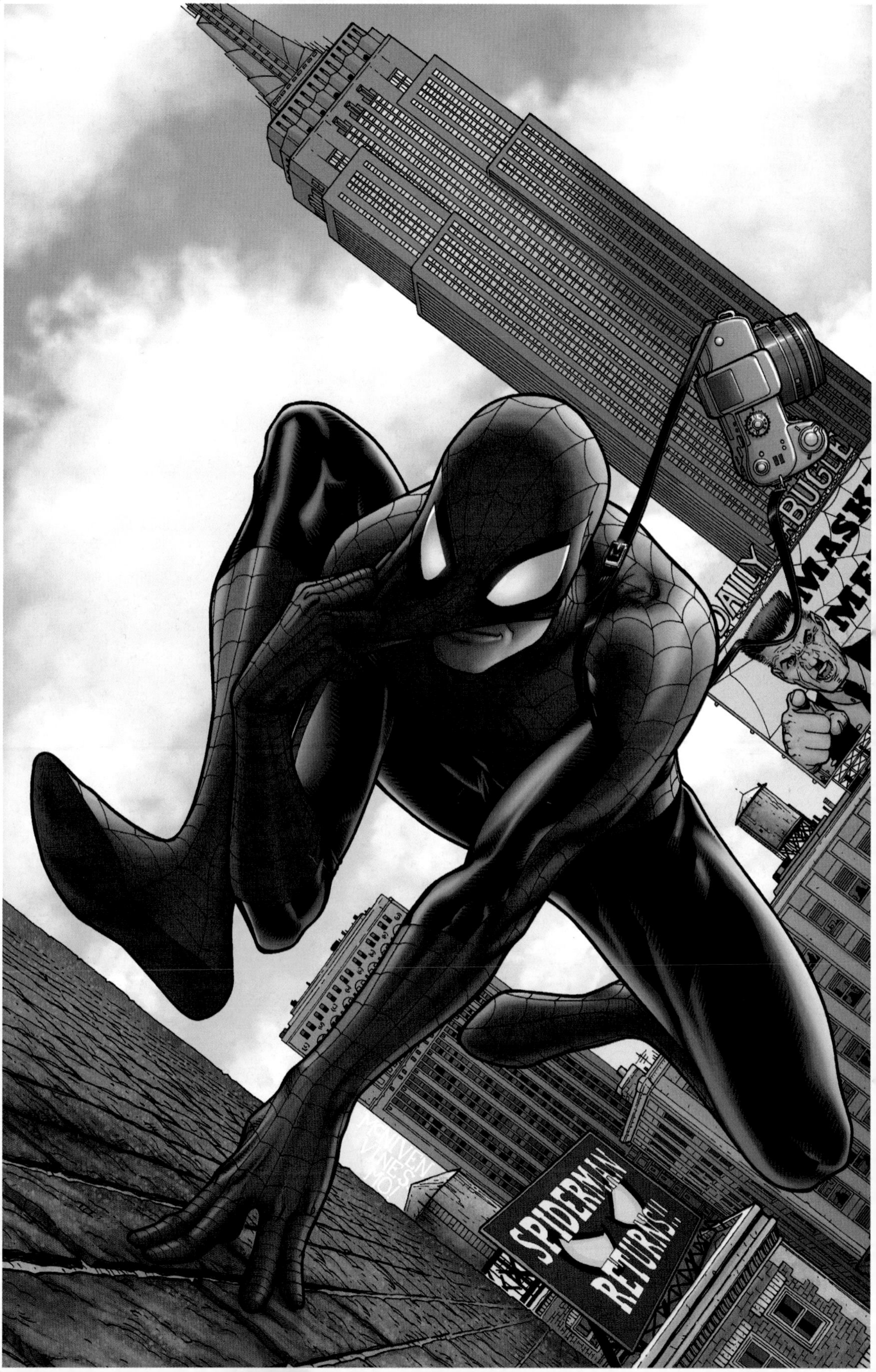
DAILY BUGLE
SPIDERMAN RETURNS!!

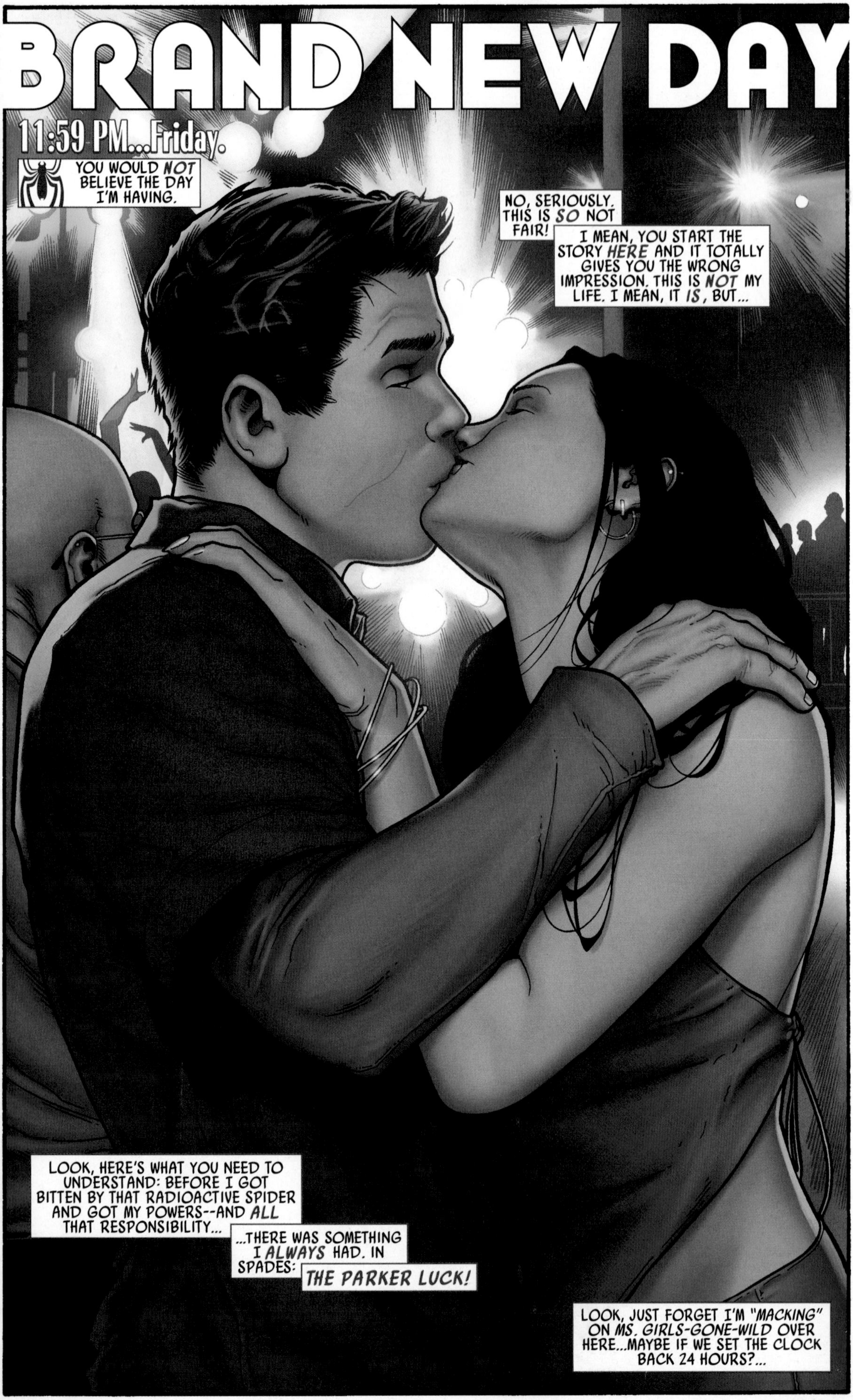
BRAND NEW DAY
11:59 PM...Friday.
YOU WOULD NOT BELIEVE THE DAY I'M HAVING.
NO, SERIOUSLY. THIS IS SO NOT FAIR!
I MEAN, YOU START THE STORY HERE AND IT TOTALLY GIVES YOU THE WRONG IMPRESSION. THIS IS NOT MY LIFE. I MEAN, IT IS, BUT...
LOOK, HERE'S WHAT YOU NEED TO UNDERSTAND: BEFORE I GOT BITTEN BY THAT RADIOACTIVE SPIDER AND GOT MY POWERS--AND ALL THAT RESPONSIBILITY...
...THERE WAS SOMETHING I ALWAYS HAD. IN SPADES:
THE PARKER LUCK!
LOOK, JUST FORGET I'M "MACKING" ON MS. GIRLS-GONE-WILD OVER HERE...MAYBE IF WE SET THE CLOCK BACK 24 HOURS?...

WHILE ATTENDING A DEMONSTRATION IN RADIOLOGY, HIGH SCHOOL STUDENT **PETER PARKER** WAS BITTEN BY A SPIDER WHICH HAD ACCIDENTALLY BEEN EXPOSED TO **RADIOACTIVE RAYS.** THROUGH A MIRACLE OF SCIENCE, PETER SOON FOUND THAT HE HAD **GAINED** THE SPIDER'S POWERS...AND HAD, IN EFFECT, BECOME A HUMAN SPIDER! FROM THAT DAY ON HE WAS...

THE AMAZING SPIDER-MAN™

DAN SLOTT WRITER
STEVE McNIVEN PENCILER
DEXTER VINES INKER
MORRY HOLLOWELL COLORS
VC'S CORY PETIT LETTERS
GALE, GUGGENHEIM, SLOTT, WELLS SPIDEY'S BRAINTRUST

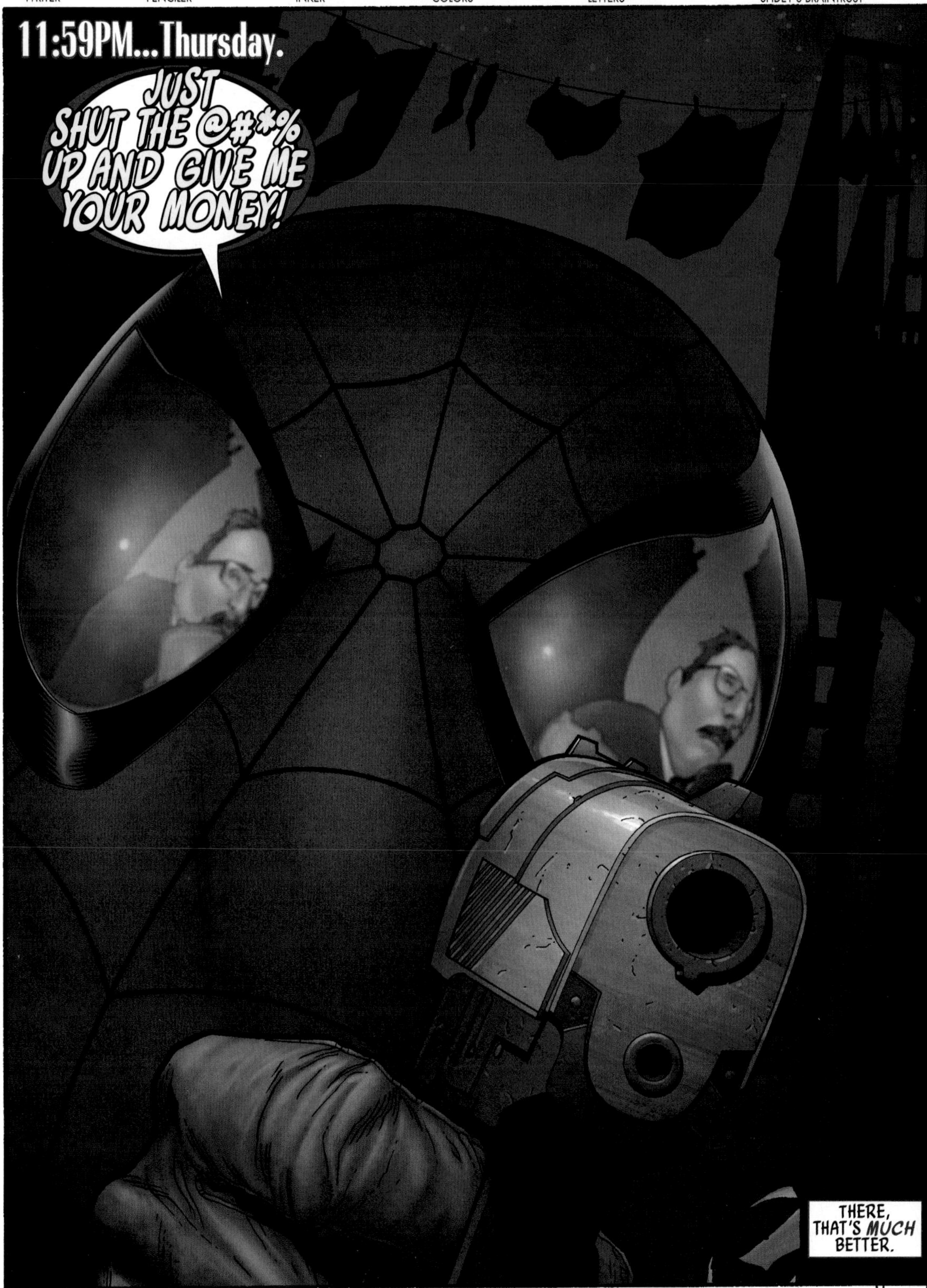

11:59PM...Thursday.
JUST SHUT THE @#*% UP AND GIVE ME YOUR MONEY!
THERE, THAT'S *MUCH* BETTER.

TOM BRENNAN ASSISTANT EDITOR
STEPHEN WACKER EDITOR
TOM BREVOORT EXECUTIVE EDITOR
JOE QUESADA EDITOR IN CHIEF
DAN BUCKLEY PUBLISHER

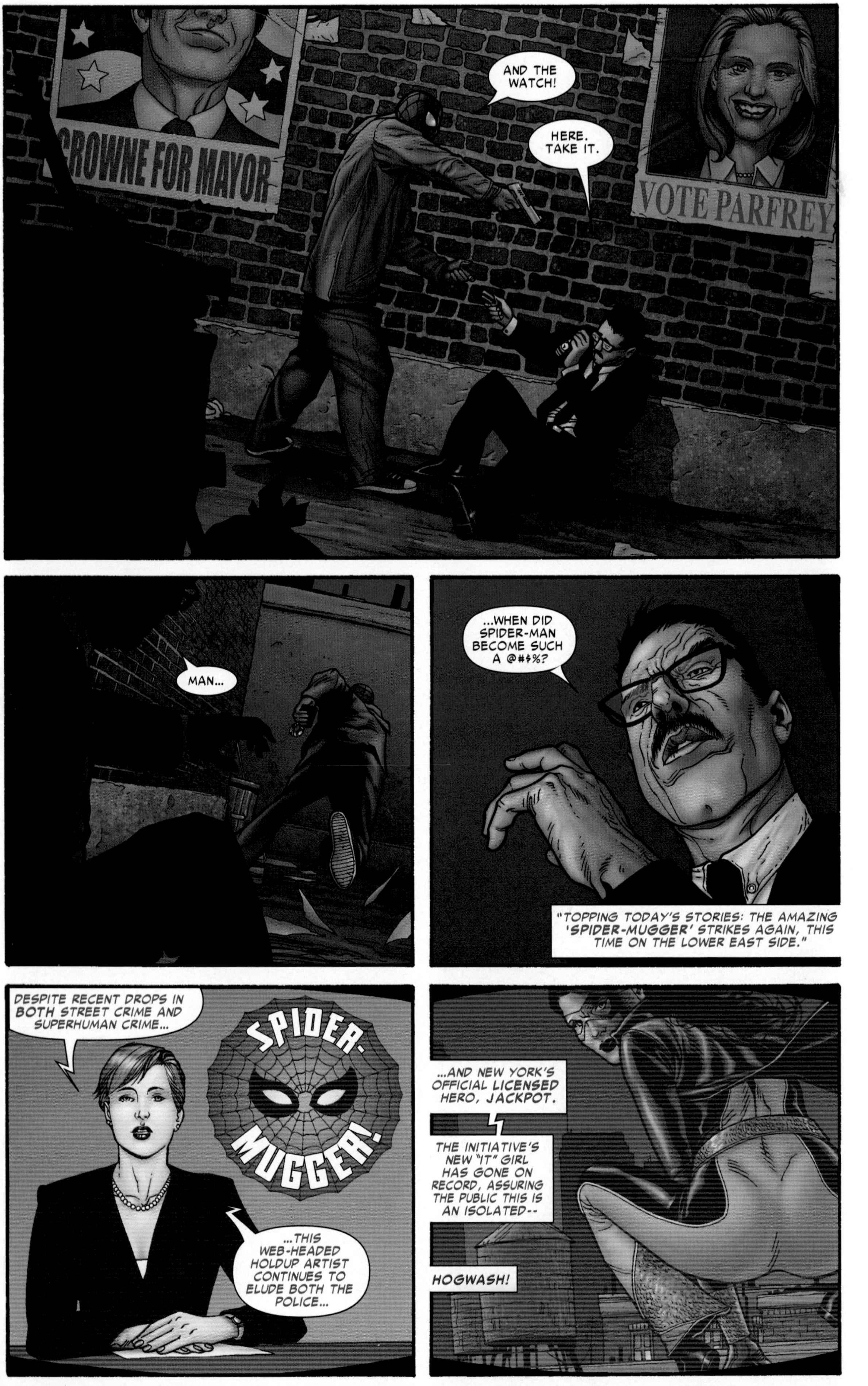
CROWNE FOR MAYOR
VOTE PARFREY
AND THE WATCH!
HERE. TAKE IT.
MAN...
...WHEN DID SPIDER-MAN BECOME SUCH A @#$%?
"TOPPING TODAY'S STORIES: THE AMAZING 'SPIDER-MUGGER' STRIKES AGAIN, THIS TIME ON THE LOWER EAST SIDE."
DESPITE RECENT DROPS IN BOTH STREET CRIME AND SUPERHUMAN CRIME...
SPIDER-MUGGER!
...THIS WEB-HEADED HOLDUP ARTIST CONTINUES TO ELUDE BOTH THE POLICE...
...AND NEW YORK'S OFFICIAL LICENSED HERO, JACKPOT.
THE INITIATIVE'S NEW "IT" GIRL HAS GONE ON RECORD, ASSURING THE PUBLIC THIS IS AN ISOLATED--
HOGWASH!

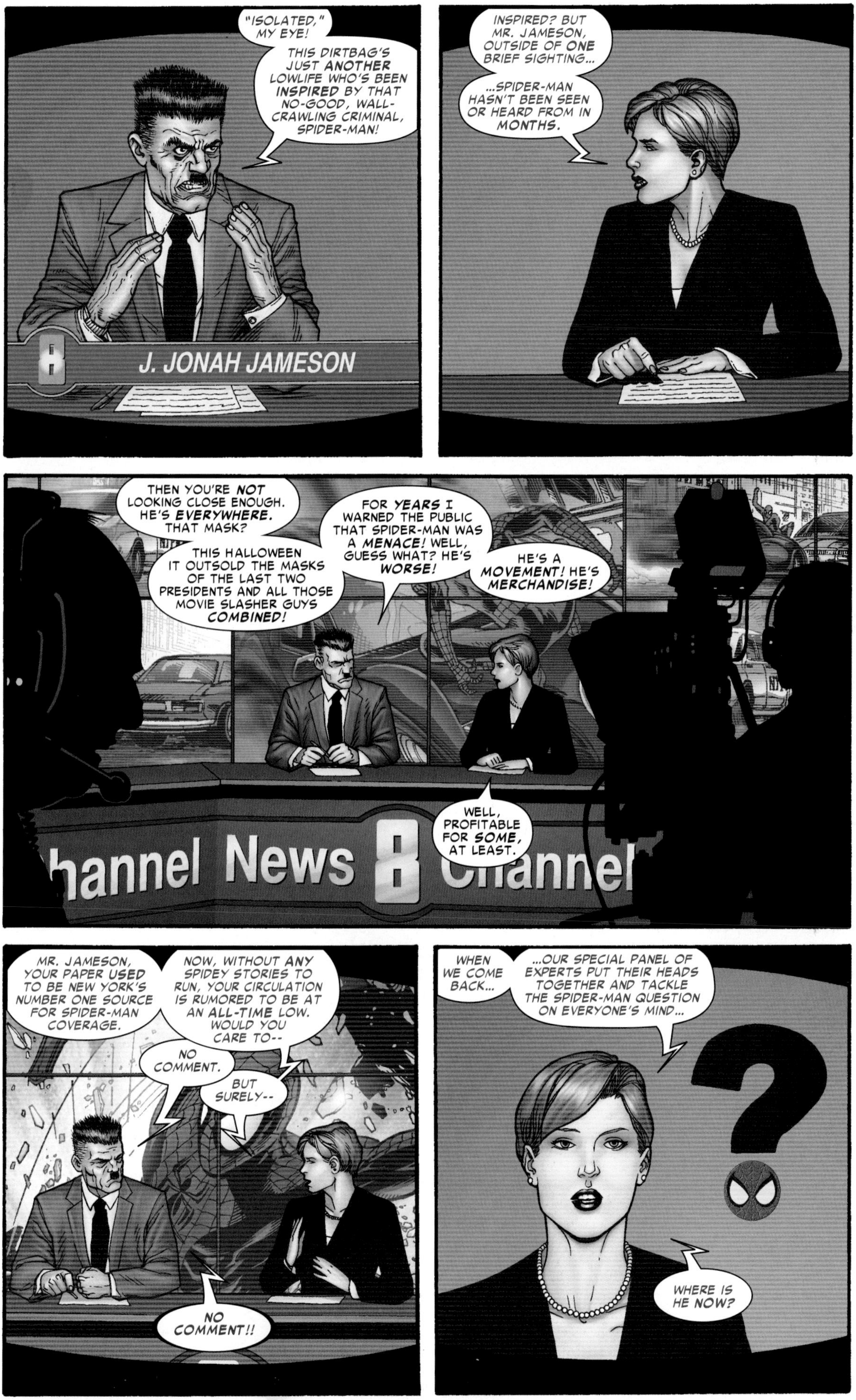
"ISOLATED," MY EYE!
THIS DIRTBAG'S JUST ANOTHER LOWLIFE WHO'S BEEN INSPIRED BY THAT NO-GOOD, WALL-CRAWLING CRIMINAL, SPIDER-MAN!
J. JONAH JAMESON
INSPIRED? BUT MR. JAMESON, OUTSIDE OF ONE BRIEF SIGHTING...
...SPIDER-MAN HASN'T BEEN SEEN OR HEARD FROM IN MONTHS.
THEN YOU'RE NOT LOOKING CLOSE ENOUGH. HE'S EVERYWHERE. THAT MASK?
THIS HALLOWEEN IT OUTSOLD THE MASKS OF THE LAST TWO PRESIDENTS AND ALL THOSE MOVIE SLASHER GUYS COMBINED!
FOR YEARS I WARNED THE PUBLIC THAT SPIDER-MAN WAS A MENACE! WELL, GUESS WHAT? HE'S WORSE!
HE'S A MOVEMENT! HE'S MERCHANDISE!
WELL, PROFITABLE FOR SOME, AT LEAST.
hannel News 8 Channel
MR. JAMESON, YOUR PAPER USED TO BE NEW YORK'S NUMBER ONE SOURCE FOR SPIDER-MAN COVERAGE.
NOW, WITHOUT ANY SPIDEY STORIES TO RUN, YOUR CIRCULATION IS RUMORED TO BE AT AN ALL-TIME LOW. WOULD YOU CARE TO--
NO COMMENT.
BUT SURELY--
NO COMMENT!!
WHEN WE COME BACK...
...OUR SPECIAL PANEL OF EXPERTS PUT THEIR HEADS TOGETHER AND TACKLE THE SPIDER-MAN QUESTION ON EVERYONE'S MIND...
WHERE IS HE NOW?

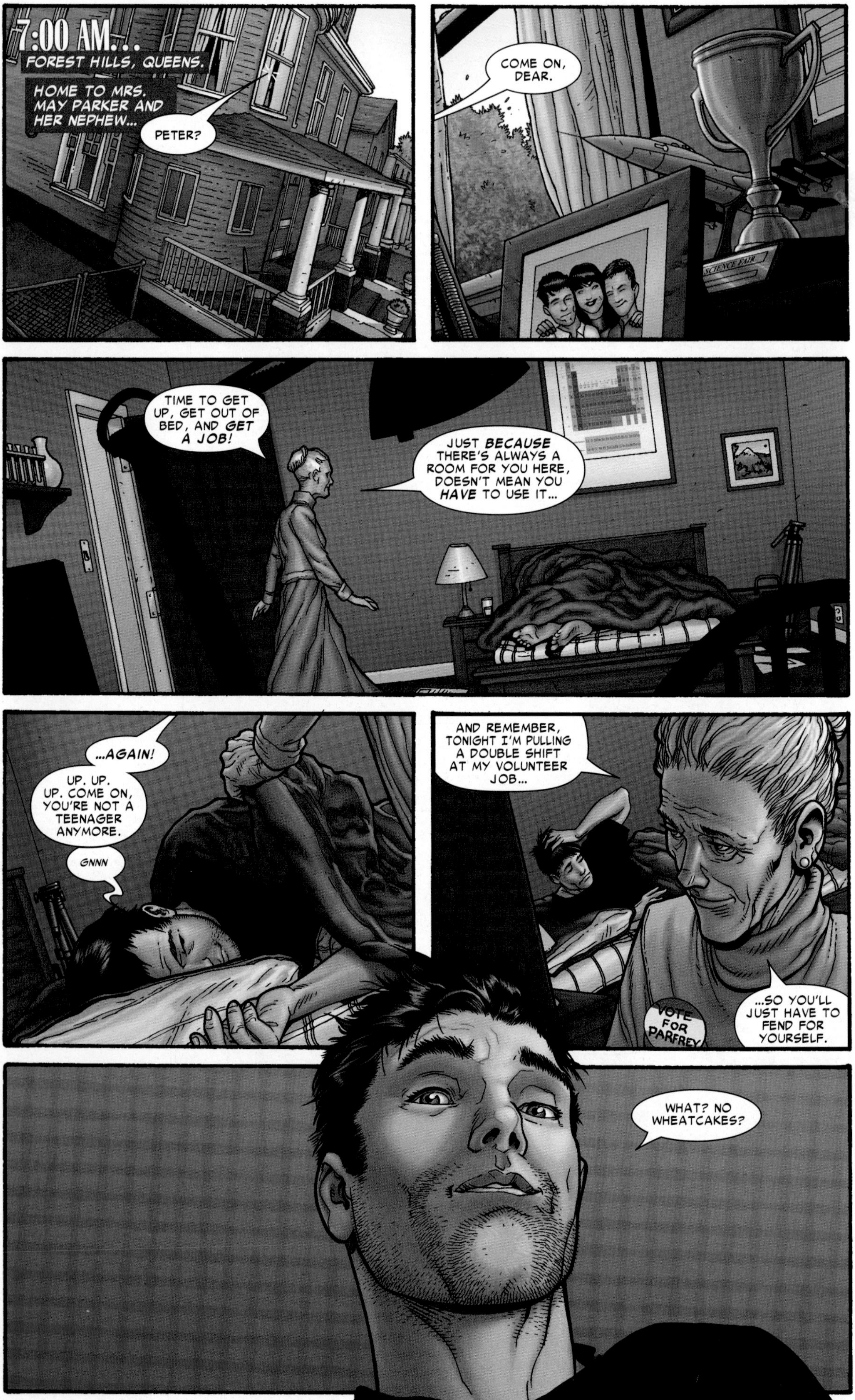
7:00 AM...
FOREST HILLS, QUEENS.
HOME TO MRS. MAY PARKER AND HER NEPHEW...
PETER?
COME ON, DEAR.
SCIENCE FAIR
TIME TO GET UP, GET OUT OF BED, AND GET A JOB!
JUST BECAUSE THERE'S ALWAYS A ROOM FOR YOU HERE, DOESN'T MEAN YOU HAVE TO USE IT...
...AGAIN!
UP. UP. UP. COME ON, YOU'RE NOT A TEENAGER ANYMORE.
GNNN
AND REMEMBER, TONIGHT I'M PULLING A DOUBLE SHIFT AT MY VOLUNTEER JOB...
VOTE FOR PARFREY
...SO YOU'LL JUST HAVE TO FEND FOR YOURSELF.
WHAT? NO WHEATCAKES?

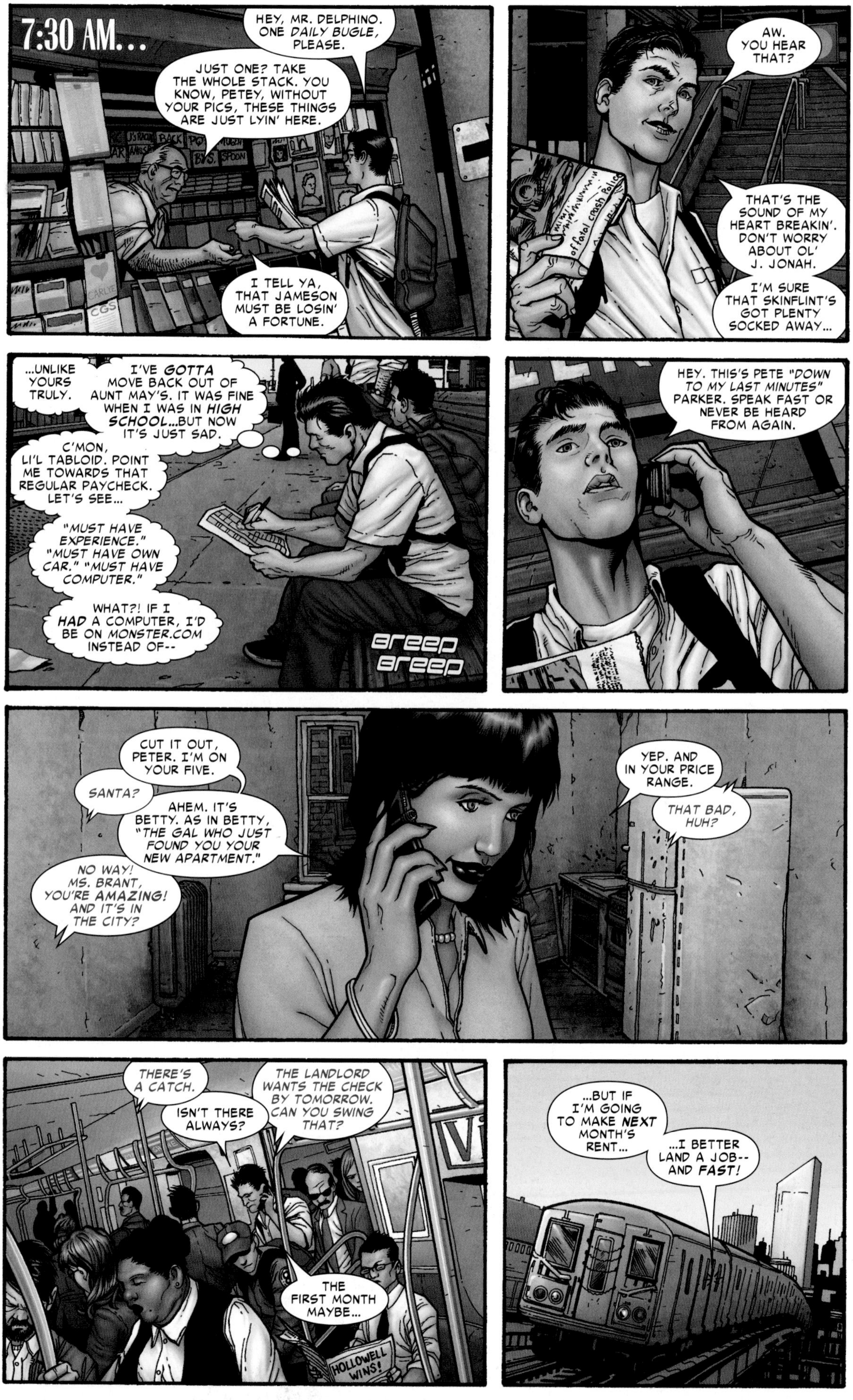
7:30 AM...
HEY, MR. DELPHINO. ONE DAILY BUGLE, PLEASE.
JUST ONE? TAKE THE WHOLE STACK. YOU KNOW, PETEY, WITHOUT YOUR PICS, THESE THINGS ARE JUST LYIN' HERE.
I TELL YA, THAT JAMESON MUST BE LOSIN' A FORTUNE.
AW. YOU HEAR THAT?
THAT'S THE SOUND OF MY HEART BREAKIN'. DON'T WORRY ABOUT OL' J. JONAH.
I'M SURE THAT SKINFLINT'S GOT PLENTY SOCKED AWAY...
...UNLIKE YOURS TRULY.
I'VE GOTTA MOVE BACK OUT OF AUNT MAY'S. IT WAS FINE WHEN I WAS IN HIGH SCHOOL...BUT NOW IT'S JUST SAD.
C'MON, LI'L TABLOID. POINT ME TOWARDS THAT REGULAR PAYCHECK. LET'S SEE...
"MUST HAVE EXPERIENCE." "MUST HAVE OWN CAR." "MUST HAVE COMPUTER."
WHAT?! IF I HAD A COMPUTER, I'D BE ON MONSTER.COM INSTEAD OF--
BREEP BREEP
HEY. THIS'S PETE "DOWN TO MY LAST MINUTES" PARKER. SPEAK FAST OR NEVER BE HEARD FROM AGAIN.
CUT IT OUT, PETER. I'M ON YOUR FIVE.
SANTA?
AHEM. IT'S BETTY. AS IN BETTY, "THE GAL WHO JUST FOUND YOU YOUR NEW APARTMENT."
NO WAY! MS. BRANT, YOU'RE AMAZING! AND IT'S IN THE CITY?
YEP. AND IN YOUR PRICE RANGE.
THAT BAD, HUH?
THERE'S A CATCH.
ISN'T THERE ALWAYS?
THE LANDLORD WANTS THE CHECK BY TOMORROW. CAN YOU SWING THAT?
THE FIRST MONTH MAYBE...
HOLLOWELL WINS!
...BUT IF I'M GOING TO MAKE NEXT MONTH'S RENT...
...I BETTER LAND A JOB-- AND FAST!

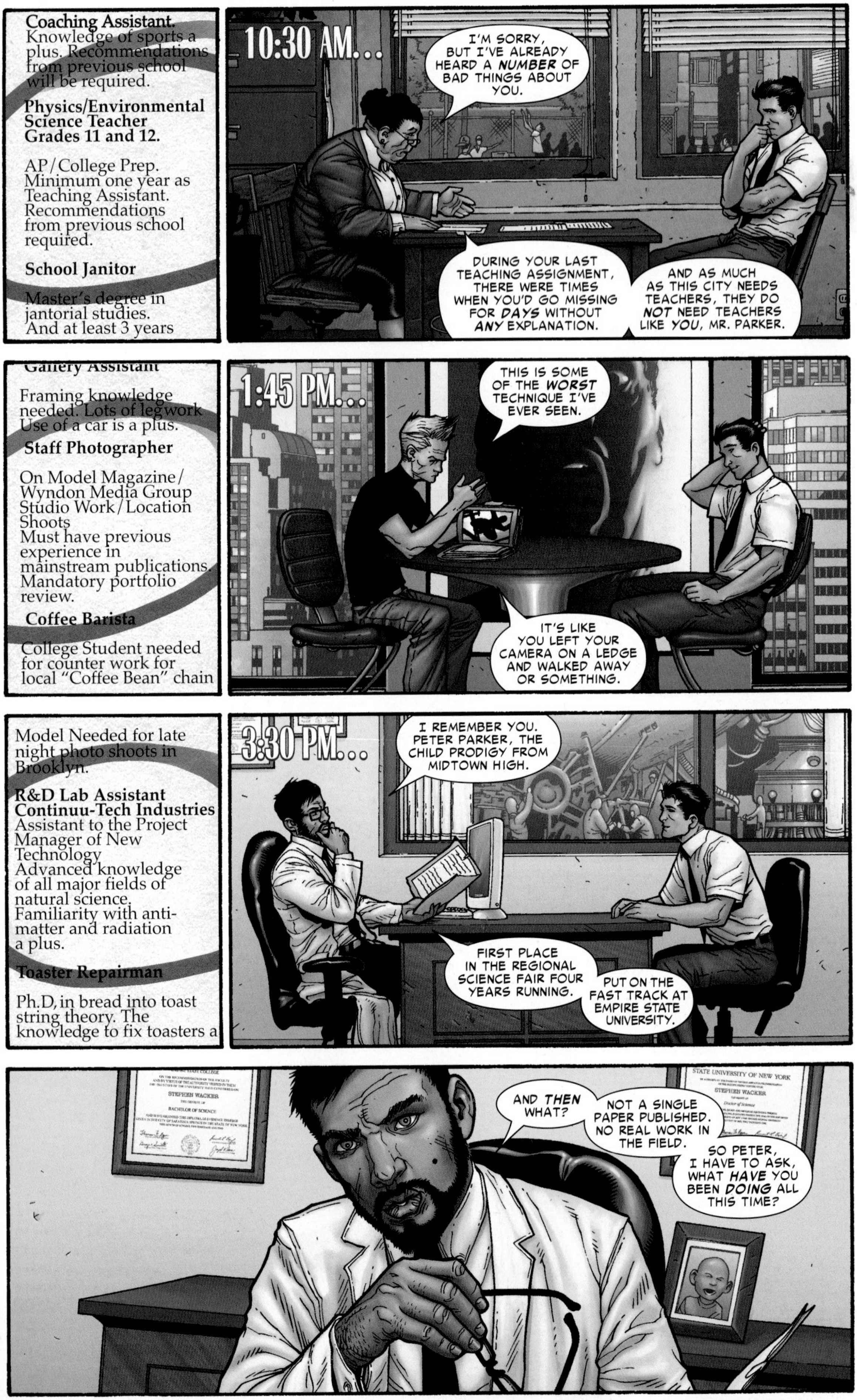
Coaching Assistant.
Knowledge of sports a plus. Recommendations from previous school will be required.
Physics/Environmental Science Teacher Grades 11 and 12.
AP/College Prep. Minimum one year as Teaching Assistant. Recommendations from previous school required.
School Janitor
Master's degree in jantorial studies. And at least 3 years
10:30 AM...
I'M SORRY, BUT I'VE ALREADY HEARD A NUMBER OF BAD THINGS ABOUT YOU.
DURING YOUR LAST TEACHING ASSIGNMENT, THERE WERE TIMES WHEN YOU'D GO MISSING FOR DAYS WITHOUT ANY EXPLANATION.
AND AS MUCH AS THIS CITY NEEDS TEACHERS, THEY DO NOT NEED TEACHERS LIKE YOU, MR. PARKER.
Gallery Assistant
Framing knowledge needed. Lots of legwork Use of a car is a plus.
Staff Photographer
On Model Magazine/ Wyndon Media Group Studio Work/Location Shoots Must have previous experience in mainstream publications. Mandatory portfolio review.
Coffee Barista
College Student needed for counter work for local "Coffee Bean" chain
1:45 PM...
THIS IS SOME OF THE WORST TECHNIQUE I'VE EVER SEEN.
IT'S LIKE YOU LEFT YOUR CAMERA ON A LEDGE AND WALKED AWAY OR SOMETHING.
Model Needed for late night photo shoots in Brooklyn.
R&D Lab Assistant Continuu-Tech Industries
Assistant to the Project Manager of New Technology Advanced knowledge of all major fields of natural science. Familiarity with anti-matter and radiation a plus.
Toaster Repairman
Ph.D, in bread into toast string theory. The knowledge to fix toasters a
3:30 PM...
I REMEMBER YOU. PETER PARKER, THE CHILD PRODIGY FROM MIDTOWN HIGH.
FIRST PLACE IN THE REGIONAL SCIENCE FAIR FOUR YEARS RUNNING.
PUT ON THE FAST TRACK AT EMPIRE STATE UNIVERSITY.
STEPHEN WACKER
BACHELOR OF SCIENCE
STATE UNIVERSITY OF NEW YORK
STEPHEN WACKER
Doctor of Science
AND THEN WHAT?
NOT A SINGLE PAPER PUBLISHED. NO REAL WORK IN THE FIELD.
SO PETER, I HAVE TO ASK, WHAT HAVE YOU BEEN DOING ALL THIS TIME?

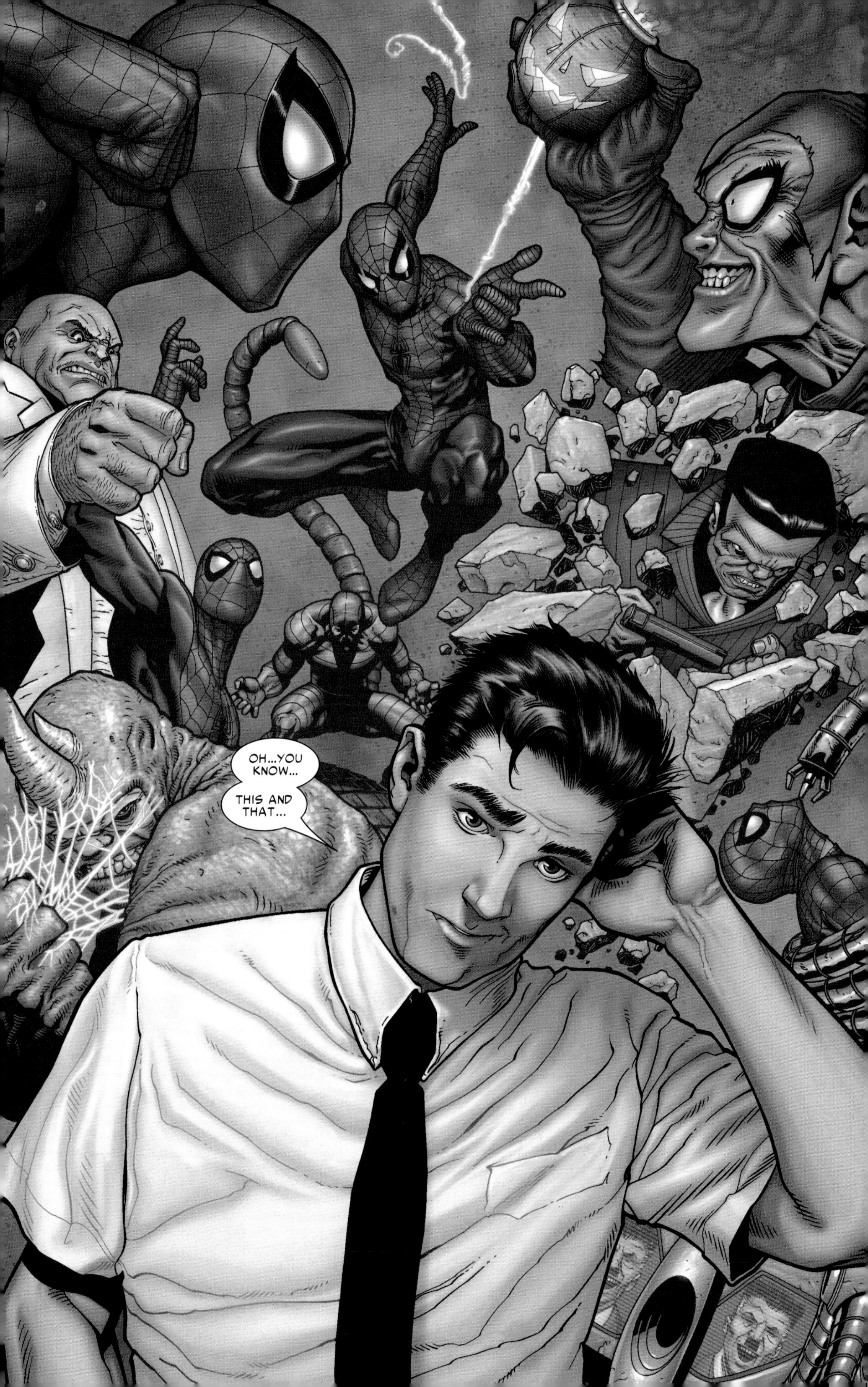
OH...YOU KNOW...
THIS AND THAT...

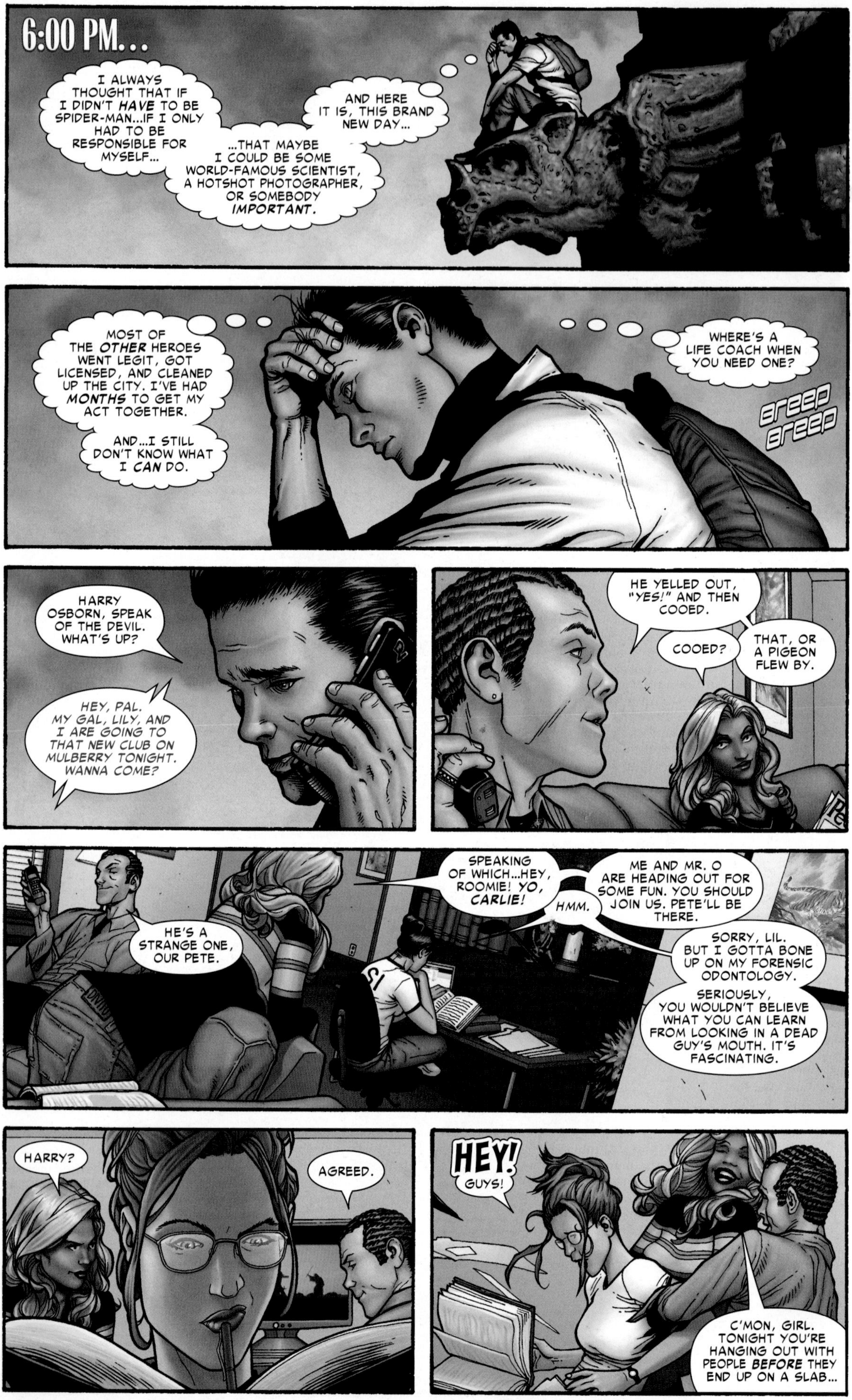
6:00 PM...
I ALWAYS THOUGHT THAT IF I DIDN'T HAVE TO BE SPIDER-MAN...IF I ONLY HAD TO BE RESPONSIBLE FOR MYSELF...
...THAT MAYBE I COULD BE SOME WORLD-FAMOUS SCIENTIST, A HOTSHOT PHOTOGRAPHER, OR SOMEBODY IMPORTANT.
AND HERE IT IS, THIS BRAND NEW DAY...
MOST OF THE OTHER HEROES WENT LEGIT, GOT LICENSED, AND CLEANED UP THE CITY. I'VE HAD MONTHS TO GET MY ACT TOGETHER.
AND...I STILL DON'T KNOW WHAT I CAN DO.
WHERE'S A LIFE COACH WHEN YOU NEED ONE?
BREEP BREEP
HARRY OSBORN, SPEAK OF THE DEVIL. WHAT'S UP?
HEY, PAL. MY GAL, LILY, AND I ARE GOING TO THAT NEW CLUB ON MULBERRY TONIGHT. WANNA COME?
HE YELLED OUT, "YES!" AND THEN COOED.
COOED?
THAT, OR A PIGEON FLEW BY.
HE'S A STRANGE ONE, OUR PETE.
SPEAKING OF WHICH...HEY, ROOMIE! YO, CARLIE!
ME AND MR. O ARE HEADING OUT FOR SOME FUN. YOU SHOULD JOIN US. PETE'LL BE THERE.
HMM.
SORRY, LIL. BUT I GOTTA BONE UP ON MY FORENSIC ODONTOLOGY.
SERIOUSLY, YOU WOULDN'T BELIEVE WHAT YOU CAN LEARN FROM LOOKING IN A DEAD GUY'S MOUTH. IT'S FASCINATING.
HARRY?
AGREED.
HEY! GUYS!
C'MON, GIRL. TONIGHT YOU'RE HANGING OUT WITH PEOPLE BEFORE THEY END UP ON A SLAB...

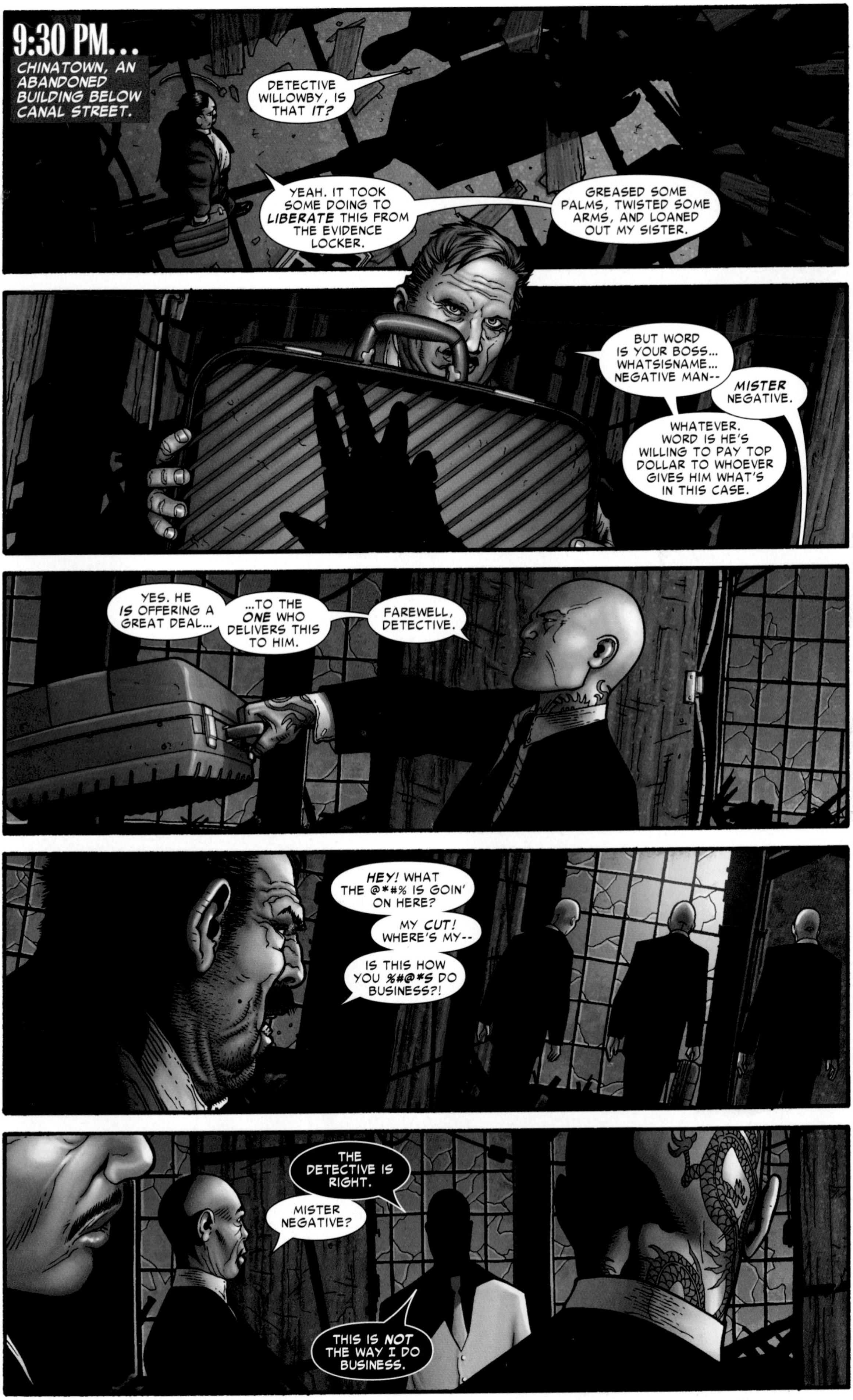
9:30 PM...
CHINATOWN, AN ABANDONED BUILDING BELOW CANAL STREET.
DETECTIVE WILLOWBY, IS THAT IT?
YEAH. IT TOOK SOME DOING TO LIBERATE THIS FROM THE EVIDENCE LOCKER.
GREASED SOME PALMS, TWISTED SOME ARMS, AND LOANED OUT MY SISTER.
BUT WORD IS YOUR BOSS... WHATSISNAME... NEGATIVE MAN--
MISTER NEGATIVE.
WHATEVER. WORD IS HE'S WILLING TO PAY TOP DOLLAR TO WHOEVER GIVES HIM WHAT'S IN THIS CASE.
YES. HE IS OFFERING A GREAT DEAL...
...TO THE ONE WHO DELIVERS THIS TO HIM.
FAREWELL, DETECTIVE.
HEY! WHAT THE @*#% IS GOIN' ON HERE?
MY CUT! WHERE'S MY--
IS THIS HOW YOU %#@*S DO BUSINESS?!
THE DETECTIVE IS RIGHT.
MISTER NEGATIVE?
THIS IS NOT THE WAY I DO BUSINESS.

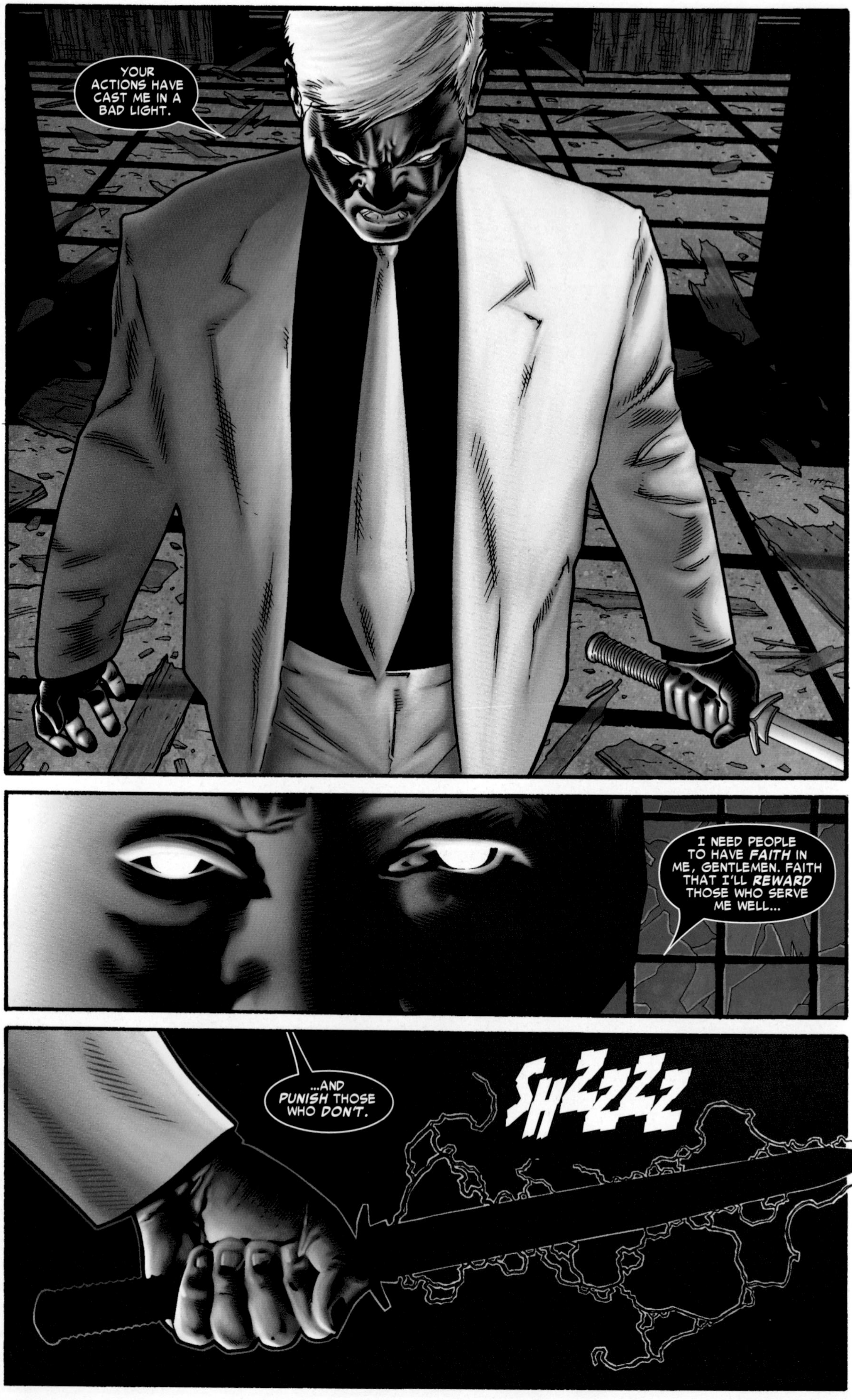
YOUR ACTIONS HAVE CAST ME IN A BAD LIGHT.
I NEED PEOPLE TO HAVE *FAITH* IN ME, GENTLEMEN. FAITH THAT I'LL *REWARD* THOSE WHO SERVE ME WELL...
...AND *PUNISH* THOSE WHO *DON'T*.
SHZZZZ

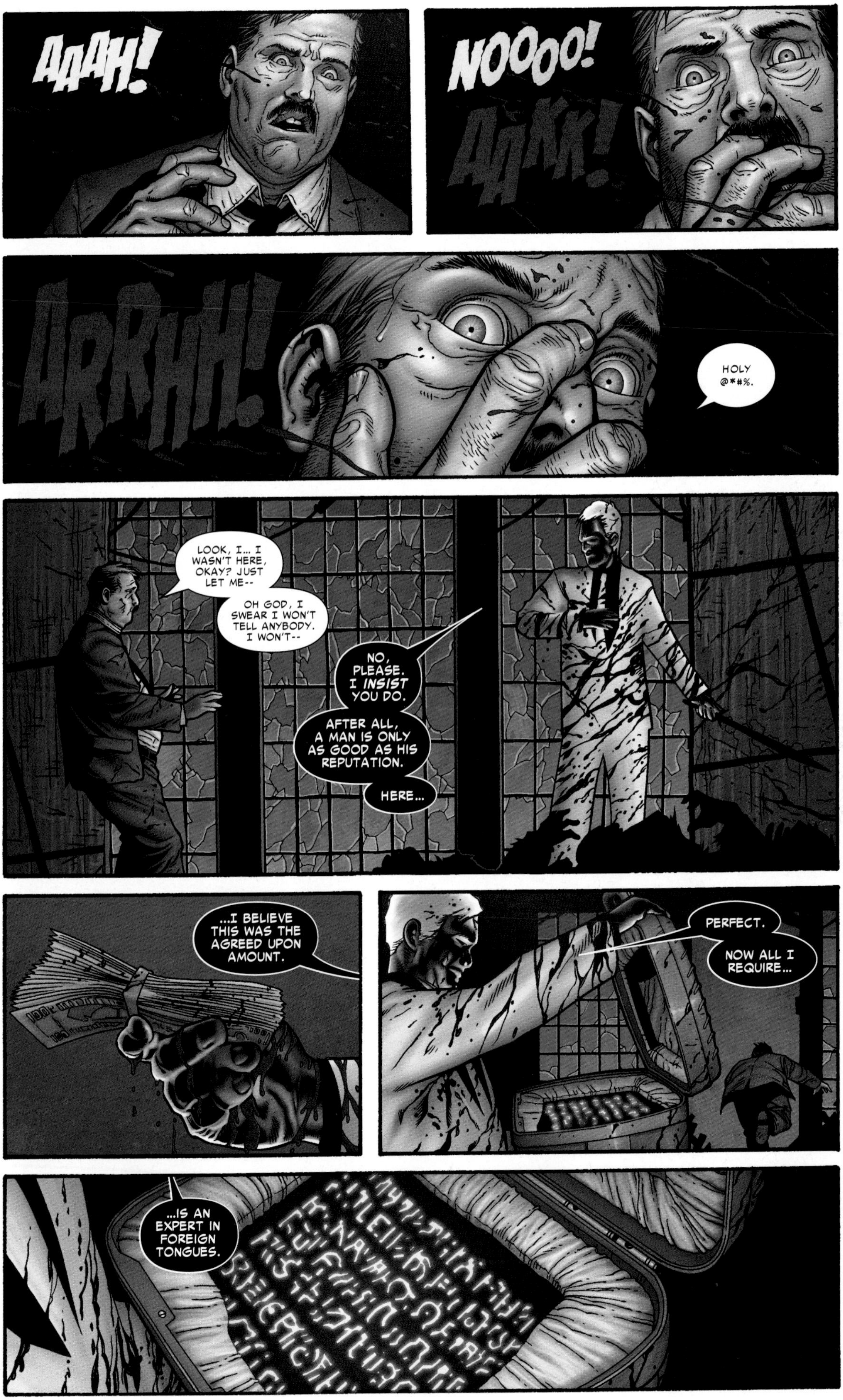

AAAH!
NOOOO!
AAKK!
ARRHH!
HOLY @*#%.
LOOK, I... I WASN'T HERE, OKAY? JUST LET ME--
OH GOD, I SWEAR I WON'T TELL ANYBODY. I WON'T--
NO, PLEASE. I *INSIST* YOU DO.
AFTER ALL, A MAN IS ONLY AS GOOD AS HIS REPUTATION.
HERE...
...I BELIEVE THIS WAS THE AGREED UPON AMOUNT.
PERFECT.
NOW ALL I REQUIRE...
...IS AN EXPERT IN FOREIGN TONGUES.

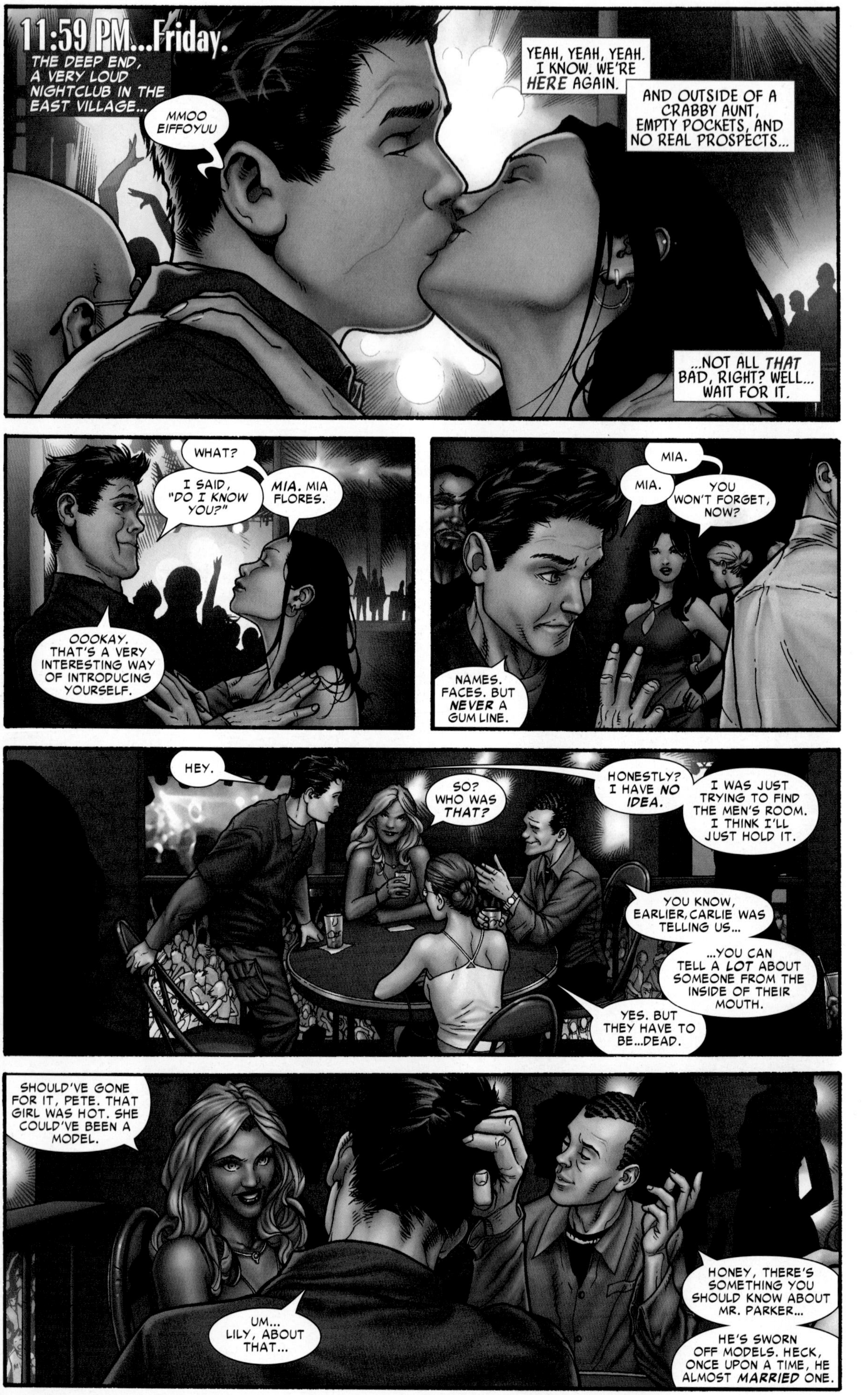
11:59 PM...Friday.
THE DEEP END, A VERY LOUD NIGHTCLUB IN THE EAST VILLAGE...
MMOO EIFFOYUU
YEAH, YEAH, YEAH. I KNOW. WE'RE HERE AGAIN.
AND OUTSIDE OF A CRABBY AUNT, EMPTY POCKETS, AND NO REAL PROSPECTS...
...NOT ALL THAT BAD, RIGHT? WELL... WAIT FOR IT.
WHAT?
I SAID, "DO I KNOW YOU?"
MIA. MIA FLORES.
OOOKAY. THAT'S A VERY INTERESTING WAY OF INTRODUCING YOURSELF.
MIA.
MIA.
YOU WON'T FORGET, NOW?
NAMES. FACES. BUT NEVER A GUM LINE.
HEY.
SO? WHO WAS THAT?
HONESTLY? I HAVE NO IDEA.
I WAS JUST TRYING TO FIND THE MEN'S ROOM. I THINK I'LL JUST HOLD IT.
YOU KNOW, EARLIER, CARLIE WAS TELLING US...
...YOU CAN TELL A LOT ABOUT SOMEONE FROM THE INSIDE OF THEIR MOUTH.
YES. BUT THEY HAVE TO BE...DEAD.
SHOULD'VE GONE FOR IT, PETE. THAT GIRL WAS HOT. SHE COULD'VE BEEN A MODEL.
UM... LILY, ABOUT THAT...
HONEY, THERE'S SOMETHING YOU SHOULD KNOW ABOUT MR. PARKER...
HE'S SWORN OFF MODELS. HECK, ONCE UPON A TIME, HE ALMOST MARRIED ONE.

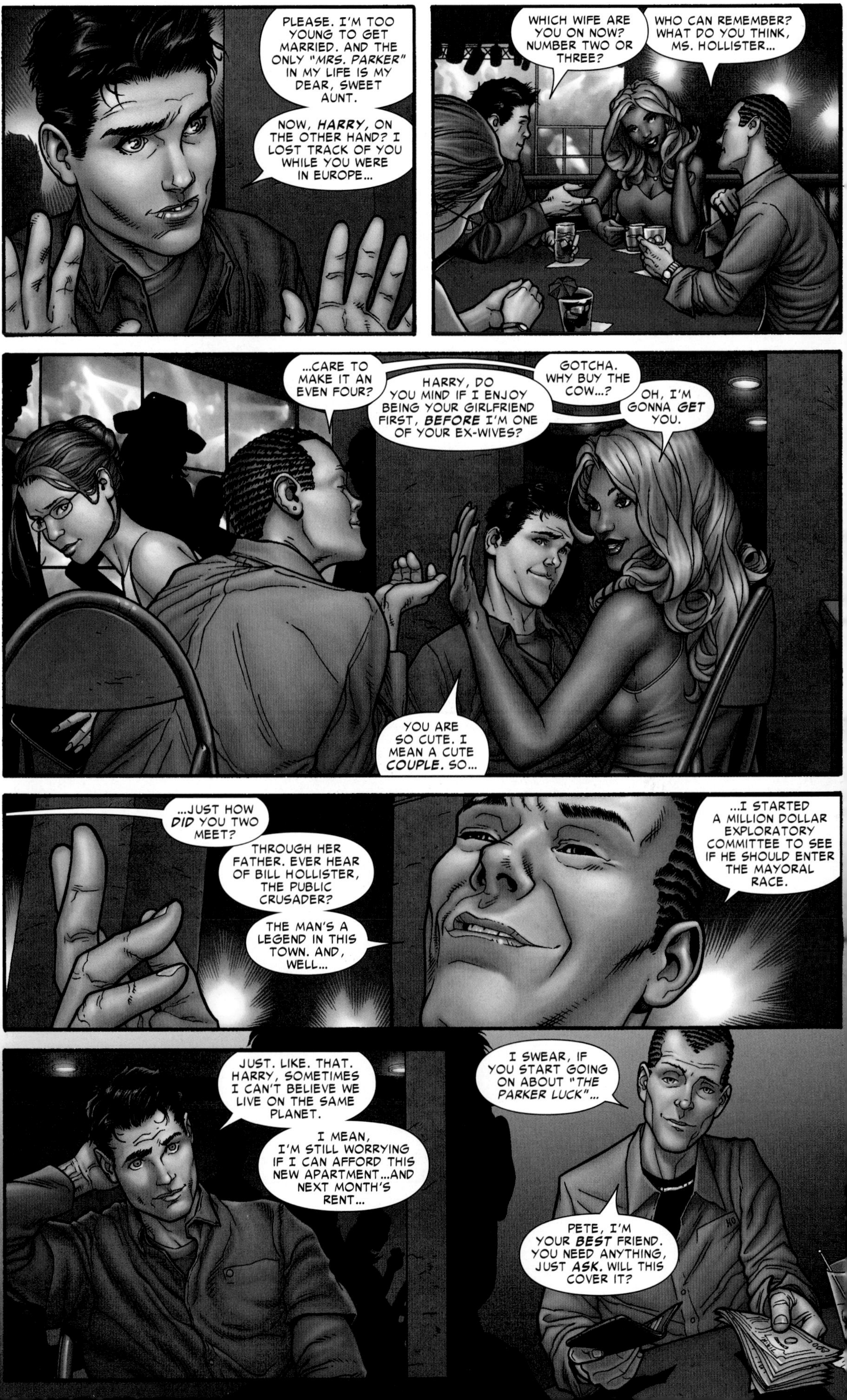
PLEASE. I'M TOO YOUNG TO GET MARRIED. AND THE ONLY "MRS. PARKER" IN MY LIFE IS MY DEAR, SWEET AUNT.
NOW, HARRY, ON THE OTHER HAND? I LOST TRACK OF YOU WHILE YOU WERE IN EUROPE...
WHICH WIFE ARE YOU ON NOW? NUMBER TWO OR THREE?
WHO CAN REMEMBER? WHAT DO YOU THINK, MS. HOLLISTER...
...CARE TO MAKE IT AN EVEN FOUR?
HARRY, DO YOU MIND IF I ENJOY BEING YOUR GIRLFRIEND FIRST, BEFORE I'M ONE OF YOUR EX-WIVES?
GOTCHA. WHY BUY THE COW...?
OH, I'M GONNA GET YOU.
YOU ARE SO CUTE. I MEAN A CUTE COUPLE. SO...
...JUST HOW DID YOU TWO MEET?
THROUGH HER FATHER. EVER HEAR OF BILL HOLLISTER, THE PUBLIC CRUSADER?
THE MAN'S A LEGEND IN THIS TOWN. AND, WELL...
...I STARTED A MILLION DOLLAR EXPLORATORY COMMITTEE TO SEE IF HE SHOULD ENTER THE MAYORAL RACE.
JUST. LIKE. THAT. HARRY, SOMETIMES I CAN'T BELIEVE WE LIVE ON THE SAME PLANET.
I MEAN, I'M STILL WORRYING IF I CAN AFFORD THIS NEW APARTMENT...AND NEXT MONTH'S RENT...
I SWEAR, IF YOU START GOING ON ABOUT "THE PARKER LUCK"...
PETE, I'M YOUR BEST FRIEND. YOU NEED ANYTHING, JUST ASK. WILL THIS COVER IT?

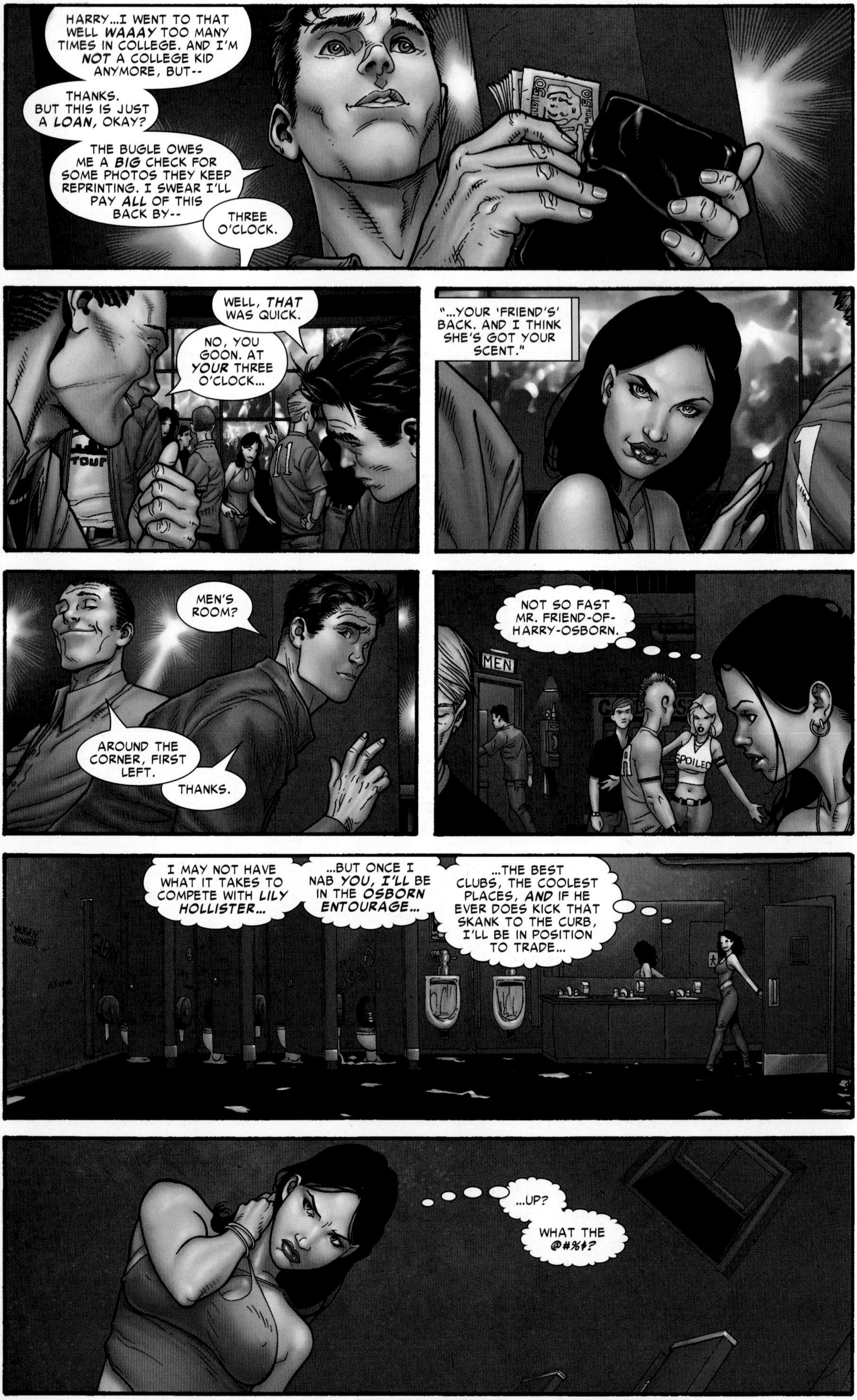
HARRY...I WENT TO THAT WELL WAAAY TOO MANY TIMES IN COLLEGE. AND I'M NOT A COLLEGE KID ANYMORE, BUT--
THANKS. BUT THIS IS JUST A LOAN, OKAY?
THE BUGLE OWES ME A BIG CHECK FOR SOME PHOTOS THEY KEEP REPRINTING. I SWEAR I'LL PAY ALL OF THIS BACK BY--
THREE O'CLOCK.
WELL, THAT WAS QUICK.
NO, YOU GOON. AT YOUR THREE O'CLOCK...
"...YOUR 'FRIEND'S' BACK. AND I THINK SHE'S GOT YOUR SCENT."
MEN'S ROOM?
AROUND THE CORNER, FIRST LEFT.
THANKS.
NOT SO FAST MR. FRIEND-OF-HARRY-OSBORN.
MEN
SPOILED
I MAY NOT HAVE WHAT IT TAKES TO COMPETE WITH LILY HOLLISTER...
...BUT ONCE I NAB YOU, I'LL BE IN THE OSBORN ENTOURAGE...
...THE BEST CLUBS, THE COOLEST PLACES, AND IF HE EVER DOES KICK THAT SKANK TO THE CURB, I'LL BE IN POSITION TO TRADE...
...UP?
WHAT THE @#%$?

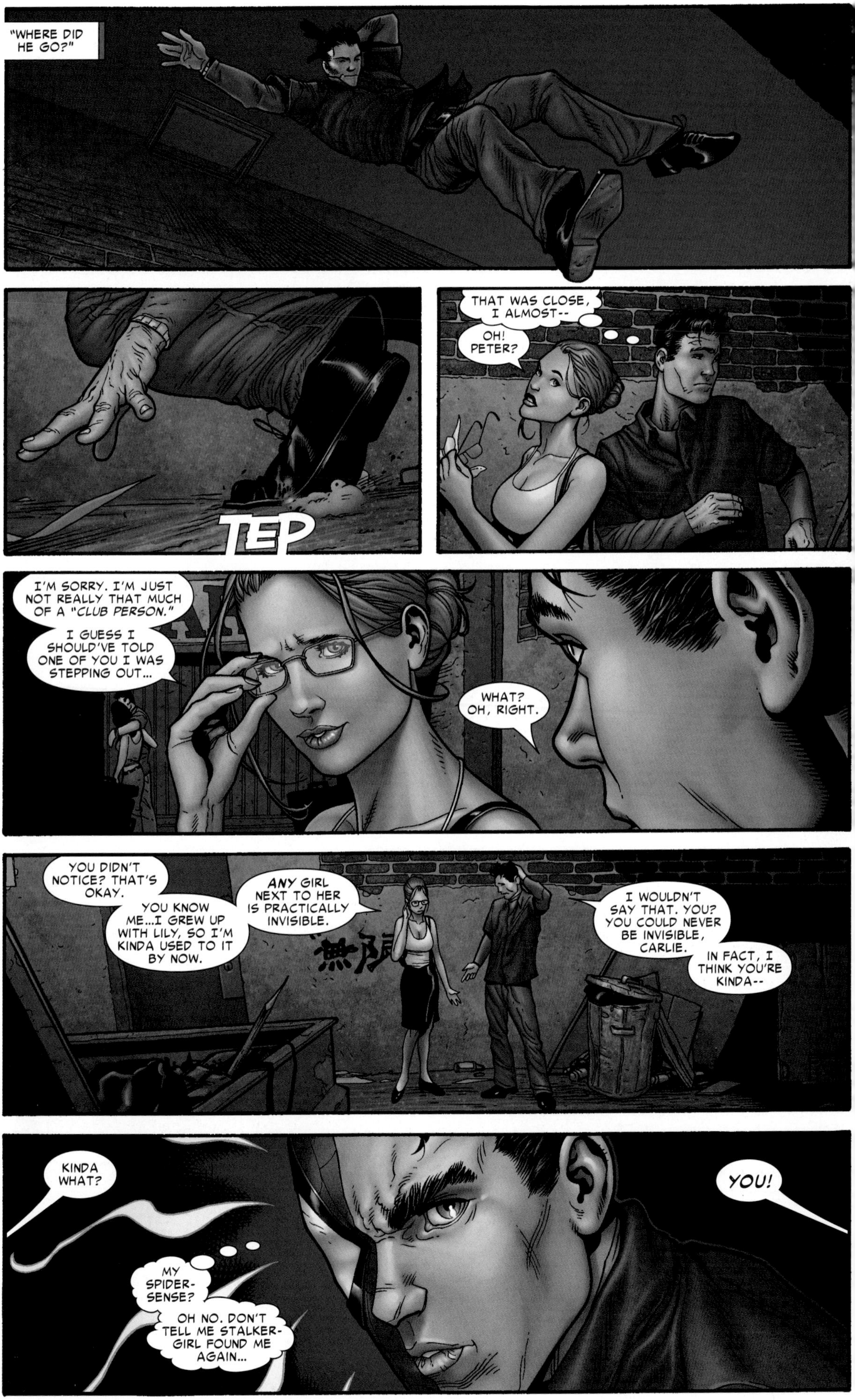
"WHERE DID HE GO?"
TEP
THAT WAS CLOSE, I ALMOST--
OH! PETER?
I'M SORRY. I'M JUST NOT REALLY THAT MUCH OF A "CLUB PERSON."
I GUESS I SHOULD'VE TOLD ONE OF YOU I WAS STEPPING OUT...
WHAT? OH, RIGHT.
YOU DIDN'T NOTICE? THAT'S OKAY.
YOU KNOW ME...I GREW UP WITH LILY, SO I'M KINDA USED TO IT BY NOW.
ANY GIRL NEXT TO HER IS PRACTICALLY INVISIBLE.
I WOULDN'T SAY THAT. YOU? YOU COULD NEVER BE INVISIBLE, CARLIE.
IN FACT, I THINK YOU'RE KINDA--
KINDA WHAT?
YOU!
MY SPIDER-SENSE?
OH NO. DON'T TELL ME STALKER-GIRL FOUND ME AGAIN...

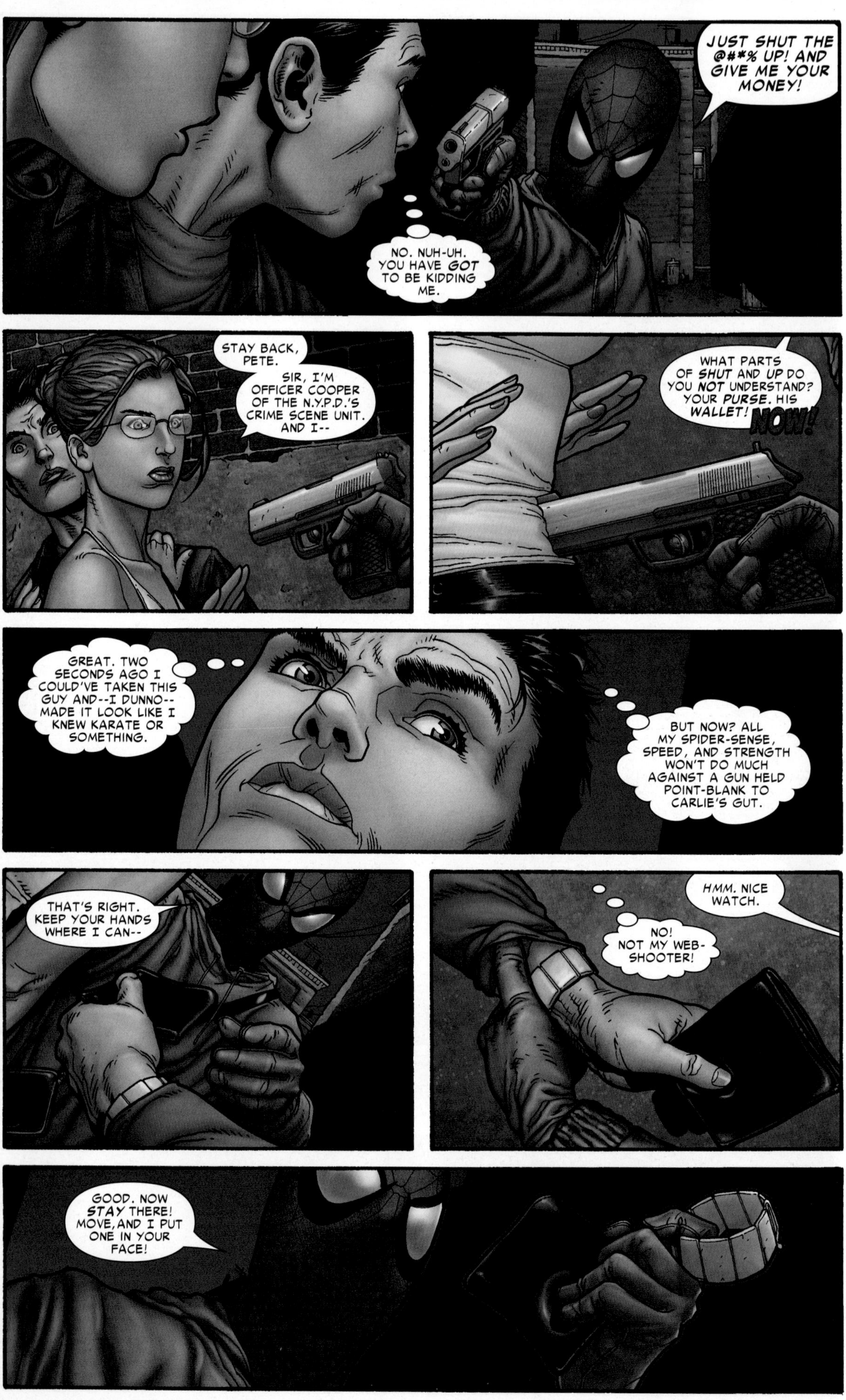
JUST SHUT THE @#*% UP! AND GIVE ME YOUR MONEY!
NO. NUH-UH. YOU HAVE GOT TO BE KIDDING ME.
STAY BACK, PETE.
SIR, I'M OFFICER COOPER OF THE N.Y.P.D.'S CRIME SCENE UNIT. AND I--
WHAT PARTS OF SHUT AND UP DO YOU NOT UNDERSTAND? YOUR PURSE. HIS WALLET! NOW!
GREAT. TWO SECONDS AGO I COULD'VE TAKEN THIS GUY AND--I DUNNO--MADE IT LOOK LIKE I KNEW KARATE OR SOMETHING.
BUT NOW? ALL MY SPIDER-SENSE, SPEED, AND STRENGTH WON'T DO MUCH AGAINST A GUN HELD POINT-BLANK TO CARLIE'S GUT.
THAT'S RIGHT. KEEP YOUR HANDS WHERE I CAN--
HMM. NICE WATCH.
NO! NOT MY WEB-SHOOTER!
GOOD. NOW STAY THERE! MOVE, AND I PUT ONE IN YOUR FACE!

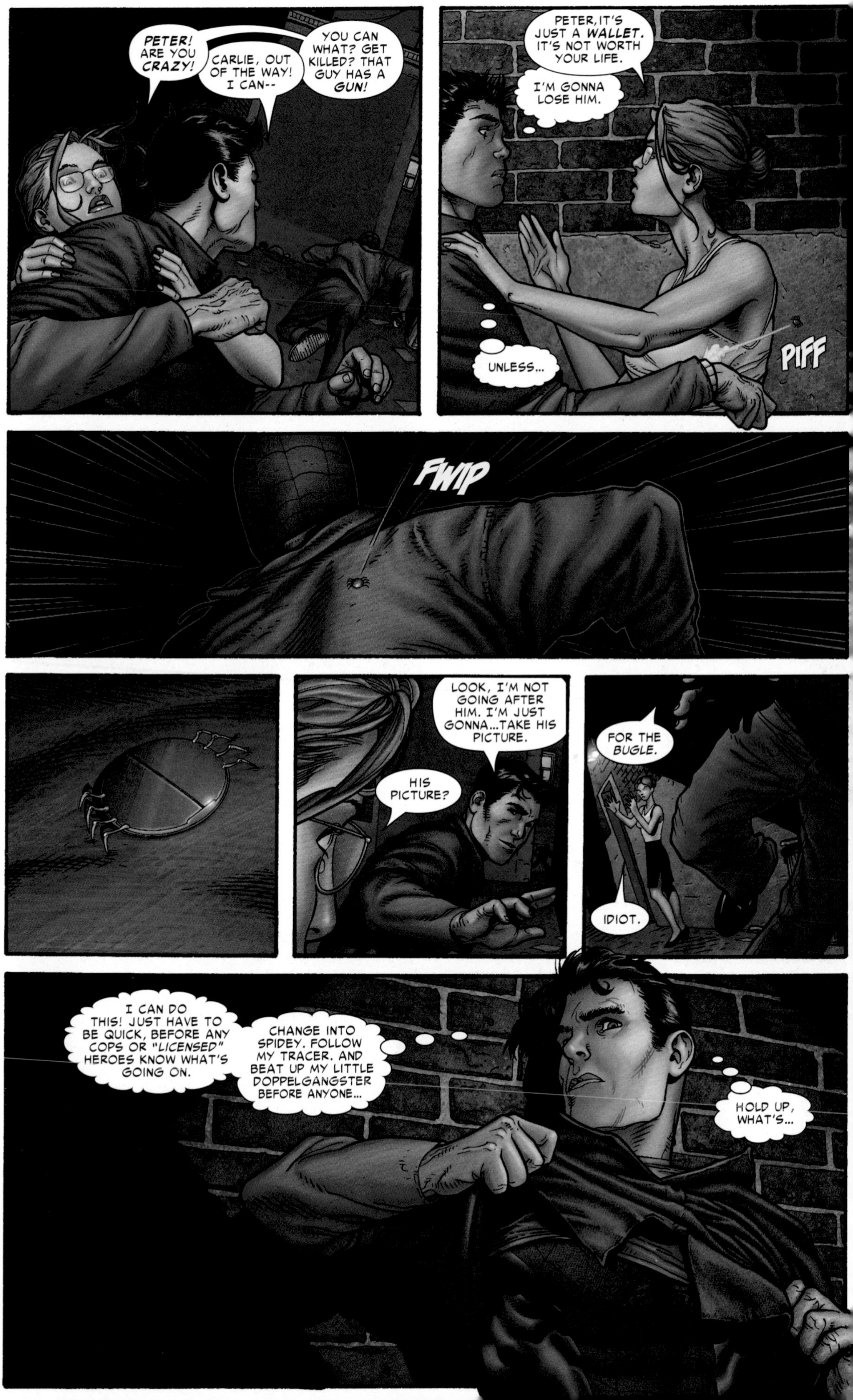
PETER! ARE YOU CRAZY!
CARLIE, OUT OF THE WAY! I CAN--
YOU CAN WHAT? GET KILLED? THAT GUY HAS A GUN!
PETER, IT'S JUST A WALLET. IT'S NOT WORTH YOUR LIFE.
I'M GONNA LOSE HIM.
UNLESS...
PIFF
FWIP
LOOK, I'M NOT GOING AFTER HIM. I'M JUST GONNA...TAKE HIS PICTURE.
HIS PICTURE?
FOR THE BUGLE.
IDIOT.
I CAN DO THIS! JUST HAVE TO BE QUICK, BEFORE ANY COPS OR "LICENSED" HEROES KNOW WHAT'S GOING ON.
CHANGE INTO SPIDEY. FOLLOW MY TRACER. AND BEAT UP MY LITTLE DOPPELGANGSTER BEFORE ANYONE...
HOLD UP, WHAT'S...

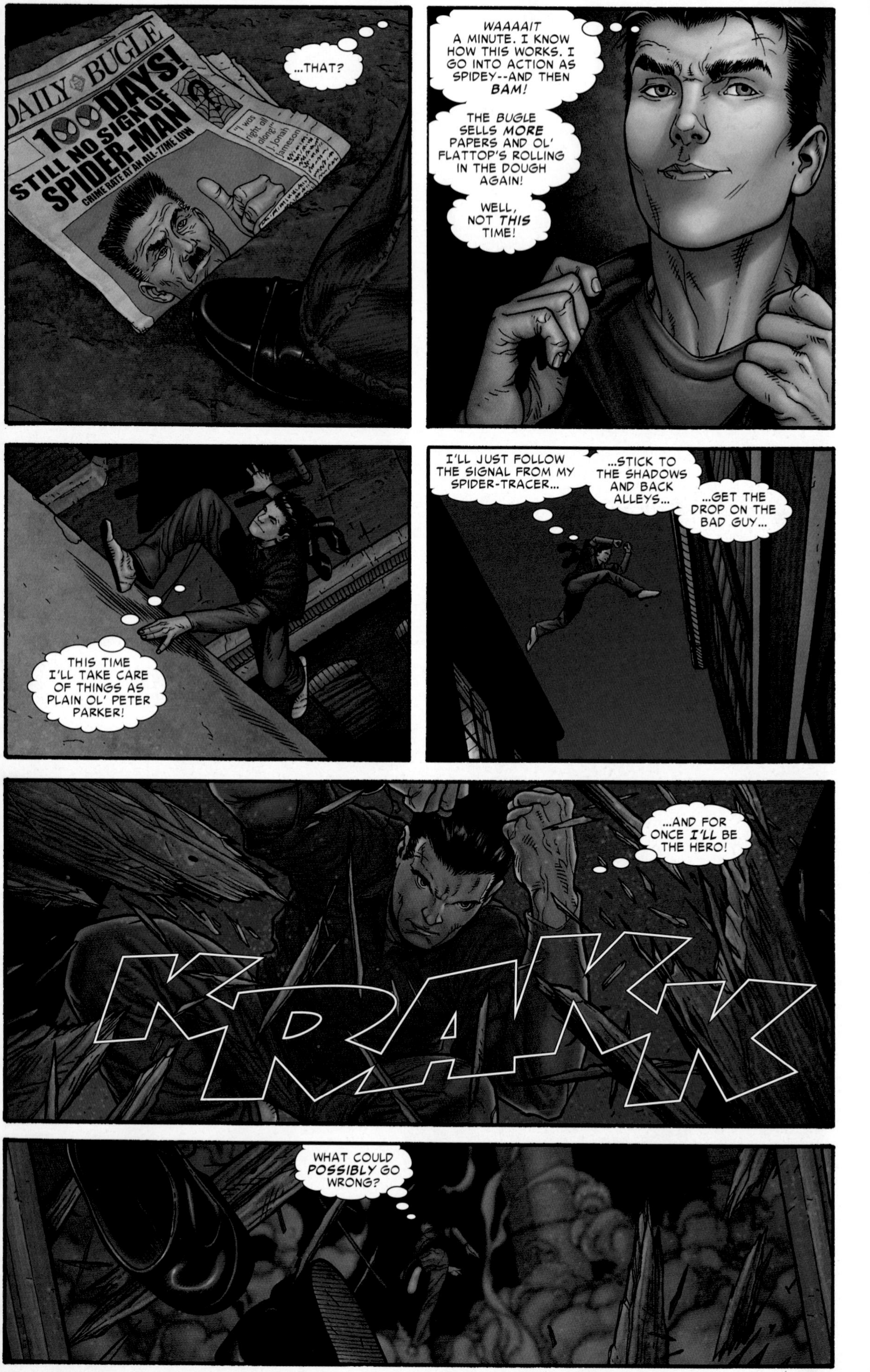
DAILY BUGLE
100 DAYS!
STILL NO SIGN OF SPIDER-MAN
CRIME RATE AT AN ALL-TIME LOW
"I was right all along!" J. Jonah Jameson
...THAT?
WAAAAIT A MINUTE. I KNOW HOW THIS WORKS. I GO INTO ACTION AS SPIDEY--AND THEN BAM!
THE BUGLE SELLS MORE PAPERS AND OL' FLATTOP'S ROLLING IN THE DOUGH AGAIN!
WELL, NOT THIS TIME!
THIS TIME I'LL TAKE CARE OF THINGS AS PLAIN OL' PETER PARKER!
I'LL JUST FOLLOW THE SIGNAL FROM MY SPIDER-TRACER...
...STICK TO THE SHADOWS AND BACK ALLEYS...
...GET THE DROP ON THE BAD GUY...
...AND FOR ONCE I'LL BE THE HERO!
KRAKK
WHAT COULD POSSIBLY GO WRONG?

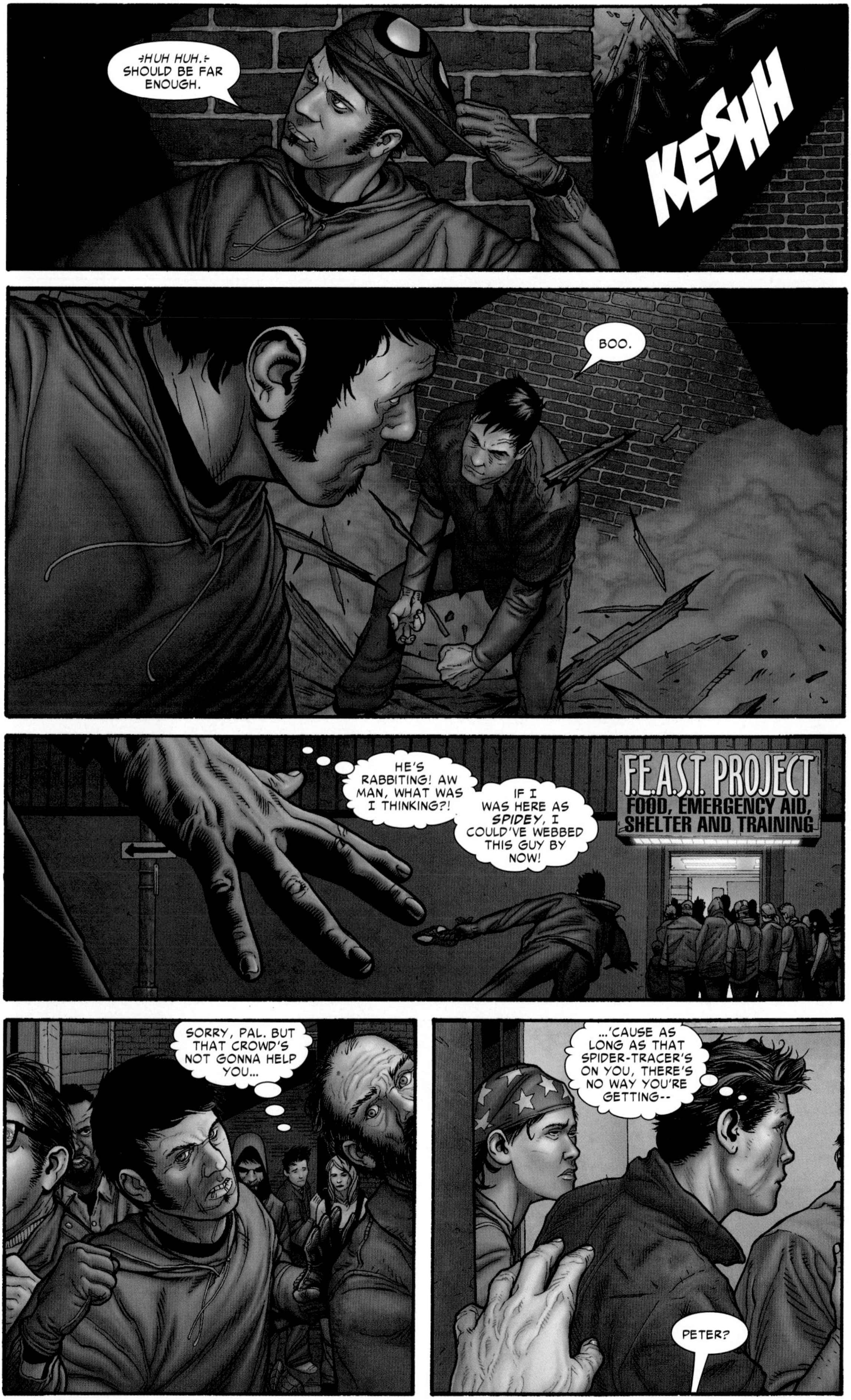

HUH HUH. SHOULD BE FAR ENOUGH.
KESHH
BOO.
HE'S RABBITING! AW MAN, WHAT WAS I THINKING?!
IF I WAS HERE AS SPIDEY, I COULD'VE WEBBED THIS GUY BY NOW!
F.E.A.S.T. PROJECT
FOOD, EMERGENCY AID, SHELTER AND TRAINING
SORRY, PAL. BUT THAT CROWD'S NOT GONNA HELP YOU...
...'CAUSE AS LONG AS THAT SPIDER-TRACER'S ON YOU, THERE'S NO WAY YOU'RE GETTING--
PETER?

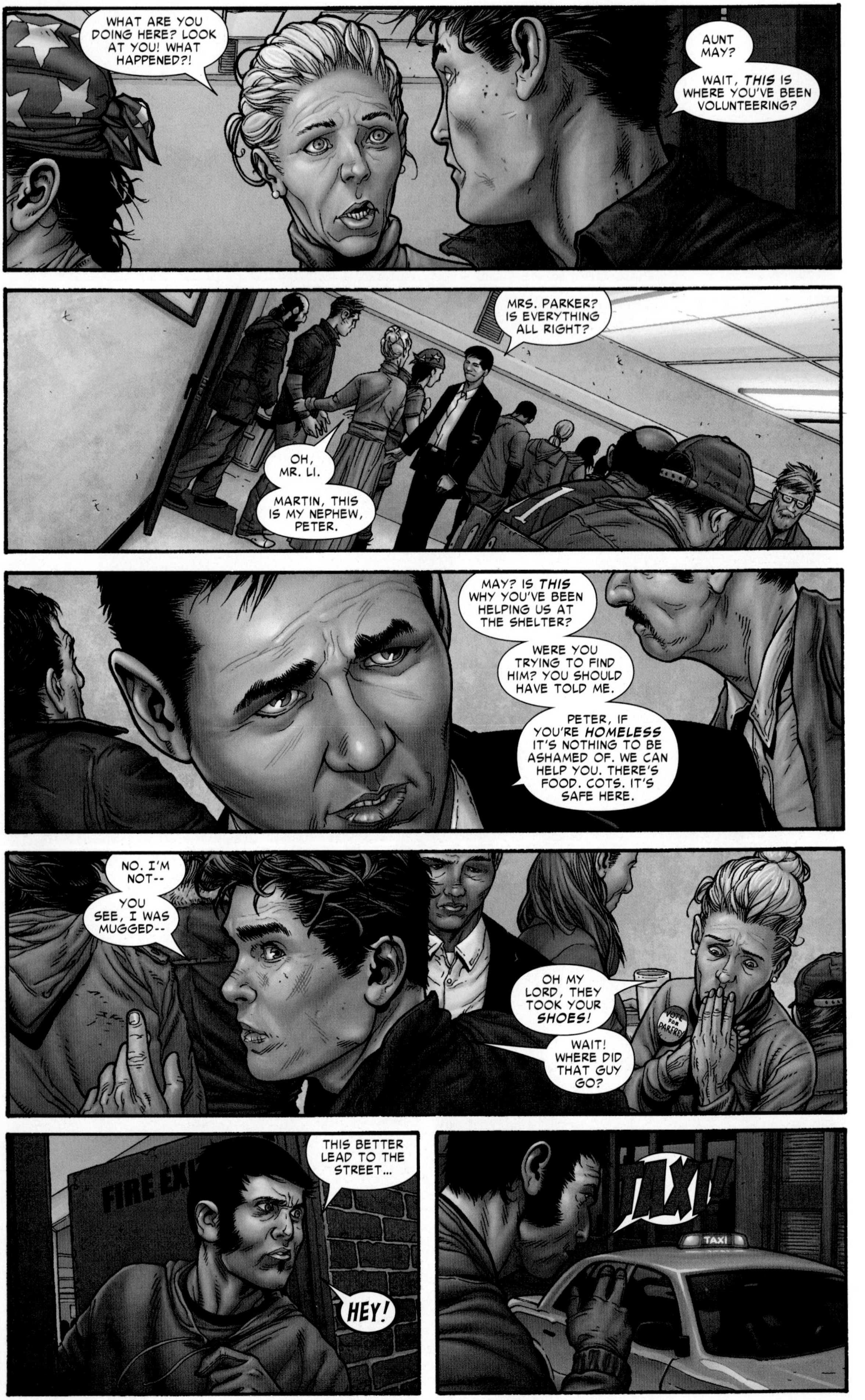
WHAT ARE YOU DOING HERE? LOOK AT YOU! WHAT HAPPENED?!
AUNT MAY?
WAIT, THIS IS WHERE YOU'VE BEEN VOLUNTEERING?
MRS. PARKER? IS EVERYTHING ALL RIGHT?
OH, MR. LI.
MARTIN, THIS IS MY NEPHEW, PETER.
MAY? IS THIS WHY YOU'VE BEEN HELPING US AT THE SHELTER?
WERE YOU TRYING TO FIND HIM? YOU SHOULD HAVE TOLD ME.
PETER, IF YOU'RE HOMELESS IT'S NOTHING TO BE ASHAMED OF. WE CAN HELP YOU. THERE'S FOOD. COTS. IT'S SAFE HERE.
NO. I'M NOT--
YOU SEE, I WAS MUGGED--
OH MY LORD, THEY TOOK YOUR SHOES!
WAIT! WHERE DID THAT GUY GO?
FIRE EX
THIS BETTER LEAD TO THE STREET...
HEY!
TAXI!
TAXI

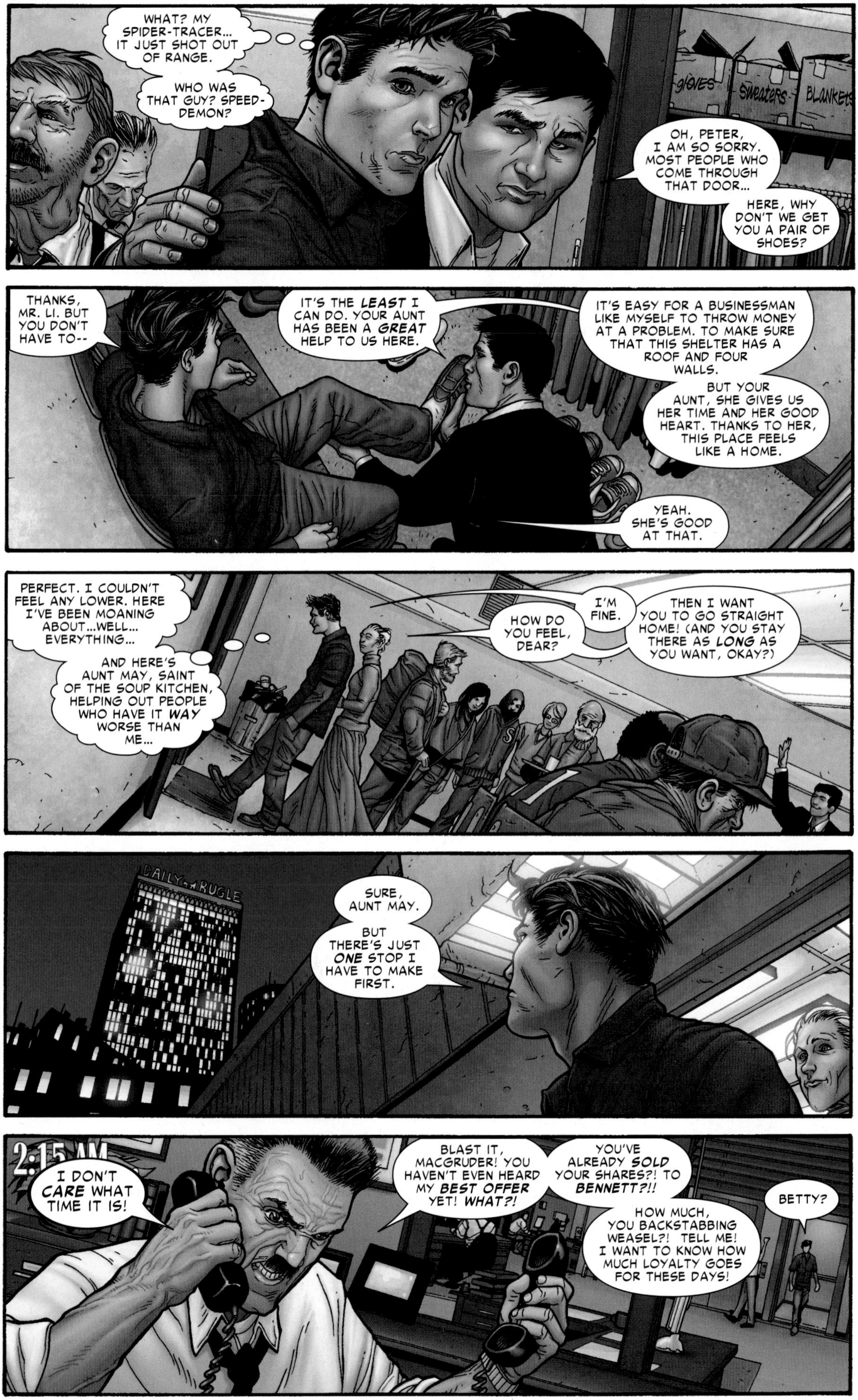
WHAT? MY SPIDER-TRACER... IT JUST SHOT OUT OF RANGE.
WHO WAS THAT GUY? SPEED-DEMON?
GLOVES
SWEATERS
BLANKETS
OH, PETER, I AM SO SORRY. MOST PEOPLE WHO COME THROUGH THAT DOOR...
HERE, WHY DON'T WE GET YOU A PAIR OF SHOES?
THANKS, MR. LI. BUT YOU DON'T HAVE TO--
IT'S THE LEAST I CAN DO. YOUR AUNT HAS BEEN A GREAT HELP TO US HERE.
IT'S EASY FOR A BUSINESSMAN LIKE MYSELF TO THROW MONEY AT A PROBLEM. TO MAKE SURE THAT THIS SHELTER HAS A ROOF AND FOUR WALLS.
BUT YOUR AUNT, SHE GIVES US HER TIME AND HER GOOD HEART. THANKS TO HER, THIS PLACE FEELS LIKE A HOME.
YEAH. SHE'S GOOD AT THAT.
PERFECT. I COULDN'T FEEL ANY LOWER. HERE I'VE BEEN MOANING ABOUT...WELL... EVERYTHING...
AND HERE'S AUNT MAY, SAINT OF THE SOUP KITCHEN, HELPING OUT PEOPLE WHO HAVE IT WAY WORSE THAN ME...
HOW DO YOU FEEL, DEAR?
I'M FINE.
THEN I WANT YOU TO GO STRAIGHT HOME! (AND YOU STAY THERE AS LONG AS YOU WANT, OKAY?)
DAILY BUGLE
SURE, AUNT MAY.
BUT THERE'S JUST ONE STOP I HAVE TO MAKE FIRST.
2:15 AM
I DON'T CARE WHAT TIME IT IS!
BLAST IT, MACGRUDER! YOU HAVEN'T EVEN HEARD MY BEST OFFER YET! WHAT?!
YOU'VE ALREADY SOLD YOUR SHARES?! TO BENNETT?!!
HOW MUCH, YOU BACKSTABBING WEASEL?! TELL ME! I WANT TO KNOW HOW MUCH LOYALTY GOES FOR THESE DAYS!
BETTY?

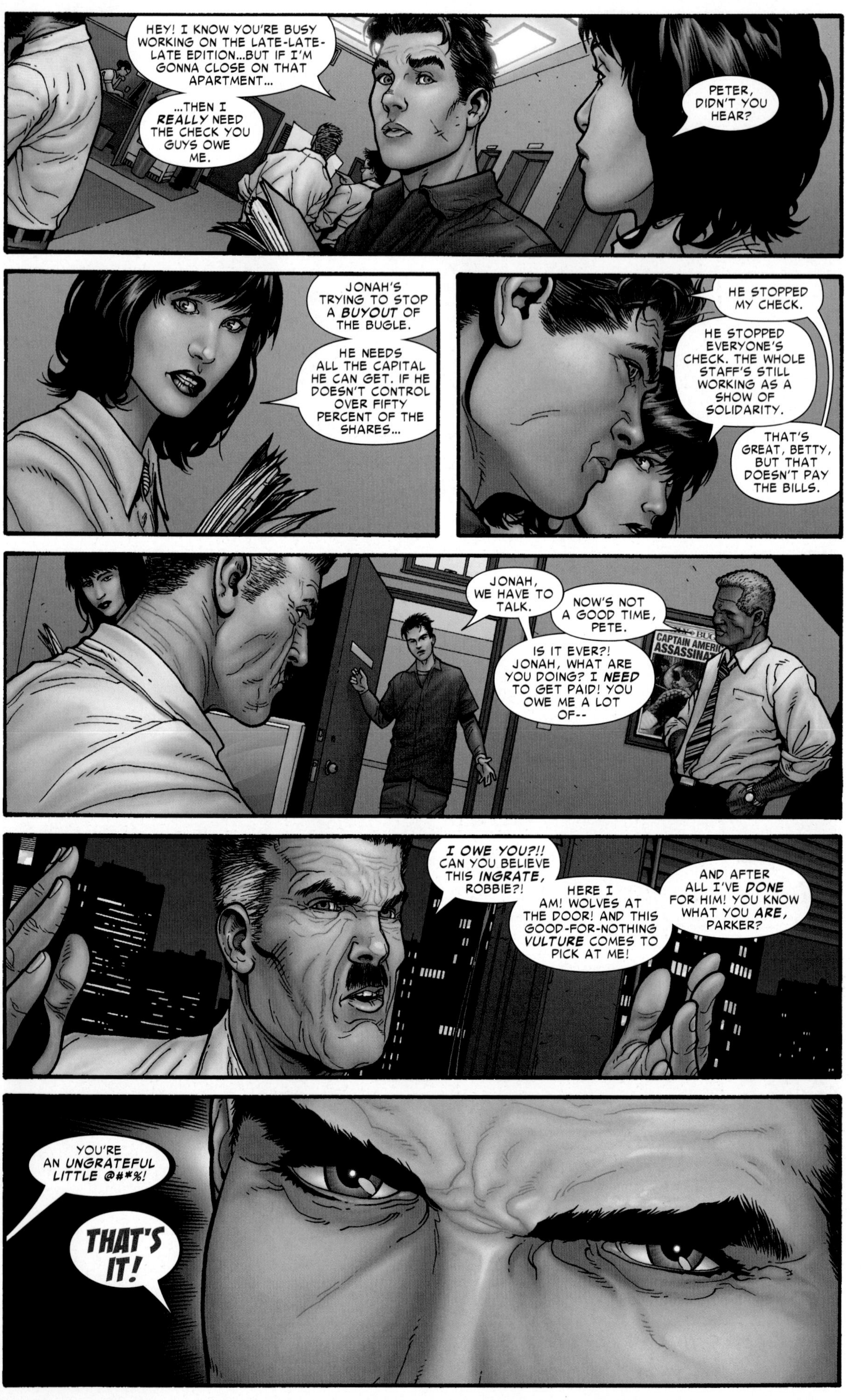
HEY! I KNOW YOU'RE BUSY WORKING ON THE LATE-LATE-LATE EDITION...BUT IF I'M GONNA CLOSE ON THAT APARTMENT...
...THEN I *REALLY* NEED THE CHECK YOU GUYS OWE ME.
PETER, DIDN'T YOU HEAR?
JONAH'S TRYING TO STOP A *BUYOUT* OF THE BUGLE.
HE NEEDS ALL THE CAPITAL HE CAN GET. IF HE DOESN'T CONTROL OVER FIFTY PERCENT OF THE SHARES...
HE STOPPED MY CHECK.
HE STOPPED EVERYONE'S CHECK. THE WHOLE STAFF'S STILL WORKING AS A SHOW OF SOLIDARITY.
THAT'S GREAT, BETTY, BUT THAT DOESN'T PAY THE BILLS.
JONAH, WE HAVE TO TALK.
NOW'S NOT A GOOD TIME, PETE.
IS IT EVER?! JONAH, WHAT ARE YOU DOING? I *NEED* TO GET PAID! YOU OWE ME A LOT OF--
CAPTAIN AMERIC
ASSASSINAT
I OWE YOU?!! CAN YOU BELIEVE THIS *INGRATE,* ROBBIE?!
HERE I AM! WOLVES AT THE DOOR! AND THIS GOOD-FOR-NOTHING *VULTURE* COMES TO PICK AT ME!
AND AFTER ALL I'VE *DONE* FOR HIM! YOU KNOW WHAT YOU *ARE,* PARKER?
YOU'RE AN *UNGRATEFUL* LITTLE @#*%!
THAT'S IT!

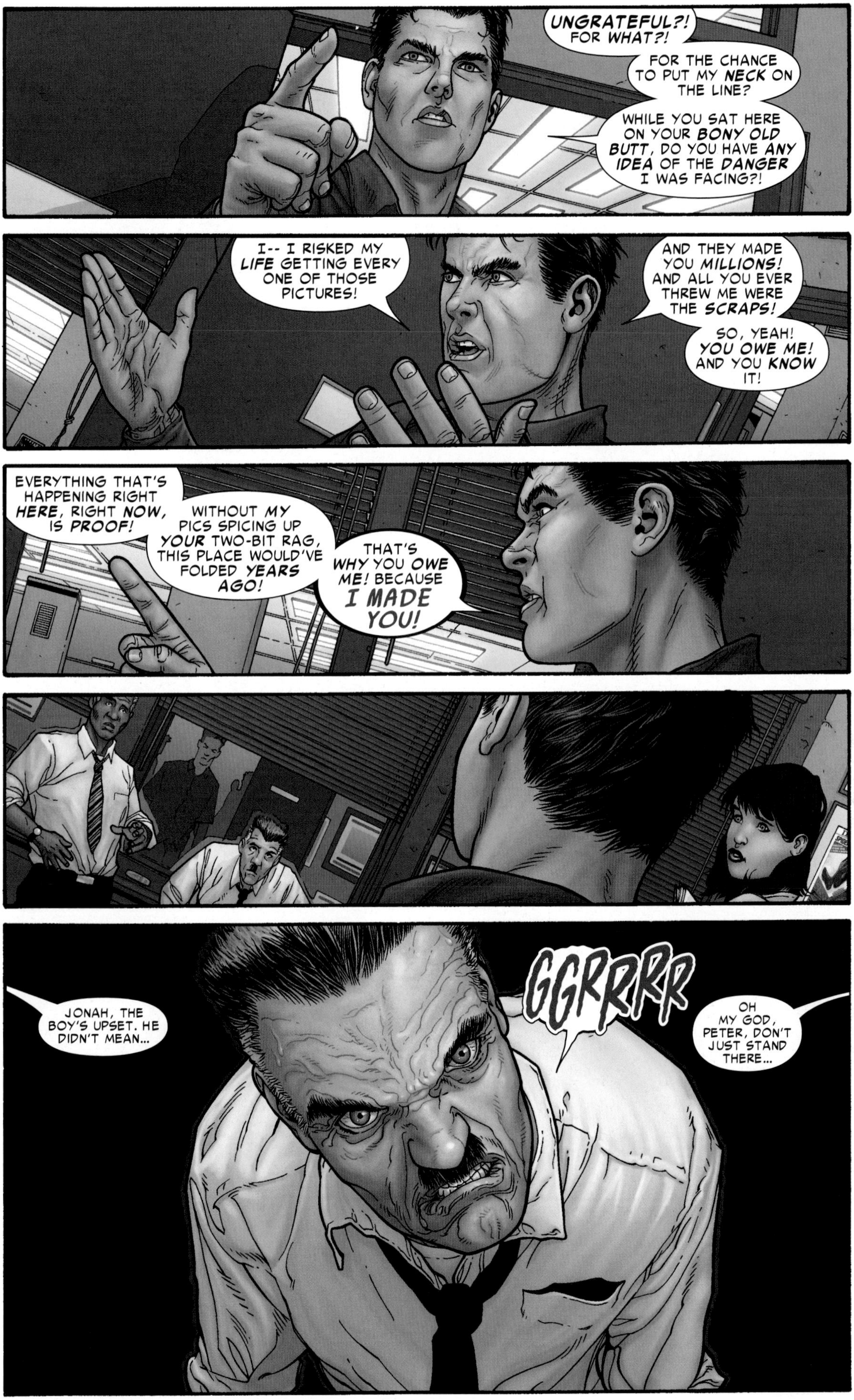
UNGRATEFUL?! FOR WHAT?!
FOR THE CHANCE TO PUT MY NECK ON THE LINE?
WHILE YOU SAT HERE ON YOUR BONY OLD BUTT, DO YOU HAVE ANY IDEA OF THE DANGER I WAS FACING?!
I-- I RISKED MY LIFE GETTING EVERY ONE OF THOSE PICTURES!
AND THEY MADE YOU MILLIONS! AND ALL YOU EVER THREW ME WERE THE SCRAPS!
SO, YEAH! YOU OWE ME! AND YOU KNOW IT!
EVERYTHING THAT'S HAPPENING RIGHT HERE, RIGHT NOW, IS PROOF!
WITHOUT MY PICS SPICING UP YOUR TWO-BIT RAG, THIS PLACE WOULD'VE FOLDED YEARS AGO!
THAT'S WHY YOU OWE ME! BECAUSE I MADE YOU!
JONAH, THE BOY'S UPSET. HE DIDN'T MEAN...
GGRRRR
OH MY GOD, PETER, DON'T JUST STAND THERE...

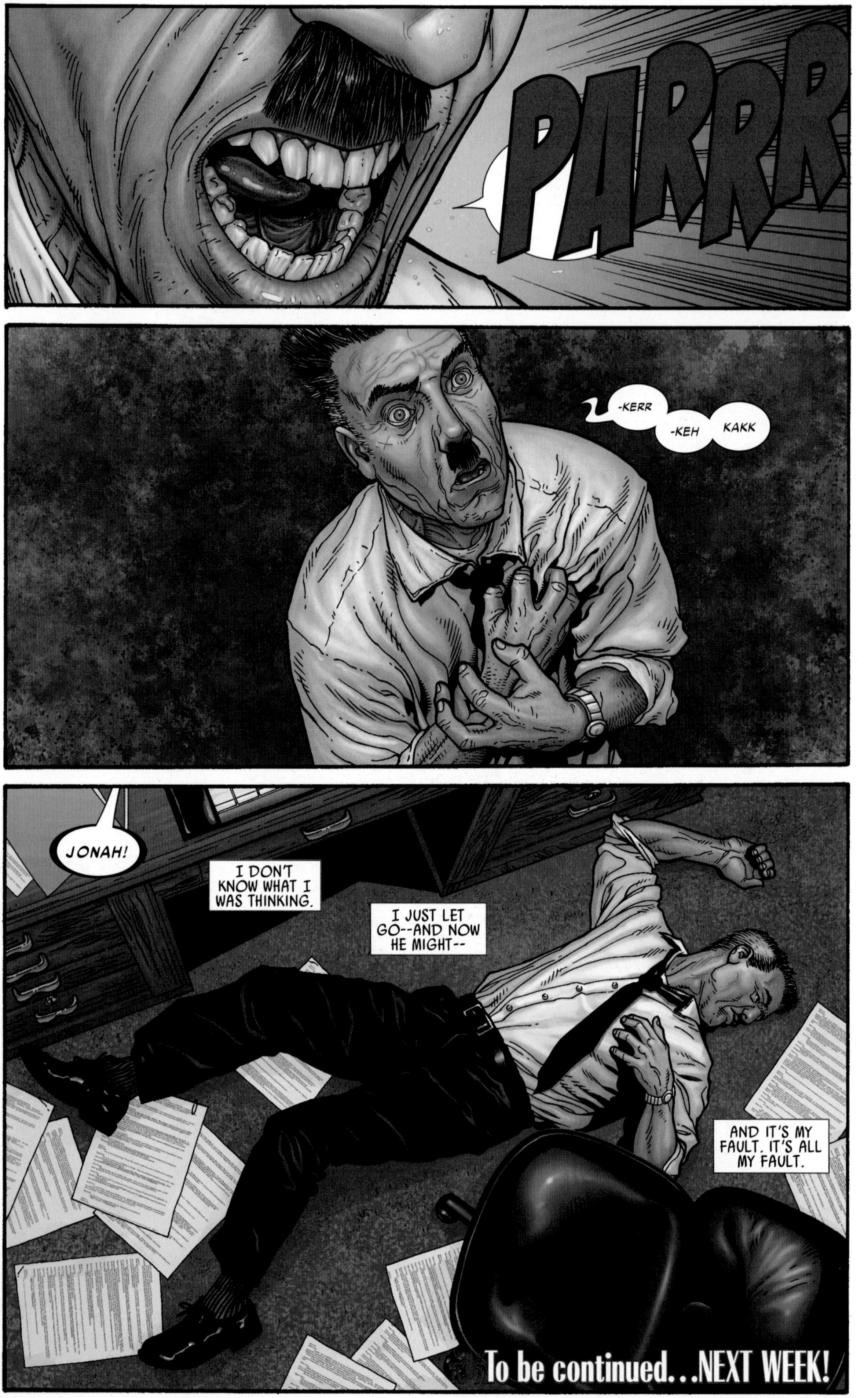
PARRR
-KERR
-KEH
KAKK
JONAH!
I DON'T KNOW WHAT I WAS THINKING.
I JUST LET GO--AND NOW HE MIGHT--
AND IT'S MY FAULT. IT'S ALL MY FAULT.
To be continued. . .NEXT WEEK!

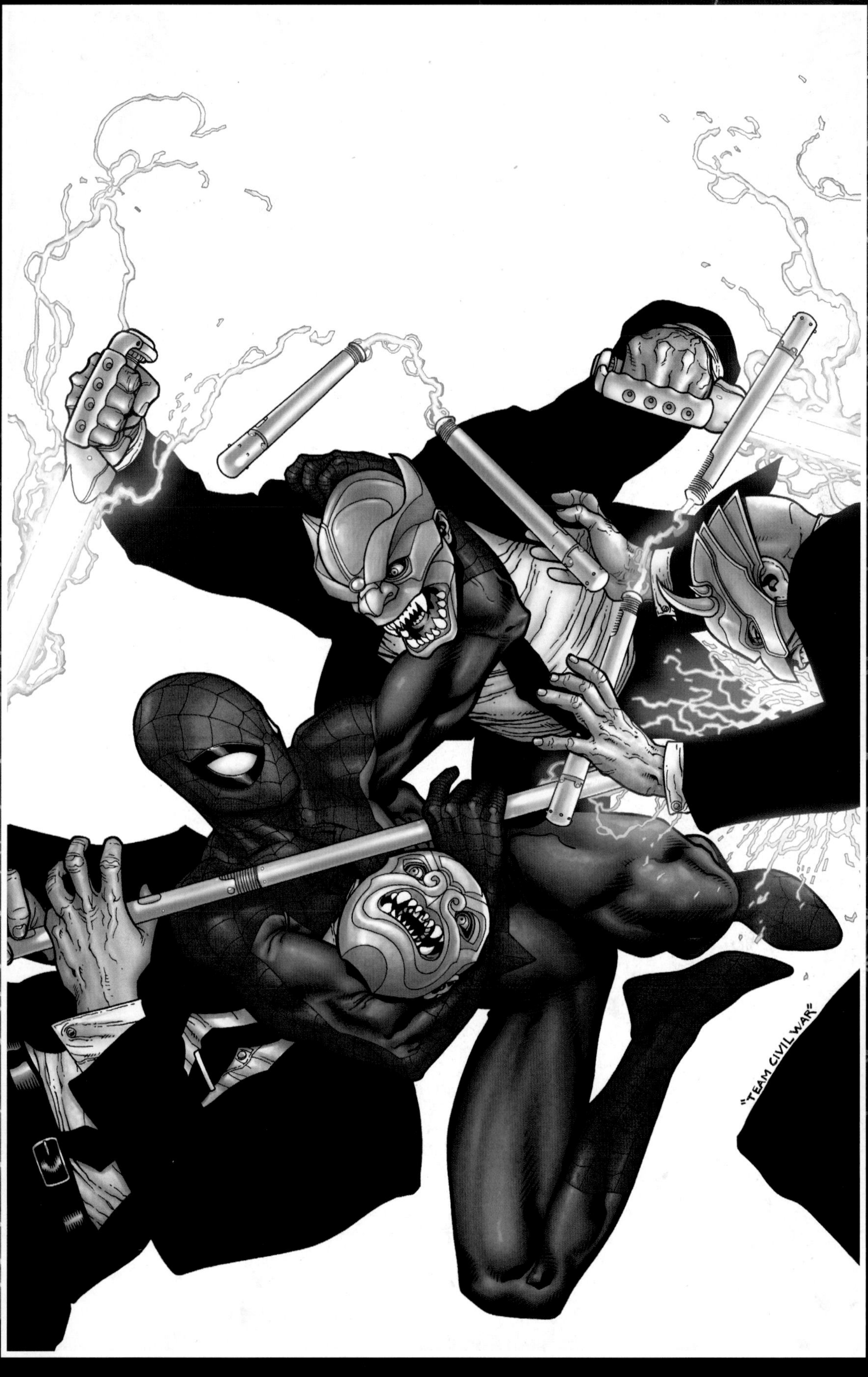
"TEAM CIVIL WAR"

AMAZING SPIDER-MAN #547

WHILE ATTENDING A DEMONSTRATION IN RADIOLOGY, HIGH SCHOOL STUDENT **PETER PARKER** WAS BITTEN BY A SPIDER WHICH HAD ACCIDENTALLY BEEN EXPOSED TO **RADIOACTIVE RAYS.** THROUGH A MIRACLE OF SCIENCE, PETER SOON FOUND THAT HE HAD **GAINED** THE SPIDER'S POWERS...AND HAD, IN EFFECT, BECOME A HUMAN SPIDER! FROM THAT DAY ON HE WAS...

THE AMAZING SPIDER-MAN™

CRIMES OF THE HEART

The Daily Bugle.

ON THE FLOOR OF PUBLISHER J. JONAH JAMESON'S OFFICE.

TRUST ME, YOU DON'T WANT TO KNOW.

FINE. HE TASTES LIKE CIGAR BUTTS AND DAY OLD COFFEE. HAPPY NOW?

SEE? THIS'S WHAT HE GETS FOR A LIFETIME OF SMOKING AND--

OH, WHO AM I KIDDING? I DID THIS. ME, PETER "KICK 'EM WHEN THEY'RE DOWN" PARKER.

I'M THE ONE WHO TORE INTO JONAH ON THE MOST STRESSFUL NIGHT OF HIS LIFE.

AND NOW HE'S HAVING A *HEART ATTACK.* AFTER YELLING OUT *MY* NAME. THAT *CAN'T* BE THE LAST THING HE EVER SAYS!

C'MON, YOU OLD COOT, *FIGHT!*

DAN SLOTT — WRITER | STEVE McNIVEN — PENCILER | DEXTER VINES — INKER | MORRY HOLLOWELL — COLORS | VC'S CORY PETIT — LETTERS | TOM BRENNAN — ASSISTANT EDITOR | STEPHEN WACKER — EDITOR | TOM BREVOORT — EXECUTIVE EDITOR | JOE QUESADA — EDITOR IN CHIEF | DAN BUCKLEY — PUBLISHER

GALE, GUGGENHEIM, SLOTT, WELLS
SPIDEY'S BRAINTRUST

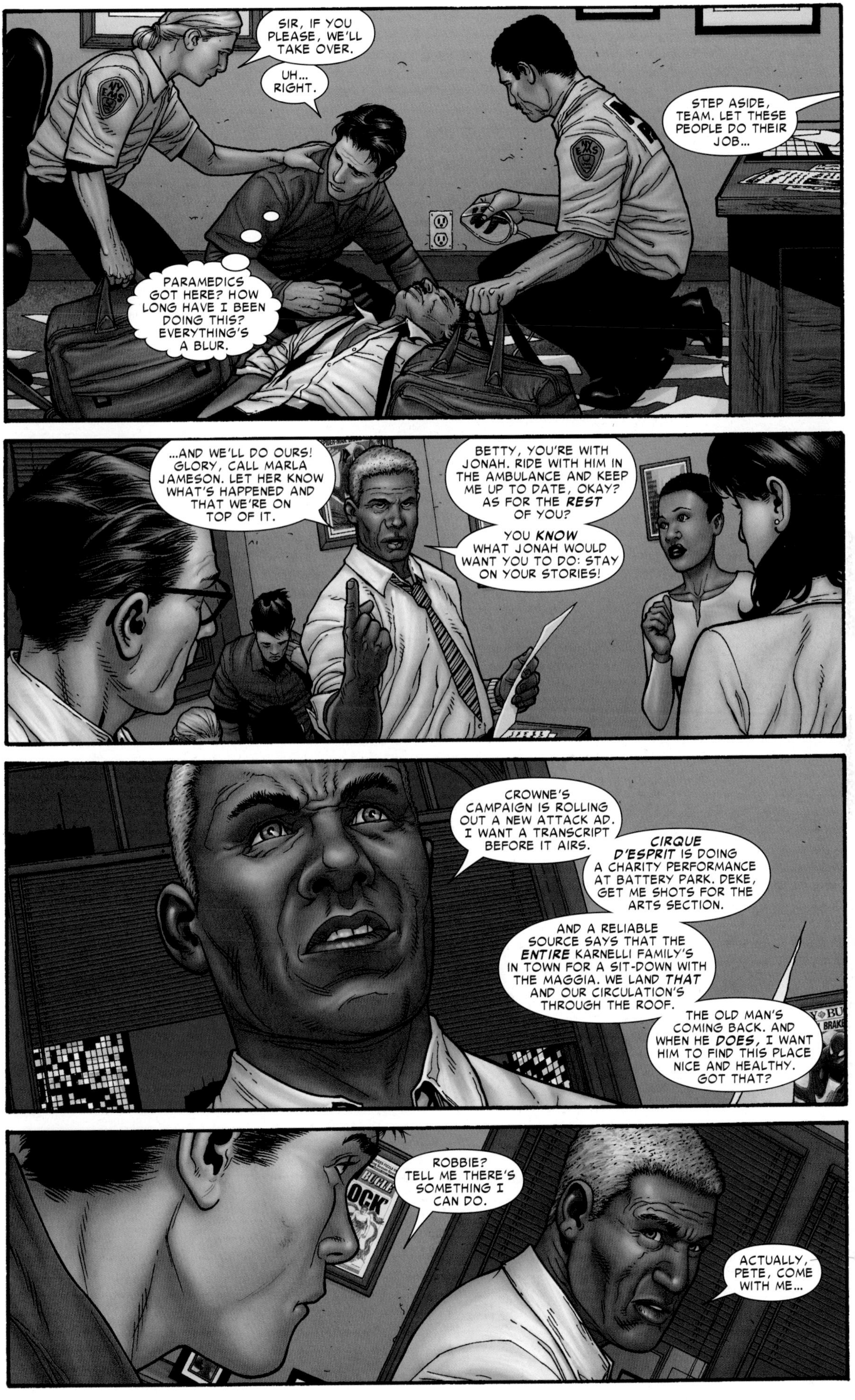
SIR, IF YOU PLEASE, WE'LL TAKE OVER.
UH... RIGHT.
STEP ASIDE, TEAM. LET THESE PEOPLE DO THEIR JOB...
PARAMEDICS GOT HERE? HOW LONG HAVE I BEEN DOING THIS? EVERYTHING'S A BLUR.
...AND WE'LL DO OURS! GLORY, CALL MARLA JAMESON. LET HER KNOW WHAT'S HAPPENED AND THAT WE'RE ON TOP OF IT.
BETTY, YOU'RE WITH JONAH. RIDE WITH HIM IN THE AMBULANCE AND KEEP ME UP TO DATE, OKAY? AS FOR THE *REST* OF YOU?
YOU *KNOW* WHAT JONAH WOULD WANT YOU TO DO: STAY ON YOUR STORIES!
CROWNE'S CAMPAIGN IS ROLLING OUT A NEW ATTACK AD. I WANT A TRANSCRIPT BEFORE IT AIRS.
CIRQUE D'ESPRIT IS DOING A CHARITY PERFORMANCE AT BATTERY PARK. DEKE, GET ME SHOTS FOR THE ARTS SECTION.
AND A RELIABLE SOURCE SAYS THAT THE *ENTIRE* KARNELLI FAMILY'S IN TOWN FOR A SIT-DOWN WITH THE MAGGIA. WE LAND *THAT* AND OUR CIRCULATION'S THROUGH THE ROOF.
THE OLD MAN'S COMING BACK. AND WHEN HE *DOES*, I WANT HIM TO FIND THIS PLACE NICE AND HEALTHY. GOT THAT?
ROBBIE? TELL ME THERE'S SOMETHING I CAN DO.
ACTUALLY, PETE, COME WITH ME...

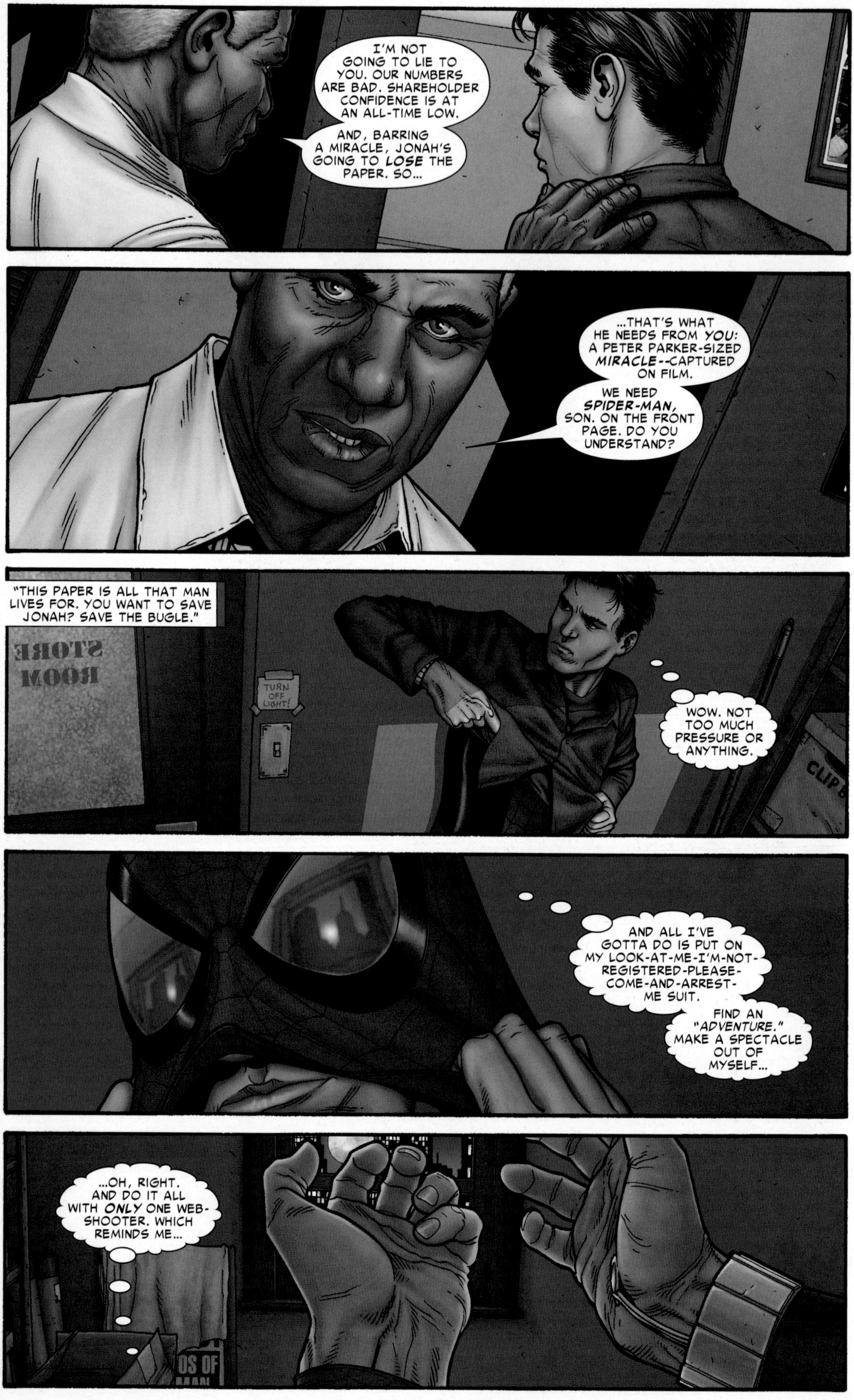
I'M NOT GOING TO LIE TO YOU. OUR NUMBERS ARE BAD. SHAREHOLDER CONFIDENCE IS AT AN ALL-TIME LOW.
AND, BARRING A MIRACLE, JONAH'S GOING TO LOSE THE PAPER. SO...
...THAT'S WHAT HE NEEDS FROM YOU: A PETER PARKER-SIZED MIRACLE--CAPTURED ON FILM.
WE NEED SPIDER-MAN, SON. ON THE FRONT PAGE. DO YOU UNDERSTAND?
"THIS PAPER IS ALL THAT MAN LIVES FOR. YOU WANT TO SAVE JONAH? SAVE THE BUGLE."
STORE ROOM
TURN OFF LIGHT!
WOW. NOT TOO MUCH PRESSURE OR ANYTHING.
AND ALL I'VE GOTTA DO IS PUT ON MY LOOK-AT-ME-I'M-NOT-REGISTERED-PLEASE-COME-AND-ARREST-ME SUIT.
FIND AN "ADVENTURE." MAKE A SPECTACLE OUT OF MYSELF...
...OH, RIGHT. AND DO IT ALL WITH ONLY ONE WEB-SHOOTER. WHICH REMINDS ME...

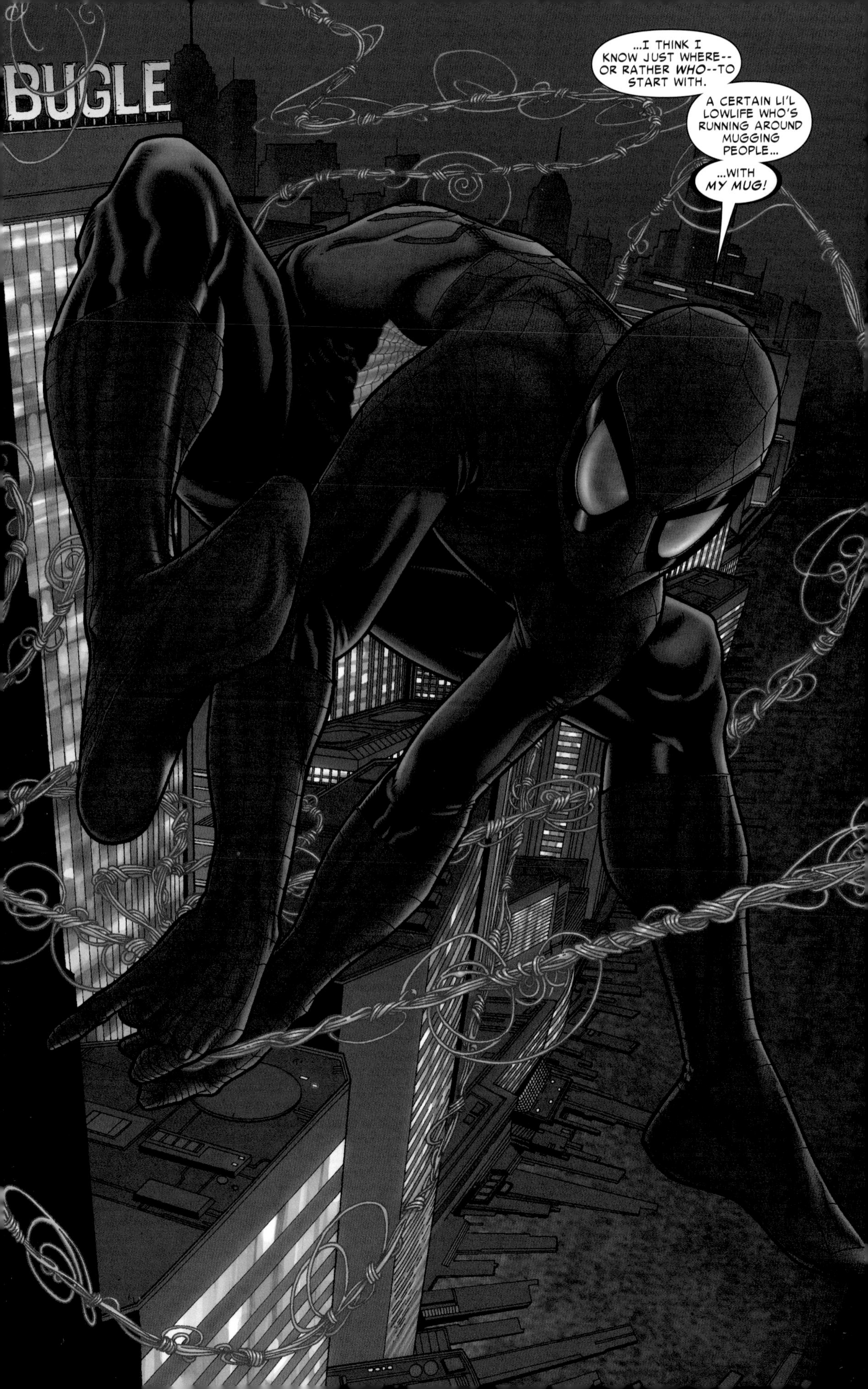
BUGLE
...I THINK I KNOW JUST WHERE--OR RATHER WHO--TO START WITH.
A CERTAIN LI'L LOWLIFE WHO'S RUNNING AROUND MUGGING PEOPLE...
...WITH MY MUG!

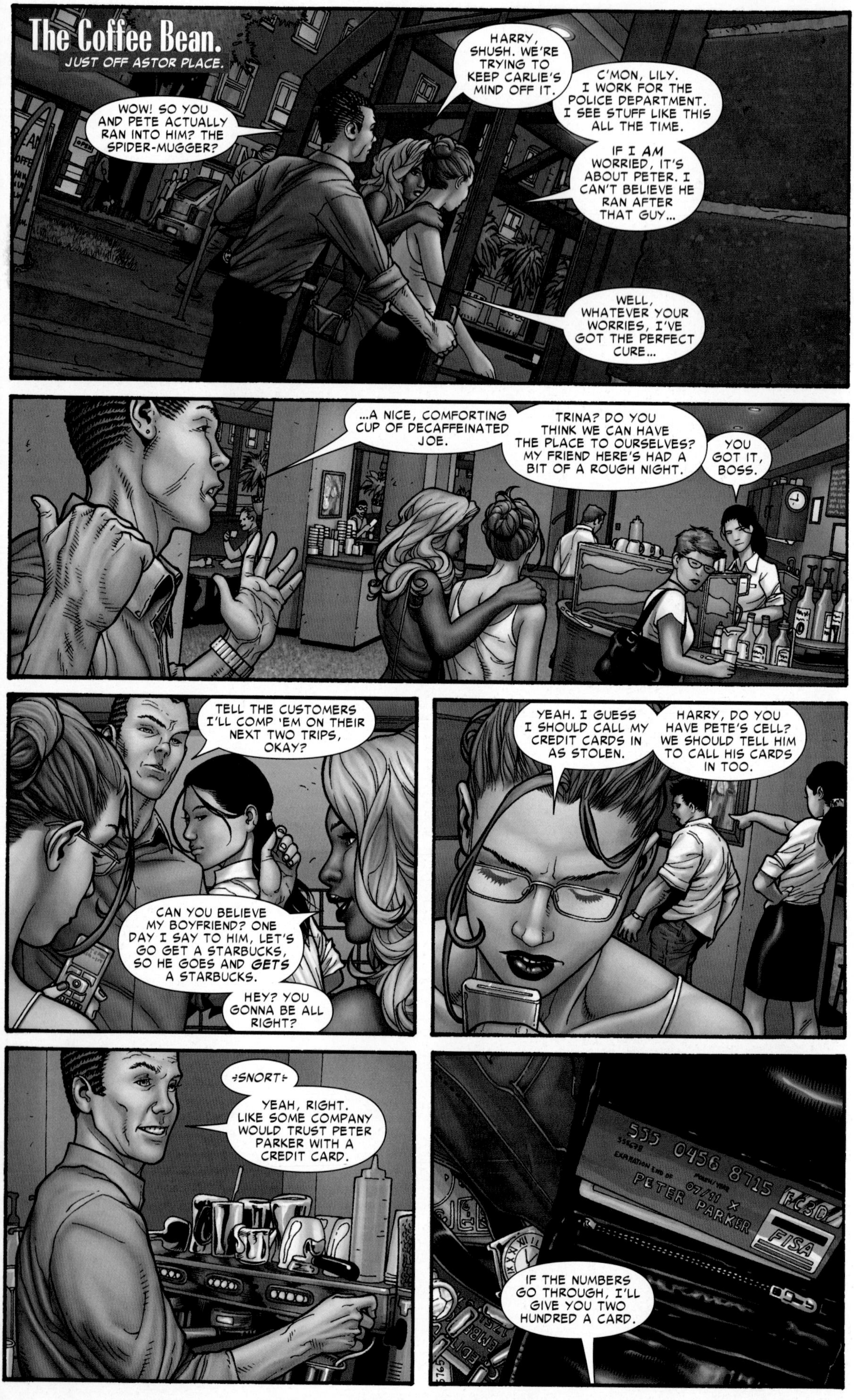
The Coffee Bean.
JUST OFF ASTOR PLACE.
WOW! SO YOU AND PETE ACTUALLY RAN INTO HIM? THE SPIDER-MUGGER?
HARRY, SHUSH. WE'RE TRYING TO KEEP CARLIE'S MIND OFF IT.
C'MON, LILY. I WORK FOR THE POLICE DEPARTMENT. I SEE STUFF LIKE THIS ALL THE TIME.
IF I AM WORRIED, IT'S ABOUT PETER. I CAN'T BELIEVE HE RAN AFTER THAT GUY...
WELL, WHATEVER YOUR WORRIES, I'VE GOT THE PERFECT CURE...
...A NICE, COMFORTING CUP OF DECAFFEINATED JOE.
TRINA? DO YOU THINK WE CAN HAVE THE PLACE TO OURSELVES? MY FRIEND HERE'S HAD A BIT OF A ROUGH NIGHT.
YOU GOT IT, BOSS.
TELL THE CUSTOMERS I'LL COMP 'EM ON THEIR NEXT TWO TRIPS, OKAY?
CAN YOU BELIEVE MY BOYFRIEND? ONE DAY I SAY TO HIM, LET'S GO GET A STARBUCKS, SO HE GOES AND GETS A STARBUCKS.
HEY? YOU GONNA BE ALL RIGHT?
YEAH. I GUESS I SHOULD CALL MY CREDIT CARDS IN AS STOLEN.
HARRY, DO YOU HAVE PETE'S CELL? WE SHOULD TELL HIM TO CALL HIS CARDS IN TOO.
SNORT
YEAH, RIGHT. LIKE SOME COMPANY WOULD TRUST PETER PARKER WITH A CREDIT CARD.
555 0456 8715
07/11
PETER PARKER
FISA
IF THE NUMBERS GO THROUGH, I'LL GIVE YOU TWO HUNDRED A CARD.

C'MON, DOOLEY. YOU'RE GONNA RUN UP A COUPLE GRAND ON EACH OF 'EM.

TAKE IT OR LEAVE IT, BOYLE.

I'LL TAKE IT, YOU CHEAP @*#%. NOW WHAT ABOUT THE JEWELRY?

The Blind Spot.
A WATERFRONT BAR WHERE NOBODY SEES NOTHIN'.

IT'S CRAP.

IT'S A LACK A' RESPECT IS WHAT IT IS, LOU.

EVERY LOUSY MEMBER OF THE TWO MAGGIA FAMILIES ARE GONNA BE THERE. ALL THE KARNELLIS. ALL THE MANFREDIS.

EVERYBODY BUT ME, LI'L BABY BRUNO! IT WAS MY FOLKS--THEIR MARRIAGE THAT BROUGHT THESE TWO SIDES TOGETHER!

I'M THE FREAKIN' HEIR APPARENT! I SHOULD BE THERE! WHAT'S UP WITH THAT?!

MAYBE IT'S 'CAUSE YOU TALK TOO MUCH, BRUNO?

HEY.

LIKE TAKE THIS WATCH. THERE'S NO WATCH ON IT.

AND IT'S JUST TIN OR SOMETHIN'. I'D GET MORE FOR A MEDIC ALERT BRACELET.

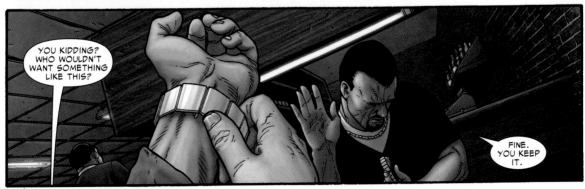

YOU KIDDING? WHO WOULDN'T WANT SOMETHING LIKE THIS?

FINE. YOU KEEP IT.

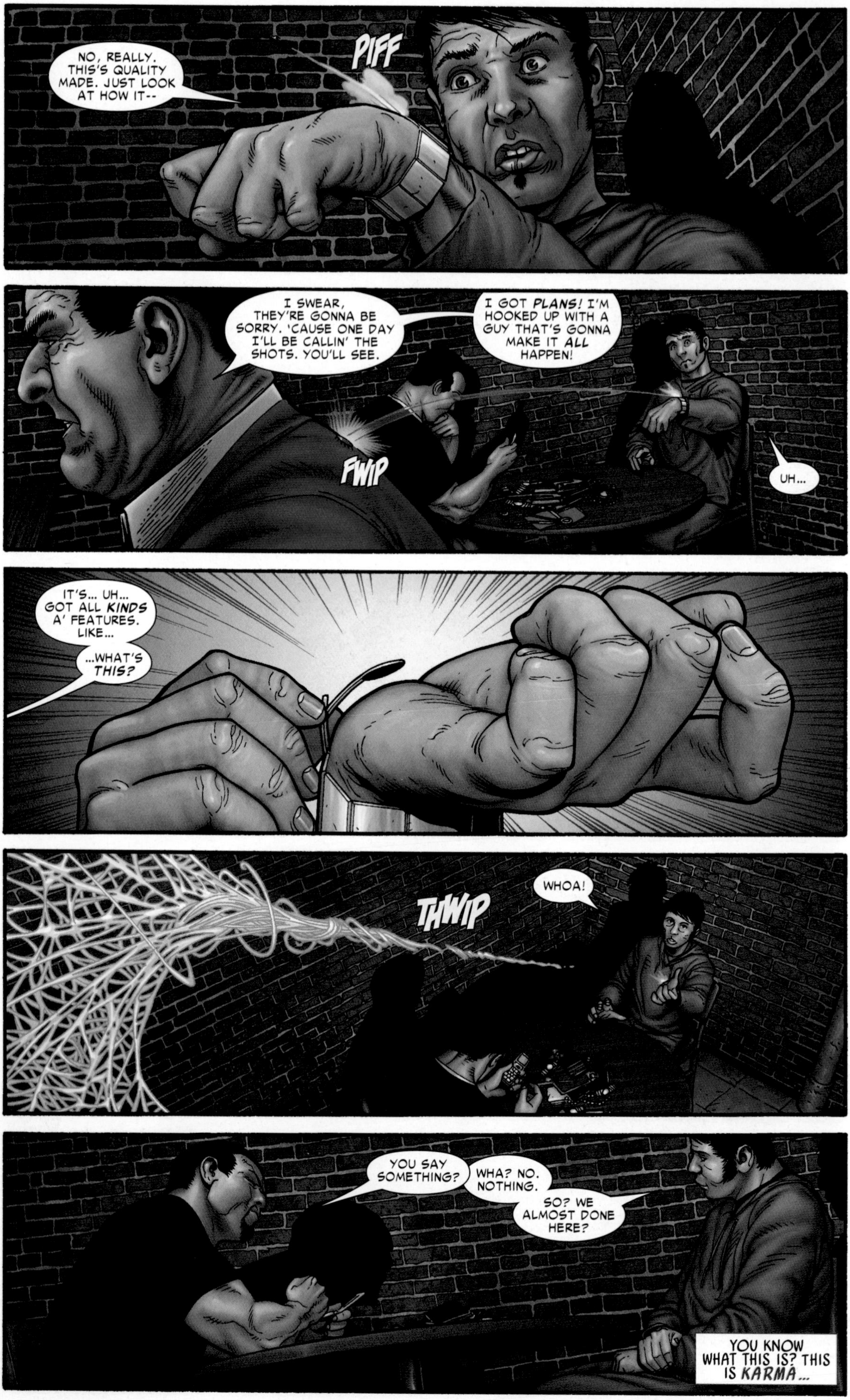
NO, REALLY. THIS'S QUALITY MADE. JUST LOOK AT HOW IT--
PIFF
I SWEAR, THEY'RE GONNA BE SORRY. 'CAUSE ONE DAY I'LL BE CALLIN' THE SHOTS. YOU'LL SEE.
I GOT PLANS! I'M HOOKED UP WITH A GUY THAT'S GONNA MAKE IT ALL HAPPEN!
FWIP
UH...
IT'S... UH... GOT ALL KINDS A' FEATURES. LIKE...
...WHAT'S THIS?
THWIP
WHOA!
YOU SAY SOMETHING?
WHA? NO. NOTHING.
SO? WE ALMOST DONE HERE?
YOU KNOW WHAT THIS IS? THIS IS KARMA...

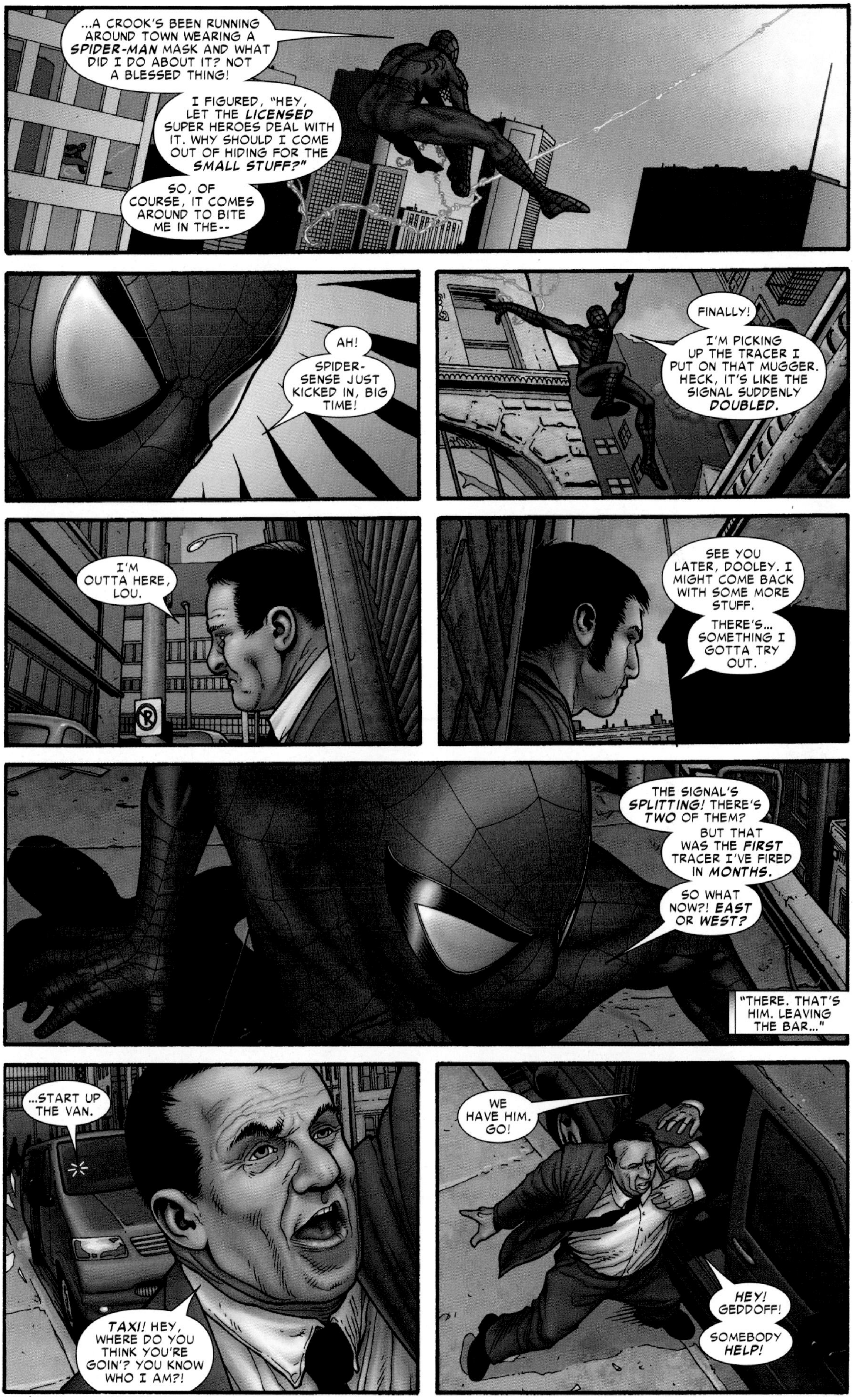

...A CROOK'S BEEN RUNNING AROUND TOWN WEARING A SPIDER-MAN MASK AND WHAT DID I DO ABOUT IT? NOT A BLESSED THING!
I FIGURED, "HEY, LET THE LICENSED SUPER HEROES DEAL WITH IT. WHY SHOULD I COME OUT OF HIDING FOR THE SMALL STUFF?"
SO, OF COURSE, IT COMES AROUND TO BITE ME IN THE--
AH!
SPIDER-SENSE JUST KICKED IN, BIG TIME!
FINALLY!
I'M PICKING UP THE TRACER I PUT ON THAT MUGGER. HECK, IT'S LIKE THE SIGNAL SUDDENLY DOUBLED.
I'M OUTTA HERE, LOU.
SEE YOU LATER, DOOLEY. I MIGHT COME BACK WITH SOME MORE STUFF.
THERE'S... SOMETHING I GOTTA TRY OUT.
THE SIGNAL'S SPLITTING! THERE'S TWO OF THEM?
BUT THAT WAS THE FIRST TRACER I'VE FIRED IN MONTHS.
SO WHAT NOW?! EAST OR WEST?
"THERE. THAT'S HIM. LEAVING THE BAR..."
...START UP THE VAN.
TAXI! HEY, WHERE DO YOU THINK YOU'RE GOIN'? YOU KNOW WHO I AM?!
WE HAVE HIM. GO!
HEY! GEDDOFF!
SOMEBODY HELP!

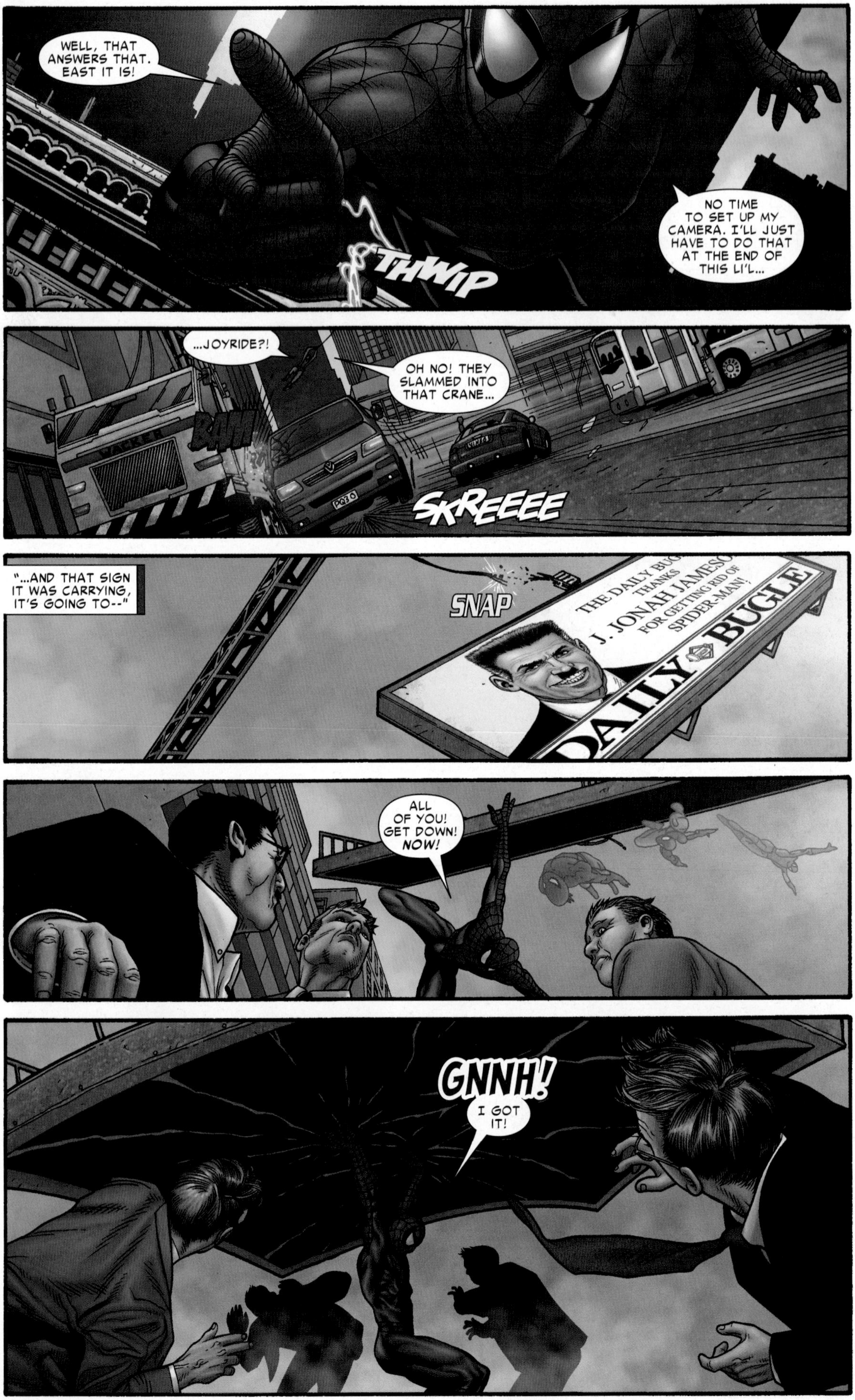
WELL, THAT ANSWERS THAT. EAST IT IS!
THWIP
NO TIME TO SET UP MY CAMERA. I'LL JUST HAVE TO DO THAT AT THE END OF THIS LI'L...
...JOYRIDE?!
OH NO! THEY SLAMMED INTO THAT CRANE...
WACKER
SKREEEEE
"...AND THAT SIGN IT WAS CARRYING, IT'S GOING TO--"
SNAP
THE DAILY BUG
THANKS
J. JONAH JAMESO
FOR GETTING RID OF
SPIDER-MAN!
DAILY BUGLE
ALL OF YOU! GET DOWN! NOW!
GNNH!
I GOT IT!

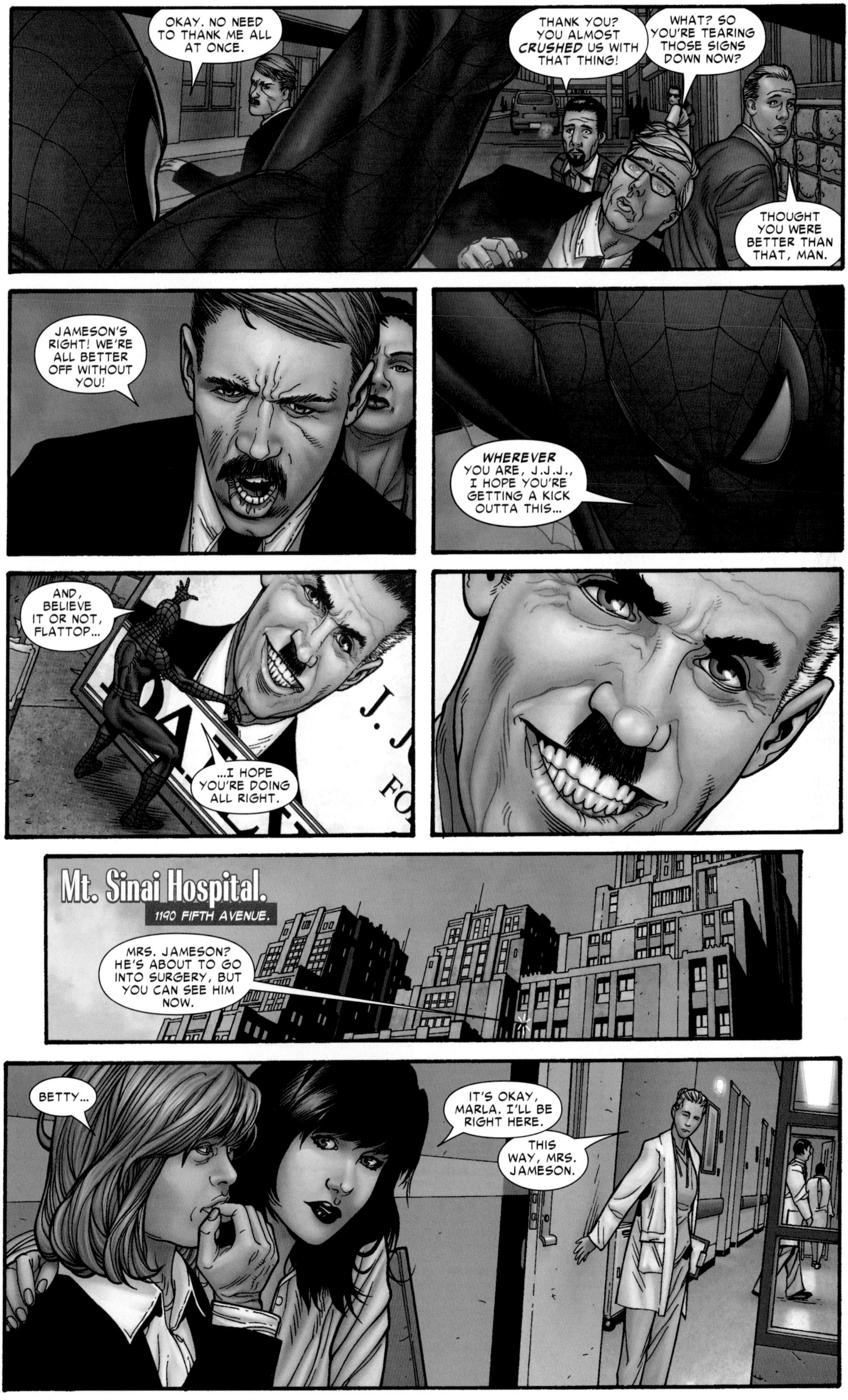
OKAY. NO NEED TO THANK ME ALL AT ONCE.
THANK YOU? YOU ALMOST *CRUSHED* US WITH THAT THING!
WHAT? SO YOU'RE TEARING THOSE SIGNS DOWN NOW?
THOUGHT YOU WERE BETTER THAN THAT, MAN.
JAMESON'S RIGHT! WE'RE ALL BETTER OFF WITHOUT YOU!
WHEREVER YOU ARE, J.J.J., I HOPE YOU'RE GETTING A KICK OUTTA THIS...
AND, BELIEVE IT OR NOT, FLATTOP...
...I HOPE YOU'RE DOING ALL RIGHT.
Mt. Sinai Hospital.
1190 FIFTH AVENUE.
MRS. JAMESON? HE'S ABOUT TO GO INTO SURGERY, BUT YOU CAN SEE HIM NOW.
BETTY...
IT'S OKAY, MARLA. I'LL BE RIGHT HERE.
THIS WAY, MRS. JAMESON.

JONAH. YOU HAVE NO IDEA.

NO IDEA HOW MANY TIMES I'VE BEEN HERE. IMAGINING THIS EXACT MOMENT.

NO GOLDEN YEARS FANTASY OF PORCH SWINGS, GRANDCHILDREN, OR WALKS ON THE BEACH.

I JUST KNEW. IT WAS ALWAYS GOING TO BE THIS. THE TUBES. THE MACHINES. TALKS OF BYPASSES, STENTS, AND GRAFTS.

AND IT WAS ALWAYS GOING TO BE *YOUR* FAULT. SOME *STUPID* THING ABOUT THE BUGLE. OR SPIDER-MAN. SOMETHING YOU'D STRESS AND OBSESS OVER.

SOMETHING *YOU* COULDN'T LET GO. AND NOTHING *I* COULD DO ABOUT--

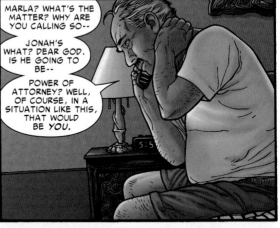

MARLA? WHAT'S THE MATTER? WHY ARE YOU CALLING SO--

JONAH'S *WHAT?* DEAR GOD. IS HE GOING TO BE--

POWER OF ATTORNEY? WELL, OF COURSE, IN A SITUATION LIKE THIS, THAT WOULD BE *YOU.*

GOOD. THEN I WANT YOU TO DRAW UP WHATEVER PAPERS YOU HAVE TO, ALLEN.

AND THEN CALL DEXTER BENNETT. TELL HIM I'M PREPARED TO SELL *ALL* OUR SHARES.

IF HE WANTS THE DAILY BUGLE SO BADLY, HE CAN *HAVE* IT.

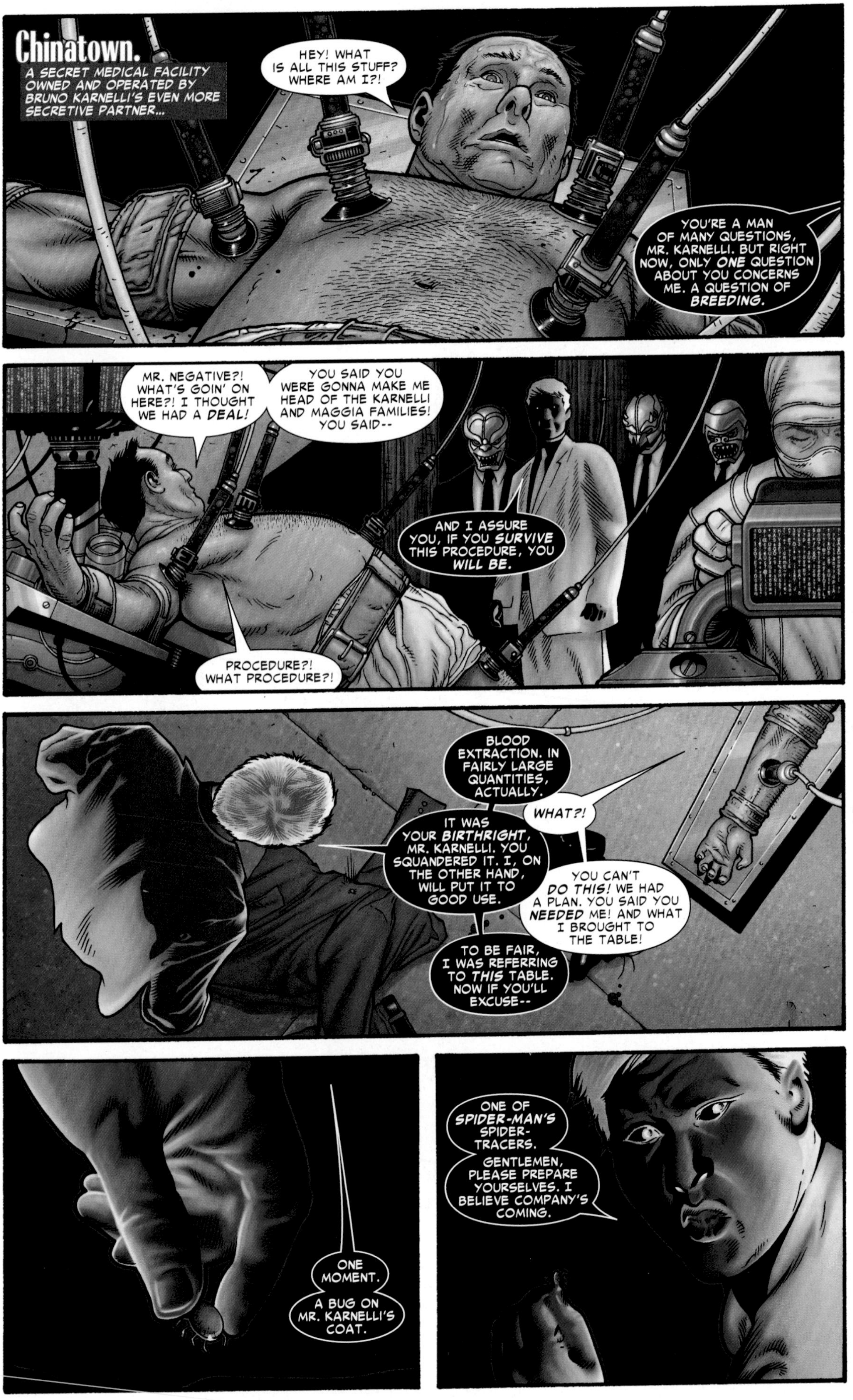
Chinatown.
A SECRET MEDICAL FACILITY OWNED AND OPERATED BY BRUNO KARNELLI'S EVEN MORE SECRETIVE PARTNER...
HEY! WHAT IS ALL THIS STUFF? WHERE AM I?!
YOU'RE A MAN OF MANY QUESTIONS, MR. KARNELLI. BUT RIGHT NOW, ONLY ONE QUESTION ABOUT YOU CONCERNS ME. A QUESTION OF BREEDING.
MR. NEGATIVE?! WHAT'S GOIN' ON HERE?! I THOUGHT WE HAD A DEAL!
YOU SAID YOU WERE GONNA MAKE ME HEAD OF THE KARNELLI AND MAGGIA FAMILIES! YOU SAID--
AND I ASSURE YOU, IF YOU SURVIVE THIS PROCEDURE, YOU WILL BE.
PROCEDURE?! WHAT PROCEDURE?!
BLOOD EXTRACTION. IN FAIRLY LARGE QUANTITIES, ACTUALLY.
WHAT?!
IT WAS YOUR BIRTHRIGHT, MR. KARNELLI. YOU SQUANDERED IT. I, ON THE OTHER HAND, WILL PUT IT TO GOOD USE.
YOU CAN'T DO THIS! WE HAD A PLAN. YOU SAID YOU NEEDED ME! AND WHAT I BROUGHT TO THE TABLE!
TO BE FAIR, I WAS REFERRING TO THIS TABLE. NOW IF YOU'LL EXCUSE--
ONE MOMENT.
A BUG ON MR. KARNELLI'S COAT.
ONE OF SPIDER-MAN'S SPIDER-TRACERS.
GENTLEMEN, PLEASE PREPARE YOURSELVES. I BELIEVE COMPANY'S COMING.

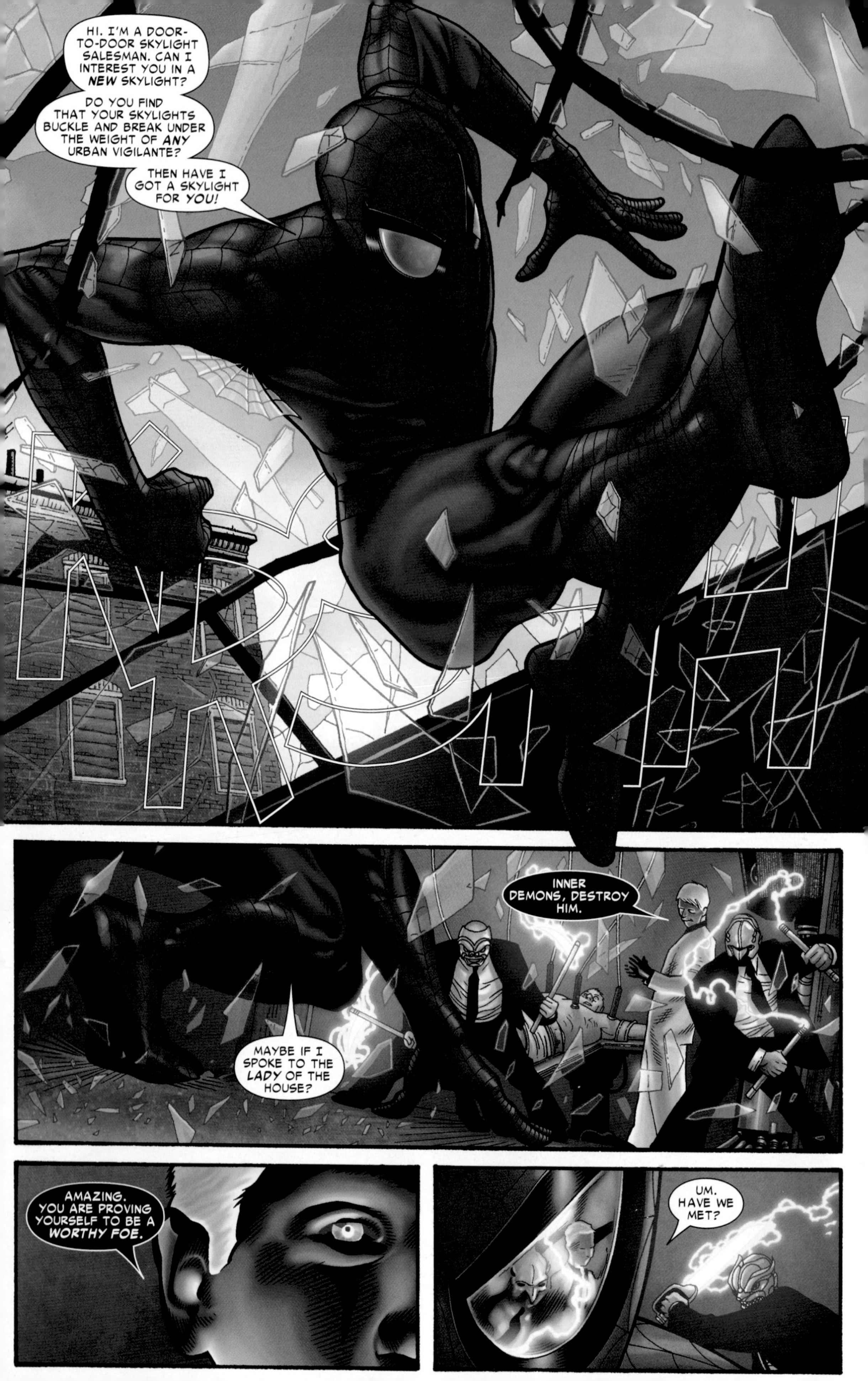
HI. I'M A DOOR-TO-DOOR SKYLIGHT SALESMAN. CAN I INTEREST YOU IN A NEW SKYLIGHT?
DO YOU FIND THAT YOUR SKYLIGHTS BUCKLE AND BREAK UNDER THE WEIGHT OF ANY URBAN VIGILANTE?
THEN HAVE I GOT A SKYLIGHT FOR YOU!
INNER DEMONS, DESTROY HIM.
MAYBE IF I SPOKE TO THE LADY OF THE HOUSE?
AMAZING. YOU ARE PROVING YOURSELF TO BE A WORTHY FOE.
UM. HAVE WE MET?

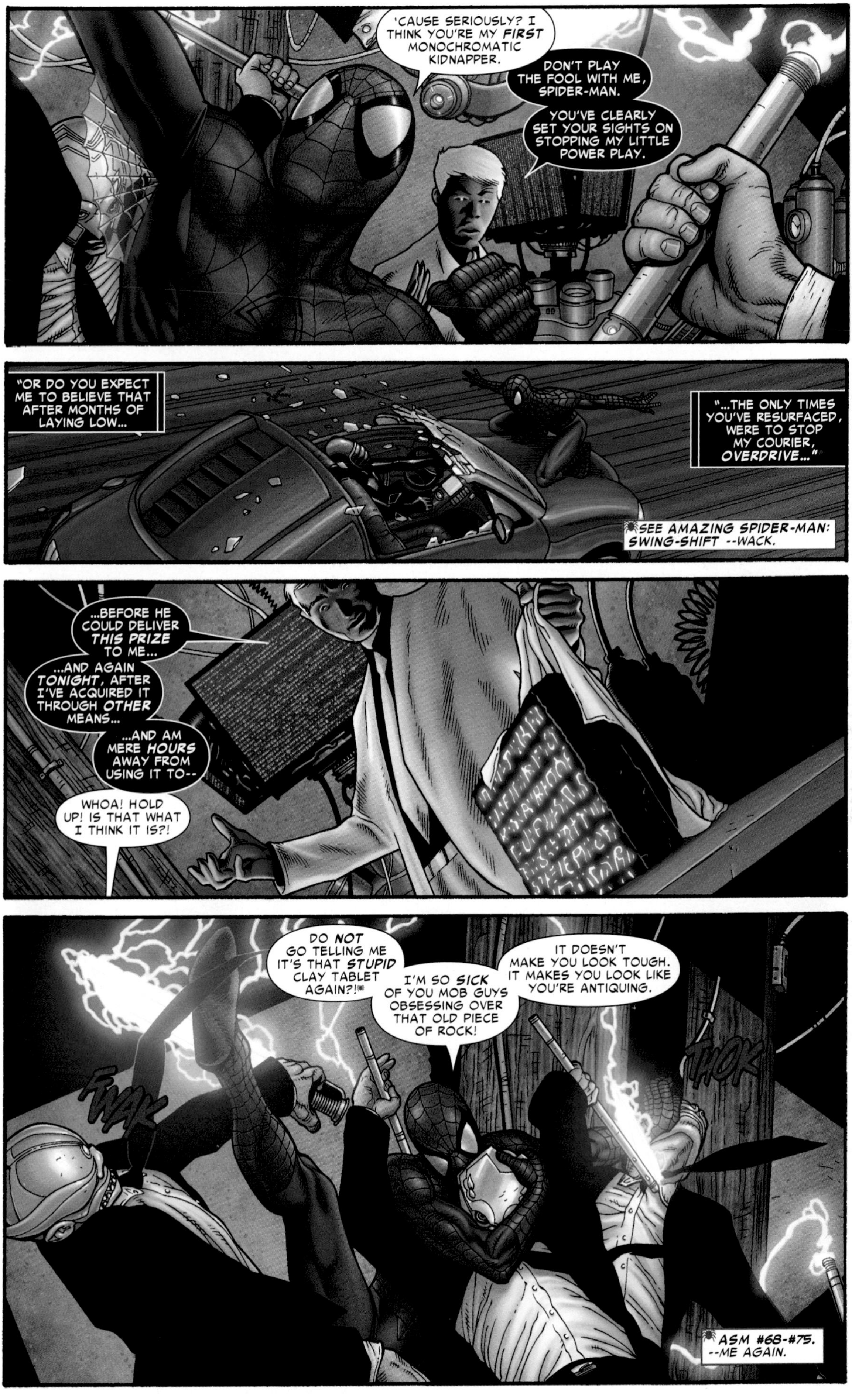
'CAUSE SERIOUSLY? I THINK YOU'RE MY *FIRST* MONOCHROMATIC KIDNAPPER.
DON'T PLAY THE FOOL WITH ME, SPIDER-MAN.
YOU'VE CLEARLY SET YOUR SIGHTS ON STOPPING MY LITTLE POWER PLAY.
"OR DO YOU EXPECT ME TO BELIEVE THAT AFTER MONTHS OF LAYING LOW...
"...THE ONLY TIMES YOU'VE RESURFACED, WERE TO STOP MY COURIER, *OVERDRIVE*..."
SEE *AMAZING SPIDER-MAN: SWING-SHIFT* --WACK.
...BEFORE HE COULD DELIVER *THIS PRIZE* TO ME...
...AND AGAIN *TONIGHT*, AFTER I'VE ACQUIRED IT THROUGH *OTHER* MEANS...
...AND AM MERE *HOURS* AWAY FROM USING IT TO--
WHOA! HOLD UP! IS THAT WHAT I THINK IT IS?!
DO *NOT* GO TELLING ME IT'S THAT *STUPID* CLAY TABLET AGAIN?!
I'M SO *SICK* OF YOU MOB GUYS OBSESSING OVER THAT OLD PIECE OF ROCK!
IT DOESN'T MAKE YOU LOOK TOUGH. IT MAKES YOU LOOK LIKE YOU'RE ANTIQUING.
FWAK
THOK
ASM #68-#75. --ME AGAIN.

GOOD EYE, SPIDER-MAN. THIS IS A LEMURIAN TABLET. BUT NOT THE ONE YOU'RE THINKING OF.

THAT WAS THE TABLET OF LIFE & TIME. THIS IS ITS SISTER, THE TABLET OF DEATH & ENTROPY.

IT CONTAINS A FORMULA FOR BREWING "THE DEVIL'S BREATH", A POISON I SHALL USE TO--

THWIP

DON'T MIND ME.

YOU WERE SAYING?

SPAKK

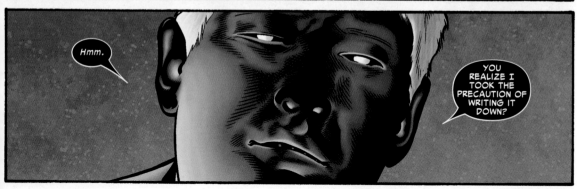

Hmm.

YOU REALIZE I TOOK THE PRECAUTION OF WRITING IT DOWN?

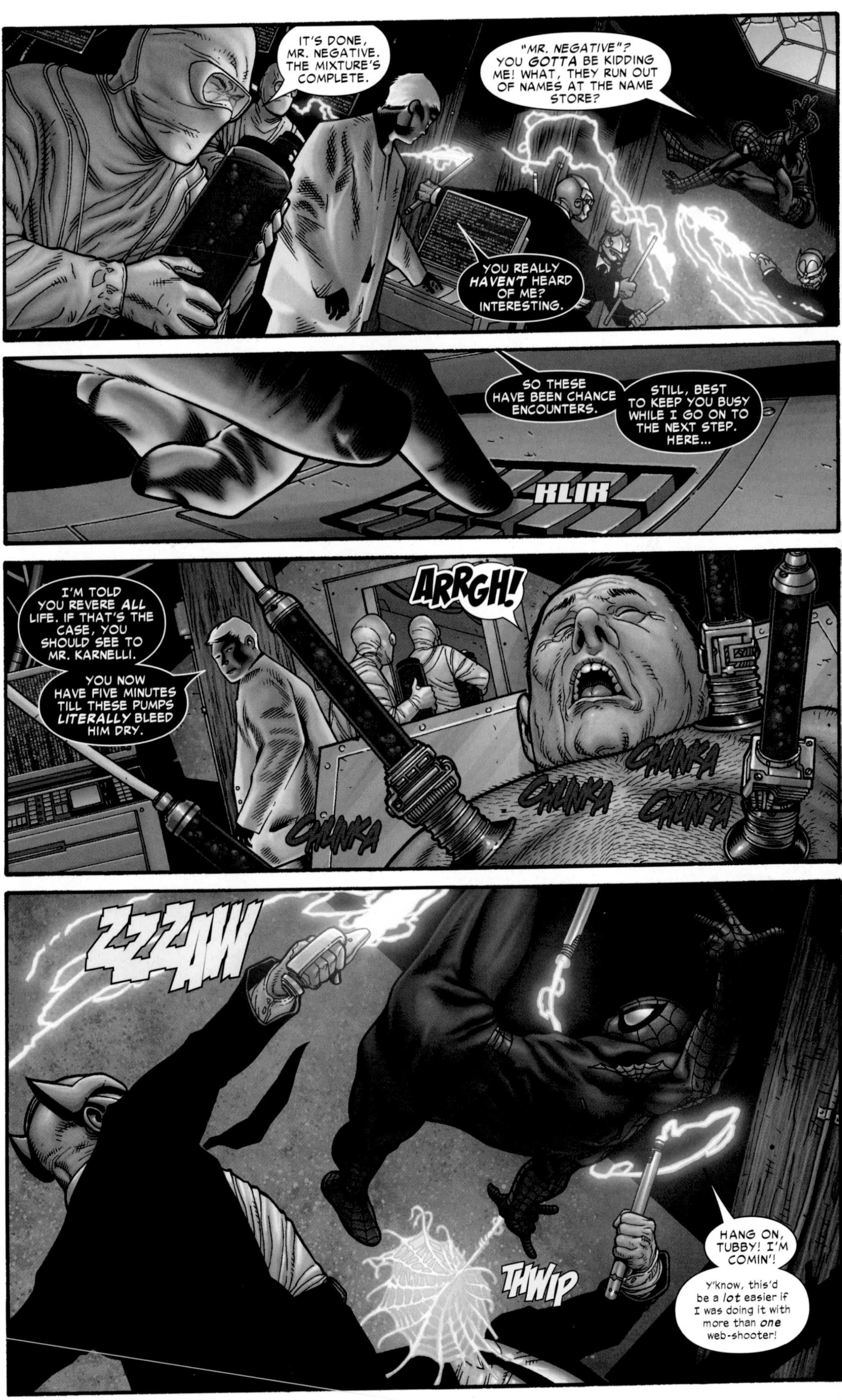
IT'S DONE, MR. NEGATIVE. THE MIXTURE'S COMPLETE.
"MR. NEGATIVE"? YOU GOTTA BE KIDDING ME! WHAT, THEY RUN OUT OF NAMES AT THE NAME STORE?
YOU REALLY HAVEN'T HEARD OF ME? INTERESTING.
SO THESE HAVE BEEN CHANCE ENCOUNTERS.
STILL, BEST TO KEEP YOU BUSY WHILE I GO ON TO THE NEXT STEP. HERE...
KLIK
I'M TOLD YOU REVERE ALL LIFE. IF THAT'S THE CASE, YOU SHOULD SEE TO MR. KARNELLI.
YOU NOW HAVE FIVE MINUTES TILL THESE PUMPS LITERALLY BLEED HIM DRY.
ARRGH!
CHUNKA
CHUNKA
CHUNKA
CHUNKA
ZZZAW
THWIP
HANG ON, TUBBY! I'M COMIN'!
Y'know, this'd be a lot easier if I was doing it with more than one web-shooter!

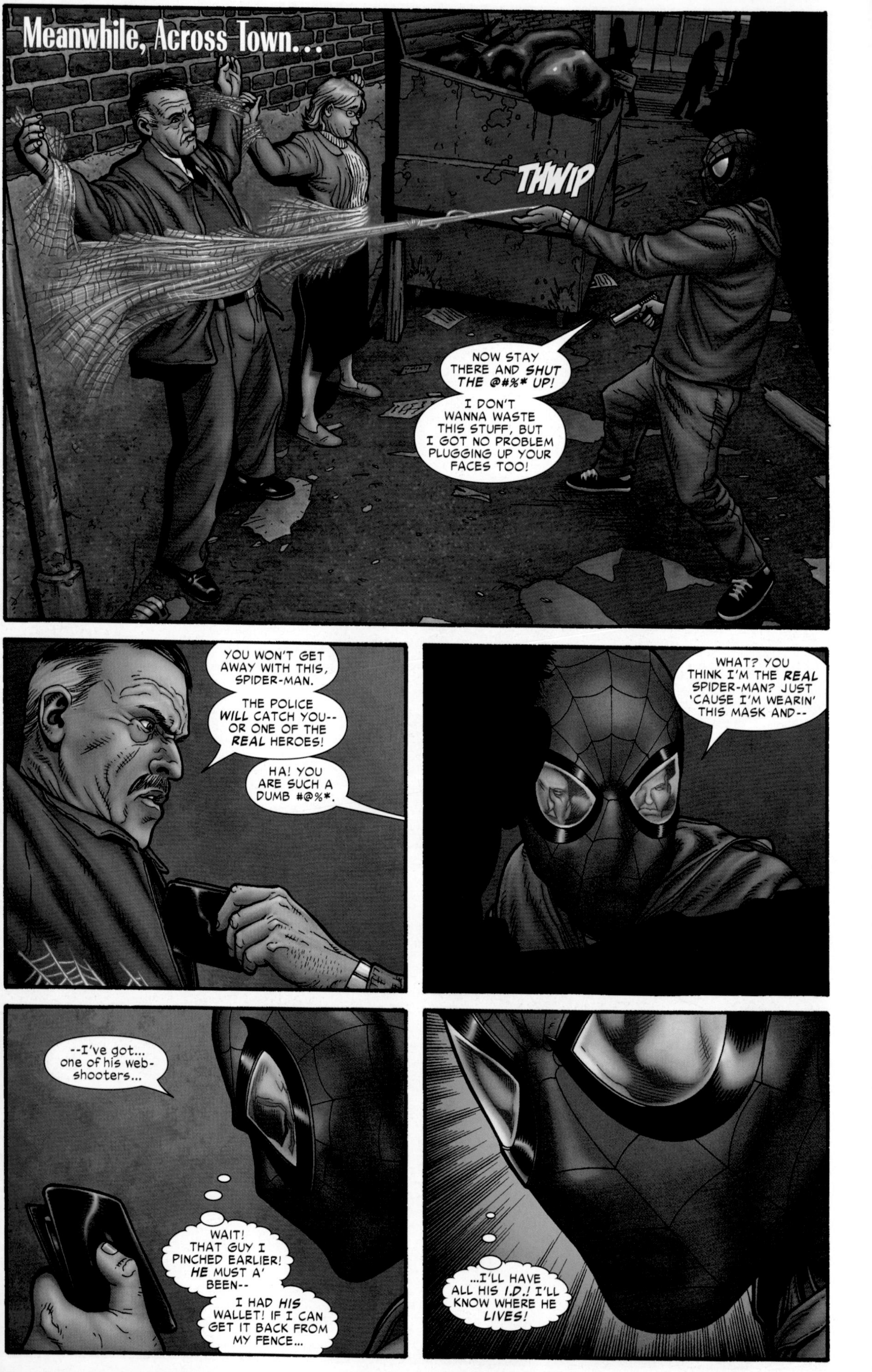
Meanwhile, Across Town...
THWIP
NOW STAY THERE AND SHUT THE @#%* UP!
I DON'T WANNA WASTE THIS STUFF, BUT I GOT NO PROBLEM PLUGGING UP YOUR FACES TOO!
YOU WON'T GET AWAY WITH THIS, SPIDER-MAN.
THE POLICE WILL CATCH YOU-- OR ONE OF THE REAL HEROES!
HA! YOU ARE SUCH A DUMB #@%*.
WHAT? YOU THINK I'M THE REAL SPIDER-MAN? JUST 'CAUSE I'M WEARIN' THIS MASK AND--
--I've got... one of his web-shooters...
WAIT! THAT GUY I PINCHED EARLIER! HE MUST A' BEEN--
I HAD HIS WALLET! IF I CAN GET IT BACK FROM MY FENCE...
...I'LL HAVE ALL HIS I.D.! I'LL KNOW WHERE HE LIVES!

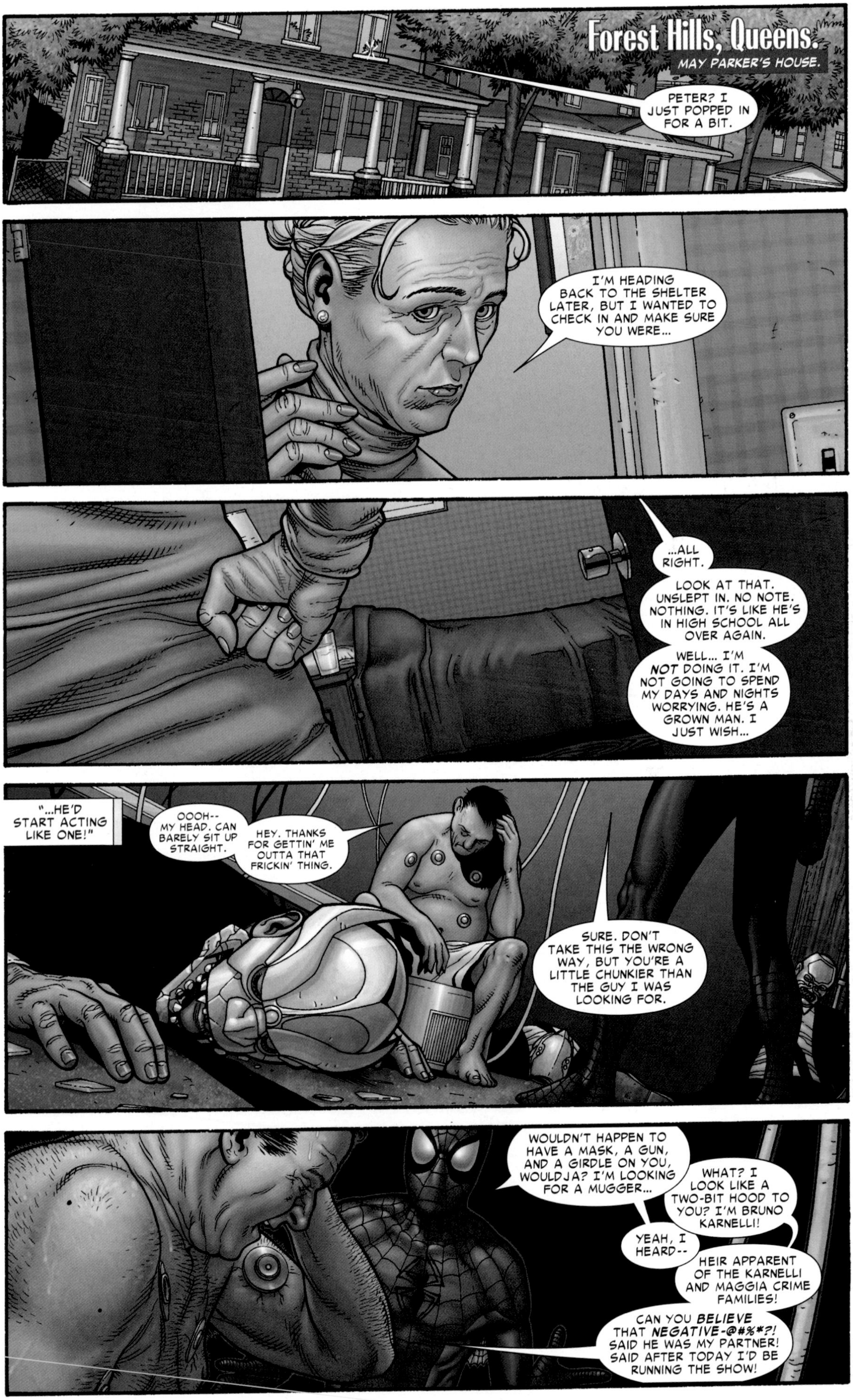

Forest Hills, Queens.
MAY PARKER'S HOUSE.
PETER? I JUST POPPED IN FOR A BIT.
I'M HEADING BACK TO THE SHELTER LATER, BUT I WANTED TO CHECK IN AND MAKE SURE YOU WERE...
...ALL RIGHT.
LOOK AT THAT. UNSLEPT IN. NO NOTE. NOTHING. IT'S LIKE HE'S IN HIGH SCHOOL ALL OVER AGAIN.
WELL... I'M *NOT* DOING IT. I'M NOT GOING TO SPEND MY DAYS AND NIGHTS WORRYING. HE'S A GROWN MAN. I JUST WISH...
"...HE'D START ACTING LIKE ONE!"
OOOH-- MY HEAD. CAN BARELY SIT UP STRAIGHT.
HEY. THANKS FOR GETTIN' ME OUTTA THAT FRICKIN' THING.
SURE. DON'T TAKE THIS THE WRONG WAY, BUT YOU'RE A LITTLE CHUNKIER THAN THE GUY I WAS LOOKING FOR.
WOULDN'T HAPPEN TO HAVE A MASK, A GUN, AND A GIRDLE ON YOU, WOULDJA? I'M LOOKING FOR A MUGGER...
WHAT? I LOOK LIKE A TWO-BIT HOOD TO YOU? I'M BRUNO KARNELLI!
YEAH, I HEARD--
HEIR APPARENT OF THE KARNELLI AND MAGGIA CRIME FAMILIES!
CAN YOU *BELIEVE* THAT *NEGATIVE-@#%*?!* SAID HE WAS MY PARTNER! SAID AFTER TODAY I'D BE RUNNING THE SHOW!

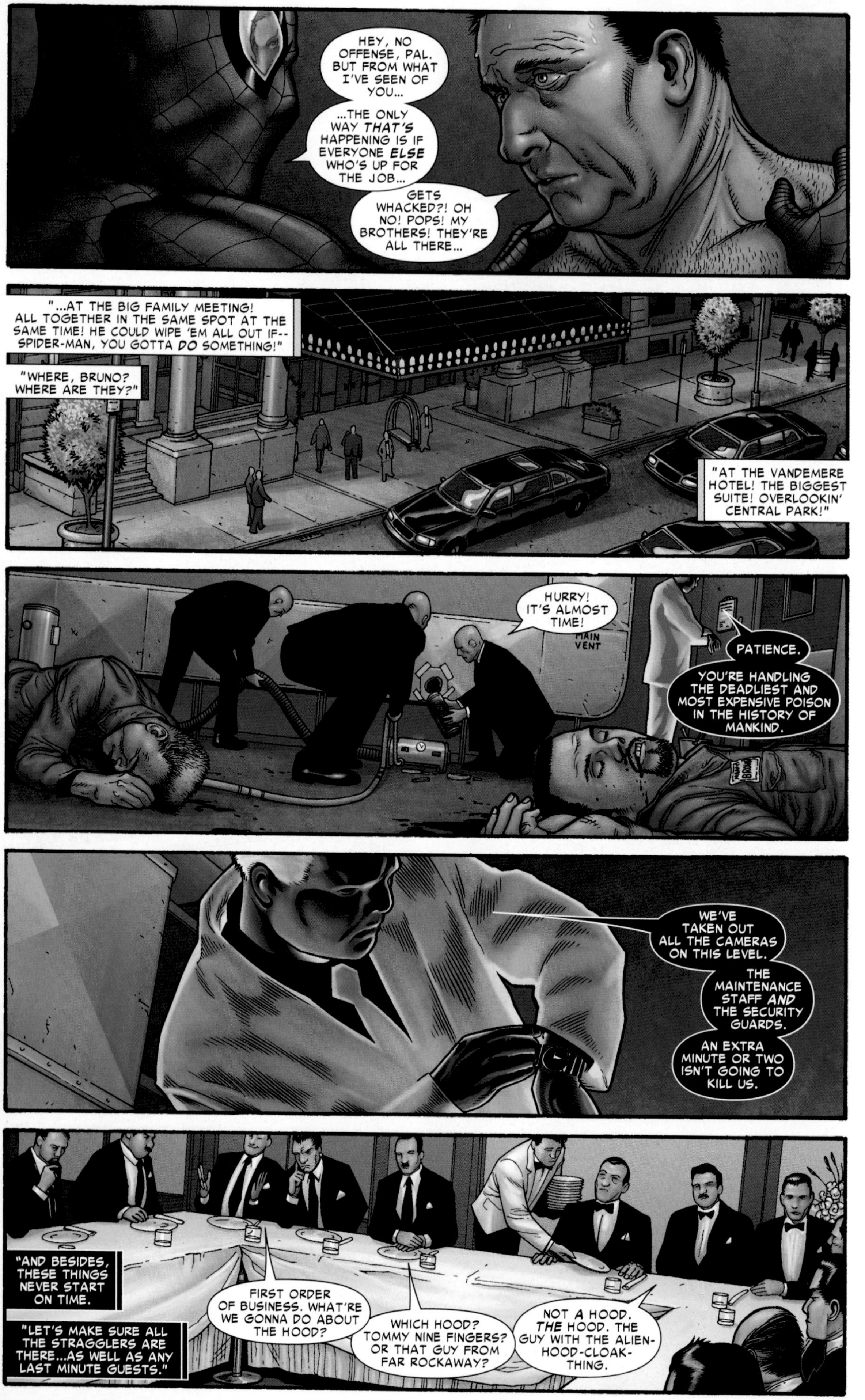
HEY, NO OFFENSE, PAL. BUT FROM WHAT I'VE SEEN OF YOU...
...THE ONLY WAY THAT'S HAPPENING IS IF EVERYONE ELSE WHO'S UP FOR THE JOB...
GETS WHACKED?! OH NO! POPS! MY BROTHERS! THEY'RE ALL THERE...
"...AT THE BIG FAMILY MEETING! ALL TOGETHER IN THE SAME SPOT AT THE SAME TIME! HE COULD WIPE 'EM ALL OUT IF-- SPIDER-MAN, YOU GOTTA DO SOMETHING!"
"WHERE, BRUNO? WHERE ARE THEY?"
"AT THE VANDEMERE HOTEL! THE BIGGEST SUITE! OVERLOOKIN' CENTRAL PARK!"
HURRY! IT'S ALMOST TIME!
MAIN VENT
PATIENCE.
YOU'RE HANDLING THE DEADLIEST AND MOST EXPENSIVE POISON IN THE HISTORY OF MANKIND.
WE'VE TAKEN OUT ALL THE CAMERAS ON THIS LEVEL.
THE MAINTENANCE STAFF AND THE SECURITY GUARDS.
AN EXTRA MINUTE OR TWO ISN'T GOING TO KILL US.
"AND BESIDES, THESE THINGS NEVER START ON TIME.
"LET'S MAKE SURE ALL THE STRAGGLERS ARE THERE...AS WELL AS ANY LAST MINUTE GUESTS."
FIRST ORDER OF BUSINESS. WHAT'RE WE GONNA DO ABOUT THE HOOD?
WHICH HOOD? TOMMY NINE FINGERS? OR THAT GUY FROM FAR ROCKAWAY?
NOT A HOOD. THE HOOD. THE GUY WITH THE ALIEN-HOOD-CLOAK-THING.

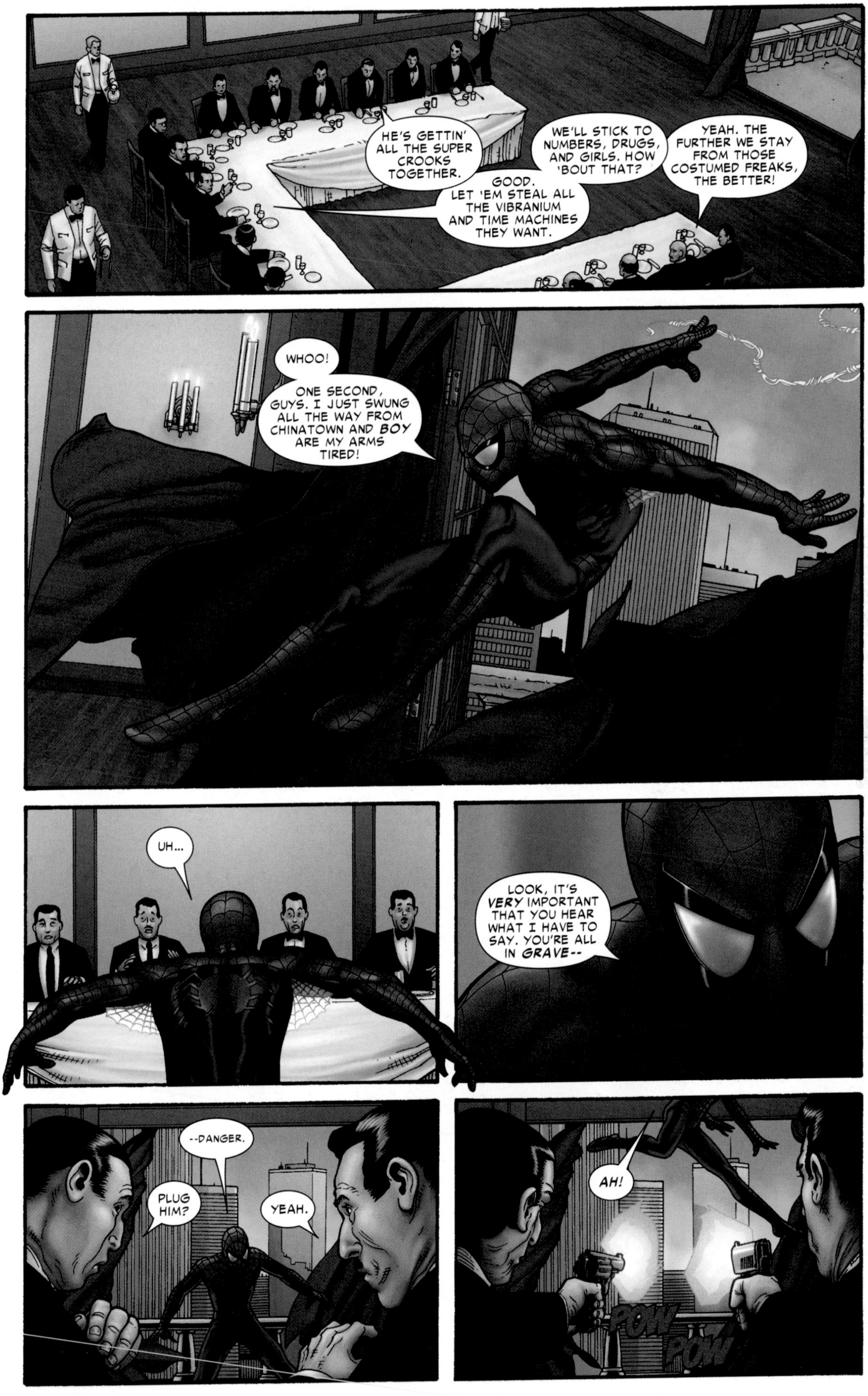
HE'S GETTIN' ALL THE SUPER CROOKS TOGETHER.
GOOD. LET 'EM STEAL ALL THE VIBRANIUM AND TIME MACHINES THEY WANT.
WE'LL STICK TO NUMBERS, DRUGS, AND GIRLS. HOW 'BOUT THAT?
YEAH. THE FURTHER WE STAY FROM THOSE COSTUMED FREAKS, THE BETTER!
WHOO!
ONE SECOND, GUYS. I JUST SWUNG ALL THE WAY FROM CHINATOWN AND BOY ARE MY ARMS TIRED!
UH...
LOOK, IT'S VERY IMPORTANT THAT YOU HEAR WHAT I HAVE TO SAY. YOU'RE ALL IN GRAVE--
--DANGER.
PLUG HIM?
YEAH.
AH!
POW
POW

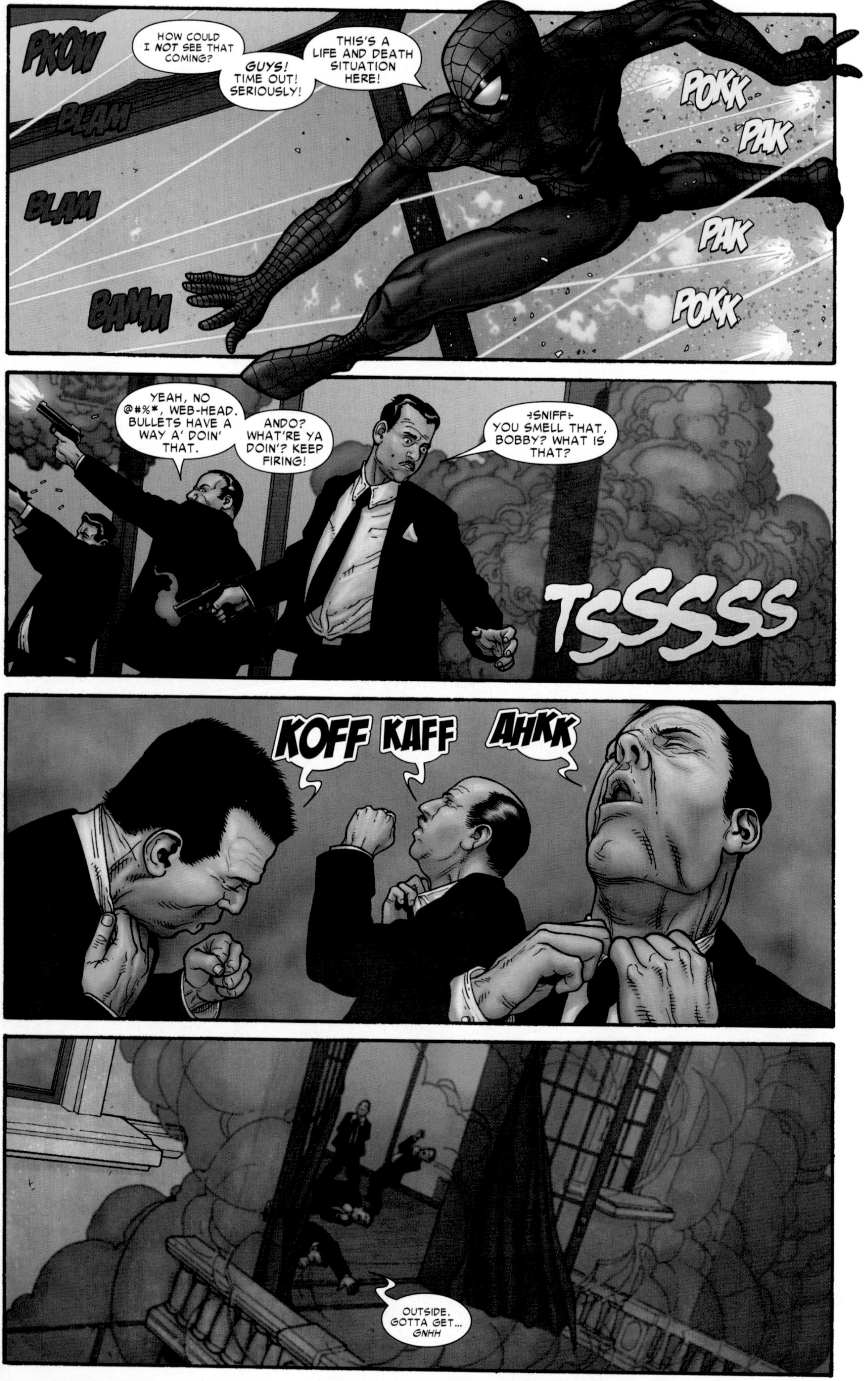
PKOW
BLAM
BLAM
BAMM
HOW COULD I NOT SEE THAT COMING?
GUYS! TIME OUT! SERIOUSLY!
THIS'S A LIFE AND DEATH SITUATION HERE!
POKK
PAK
PAK
POKK
YEAH, NO @#%*, WEB-HEAD. BULLETS HAVE A WAY A' DOIN' THAT.
ANDO? WHAT'RE YA DOIN'? KEEP FIRING!
SNIFF
YOU SMELL THAT, BOBBY? WHAT IS THAT?
TSSSSS
KOFF
KAFF
AHKK
OUTSIDE. GOTTA GET... GNHH

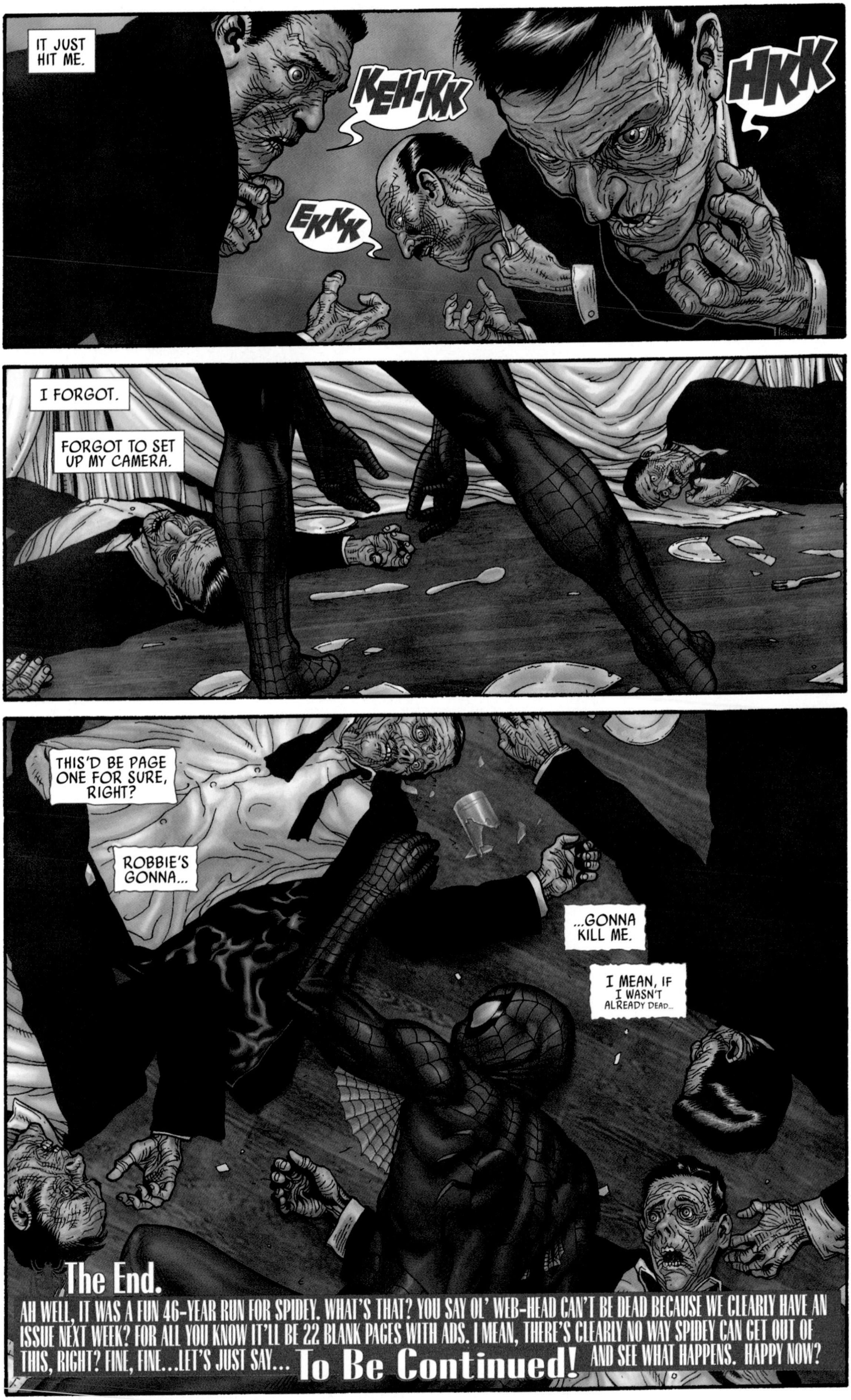

IT JUST HIT ME.
KEH-KK
HKK
EKKK
I FORGOT.
FORGOT TO SET UP MY CAMERA.
THIS'D BE PAGE ONE FOR SURE, RIGHT?
ROBBIE'S GONNA...
...GONNA KILL ME.
I MEAN, IF I WASN'T ALREADY DEAD...
The End.
AH WELL, IT WAS A FUN 46-YEAR RUN FOR SPIDEY. WHAT'S THAT? YOU SAY OL' WEB-HEAD CAN'T BE DEAD BECAUSE WE CLEARLY HAVE AN ISSUE NEXT WEEK? FOR ALL YOU KNOW IT'LL BE 22 BLANK PAGES WITH ADS. I MEAN, THERE'S CLEARLY NO WAY SPIDEY CAN GET OUT OF THIS, RIGHT? FINE, FINE...LET'S JUST SAY... To Be Continued! AND SEE WHAT HAPPENS. HAPPY NOW?

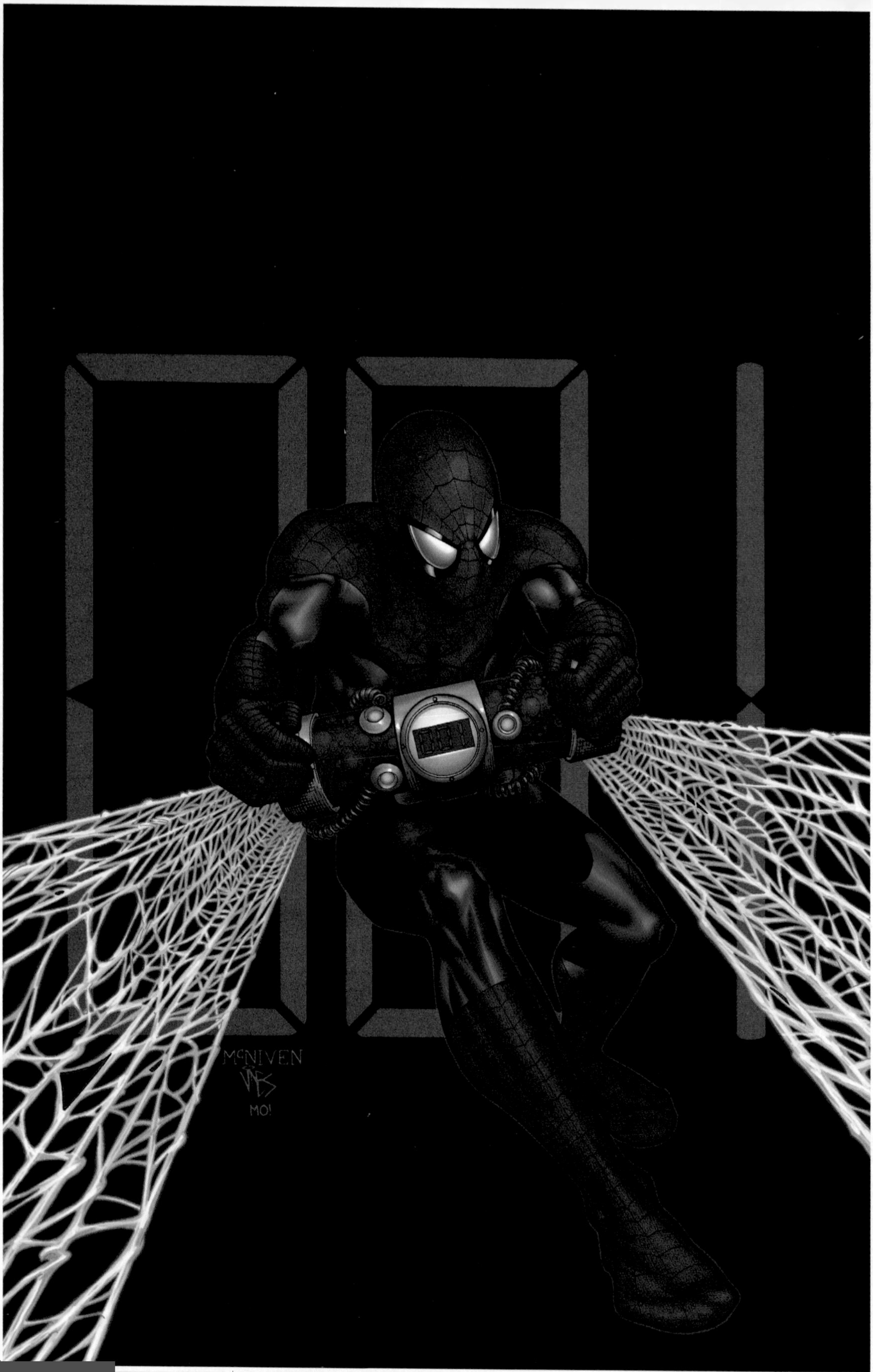
McNIVEN
MO!

G SPIDER

WHILE ATTENDING A DEMONSTRATION IN RADIOLOGY, HIGH SCHOOL STUDENT **PETER PARKER** WAS BITTEN BY A SPIDER WHICH HAD ACCIDENTALLY BEEN EXPOSED TO **RADIOACTIVE RAYS.** THROUGH A MIRACLE OF SCIENCE, PETER SOON FOUND THAT HE HAD **GAINED** THE SPIDER'S POWERS...AND HAD, IN EFFECT, BECOME A HUMAN SPIDER! FROM THAT DAY ON HE WAS...

THE AMAZING SPIDER-MAN™

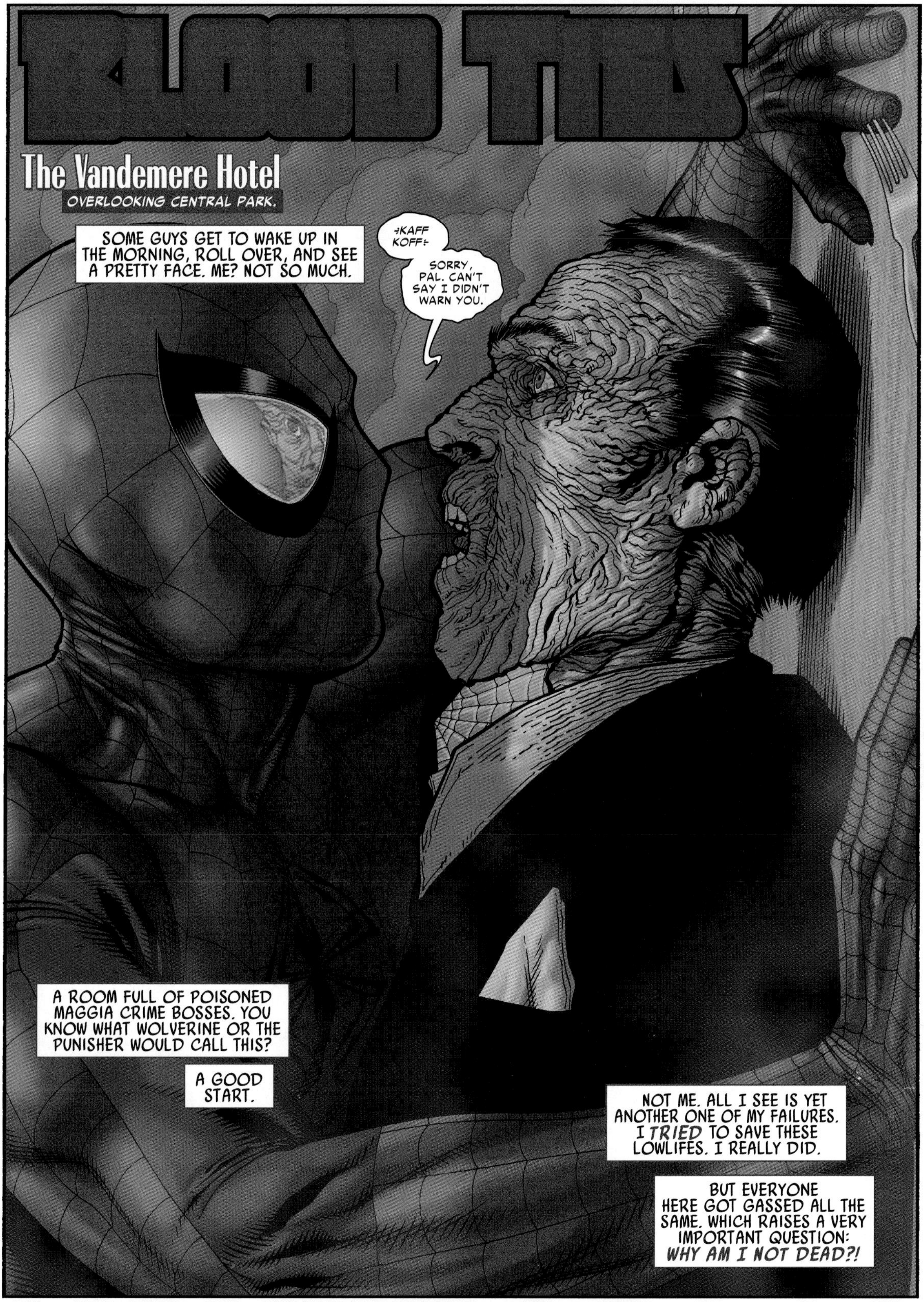
BLOOD TIES
The Vandemere Hotel
OVERLOOKING CENTRAL PARK.
SOME GUYS GET TO WAKE UP IN THE MORNING, ROLL OVER, AND SEE A PRETTY FACE. ME? NOT SO MUCH.
÷KAFF KOFF÷
SORRY, PAL. CAN'T SAY I DIDN'T WARN YOU.
A ROOM FULL OF POISONED MAGGIA CRIME BOSSES. YOU KNOW WHAT WOLVERINE OR THE PUNISHER WOULD CALL THIS?
A GOOD START.
NOT ME. ALL I SEE IS YET ANOTHER ONE OF MY FAILURES. I *TRIED* TO SAVE THESE LOWLIFES. I REALLY DID.
BUT EVERYONE HERE GOT GASSED ALL THE SAME. WHICH RAISES A VERY IMPORTANT QUESTION: *WHY AM I NOT DEAD?!*

DAN SLOTT	STEVE McNIVEN	DEXTER VINES	DAVE STEWART	VC'S CORY PETIT	GALE, GUGGENHEIM, SLOTT, WELLS	TOM BRENNAN	STEPHEN WACKER	TOM BREVOORT	JOE QUESADA	DAN BUCKLEY
WRITER	PENCILER	INKER	COLORS	LETTERS	SPIDEY'S BRAINTRUST	ASSISTANT EDITOR	EDITOR	EXECUTIVE EDITOR	EDITOR IN CHIEF	PUBLISHER

WAIT. LET'S REPHRASE THAT...

THE GUYS FROM ROOM SERVICE, THEY'RE OKAY, TOO. RELATIVELY SPEAKING.

SO WHAT MAKES US SO SPECIAL?

HAKK KA

AKK AH

OH NO! THE DOORS TO THE BALCONY ARE OPEN! THAT GAS...

...WHAT DID MR. NEGATIVE CALL IT? THE DEVIL'S BREATH...

...IT'S GOING OUT INTO THE STREET! I HAVE TO--

I SWEAR, BOBBY, I'LL FIND WHOEVER DID THIS. I'LL MAKE THEM PAY!

I SWEAR A VENDETTA! A BLOOD FEUD ON--

WAIT! BLOOD! THAT'S IT!

THE KEY INGREDIENT IN NEGATIVE'S POISON WAS BRUNO KARNELLI'S BLOOD!

AND HE'S THE ONLY ONE IN THE MAGGIA WHO BELONGS TO BOTH OF THEIR FAMILIES...

SO WHY IS THIS WISE-GUY...?

HEY, YOU! GOODFELLA!

WHATEVER. JUST ANSWER THIS: HOW CAN YOU SWEAR A KARNELLI BLOOD FEUD...

IT'S CARMINE, BUG. CARMINE KARNELLI. SHOW SOME RESPECT.

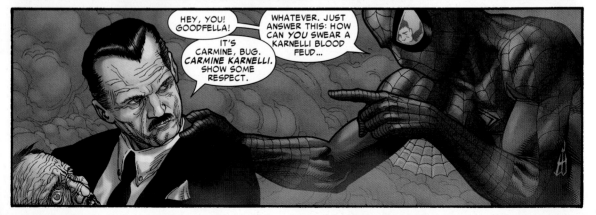

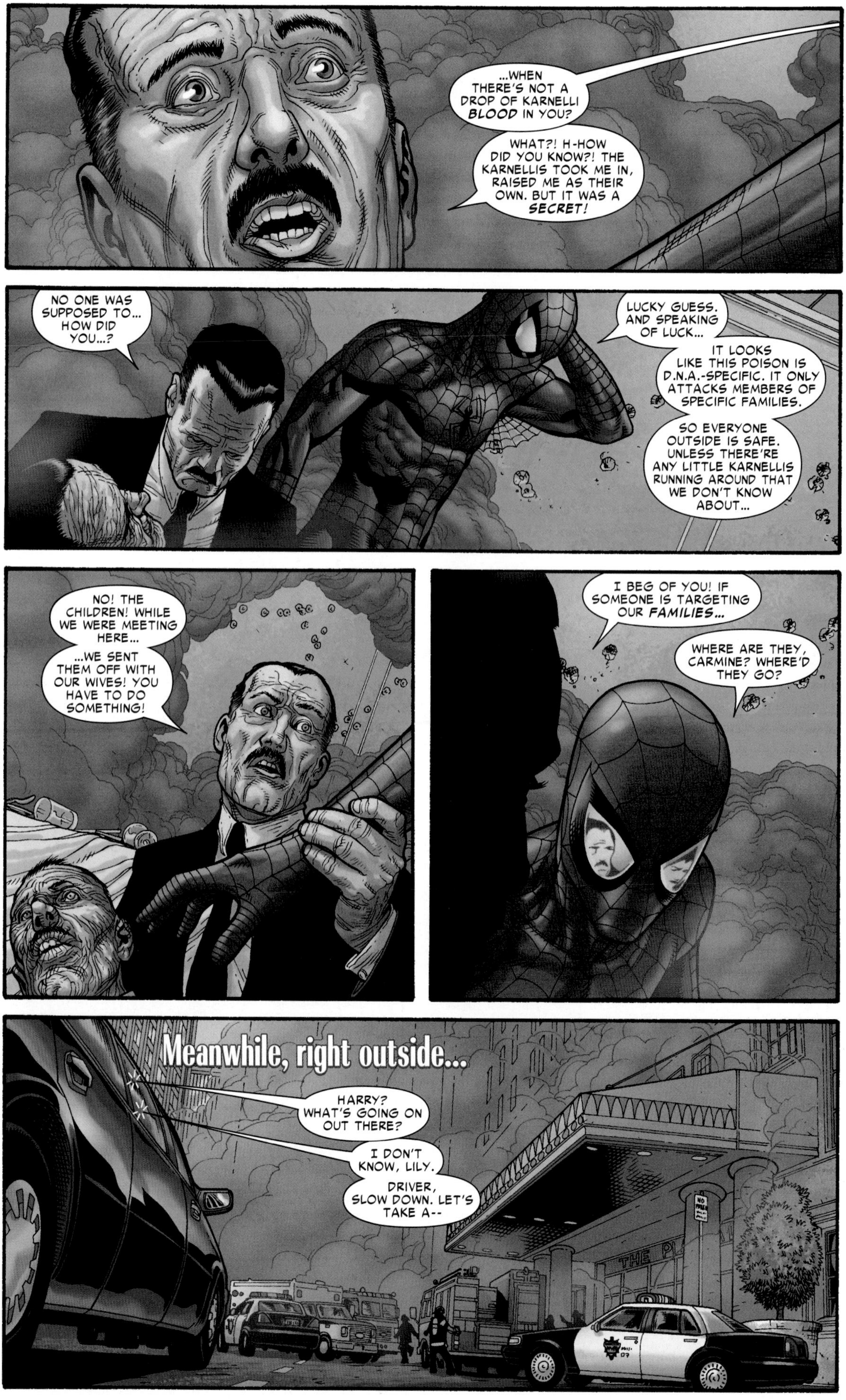
...WHEN THERE'S NOT A DROP OF KARNELLI BLOOD IN YOU?
WHAT?! H-HOW DID YOU KNOW?! THE KARNELLIS TOOK ME IN, RAISED ME AS THEIR OWN. BUT IT WAS A SECRET!
NO ONE WAS SUPPOSED TO... HOW DID YOU...?
LUCKY GUESS. AND SPEAKING OF LUCK...
IT LOOKS LIKE THIS POISON IS D.N.A.-SPECIFIC. IT ONLY ATTACKS MEMBERS OF SPECIFIC FAMILIES.
SO EVERYONE OUTSIDE IS SAFE. UNLESS THERE'RE ANY LITTLE KARNELLIS RUNNING AROUND THAT WE DON'T KNOW ABOUT...
NO! THE CHILDREN! WHILE WE WERE MEETING HERE...
...WE SENT THEM OFF WITH OUR WIVES! YOU HAVE TO DO SOMETHING!
I BEG OF YOU! IF SOMEONE IS TARGETING OUR FAMILIES...
WHERE ARE THEY, CARMINE? WHERE'D THEY GO?
Meanwhile, right outside...
HARRY? WHAT'S GOING ON OUT THERE?
I DON'T KNOW, LILY.
DRIVER, SLOW DOWN. LET'S TAKE A--

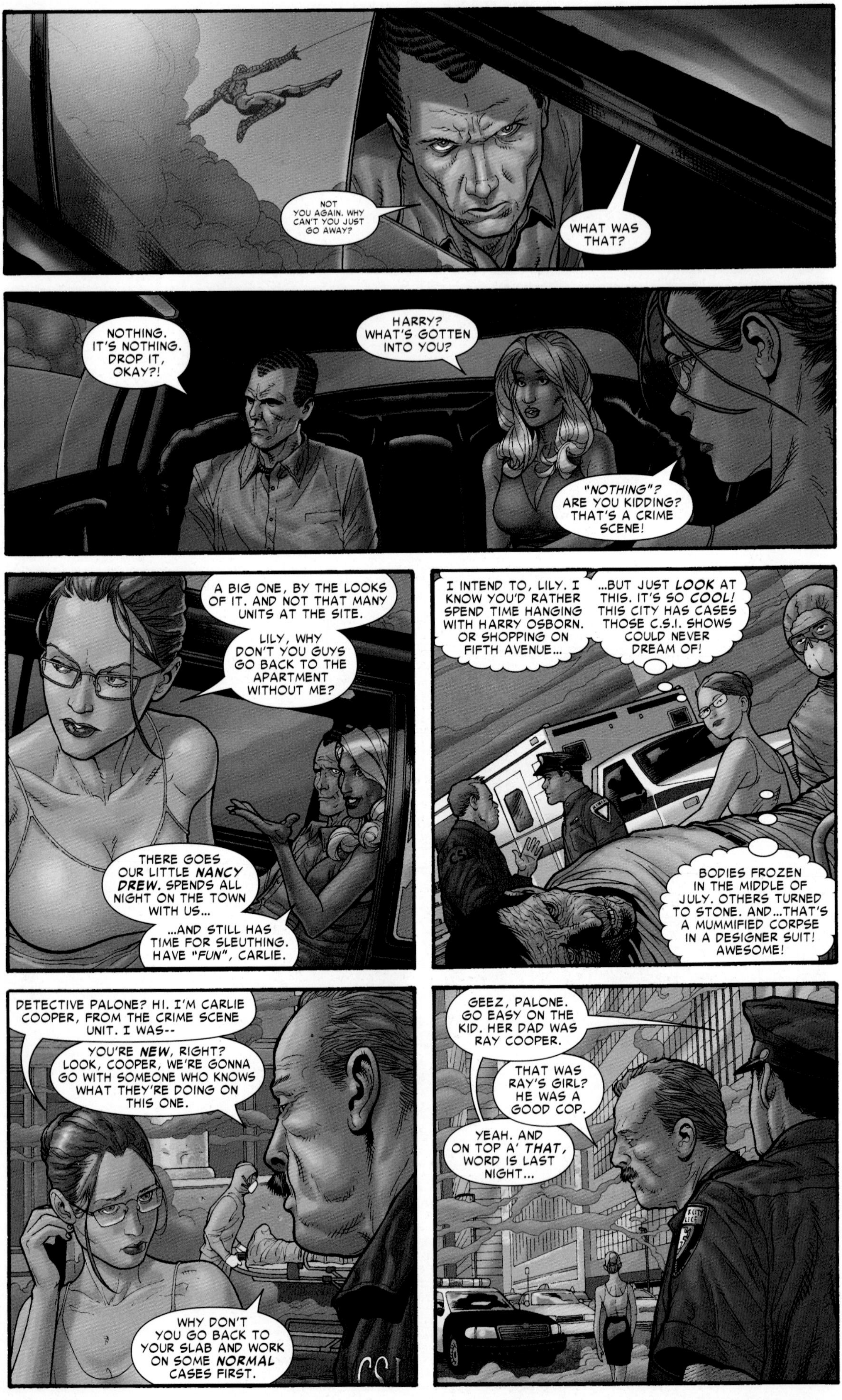
NOT YOU AGAIN. WHY CAN'T YOU JUST GO AWAY?
WHAT WAS THAT?
NOTHING. IT'S NOTHING. DROP IT, OKAY?!
HARRY? WHAT'S GOTTEN INTO YOU?
"NOTHING"? ARE YOU KIDDING? THAT'S A CRIME SCENE!
A BIG ONE, BY THE LOOKS OF IT. AND NOT THAT MANY UNITS AT THE SITE.
LILY, WHY DON'T YOU GUYS GO BACK TO THE APARTMENT WITHOUT ME?
THERE GOES OUR LITTLE NANCY DREW. SPENDS ALL NIGHT ON THE TOWN WITH US...
...AND STILL HAS TIME FOR SLEUTHING. HAVE "FUN", CARLIE.
I INTEND TO, LILY. I KNOW YOU'D RATHER SPEND TIME HANGING WITH HARRY OSBORN. OR SHOPPING ON FIFTH AVENUE...
...BUT JUST LOOK AT THIS. IT'S SO COOL! THIS CITY HAS CASES THOSE C.S.I. SHOWS COULD NEVER DREAM OF!
BODIES FROZEN IN THE MIDDLE OF JULY. OTHERS TURNED TO STONE. AND...THAT'S A MUMMIFIED CORPSE IN A DESIGNER SUIT! AWESOME!
DETECTIVE PALONE? HI. I'M CARLIE COOPER, FROM THE CRIME SCENE UNIT. I WAS--
YOU'RE NEW, RIGHT? LOOK, COOPER, WE'RE GONNA GO WITH SOMEONE WHO KNOWS WHAT THEY'RE DOING ON THIS ONE.
WHY DON'T YOU GO BACK TO YOUR SLAB AND WORK ON SOME NORMAL CASES FIRST.
GEEZ, PALONE. GO EASY ON THE KID. HER DAD WAS RAY COOPER.
THAT WAS RAY'S GIRL? HE WAS A GOOD COP.
YEAH. AND ON TOP A' THAT, WORD IS LAST NIGHT...

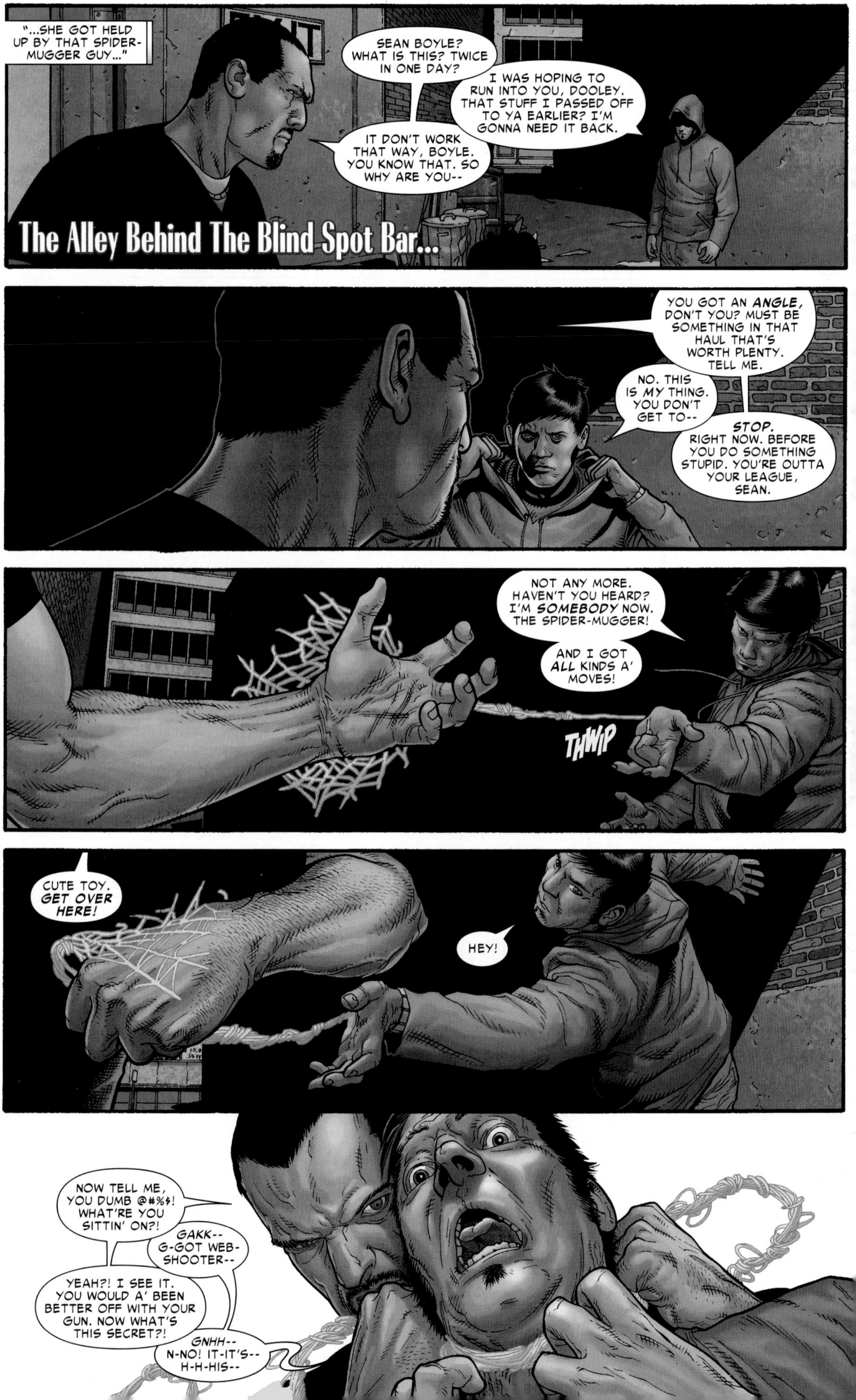
"...SHE GOT HELD UP BY THAT SPIDER-MUGGER GUY..."
SEAN BOYLE? WHAT IS THIS? TWICE IN ONE DAY?
I WAS HOPING TO RUN INTO YOU, DOOLEY. THAT STUFF I PASSED OFF TO YA EARLIER? I'M GONNA NEED IT BACK.
IT DON'T WORK THAT WAY, BOYLE. YOU KNOW THAT. SO WHY ARE YOU--
The Alley Behind The Blind Spot Bar...
YOU GOT AN ANGLE, DON'T YOU? MUST BE SOMETHING IN THAT HAUL THAT'S WORTH PLENTY. TELL ME.
NO. THIS IS MY THING. YOU DON'T GET TO--
STOP. RIGHT NOW. BEFORE YOU DO SOMETHING STUPID. YOU'RE OUTTA YOUR LEAGUE, SEAN.
NOT ANY MORE. HAVEN'T YOU HEARD? I'M SOMEBODY NOW. THE SPIDER-MUGGER!
AND I GOT ALL KINDS A' MOVES!
THWIP
CUTE TOY. GET OVER HERE!
HEY!
NOW TELL ME, YOU DUMB @#%$! WHAT'RE YOU SITTIN' ON?!
GAKK-- G-GOT WEB-SHOOTER--
YEAH?! I SEE IT. YOU WOULD A' BEEN BETTER OFF WITH YOUR GUN. NOW WHAT'S THIS SECRET?!
GNHH-- N-NO! IT-IT'S-- H-H-HIS--

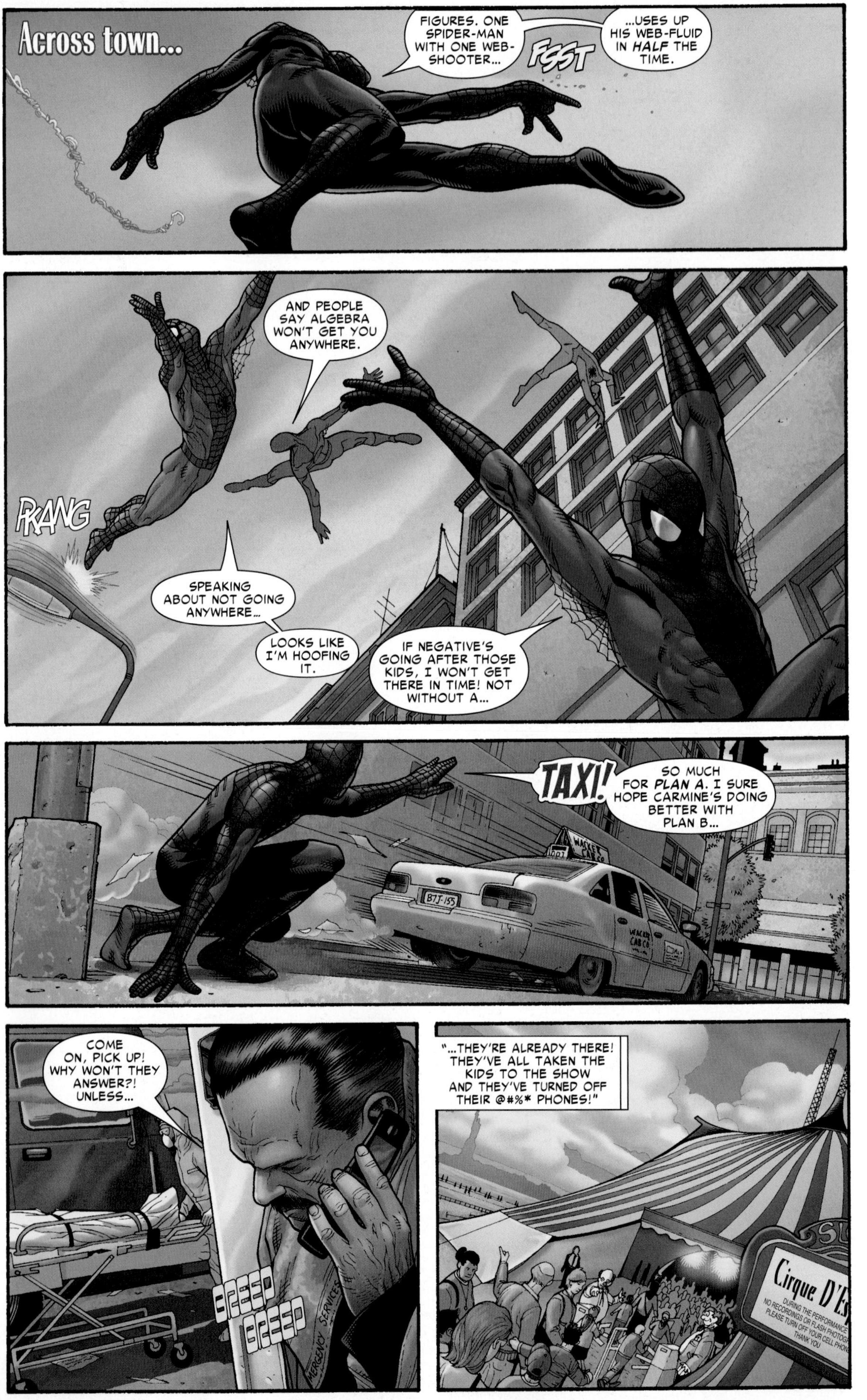
Across town...
FIGURES. ONE SPIDER-MAN WITH ONE WEB-SHOOTER...
FSST
...USES UP HIS WEB-FLUID IN HALF THE TIME.
AND PEOPLE SAY ALGEBRA WON'T GET YOU ANYWHERE.
PKANG
SPEAKING ABOUT NOT GOING ANYWHERE...
LOOKS LIKE I'M HOOFING IT.
IF NEGATIVE'S GOING AFTER THOSE KIDS, I WON'T GET THERE IN TIME! NOT WITHOUT A...
TAXI!
SO MUCH FOR PLAN A. I SURE HOPE CARMINE'S DOING BETTER WITH PLAN B...
COME ON, PICK UP! WHY WON'T THEY ANSWER?! UNLESS...
BREEP BREEP
"...THEY'RE ALREADY THERE! THEY'VE ALL TAKEN THE KIDS TO THE SHOW AND THEY'VE TURNED OFF THEIR @#%* PHONES!"
Cirque D'Es
DURING THE PERFORMANCE NO RECORDINGS OR FLASH PHOTOG PLEASE TURN OFF YOUR CELL PHON THANK YOU

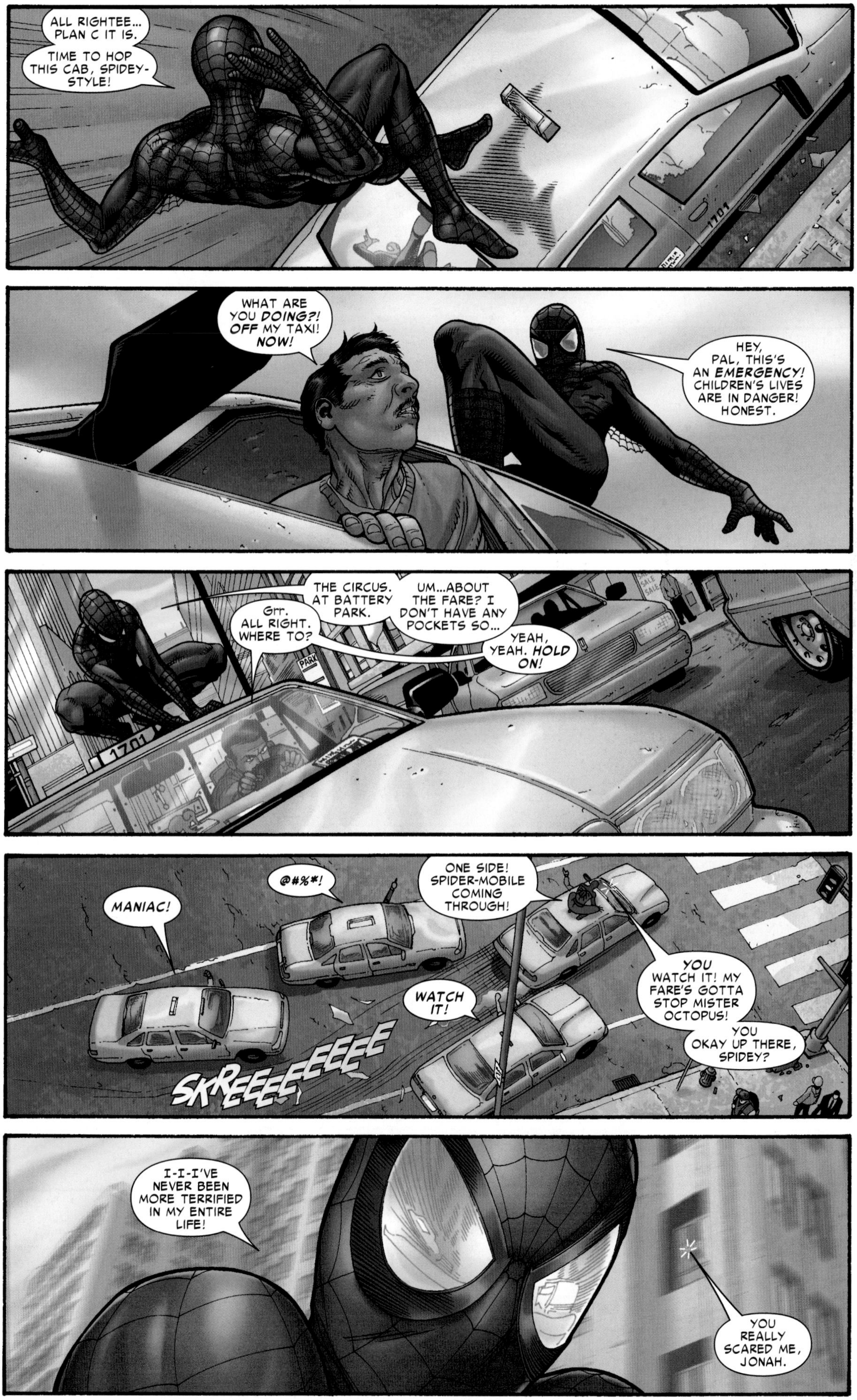
ALL RIGHTEE... PLAN C IT IS.
TIME TO HOP THIS CAB, SPIDEY-STYLE!
1701
WHAT ARE YOU DOING?! OFF MY TAXI! NOW!
HEY, PAL, THIS'S AN EMERGENCY! CHILDREN'S LIVES ARE IN DANGER! HONEST.
Grr. ALL RIGHT. WHERE TO?
THE CIRCUS. AT BATTERY PARK.
UM...ABOUT THE FARE? I DON'T HAVE ANY POCKETS SO...
YEAH, YEAH. HOLD ON!
PARK
1701
MANIAC!
@#%*!
ONE SIDE! SPIDER-MOBILE COMING THROUGH!
WATCH IT!
YOU WATCH IT! MY FARE'S GOTTA STOP MISTER OCTOPUS!
YOU OKAY UP THERE, SPIDEY?
SKREEEEEEEEEEE
I-I-I'VE NEVER BEEN MORE TERRIFIED IN MY ENTIRE LIFE!
YOU REALLY SCARED ME, JONAH.

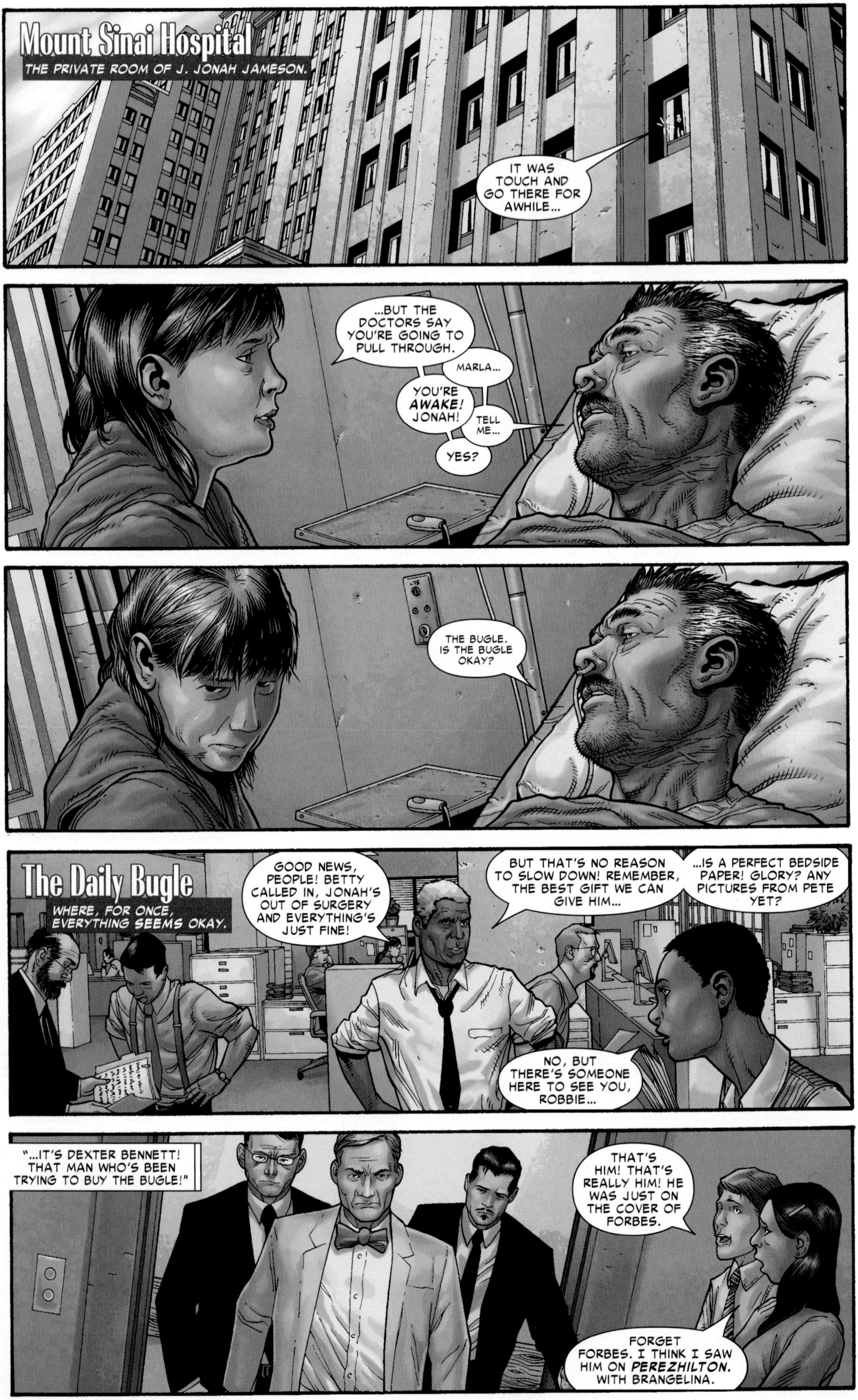
Mount Sinai Hospital
THE PRIVATE ROOM OF J. JONAH JAMESON.
IT WAS TOUCH AND GO THERE FOR AWHILE...
...BUT THE DOCTORS SAY YOU'RE GOING TO PULL THROUGH.
MARLA...
YOU'RE AWAKE! JONAH!
TELL ME...
YES?
THE BUGLE. IS THE BUGLE OKAY?
The Daily Bugle
WHERE, FOR ONCE, EVERYTHING SEEMS OKAY.
GOOD NEWS, PEOPLE! BETTY CALLED IN, JONAH'S OUT OF SURGERY AND EVERYTHING'S JUST FINE!
BUT THAT'S NO REASON TO SLOW DOWN! REMEMBER, THE BEST GIFT WE CAN GIVE HIM...
...IS A PERFECT BEDSIDE PAPER! GLORY? ANY PICTURES FROM PETE YET?
NO, BUT THERE'S SOMEONE HERE TO SEE YOU, ROBBIE...
"...IT'S DEXTER BENNETT! THAT MAN WHO'S BEEN TRYING TO BUY THE BUGLE!"
THAT'S HIM! THAT'S REALLY HIM! HE WAS JUST ON THE COVER OF FORBES.
FORGET FORBES. I THINK I SAW HIM ON PEREZHILTON. WITH BRANGELINA.

MR. BENNETT, I DON'T KNOW WHAT YOU THINK YOU'RE DOING HERE, BUT--

FIRST, LOSE THE LIGHTS. FLUORESCENTS SUCK THE *VITAMIN D* RIGHT OUT OF YOU.

SIR, WE'RE VERY BUSY. I'M GOING TO HAVE TO ASK YOU TO--

AND THAT? THAT THING. I DON'T KNOW WHAT IT IS, BUT IT'S GONE.

NO WONDER JAMESON DIDN'T CROAK. NO ONE WOULD BE CAUGHT *DEAD* HERE.

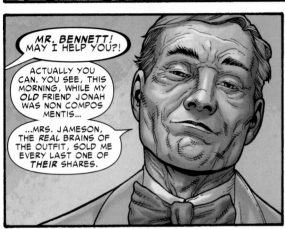

MR. BENNETT! MAY I HELP YOU?!

ACTUALLY YOU CAN. YOU SEE, THIS MORNING, WHILE MY *OLD* FRIEND JONAH WAS NON COMPOS MENTIS...

...MRS. JAMESON, THE *REAL* BRAINS OF THE OUTFIT, SOLD ME EVERY LAST ONE OF *THEIR* SHARES.

WHICH MEANS YOU'RE ALL WORKING FOR ME NOW. SO IF YOU WERE SERIOUS ABOUT THAT HELP...

I COULD REALLY GO FOR A TURKEY CLUB, NO MAYO, AND A DIET PEPSI. NOT A COKE, A *PEPSI*.

IF THEY DON'T HAVE PEPSI, THEN A SNAPPLE.

MISTER BENNETT, MY NAME'S JOE ROBERTSON. I *AM* THE EDITOR IN CHIEF HERE. AND FOR YOUR OWN PERSONAL WELL-BEING...

...I'M GOING TO PRETEND THESE LAST TWO MINUTES DIDN'T HAPPEN...

"...AND THAT I WAS SOMEWHERE ELSE."

JAMAAL, THAT WAS *INTENSE!* I'VE BEEN IN QUINJETS SLOWER THAN THAT!

WHATEVER. JUST BE QUICK. I'M GONNA CALL THE COPS...

...AND THEY DON'T LIKE YOU MUCH THESE DAYS.

YOU KNOW, YOU REALLY SHOULD GET LICENSED.

YEAH, THAT'S ME ALL OVER. THE GYPSY CAB OF SUPER HEROES.

AS-SALAMU ALAIKUM, SPIDER-MAN.

WA ALAIKUM AS-SALAAM, JAMAAL! I OWE YOU ONE.

I LOVE THIS CITY.

SPIDER-MAN. THIS IS BECOMING AN ALL-TOO-REGULAR OCCURRENCE.

I SEE NOW. HE MUST BE BROKEN. BEATEN. DESTROYED.

HURRY! HERE IS WHAT YOU NEED TO DO.

KEEP HIM BUSY LONG ENOUGH FOR THE DEVICE TO GO OFF. I WANT HIM TO BE THERE.

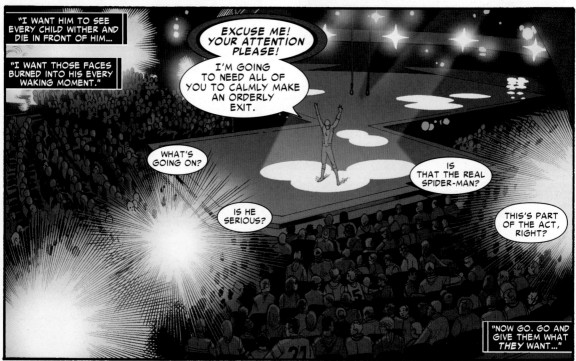

"I WANT HIM TO SEE EVERY CHILD WITHER AND DIE IN FRONT OF HIM...

"I WANT THOSE FACES BURNED INTO HIS EVERY WAKING MOMENT."

EXCUSE ME! YOUR ATTENTION PLEASE!

I'M GOING TO NEED ALL OF YOU TO CALMLY MAKE AN ORDERLY EXIT.

WHAT'S GOING ON?

IS THAT THE REAL SPIDER-MAN?

IS HE SERIOUS?

THIS'S PART OF THE ACT, RIGHT?

"NOW GO. GO AND GIVE THEM WHAT THEY WANT..."

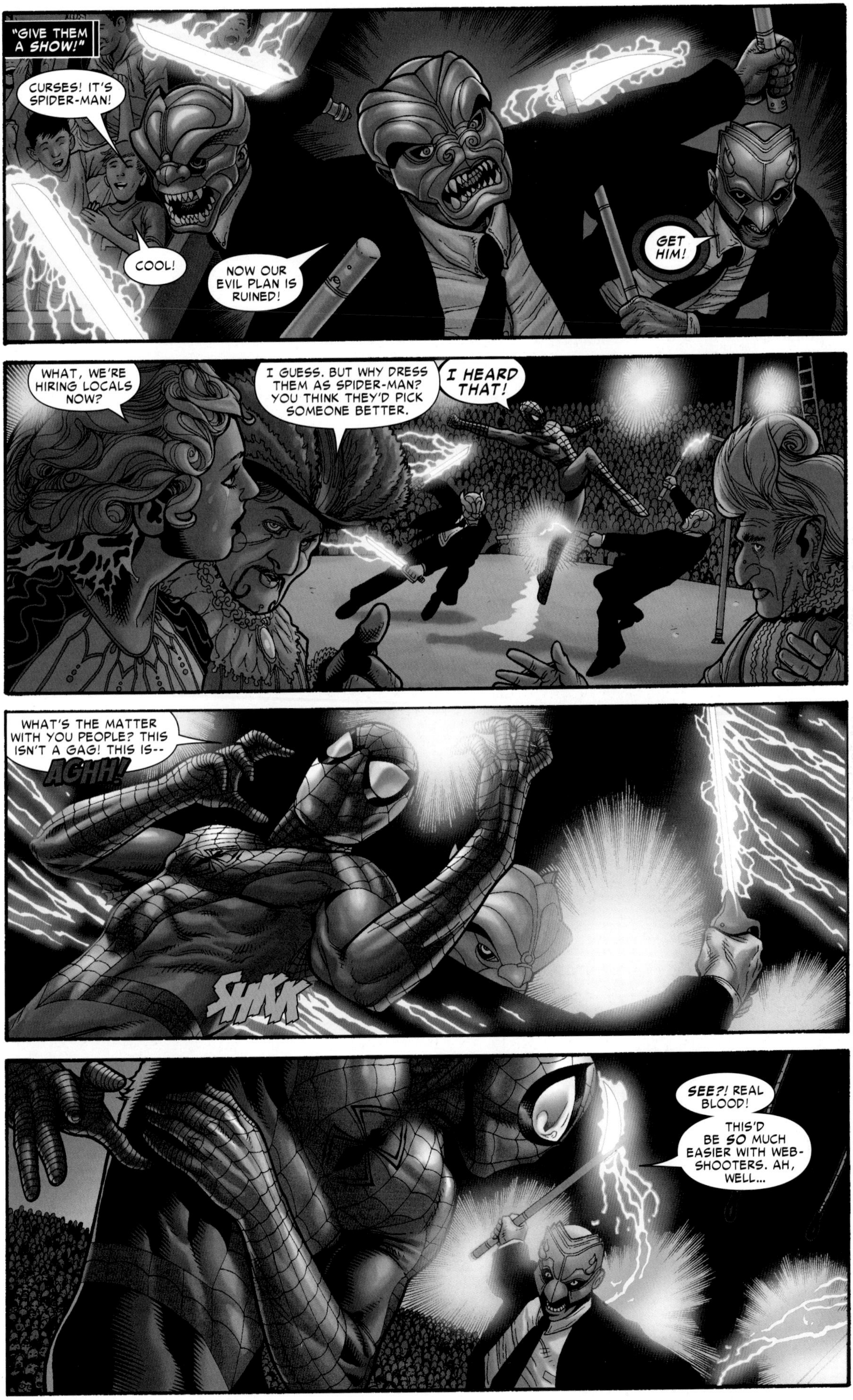
"GIVE THEM A SHOW!"
CURSES! IT'S SPIDER-MAN!
COOL!
NOW OUR EVIL PLAN IS RUINED!
GET HIM!
WHAT, WE'RE HIRING LOCALS NOW?
I GUESS. BUT WHY DRESS THEM AS SPIDER-MAN? YOU THINK THEY'D PICK SOMEONE BETTER.
I HEARD THAT!
WHAT'S THE MATTER WITH YOU PEOPLE? THIS ISN'T A GAG! THIS IS--
AGHH!
SHKK
SEE?! REAL BLOOD!
THIS'D BE SO MUCH EASIER WITH WEB-SHOOTERS. AH, WELL...

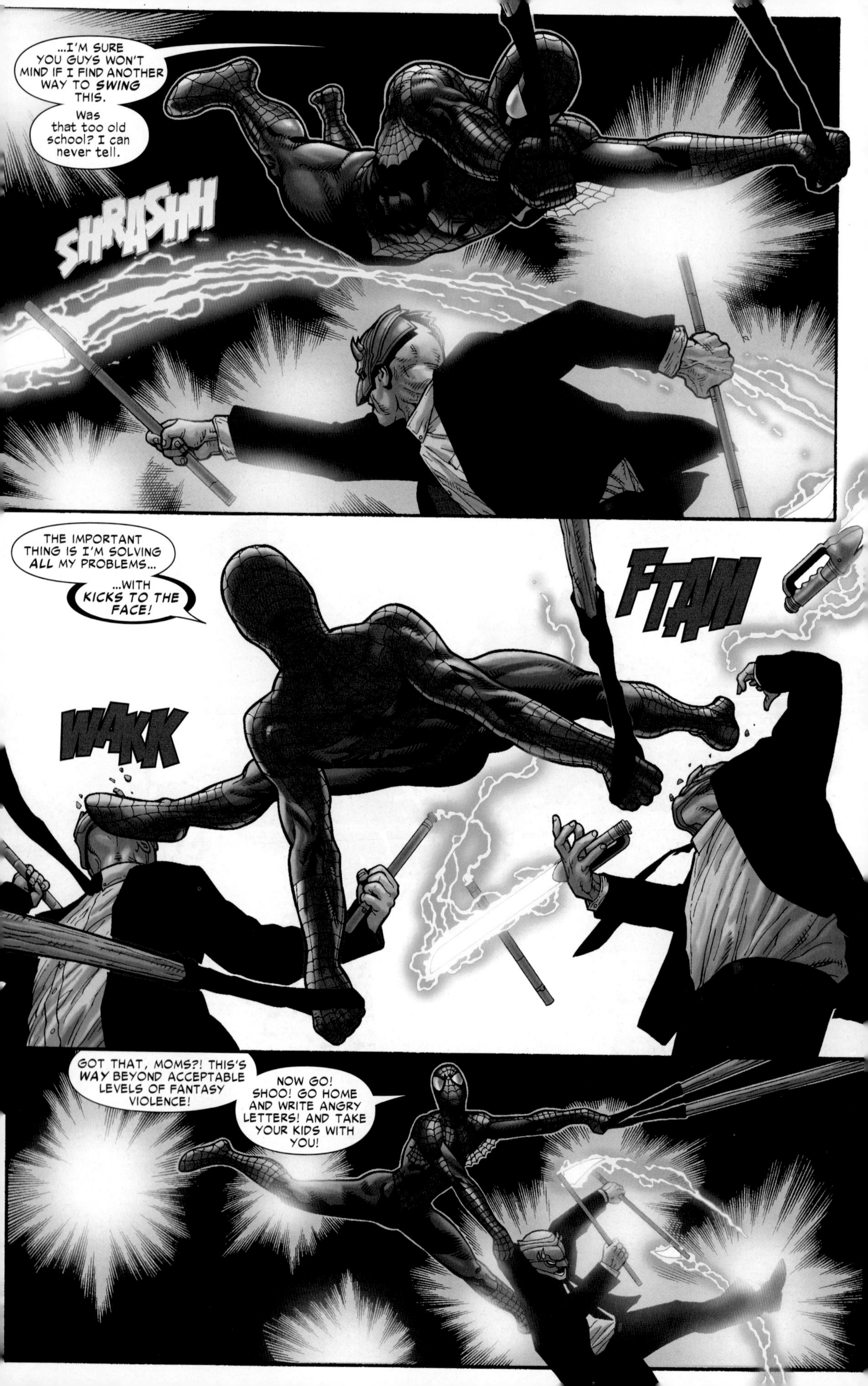
...I'M SURE YOU GUYS WON'T MIND IF I FIND ANOTHER WAY TO SWING THIS.
Was that too old school? I can never tell.
SHRASHH
THE IMPORTANT THING IS I'M SOLVING ALL MY PROBLEMS...
...WITH KICKS TO THE FACE!
FTAM
WAKK
GOT THAT, MOMS?! THIS'S WAY BEYOND ACCEPTABLE LEVELS OF FANTASY VIOLENCE!
NOW GO! SHOO! GO HOME AND WRITE ANGRY LETTERS! AND TAKE YOUR KIDS WITH YOU!

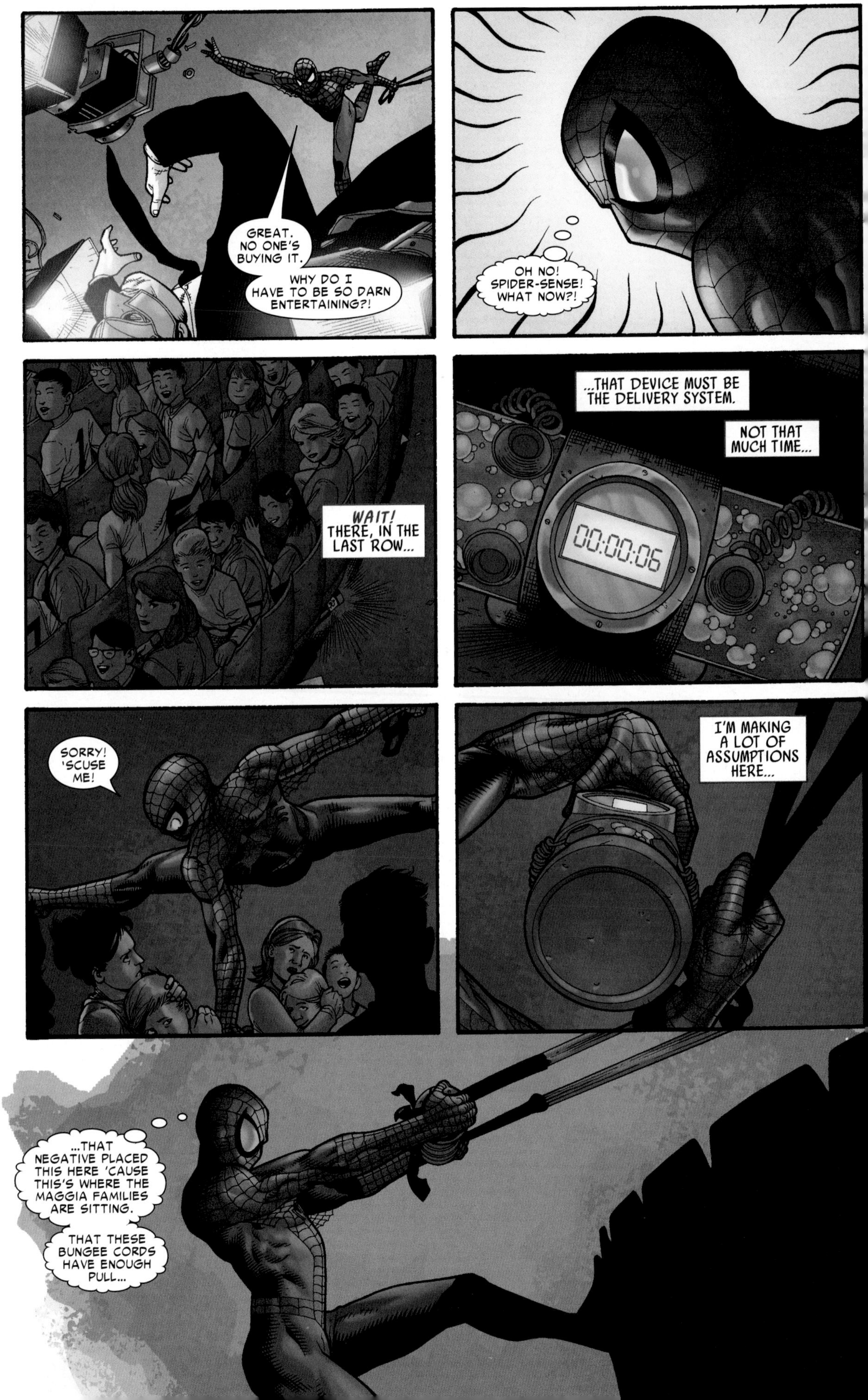
GREAT. NO ONE'S BUYING IT.
WHY DO I HAVE TO BE SO DARN ENTERTAINING?!
OH NO! SPIDER-SENSE! WHAT NOW?!
WAIT! THERE, IN THE LAST ROW...
...THAT DEVICE MUST BE THE DELIVERY SYSTEM.
NOT THAT MUCH TIME...
00:00:06
SORRY! 'SCUSE ME!
I'M MAKING A LOT OF ASSUMPTIONS HERE...
...THAT NEGATIVE PLACED THIS HERE 'CAUSE THIS'S WHERE THE MAGGIA FAMILIES ARE SITTING.
THAT THESE BUNGEE CORDS HAVE ENOUGH PULL...

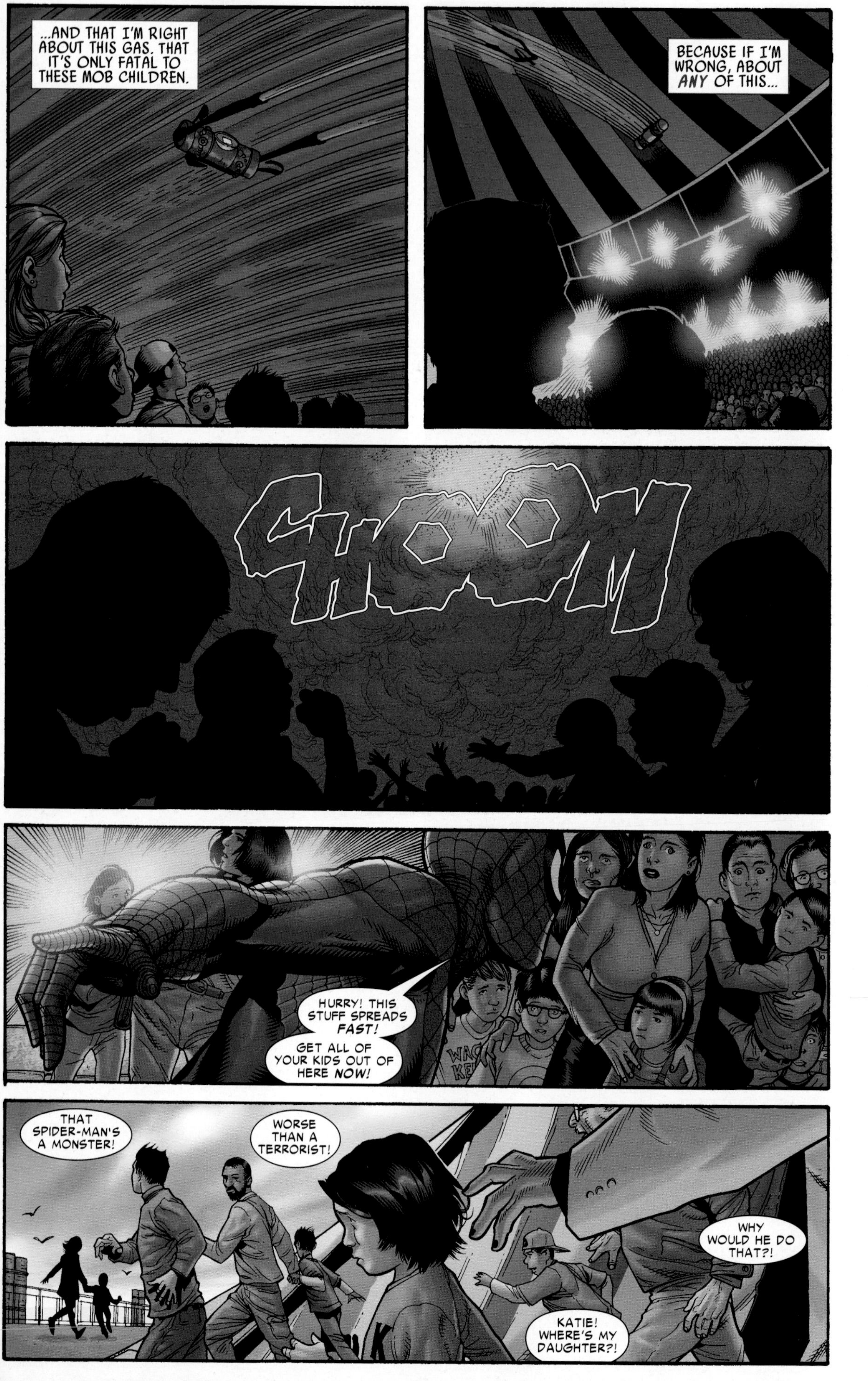
...AND THAT I'M RIGHT ABOUT THIS GAS. THAT IT'S ONLY FATAL TO THESE MOB CHILDREN.
BECAUSE IF I'M WRONG, ABOUT ANY OF THIS...
SHOOOM
HURRY! THIS STUFF SPREADS FAST!
GET ALL OF YOUR KIDS OUT OF HERE NOW!
THAT SPIDER-MAN'S A MONSTER!
WORSE THAN A TERRORIST!
WHY WOULD HE DO THAT?!
KATIE! WHERE'S MY DAUGHTER?!

HOLD YOUR BREATH! WHATEVER YOU DO, DON'T BREATHE. AND GET AS FAR AWAY FROM THE TENT AS POSSIBLE!

IS THAT IT? IS THAT ALL THE KARNELLI AND MANFREDI KIDS?

YES. WE'RE THE LAST ONES.

NICELY DONE, SPIDER-MAN. BUT YOU MISSED ONE.

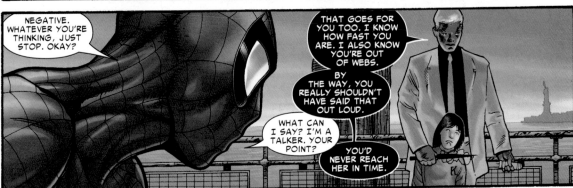

NEGATIVE. WHATEVER YOU'RE THINKING, JUST STOP. OKAY?

THAT GOES FOR YOU TOO. I KNOW HOW FAST YOU ARE. I ALSO KNOW YOU'RE OUT OF WEBS.

BY THE WAY, YOU REALLY SHOULDN'T HAVE SAID THAT OUT LOUD.

WHAT CAN I SAY? I'M A TALKER. YOUR POINT?

YOU'D NEVER REACH HER IN TIME.

SO WHAT NOW? WHAT DO YOU WANT? I DON'T GET IT. YOU KILLED ALL THE MAGGIA DONS. WHY GO AFTER THEIR CHILDREN?

WHAT KIND OF SICK FREAK WOULD DO SOMETHING LIKE THAT?! WHAT COULD YOU POSSIBLY HOPE TO GAIN?!

THEIR *FAMILY* BUSINESS. ONE WHERE I'VE MADE MANY INROADS. AND A BUSINESS THAT I INTEND TO KEEP...

...WELL INTO MY OLD AGE. I THOUGHT IT BEST TO TEND TO MY GARDEN WHILE THE WEEDS WERE STILL YOUNG.

BUT NOW, THANKS TO *YOU*, THAT WILL HAVE TO WAIT. YOU SEE, DEVIL'S BREATH CONTAINS MANY RARE AND COSTLY INGREDIENTS.

THERE'S BARELY ENOUGH LEFT FOR *ONE* DOSE.

YOUR BLOOD, SPIDER-MAN. GIVE IT TO ME, AND I RELEASE THE GIRL.

YOU'RE NOT KIDDING, ARE YOU?

NO. THIS IS A SERIOUS TRANSACTION.

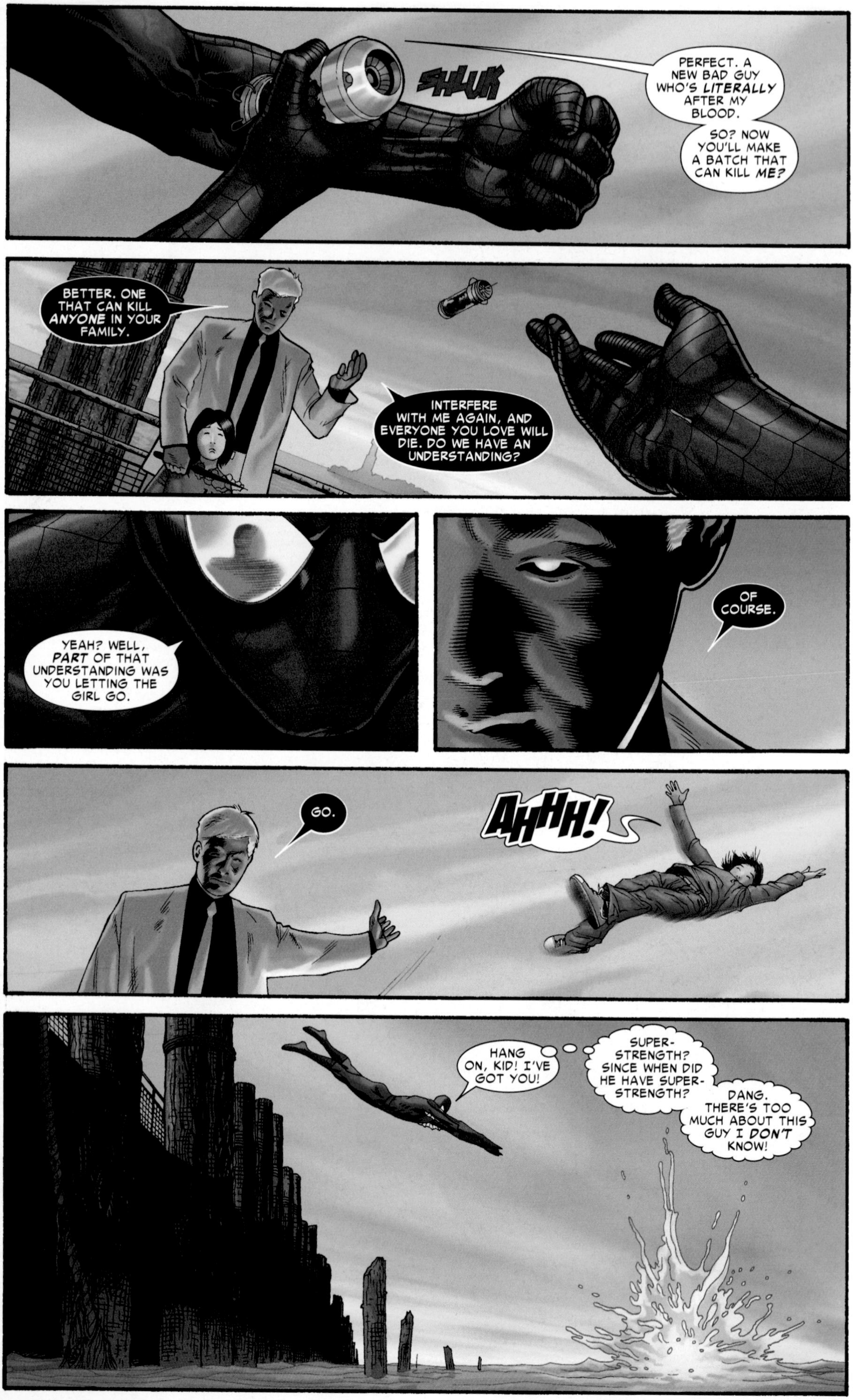
PERFECT. A NEW BAD GUY WHO'S LITERALLY AFTER MY BLOOD.
SHLUK
SO? NOW YOU'LL MAKE A BATCH THAT CAN KILL ME?
BETTER. ONE THAT CAN KILL ANYONE IN YOUR FAMILY.
INTERFERE WITH ME AGAIN, AND EVERYONE YOU LOVE WILL DIE. DO WE HAVE AN UNDERSTANDING?
YEAH? WELL, PART OF THAT UNDERSTANDING WAS YOU LETTING THE GIRL GO.
OF COURSE.
GO.
AHHH!
HANG ON, KID! I'VE GOT YOU!
SUPER-STRENGTH? SINCE WHEN DID HE HAVE SUPER-STRENGTH?
DANG. THERE'S TOO MUCH ABOUT THIS GUY I DON'T KNOW!

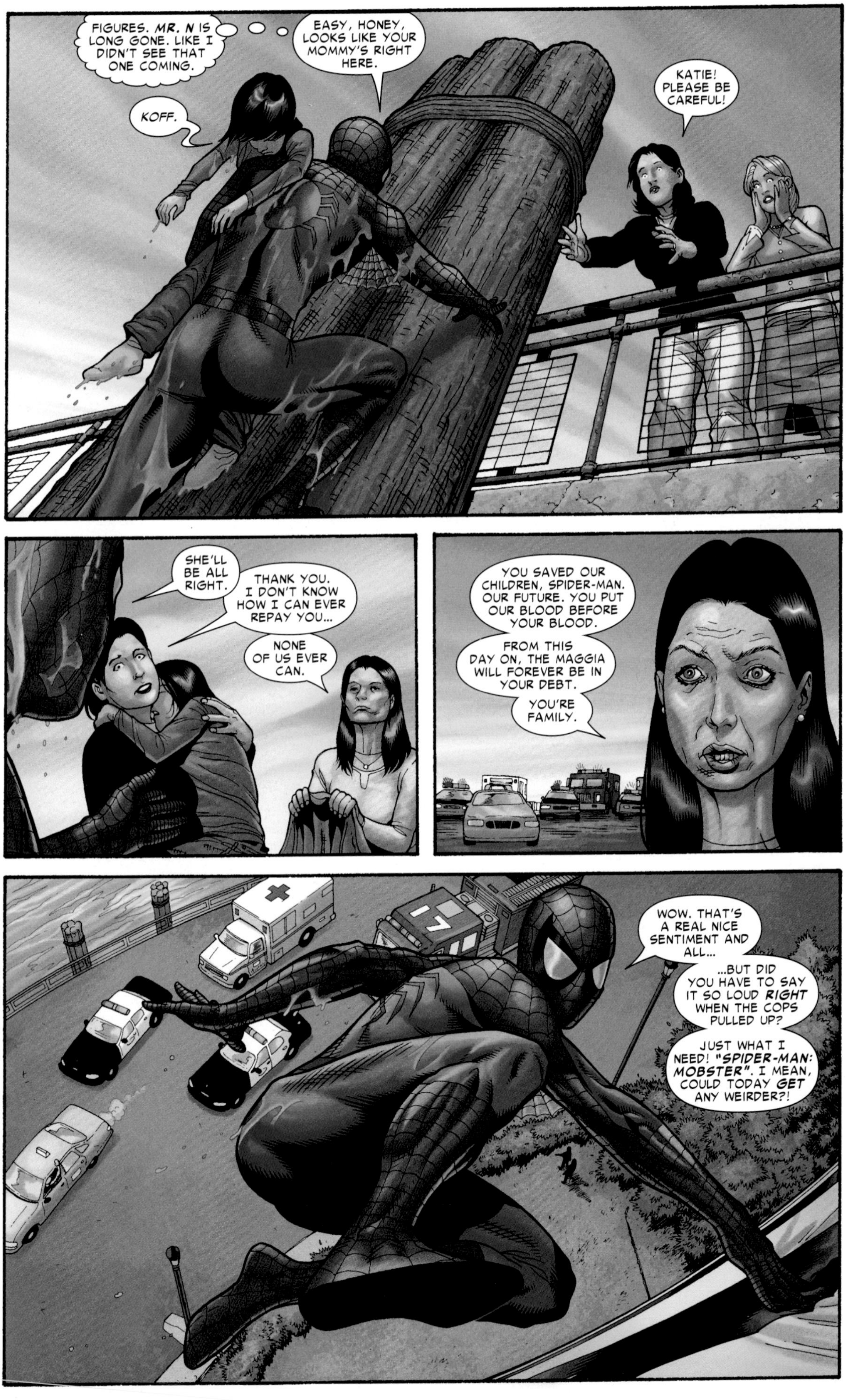
FIGURES. MR. N IS LONG GONE. LIKE I DIDN'T SEE THAT ONE COMING.
EASY, HONEY, LOOKS LIKE YOUR MOMMY'S RIGHT HERE.
KOFF.
KATIE! PLEASE BE CAREFUL!
SHE'LL BE ALL RIGHT.
THANK YOU. I DON'T KNOW HOW I CAN EVER REPAY YOU...
NONE OF US EVER CAN.
YOU SAVED OUR CHILDREN, SPIDER-MAN. OUR FUTURE. YOU PUT OUR BLOOD BEFORE YOUR BLOOD.
FROM THIS DAY ON, THE MAGGIA WILL FOREVER BE IN YOUR DEBT.
YOU'RE FAMILY.
WOW. THAT'S A REAL NICE SENTIMENT AND ALL...
...BUT DID YOU HAVE TO SAY IT SO LOUD RIGHT WHEN THE COPS PULLED UP?
JUST WHAT I NEED! "SPIDER-MAN: MOBSTER". I MEAN, COULD TODAY GET ANY WEIRDER?!

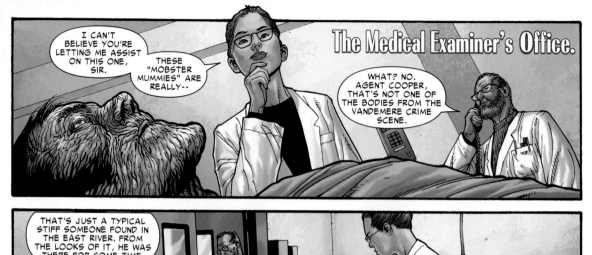

The Medical Examiner's Office.
I CAN'T BELIEVE YOU'RE LETTING ME ASSIST ON THIS ONE, SIR.
THESE "MOBSTER MUMMIES" ARE REALLY--
WHAT? NO. AGENT COOPER, THAT'S NOT ONE OF THE BODIES FROM THE VANDEMERE CRIME SCENE.
THAT'S JUST A TYPICAL STIFF SOMEONE FOUND IN THE EAST RIVER. FROM THE LOOKS OF IT, HE WAS THERE FOR SOME TIME.
BEFORE YOU WORK ON THE MORE "EXOTIC" CASES, YOU HAVE TO START AT THE BOTTOM.
ALL RIGHT. SHOULD I...?
COOPER, SHORT OF PREPPING THE SUBJECT, I DON'T WANT YOU DOING A THING UNTIL I GET BACK.
FINE.
HMM.
LOOKS LIKE THERE'S SOMETHING IN HIS MOUTH... AN INSECT?
MY ENTOMOLOGY'S PRETTY GOOD, MAYBE IF I CAN PLACE THE BUG, I CAN DETERMINE--
WHAT? THAT'S NO--
THAT'S A SPIDER-TRACER!
WHO IS THIS GUY? AND...

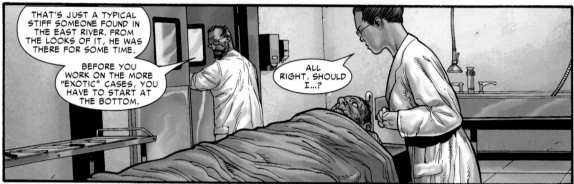

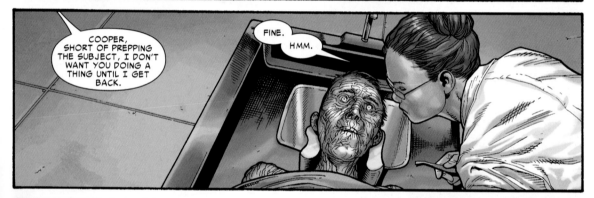

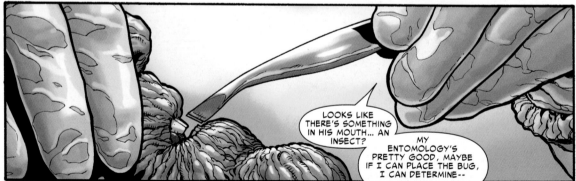

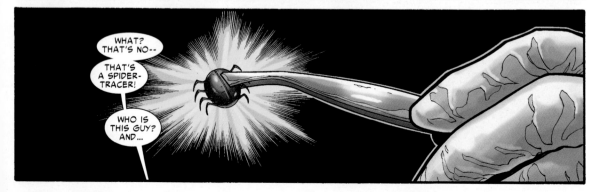

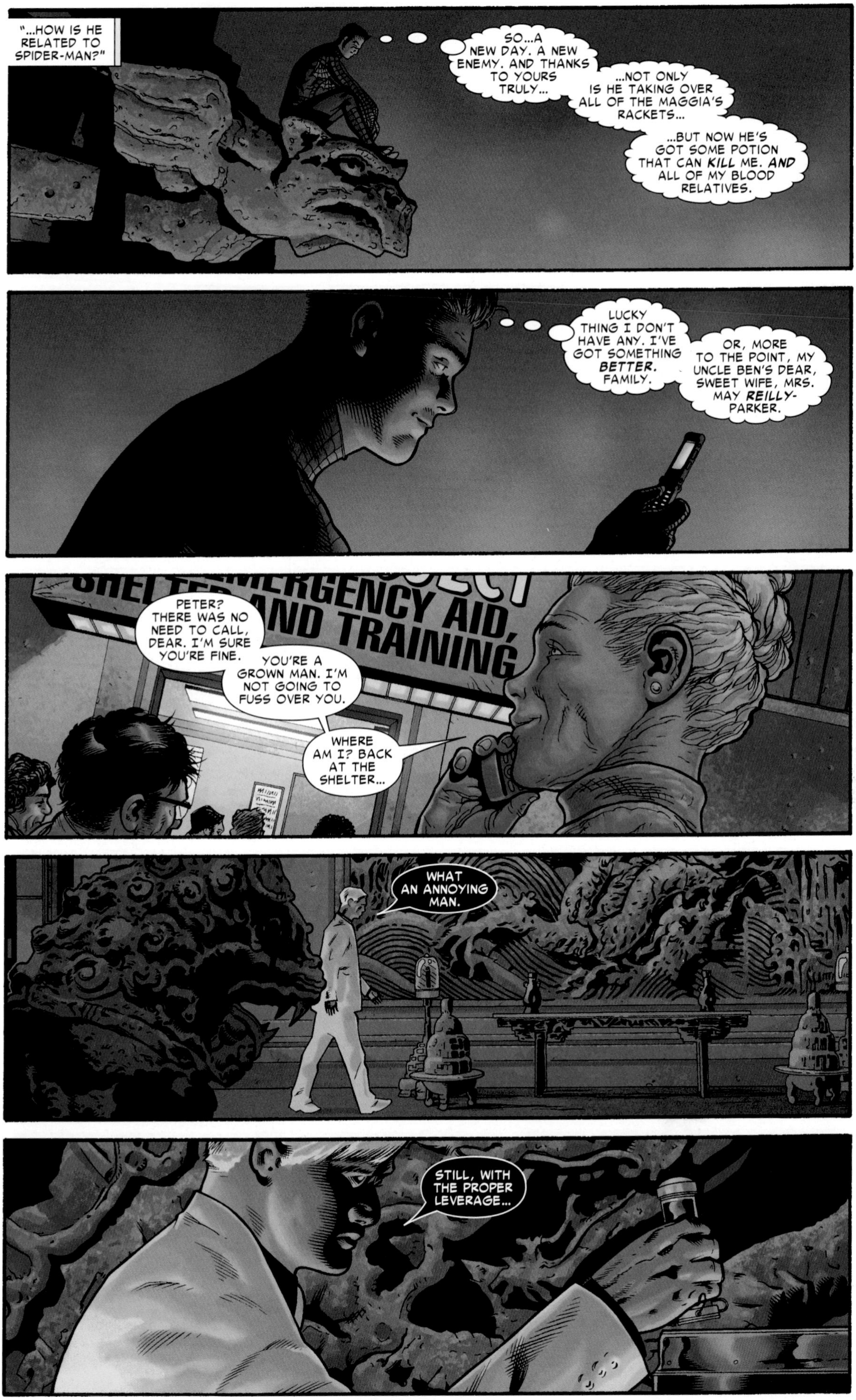
"...HOW IS HE RELATED TO SPIDER-MAN?"
SO...A NEW DAY. A NEW ENEMY. AND THANKS TO YOURS TRULY...
...NOT ONLY IS HE TAKING OVER ALL OF THE MAGGIA'S RACKETS...
...BUT NOW HE'S GOT SOME POTION THAT CAN KILL ME. AND ALL OF MY BLOOD RELATIVES.
LUCKY THING I DON'T HAVE ANY. I'VE GOT SOMETHING BETTER. FAMILY.
OR, MORE TO THE POINT, MY UNCLE BEN'S DEAR, SWEET WIFE, MRS. MAY REILLY-PARKER.
EMERGENCY AID, AND TRAINING
PETER? THERE WAS NO NEED TO CALL, DEAR. I'M SURE YOU'RE FINE.
YOU'RE A GROWN MAN. I'M NOT GOING TO FUSS OVER YOU.
WHERE AM I? BACK AT THE SHELTER...
WHAT AN ANNOYING MAN.
STILL, WITH THE PROPER LEVERAGE...

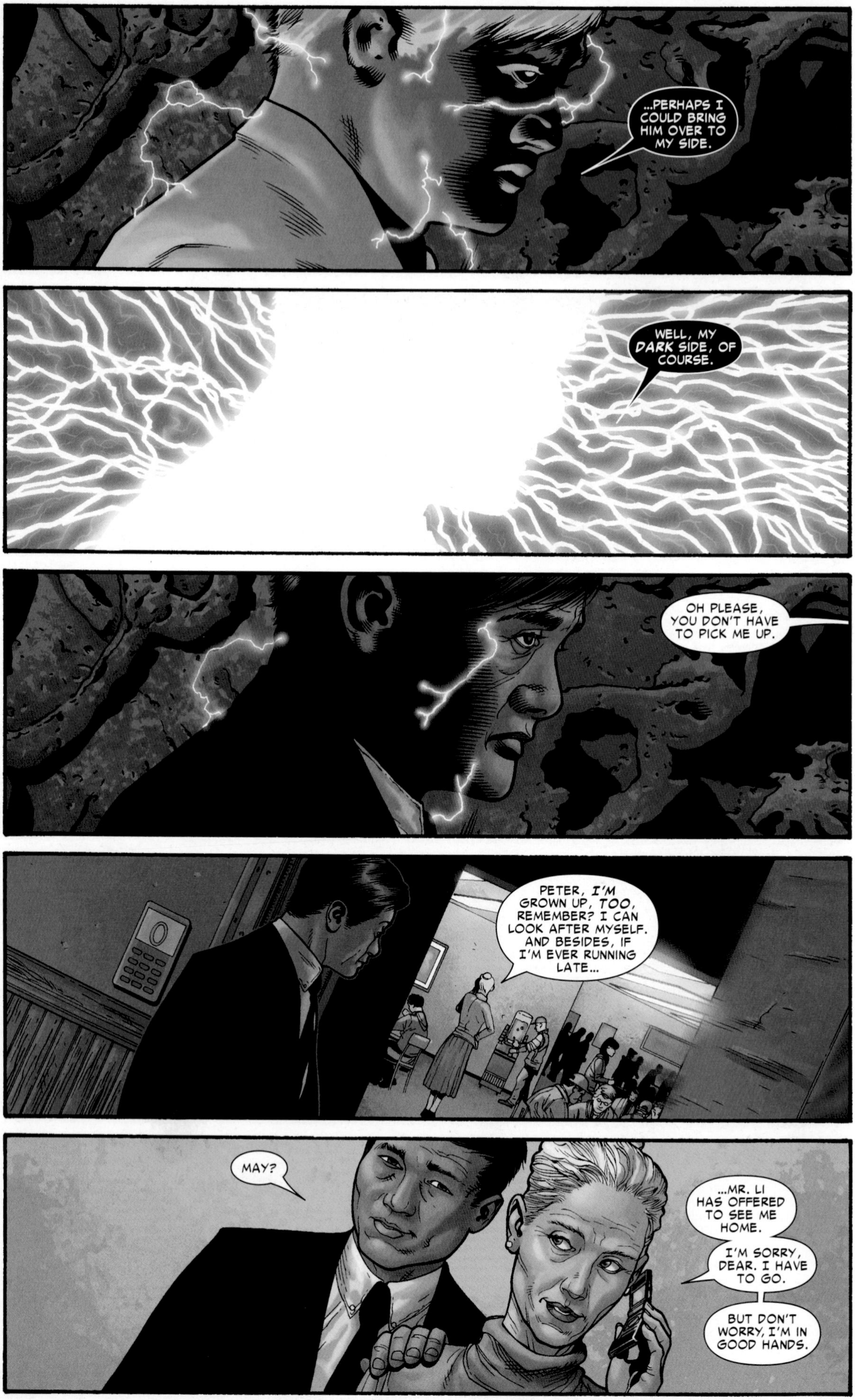
...PERHAPS I COULD BRING HIM OVER TO MY SIDE.
WELL, MY DARK SIDE, OF COURSE.
OH PLEASE, YOU DON'T HAVE TO PICK ME UP.
PETER, I'M GROWN UP, TOO, REMEMBER? I CAN LOOK AFTER MYSELF. AND BESIDES, IF I'M EVER RUNNING LATE...
MAY?
...MR. LI HAS OFFERED TO SEE ME HOME.
I'M SORRY, DEAR. I HAVE TO GO.
BUT DON'T WORRY, I'M IN GOOD HANDS.

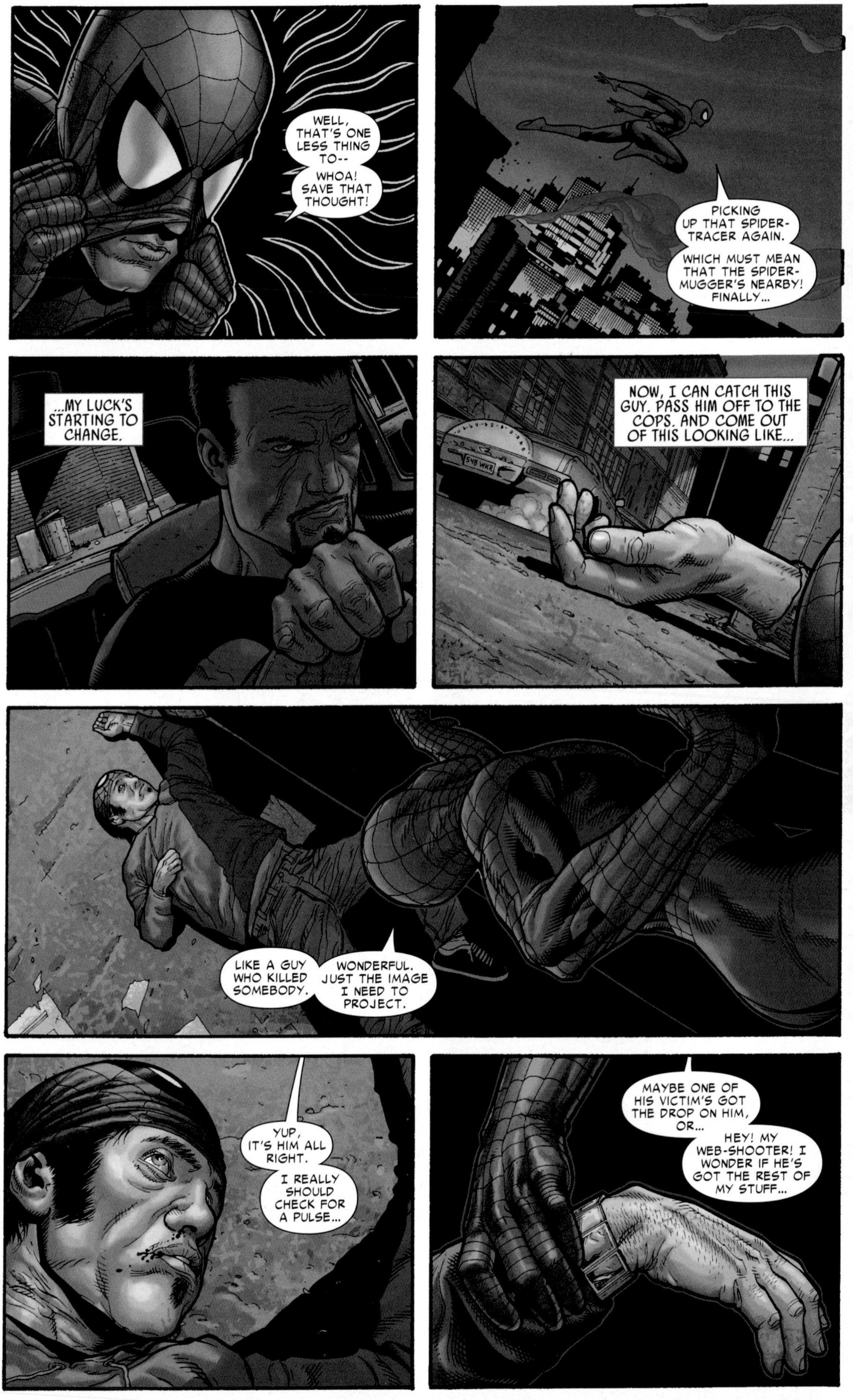
WELL, THAT'S ONE LESS THING TO--
WHOA! SAVE THAT THOUGHT!
PICKING UP THAT SPIDER-TRACER AGAIN.
WHICH MUST MEAN THAT THE SPIDER-MUGGER'S NEARBY! FINALLY...
...MY LUCK'S STARTING TO CHANGE.
NOW, I CAN CATCH THIS GUY. PASS HIM OFF TO THE COPS. AND COME OUT OF THIS LOOKING LIKE...
548 WKR
LIKE A GUY WHO KILLED SOMEBODY.
WONDERFUL. JUST THE IMAGE I NEED TO PROJECT.
YUP, IT'S HIM ALL RIGHT.
I REALLY SHOULD CHECK FOR A PULSE...
MAYBE ONE OF HIS VICTIM'S GOT THE DROP ON HIM, OR...
HEY! MY WEB-SHOOTER! I WONDER IF HE'S GOT THE REST OF MY STUFF...

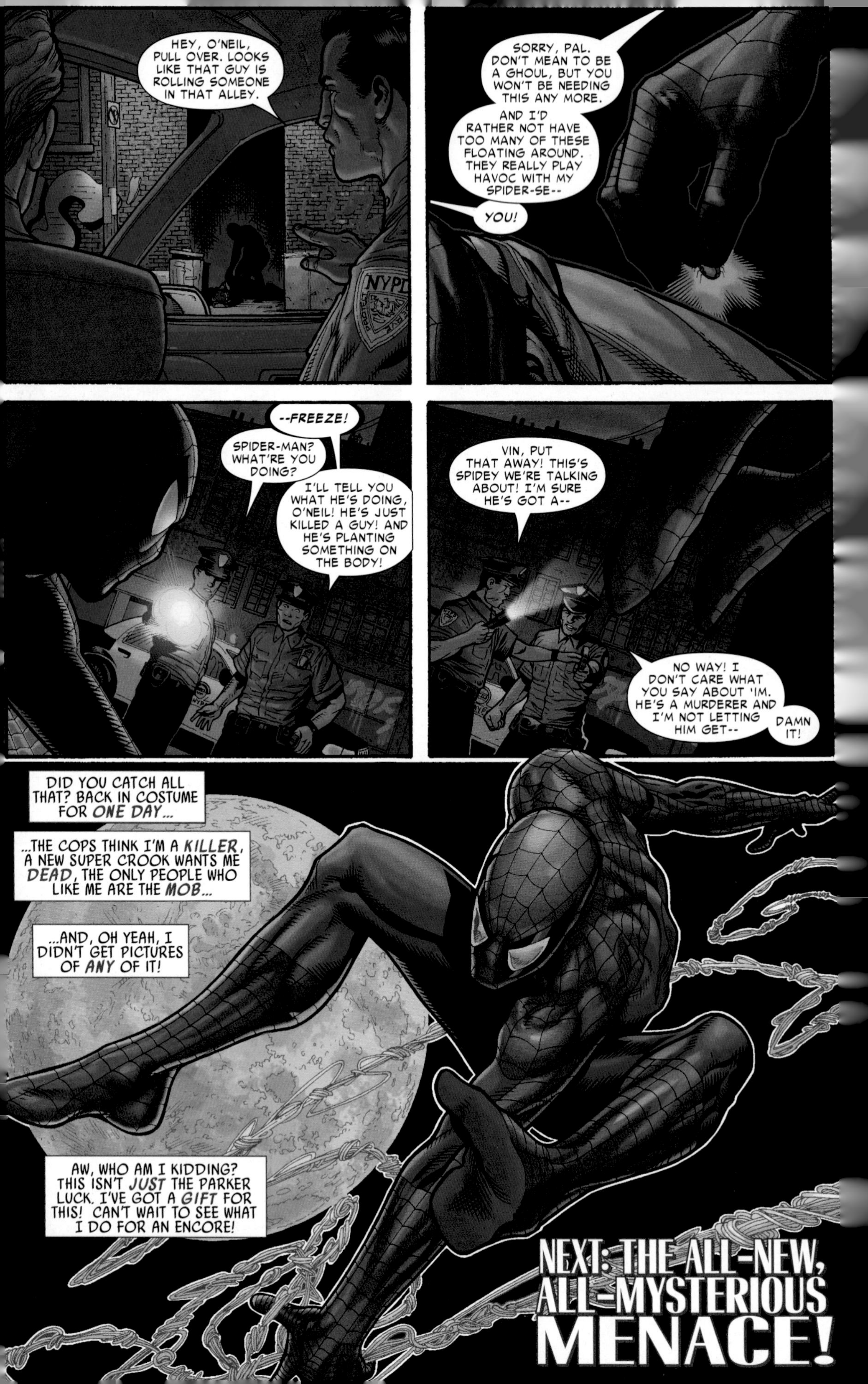
HEY, O'NEIL, PULL OVER. LOOKS LIKE THAT GUY IS ROLLING SOMEONE IN THAT ALLEY.
SORRY, PAL. DON'T MEAN TO BE A GHOUL, BUT YOU WON'T BE NEEDING THIS ANY MORE.
AND I'D RATHER NOT HAVE TOO MANY OF THESE FLOATING AROUND. THEY REALLY PLAY HAVOC WITH MY SPIDER-SE--
YOU!
--FREEZE!
SPIDER-MAN? WHAT'RE YOU DOING?
I'LL TELL YOU WHAT HE'S DOING, O'NEIL! HE'S JUST KILLED A GUY! AND HE'S PLANTING SOMETHING ON THE BODY!
VIN, PUT THAT AWAY! THIS'S SPIDEY WE'RE TALKING ABOUT! I'M SURE HE'S GOT A--
NO WAY! I DON'T CARE WHAT YOU SAY ABOUT 'IM. HE'S A MURDERER AND I'M NOT LETTING HIM GET--
DAMN IT!
DID YOU CATCH ALL THAT? BACK IN COSTUME FOR ONE DAY...
...THE COPS THINK I'M A KILLER, A NEW SUPER CROOK WANTS ME DEAD, THE ONLY PEOPLE WHO LIKE ME ARE THE MOB...
...AND, OH YEAH, I DIDN'T GET PICTURES OF ANY OF IT!
AW, WHO AM I KIDDING? THIS ISN'T JUST THE PARKER LUCK. I'VE GOT A GIFT FOR THIS! CAN'T WAIT TO SEE WHAT I DO FOR AN ENCORE!
NEXT: THE ALL-NEW, ALL-MYSTERIOUS MENACE!

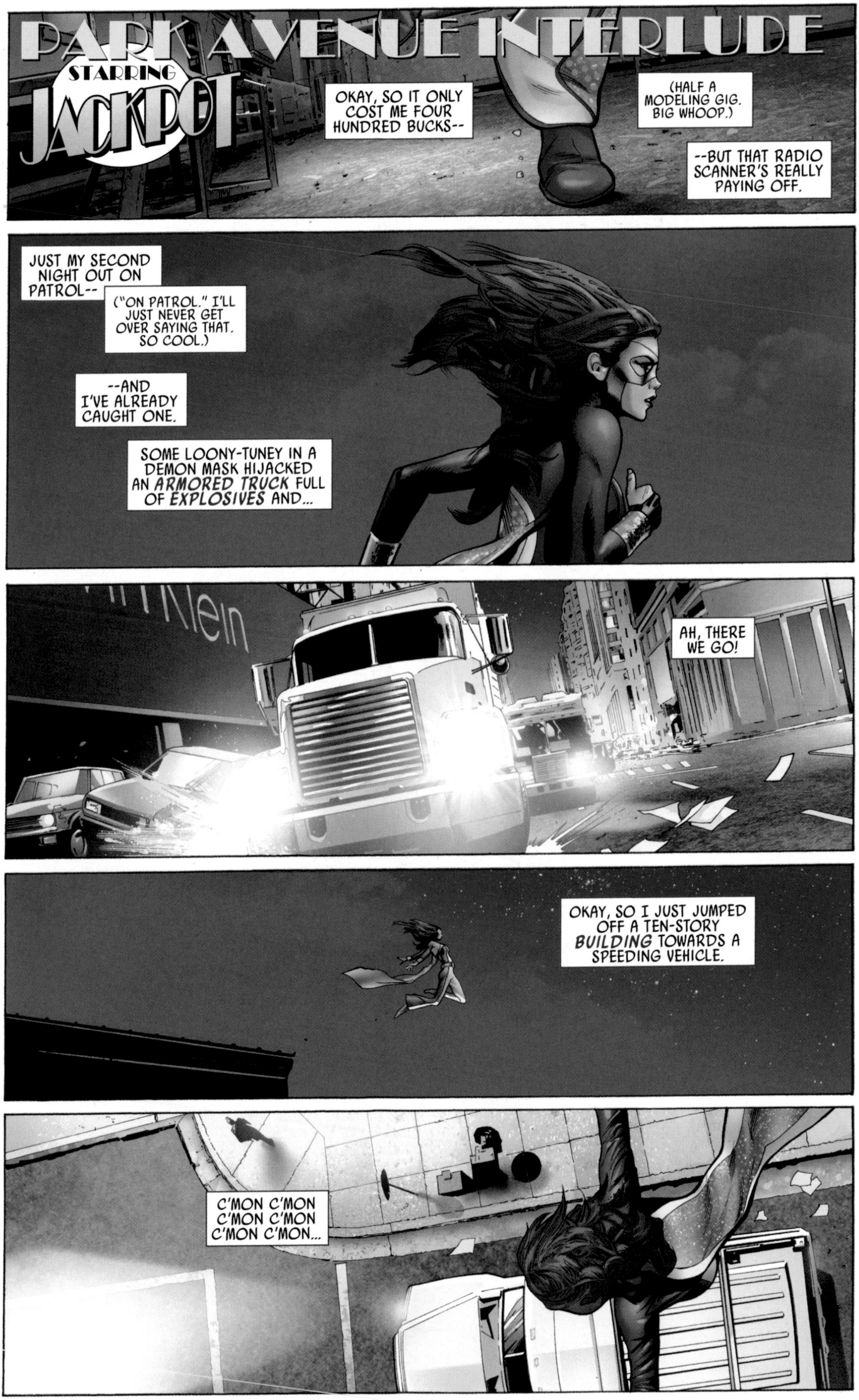
PARK AVENUE INTERLUDE
STARRING JACKPOT
OKAY, SO IT ONLY COST ME FOUR HUNDRED BUCKS--
(HALF A MODELING GIG. BIG WHOOP.)
--BUT THAT RADIO SCANNER'S REALLY PAYING OFF.
JUST MY SECOND NIGHT OUT ON PATROL--
("ON PATROL." I'LL JUST NEVER GET OVER SAYING THAT. SO COOL.)
--AND I'VE ALREADY CAUGHT ONE.
SOME LOONY-TUNEY IN A DEMON MASK HIJACKED AN ARMORED TRUCK FULL OF EXPLOSIVES AND...
AH, THERE WE GO!
OKAY, SO I JUST JUMPED OFF A TEN-STORY BUILDING TOWARDS A SPEEDING VEHICLE.
C'MON C'MON C'MON C'MON C'MON C'MON...

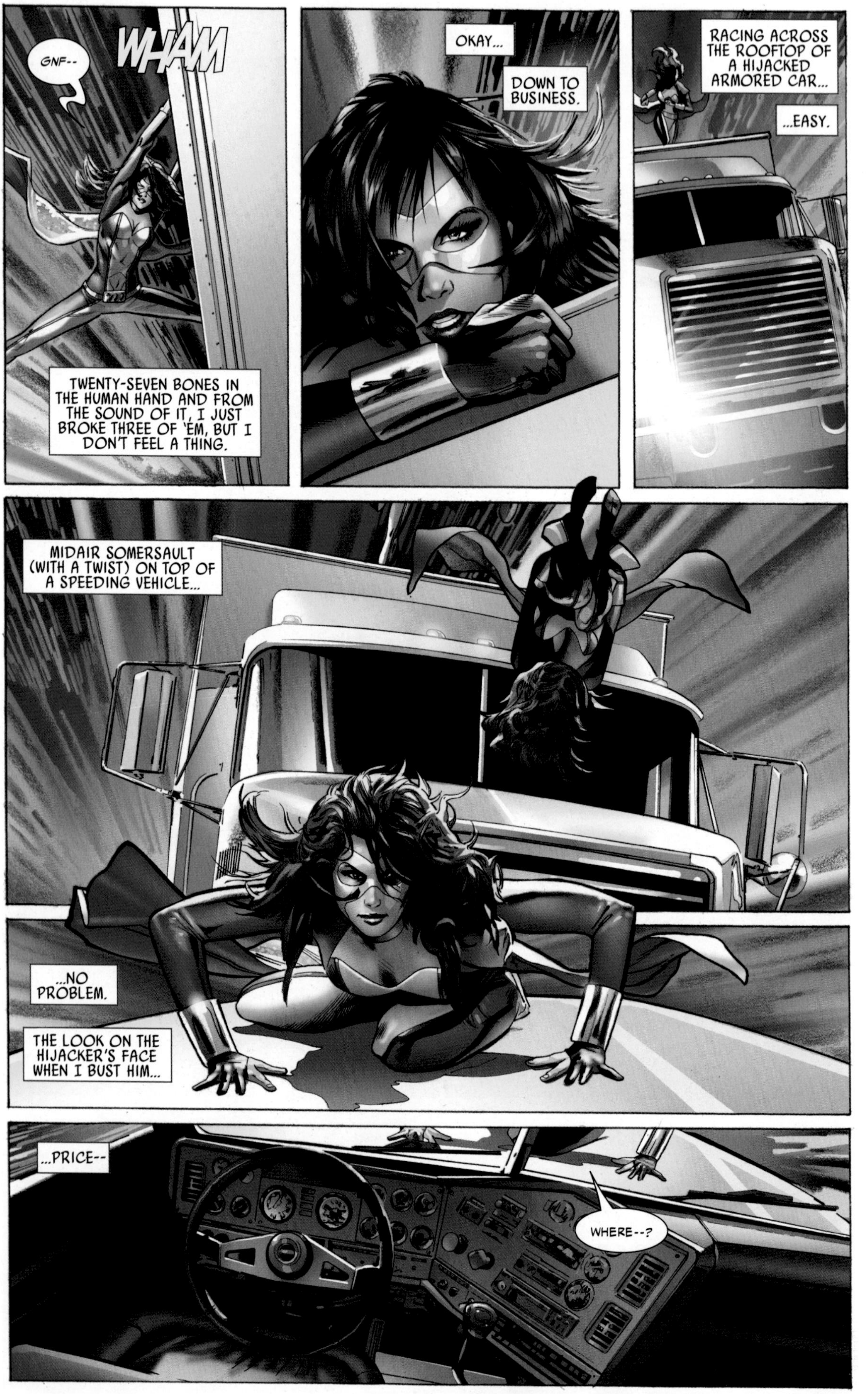
GNF--
WHAM
TWENTY-SEVEN BONES IN THE HUMAN HAND AND FROM THE SOUND OF IT, I JUST BROKE THREE OF 'EM, BUT I DON'T FEEL A THING.
OKAY...
DOWN TO BUSINESS.
RACING ACROSS THE ROOFTOP OF A HIJACKED ARMORED CAR...
...EASY.
MIDAIR SOMERSAULT (WITH A TWIST) ON TOP OF A SPEEDING VEHICLE...
...NO PROBLEM.
THE LOOK ON THE HIJACKER'S FACE WHEN I BUST HIM...
...PRICE--
WHERE--?

OKAY, SO MAYBE THIS IS A FEW DIFFERENT KINDS OF BAD.

CRAASH

KEEP IT TOGETHER... KEEP IT TOGETHER...

BRAKE PEDAL... BRAKE PEDAL...

HA! HA! HA! HA! HA!

CLANG

SHREEOOOO

SKREEEEEECH

THIS GUY'S A $%^#ING MENACE...

WELL, I'M GONNA GET YOU, TIGER. COUNT ON IT...

UNFORTUNATELY, TRUE BELIEVER, YOU'LL HAVE TO WAIT 'TIL NEXT MONTH TO SEE HER TRY!

MARC GUGGENHEIM
WRITER

GREG LAND
PENCILER

JAY LEISTEN
INKER

JUSTIN PONSOR
COLORS

VC'S CORY PETIT
LETTERS

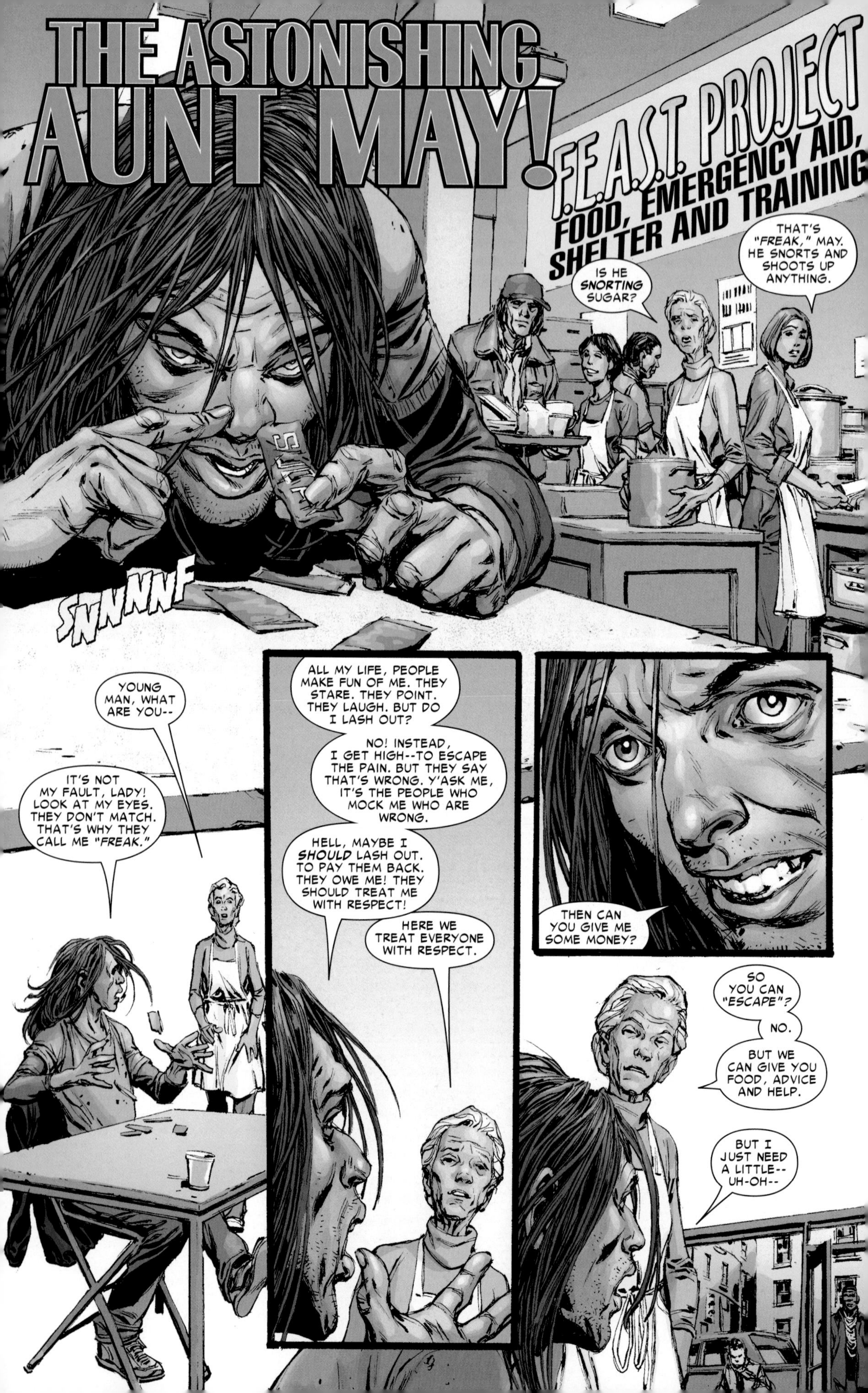
THE ASTONISHING AUNT MAY!
F.E.A.S.T. PROJECT
FOOD, EMERGENCY AID, SHELTER AND TRAINING
IS HE SNORTING SUGAR?
THAT'S "FREAK," MAY. HE SNORTS AND SHOOTS UP ANYTHING.
SNNNNF
YOUNG MAN, WHAT ARE YOU--
IT'S NOT MY FAULT, LADY! LOOK AT MY EYES. THEY DON'T MATCH. THAT'S WHY THEY CALL ME "FREAK."
ALL MY LIFE, PEOPLE MAKE FUN OF ME. THEY STARE. THEY POINT. THEY LAUGH. BUT DO I LASH OUT?
NO! INSTEAD, I GET HIGH--TO ESCAPE THE PAIN. BUT THEY SAY THAT'S WRONG. Y'ASK ME, IT'S THE PEOPLE WHO MOCK ME WHO ARE WRONG.
HELL, MAYBE I SHOULD LASH OUT. TO PAY THEM BACK. THEY OWE ME! THEY SHOULD TREAT ME WITH RESPECT!
HERE WE TREAT EVERYONE WITH RESPECT.
THEN CAN YOU GIVE ME SOME MONEY?
SO YOU CAN "ESCAPE"?
NO.
BUT WE CAN GIVE YOU FOOD, ADVICE AND HELP.
BUT I JUST NEED A LITTLE-- UH-OH--

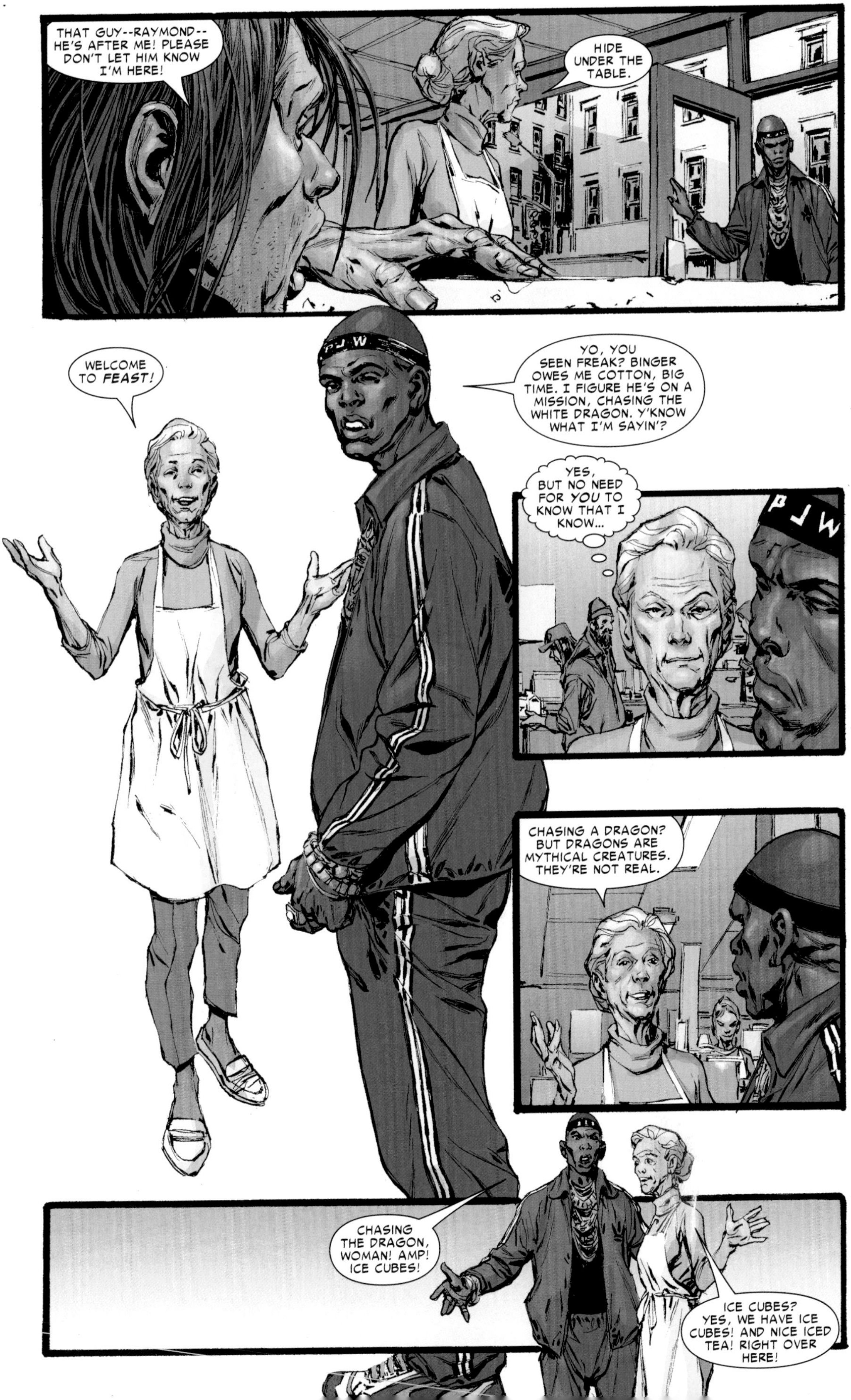

THAT GUY--RAYMOND--HE'S AFTER ME! PLEASE DON'T LET HIM KNOW I'M HERE!
HIDE UNDER THE TABLE.
WELCOME TO FEAST!
YO, YOU SEEN FREAK? BINGER OWES ME COTTON, BIG TIME. I FIGURE HE'S ON A MISSION, CHASING THE WHITE DRAGON. Y'KNOW WHAT I'M SAYIN'?
YES, BUT NO NEED FOR YOU TO KNOW THAT I KNOW...
CHASING A DRAGON? BUT DRAGONS ARE MYTHICAL CREATURES. THEY'RE NOT REAL.
CHASING THE DRAGON, WOMAN! AMP! ICE CUBES!
ICE CUBES? YES, WE HAVE ICE CUBES! AND NICE ICED TEA! RIGHT OVER HERE!

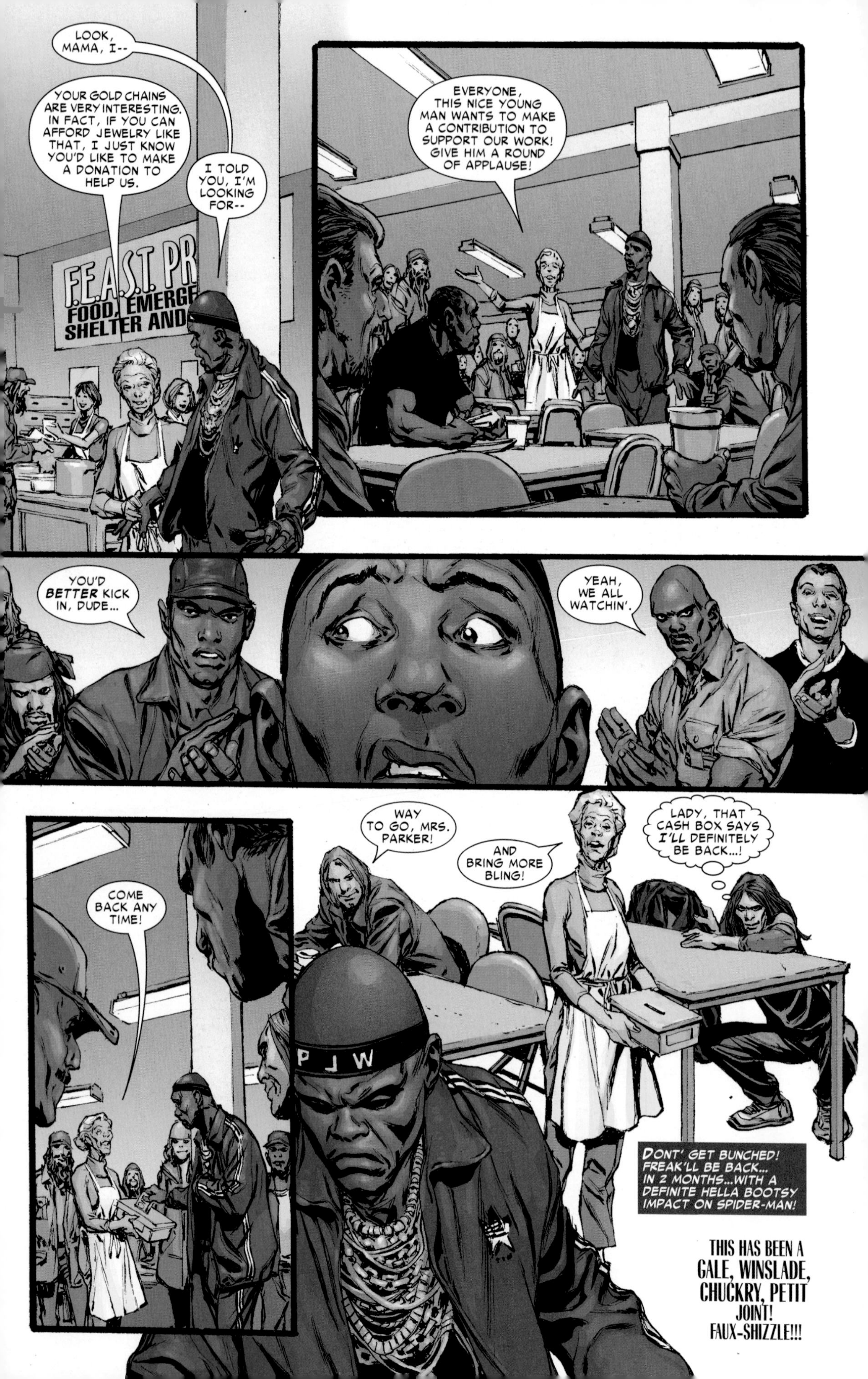
LOOK, MAMA, I--
YOUR GOLD CHAINS ARE VERY INTERESTING. IN FACT, IF YOU CAN AFFORD JEWELRY LIKE THAT, I JUST KNOW YOU'D LIKE TO MAKE A DONATION TO HELP US.
I TOLD YOU, I'M LOOKING FOR--
F.E.A.S.T. PR
FOOD, EMERGE
SHELTER AND
EVERYONE, THIS NICE YOUNG MAN WANTS TO MAKE A CONTRIBUTION TO SUPPORT OUR WORK! GIVE HIM A ROUND OF APPLAUSE!
YOU'D BETTER KICK IN, DUDE...
YEAH, WE ALL WATCHIN'.
COME BACK ANY TIME!
WAY TO GO, MRS. PARKER!
AND BRING MORE BLING!
LADY, THAT CASH BOX SAYS I'LL DEFINITELY BE BACK...!
PLW
DONT' GET BUNCHED! FREAK'LL BE BACK... IN 2 MONTHS...WITH A DEFINITE HELLA BOOTSY IMPACT ON SPIDER-MAN!
THIS HAS BEEN A GALE, WINSLADE, CHUCKRY, PETIT JOINT! FAUX-SHIZZLE!!!

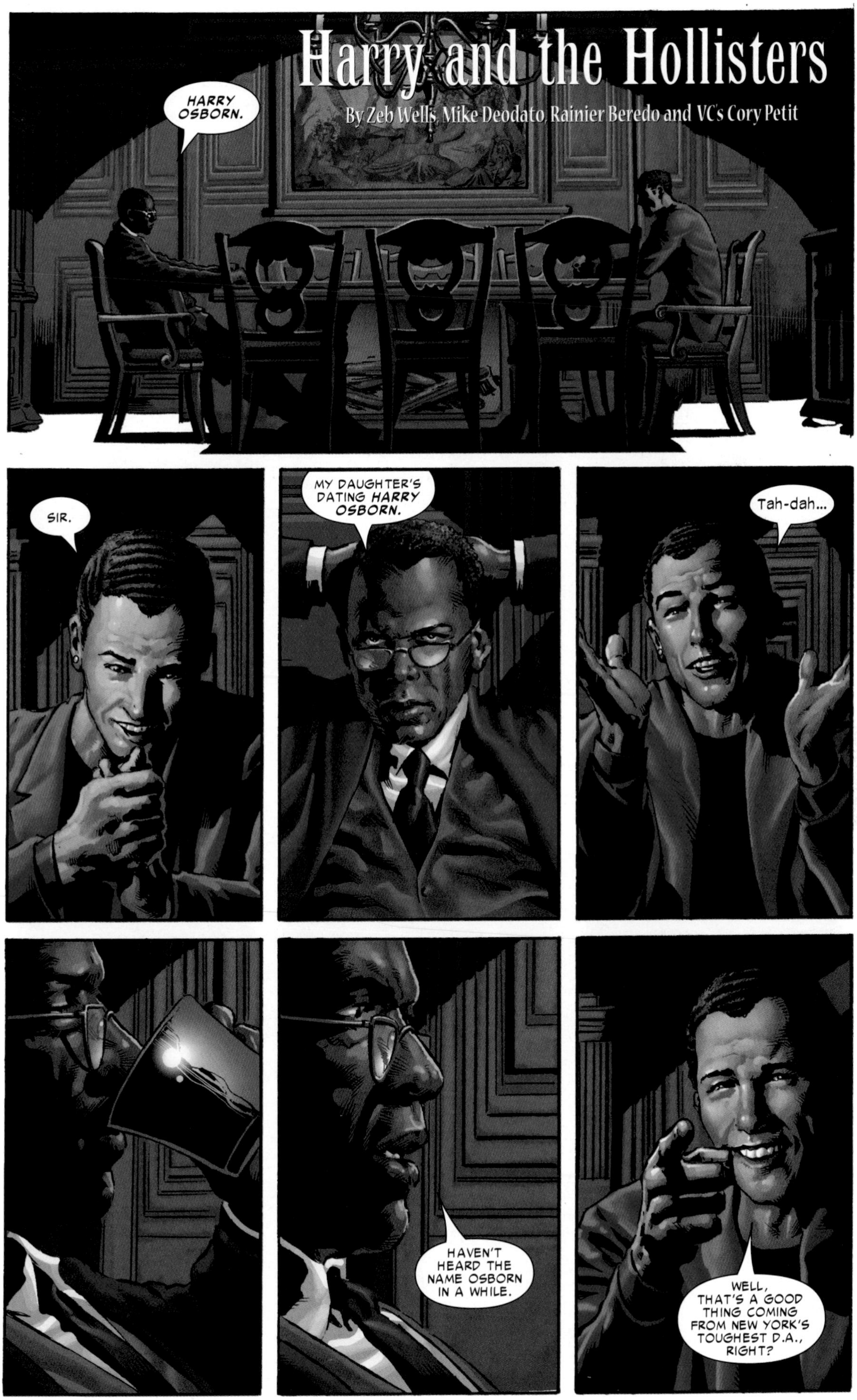
Harry and the Hollisters
By Zeb Wells, Mike Deodato, Rainier Beredo and VC's Cory Petit
HARRY OSBORN.
SIR.
MY DAUGHTER'S DATING HARRY OSBORN.
Tah-dah...
HAVEN'T HEARD THE NAME OSBORN IN A WHILE.
WELL, THAT'S A GOOD THING COMING FROM NEW YORK'S TOUGHEST D.A., RIGHT?

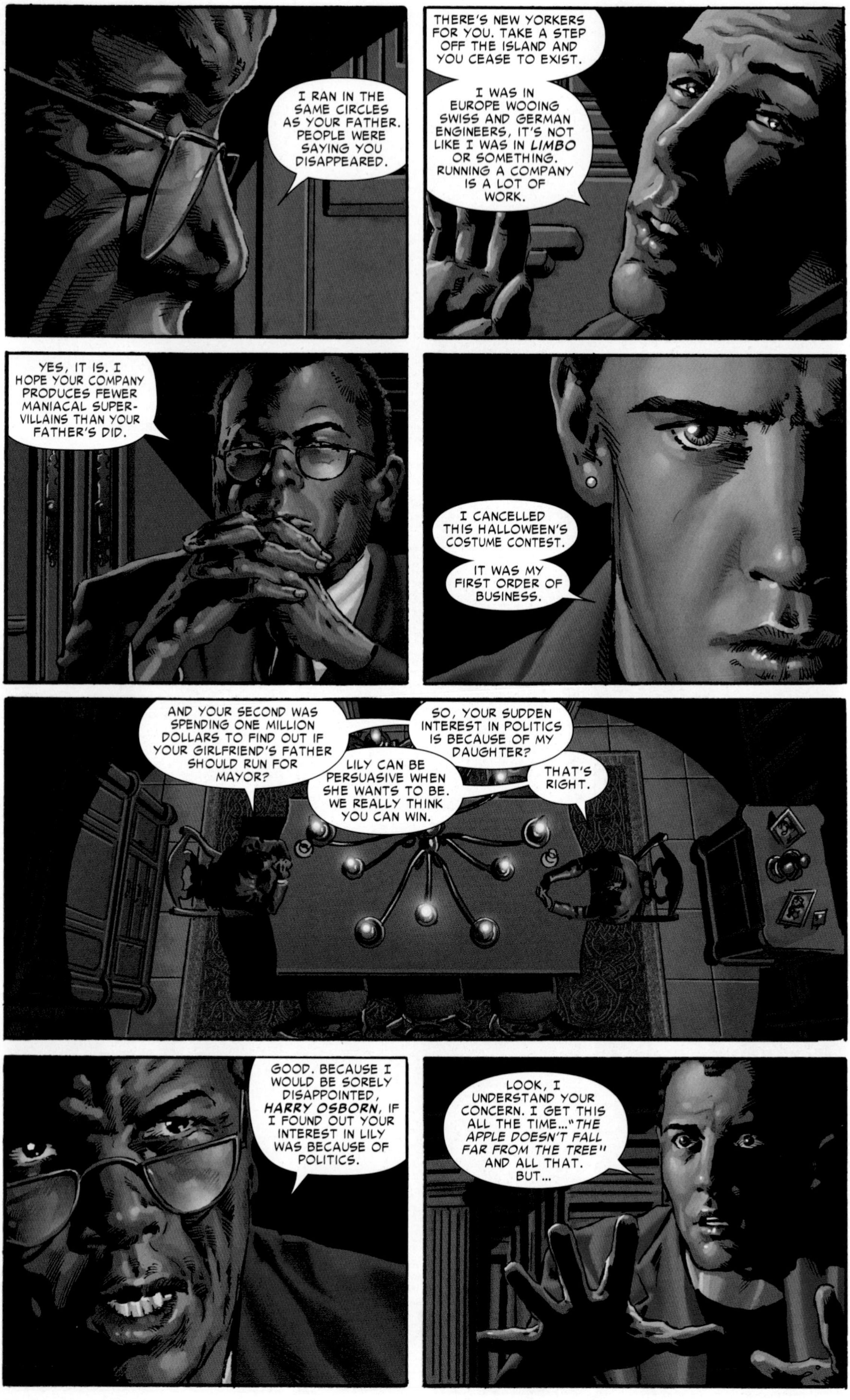
I RAN IN THE SAME CIRCLES AS YOUR FATHER. PEOPLE WERE SAYING YOU DISAPPEARED.
THERE'S NEW YORKERS FOR YOU. TAKE A STEP OFF THE ISLAND AND YOU CEASE TO EXIST.
I WAS IN EUROPE WOOING SWISS AND GERMAN ENGINEERS, IT'S NOT LIKE I WAS IN *LIMBO* OR SOMETHING. RUNNING A COMPANY IS A LOT OF WORK.
YES, IT IS. I HOPE YOUR COMPANY PRODUCES FEWER MANIACAL SUPER-VILLAINS THAN YOUR FATHER'S DID.
I CANCELLED THIS HALLOWEEN'S COSTUME CONTEST.
IT WAS MY FIRST ORDER OF BUSINESS.
AND YOUR SECOND WAS SPENDING ONE MILLION DOLLARS TO FIND OUT IF YOUR GIRLFRIEND'S FATHER SHOULD RUN FOR MAYOR?
SO, YOUR SUDDEN INTEREST IN POLITICS IS BECAUSE OF MY DAUGHTER?
LILY CAN BE PERSUASIVE WHEN SHE WANTS TO BE. WE REALLY THINK YOU CAN WIN.
THAT'S RIGHT.
GOOD. BECAUSE I WOULD BE SORELY DISAPPOINTED, ***HARRY OSBORN***, IF I FOUND OUT YOUR INTEREST IN LILY WAS BECAUSE OF POLITICS.
LOOK, I UNDERSTAND YOUR CONCERN. I GET THIS ALL THE TIME... "*THE APPLE DOESN'T FALL FAR FROM THE TREE*" AND ALL THAT. BUT...

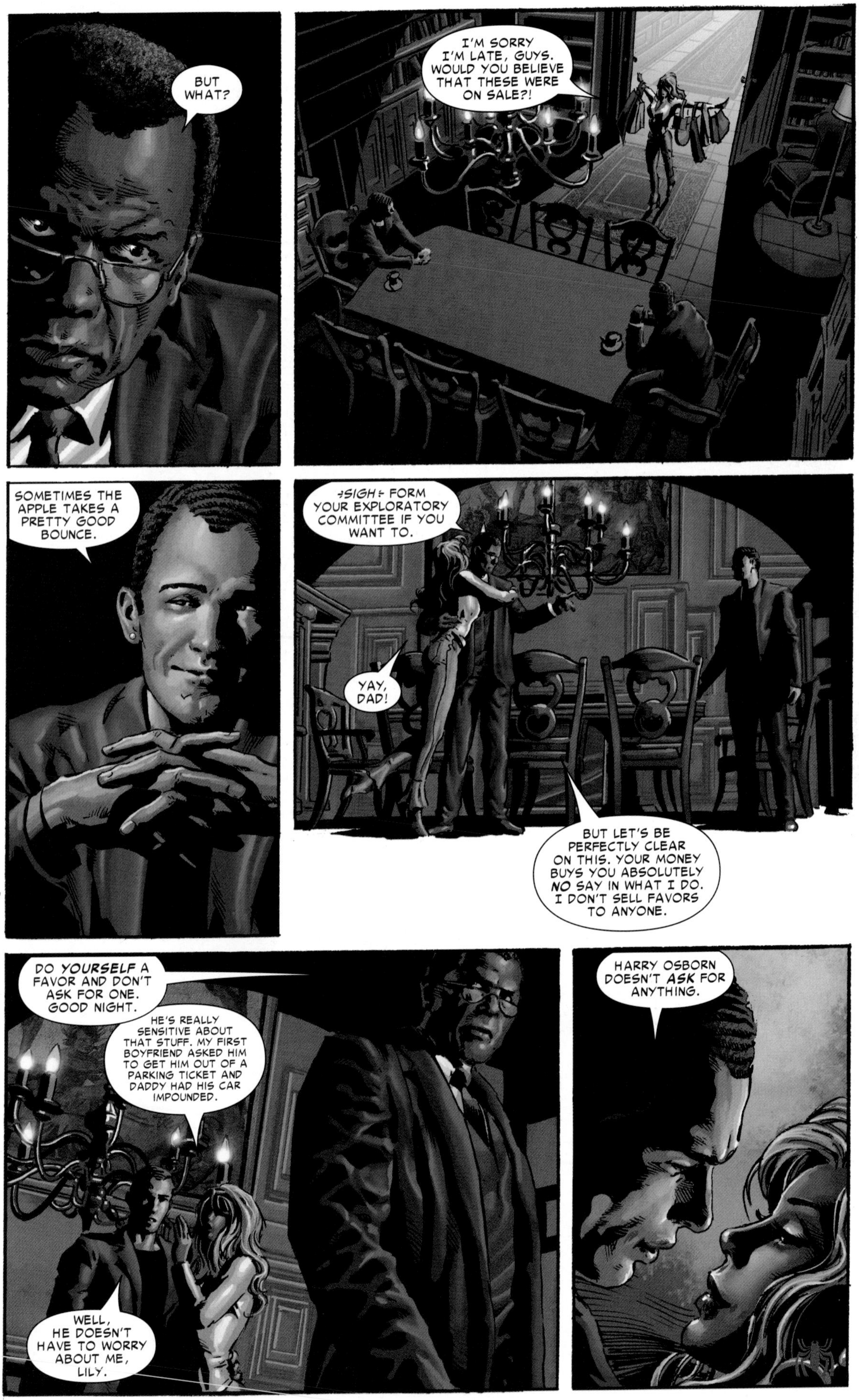

BUT WHAT?
I'M SORRY I'M LATE, GUYS. WOULD YOU BELIEVE THAT THESE WERE ON SALE?!
SOMETIMES THE APPLE TAKES A PRETTY GOOD BOUNCE.
⸗SIGH⸗ FORM YOUR EXPLORATORY COMMITTEE IF YOU WANT TO.
YAY, DAD!
BUT LET'S BE PERFECTLY CLEAR ON THIS. YOUR MONEY BUYS YOU ABSOLUTELY NO SAY IN WHAT I DO. I DON'T SELL FAVORS TO ANYONE.
DO YOURSELF A FAVOR AND DON'T ASK FOR ONE. GOOD NIGHT.
HE'S REALLY SENSITIVE ABOUT THAT STUFF. MY FIRST BOYFRIEND ASKED HIM TO GET HIM OUT OF A PARKING TICKET AND DADDY HAD HIS CAR IMPOUNDED.
WELL, HE DOESN'T HAVE TO WORRY ABOUT ME, LILY.
HARRY OSBORN DOESN'T ASK FOR ANYTHING.

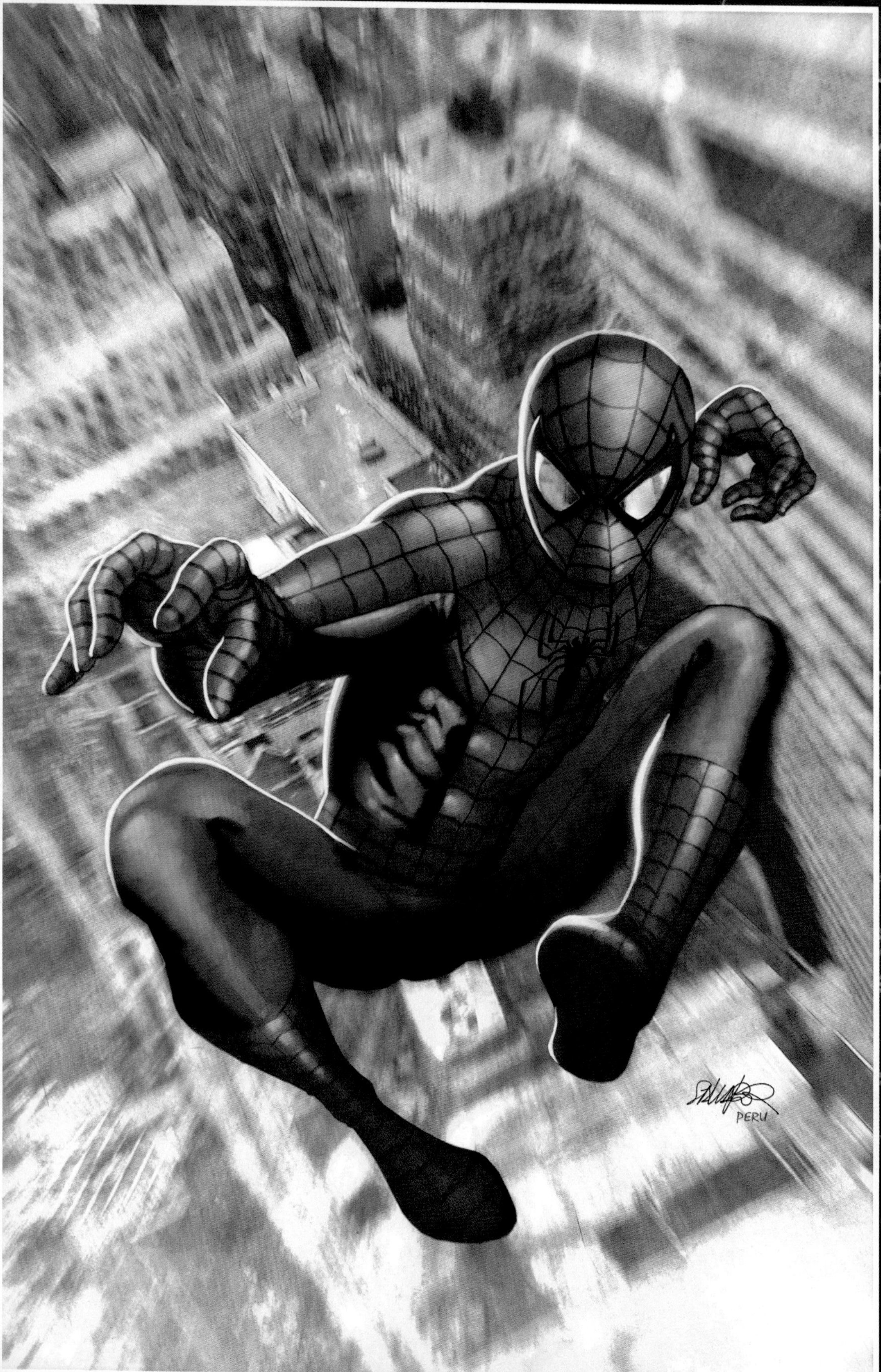
PERU

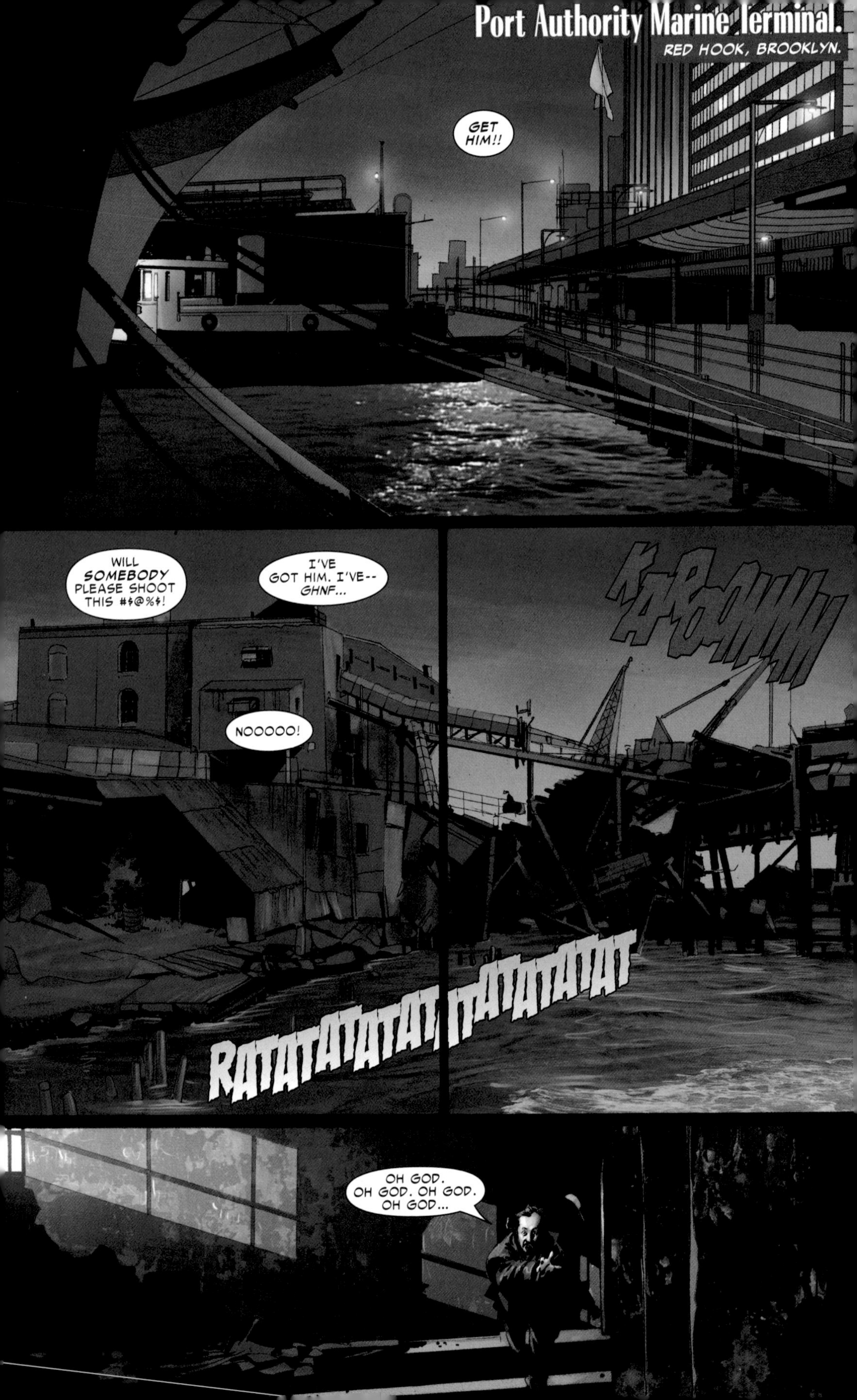

Port Authority Marine Terminal.
RED HOOK, BROOKLYN.
GET HIM!!
WILL SOMEBODY PLEASE SHOOT THIS #$@%$!
I'VE GOT HIM. I'VE-- GHNF...
NOOOOO!
KA-BOOMMM
RATATATATATATATATATAT
OH GOD. OH GOD. OH GOD. OH GOD...

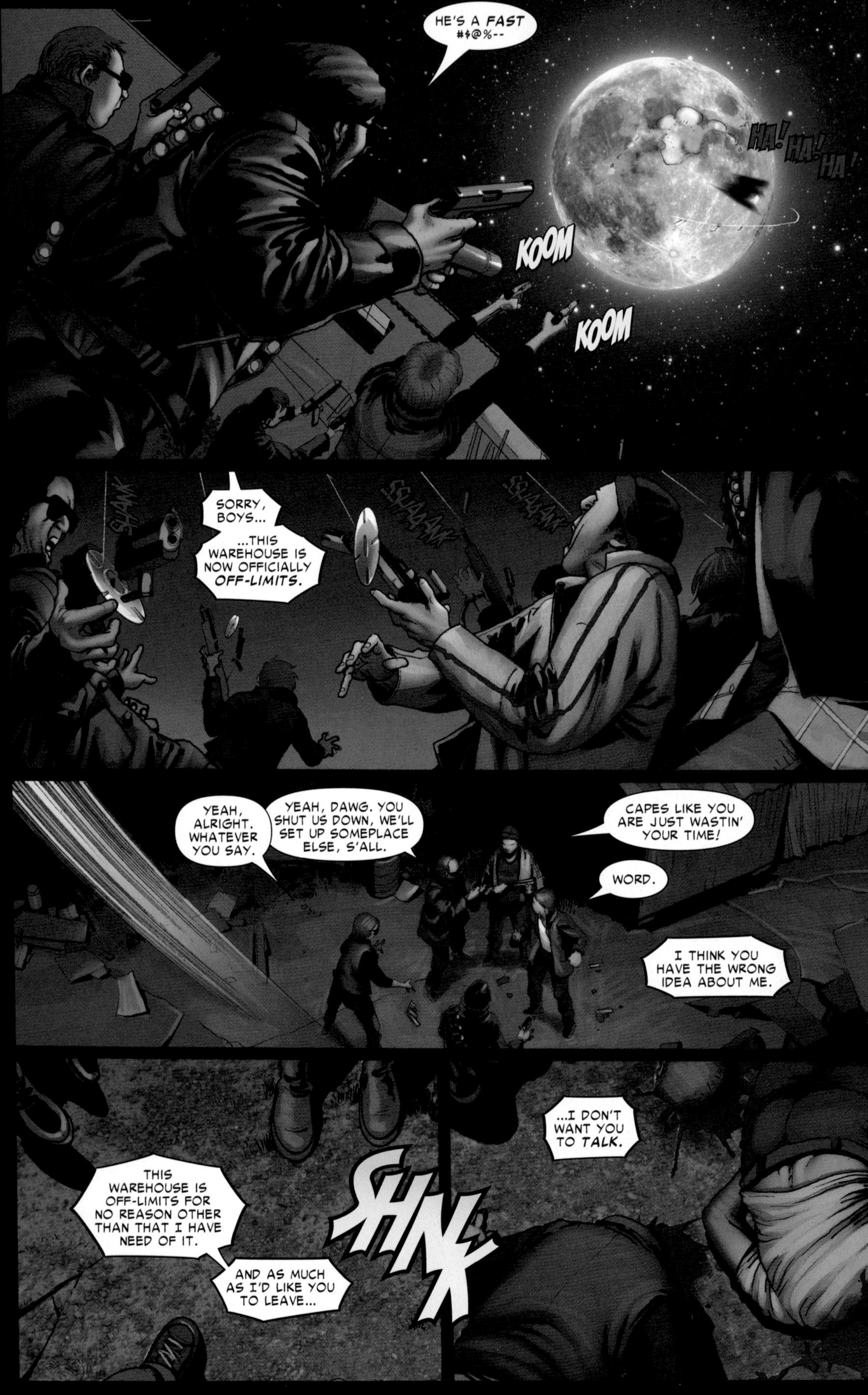
HE'S A FAST #$@%--
KOOM
KOOM
HA! HA! HA!
SORRY, BOYS...
...THIS WAREHOUSE IS NOW OFFICIALLY OFF-LIMITS.
SHAAANK
SHAAANK
YEAH, ALRIGHT. WHATEVER YOU SAY.
YEAH, DAWG. YOU SHUT US DOWN, WE'LL SET UP SOMEPLACE ELSE, S'ALL.
CAPES LIKE YOU ARE JUST WASTIN' YOUR TIME!
WORD.
I THINK YOU HAVE THE WRONG IDEA ABOUT ME.
THIS WAREHOUSE IS OFF-LIMITS FOR NO REASON OTHER THAN THAT I HAVE NEED OF IT.
AND AS MUCH AS I'D LIKE YOU TO LEAVE...
...I DON'T WANT YOU TO TALK.
SHNK

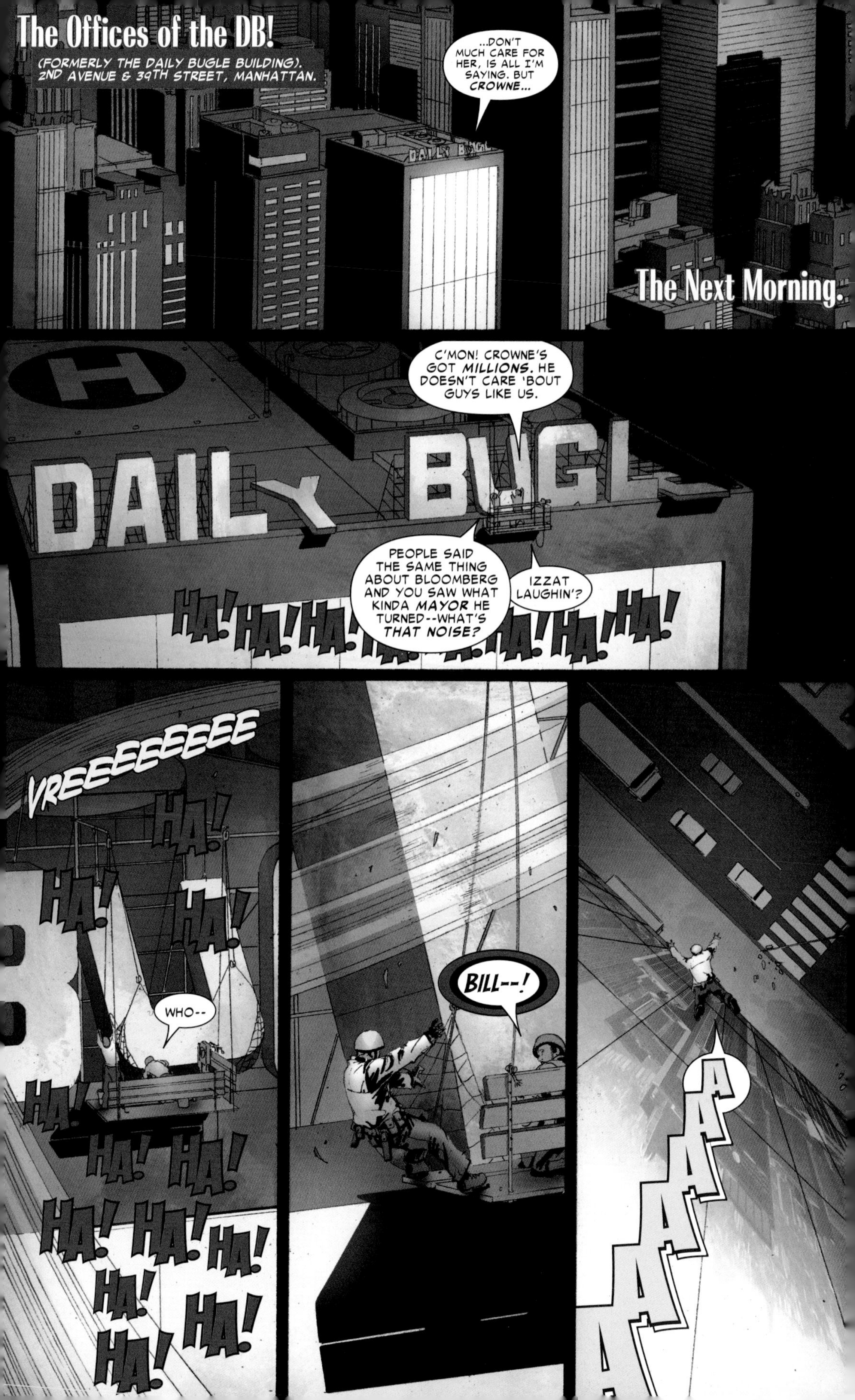
The Offices of the DB!
(FORMERLY THE DAILY BUGLE BUILDING). 2ND AVENUE & 39TH STREET, MANHATTAN.
...DON'T MUCH CARE FOR HER, IS ALL I'M SAYING. BUT CROWNE...
DAILY BUGLE
The Next Morning.
C'MON! CROWNE'S GOT MILLIONS. HE DOESN'T CARE 'BOUT GUYS LIKE US.
DAILY BUGL
PEOPLE SAID THE SAME THING ABOUT BLOOMBERG AND YOU SAW WHAT KINDA MAYOR HE TURNED--WHAT'S THAT NOISE?
IZZAT LAUGHIN'?
HA! HA! HA! HA! HA! HA! HA! HA!
VREEEEEEEEEE
HA! HA! HA!
WHO--
HA! HA! HA! HA! HA! HA! HA! HA! HA!
BILL--!
AAAAAAAAA

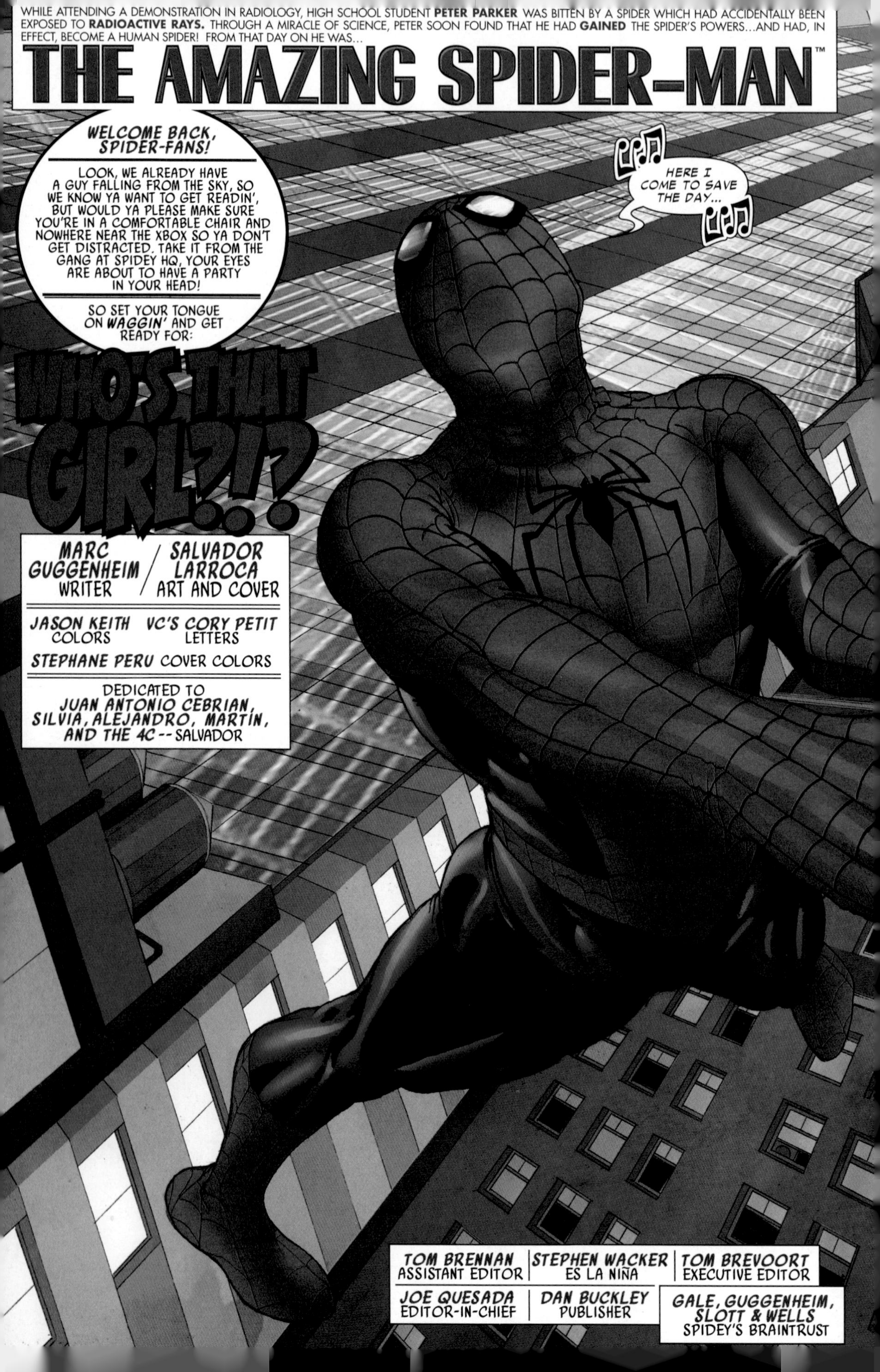

WHILE ATTENDING A DEMONSTRATION IN RADIOLOGY, HIGH SCHOOL STUDENT PETER PARKER WAS BITTEN BY A SPIDER WHICH HAD ACCIDENTALLY BEEN EXPOSED TO RADIOACTIVE RAYS. THROUGH A MIRACLE OF SCIENCE, PETER SOON FOUND THAT HE HAD GAINED THE SPIDER'S POWERS...AND HAD, IN EFFECT, BECOME A HUMAN SPIDER! FROM THAT DAY ON HE WAS...
THE AMAZING SPIDER-MAN™
WELCOME BACK, SPIDER-FANS!
LOOK, WE ALREADY HAVE A GUY FALLING FROM THE SKY, SO WE KNOW YA WANT TO GET READIN', BUT WOULD YA PLEASE MAKE SURE YOU'RE IN A COMFORTABLE CHAIR AND NOWHERE NEAR THE XBOX SO YA DON'T GET DISTRACTED. TAKE IT FROM THE GANG AT SPIDEY HQ, YOUR EYES ARE ABOUT TO HAVE A PARTY IN YOUR HEAD!
SO SET YOUR TONGUE ON WAGGIN' AND GET READY FOR:
WHO'S THAT GIRL?!?
HERE I COME TO SAVE THE DAY...
MARC GUGGENHEIM WRITER / SALVADOR LARROCA ART AND COVER
JASON KEITH COLORS VC'S CORY PETIT LETTERS
STEPHANE PERU COVER COLORS
DEDICATED TO JUAN ANTONIO CEBRIAN, SILVIA, ALEJANDRO, MARTÍN, AND THE 4C -- SALVADOR
TOM BRENNAN ASSISTANT EDITOR
STEPHEN WACKER ES LA NIÑA
TOM BREVOORT EXECUTIVE EDITOR
JOE QUESADA EDITOR-IN-CHIEF
DAN BUCKLEY PUBLISHER
GALE, GUGGENHEIM, SLOTT & WELLS SPIDEY'S BRAINTRUST

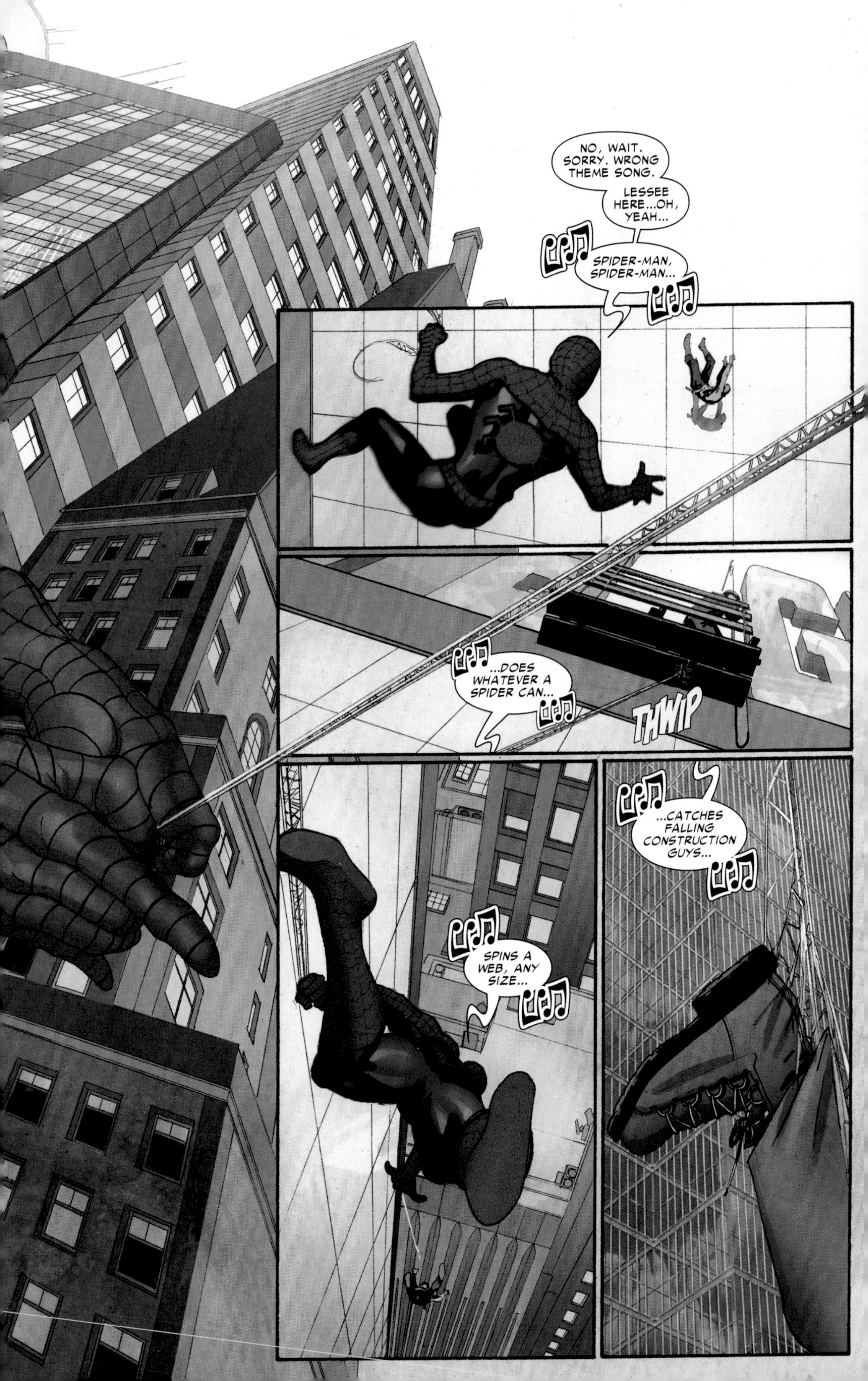
NO, WAIT. SORRY. WRONG THEME SONG.
LESSEE HERE...OH, YEAH...
SPIDER-MAN, SPIDER-MAN...
...DOES WHATEVER A SPIDER CAN...
THWIP
SPINS A WEB, ANY SIZE...
...CATCHES FALLING CONSTRUCTION GUYS...

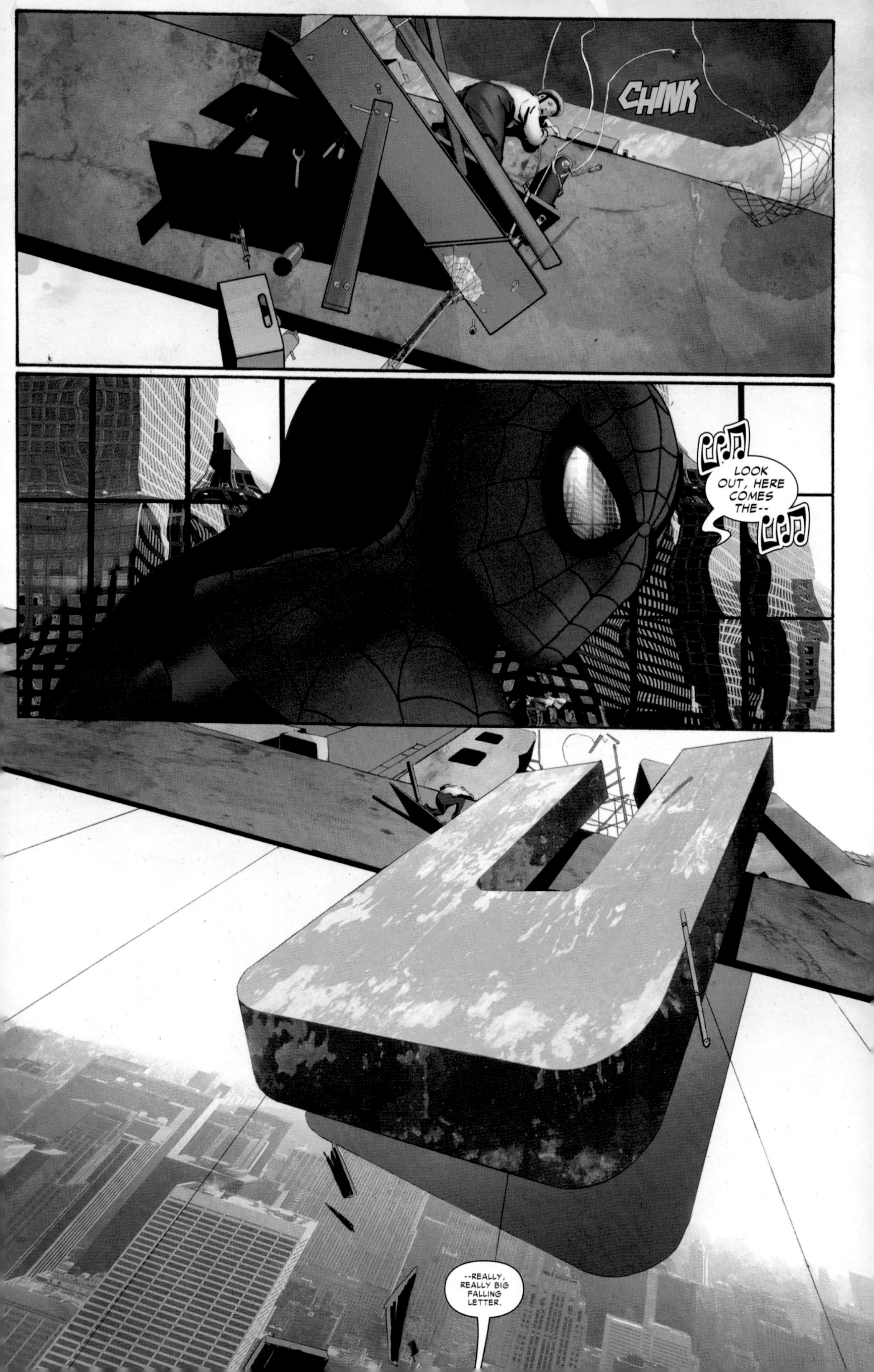
CHINK
LOOK OUT, HERE COMES THE--
--REALLY, REALLY BIG FALLING LETTER.

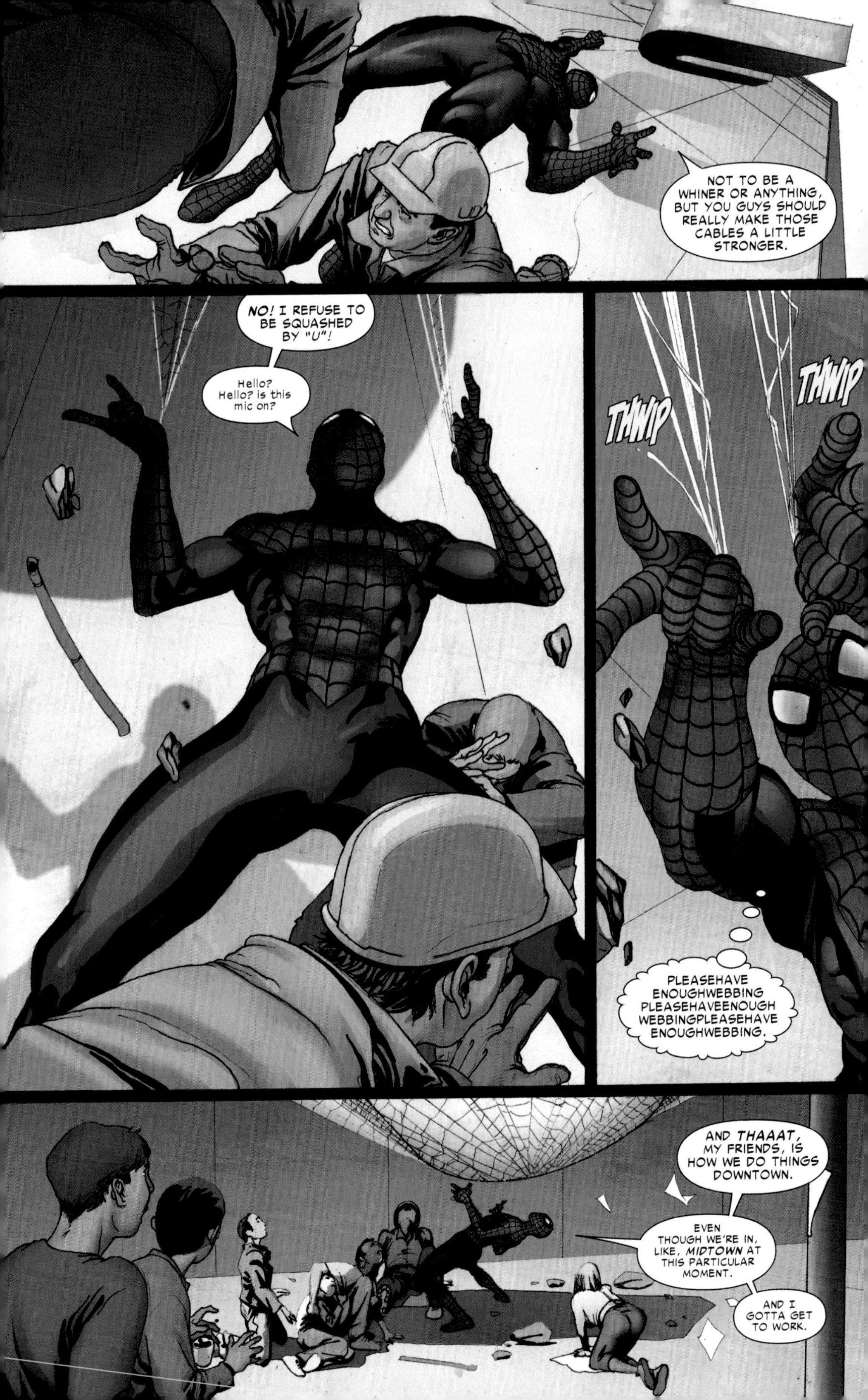

NOT TO BE A WHINER OR ANYTHING, BUT YOU GUYS SHOULD REALLY MAKE THOSE CABLES A LITTLE STRONGER.
NO! I REFUSE TO BE SQUASHED BY "U"!
Hello? Hello? is this mic on?
THWIP
THWIP
PLEASEHAVE ENOUGHWEBBING PLEASEHAVEENOUGH WEBBINGPLEASEHAVE ENOUGHWEBBING.
AND THAAAT, MY FRIENDS, IS HOW WE DO THINGS DOWNTOWN.
EVEN THOUGH WE'RE IN, LIKE, MIDTOWN AT THIS PARTICULAR MOMENT.
AND I GOTTA GET TO WORK.

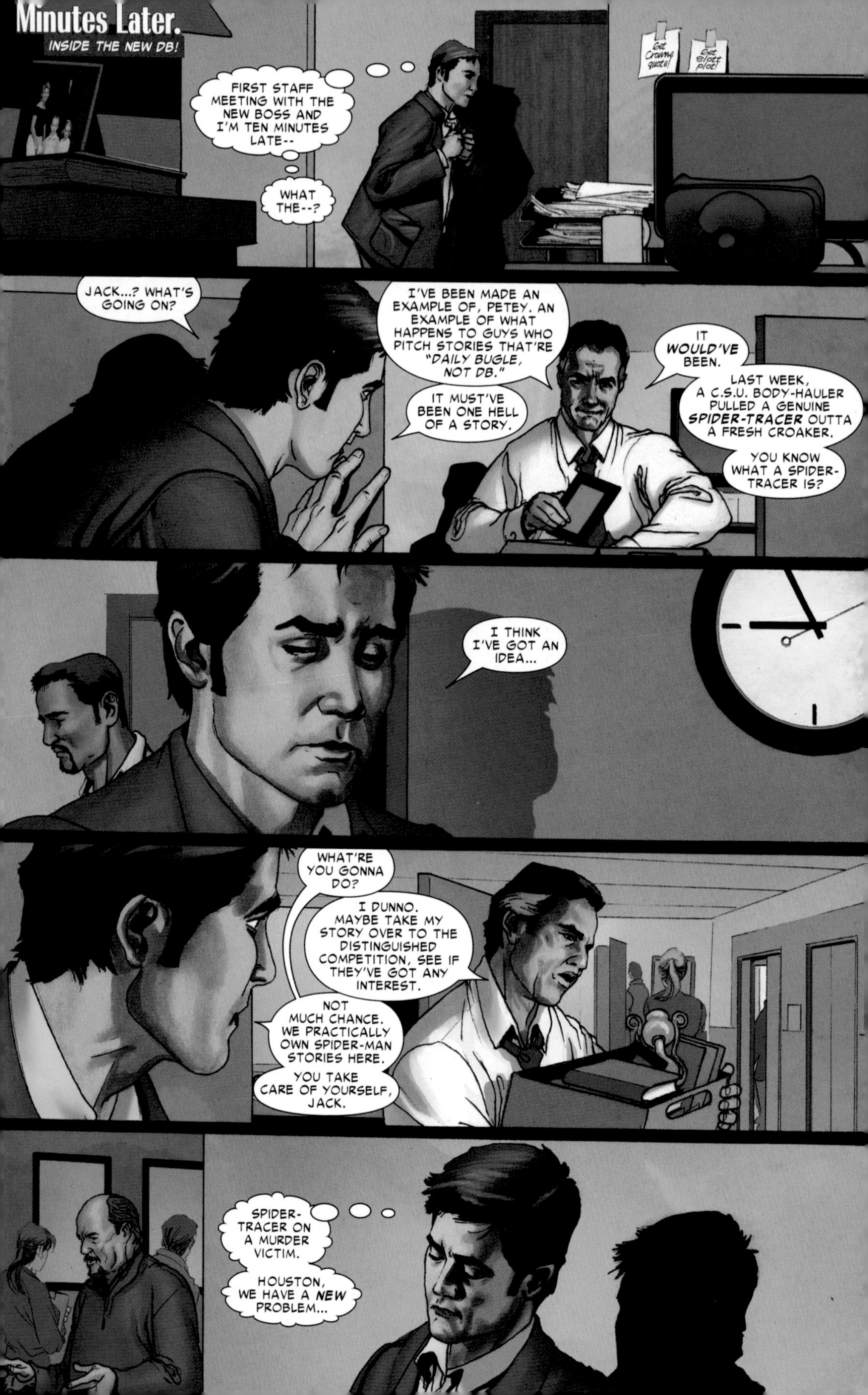
Minutes Later.
INSIDE THE NEW DB!
FIRST STAFF MEETING WITH THE NEW BOSS AND I'M TEN MINUTES LATE--
WHAT THE--?
Get Crowne quote!
Get Slott plot!
JACK...? WHAT'S GOING ON?
I'VE BEEN MADE AN EXAMPLE OF, PETEY. AN EXAMPLE OF WHAT HAPPENS TO GUYS WHO PITCH STORIES THAT'RE "DAILY BUGLE, NOT DB."
IT MUST'VE BEEN ONE HELL OF A STORY.
IT WOULD'VE BEEN.
LAST WEEK, A C.S.U. BODY-HAULER PULLED A GENUINE SPIDER-TRACER OUTTA A FRESH CROAKER.
YOU KNOW WHAT A SPIDER-TRACER IS?
I THINK I'VE GOT AN IDEA...
WHAT'RE YOU GONNA DO?
I DUNNO. MAYBE TAKE MY STORY OVER TO THE DISTINGUISHED COMPETITION, SEE IF THEY'VE GOT ANY INTEREST.
NOT MUCH CHANCE. WE PRACTICALLY OWN SPIDER-MAN STORIES HERE.
YOU TAKE CARE OF YOURSELF, JACK.
SPIDER-TRACER ON A MURDER VICTIM.
HOUSTON, WE HAVE A NEW PROBLEM...

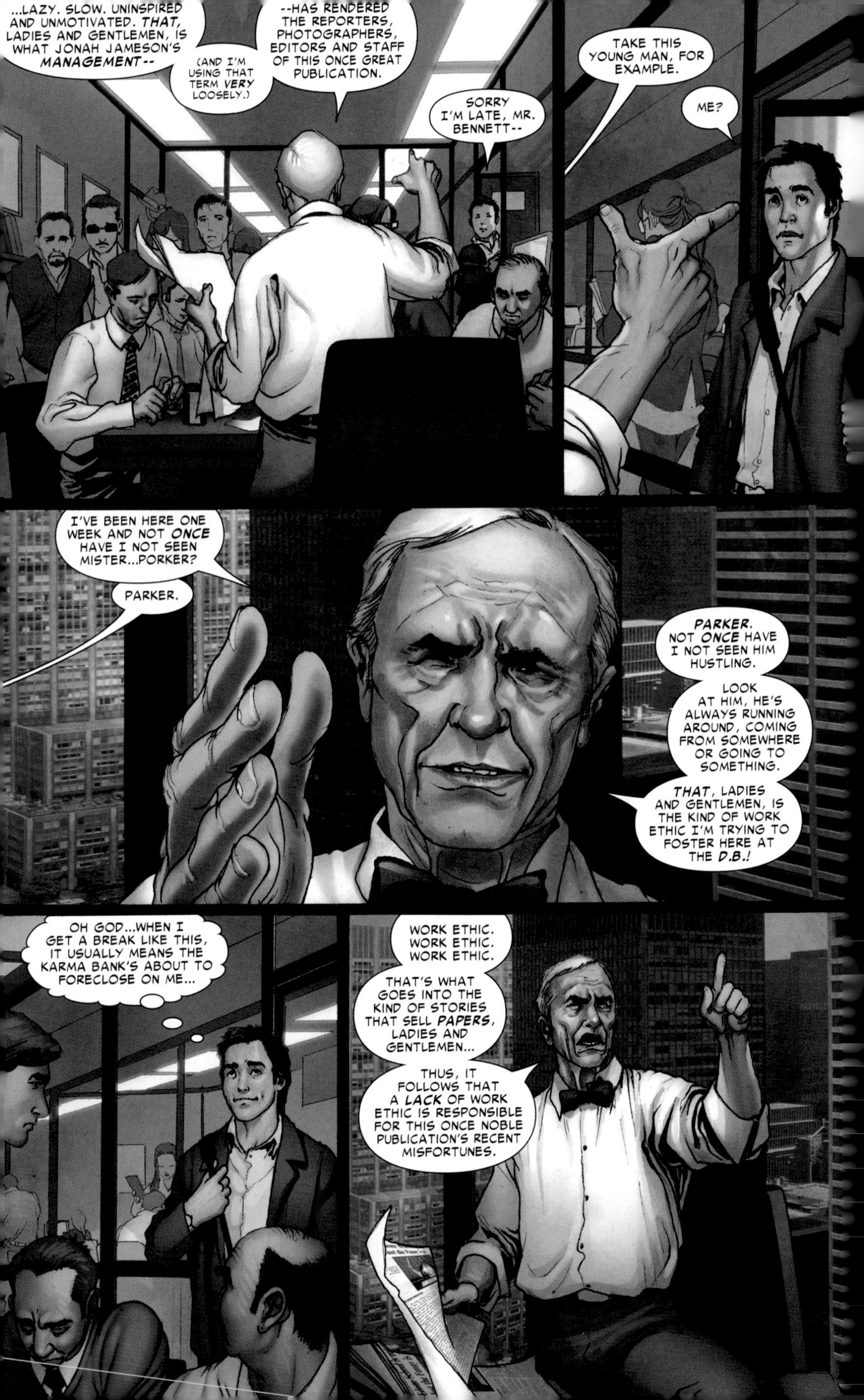
...LAZY. SLOW. UNINSPIRED AND UNMOTIVATED. THAT, LADIES AND GENTLEMEN, IS WHAT JONAH JAMESON'S MANAGEMENT--
(AND I'M USING THAT TERM VERY LOOSELY.)
--HAS RENDERED THE REPORTERS, PHOTOGRAPHERS, EDITORS AND STAFF OF THIS ONCE GREAT PUBLICATION.
SORRY I'M LATE, MR. BENNETT--
TAKE THIS YOUNG MAN, FOR EXAMPLE.
ME?
I'VE BEEN HERE ONE WEEK AND NOT ONCE HAVE I NOT SEEN MISTER...PORKER?
PARKER.
PARKER. NOT ONCE HAVE I NOT SEEN HIM HUSTLING.
LOOK AT HIM, HE'S ALWAYS RUNNING AROUND, COMING FROM SOMEWHERE OR GOING TO SOMETHING.
THAT, LADIES AND GENTLEMEN, IS THE KIND OF WORK ETHIC I'M TRYING TO FOSTER HERE AT THE D.B.!
OH GOD...WHEN I GET A BREAK LIKE THIS, IT USUALLY MEANS THE KARMA BANK'S ABOUT TO FORECLOSE ON ME...
WORK ETHIC. WORK ETHIC. WORK ETHIC.
THAT'S WHAT GOES INTO THE KIND OF STORIES THAT SELL PAPERS, LADIES AND GENTLEMEN...
THUS, IT FOLLOWS THAT A LACK OF WORK ETHIC IS RESPONSIBLE FOR THIS ONCE NOBLE PUBLICATION'S RECENT MISFORTUNES.

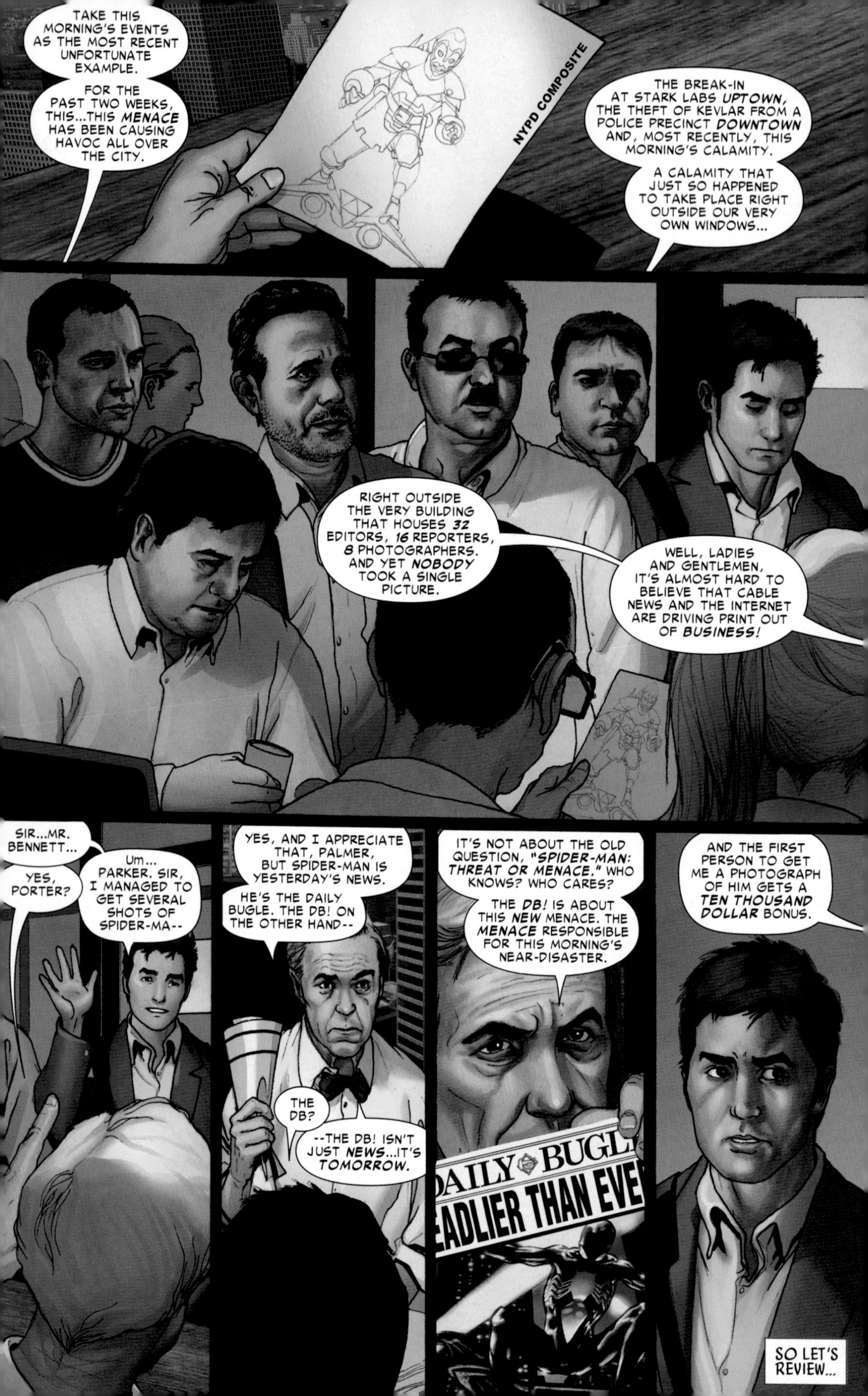
TAKE THIS MORNING'S EVENTS AS THE MOST RECENT UNFORTUNATE EXAMPLE.
FOR THE PAST TWO WEEKS, THIS...THIS MENACE HAS BEEN CAUSING HAVOC ALL OVER THE CITY.
NYPD COMPOSITE
THE BREAK-IN AT STARK LABS UPTOWN, THE THEFT OF KEVLAR FROM A POLICE PRECINCT DOWNTOWN AND, MOST RECENTLY, THIS MORNING'S CALAMITY.
A CALAMITY THAT JUST SO HAPPENED TO TAKE PLACE RIGHT OUTSIDE OUR VERY OWN WINDOWS...
RIGHT OUTSIDE THE VERY BUILDING THAT HOUSES 32 EDITORS, 16 REPORTERS, 8 PHOTOGRAPHERS. AND YET NOBODY TOOK A SINGLE PICTURE.
WELL, LADIES AND GENTLEMEN, IT'S ALMOST HARD TO BELIEVE THAT CABLE NEWS AND THE INTERNET ARE DRIVING PRINT OUT OF BUSINESS!
SIR...MR. BENNETT...
YES, PORTER?
Um... PARKER. SIR, I MANAGED TO GET SEVERAL SHOTS OF SPIDER-MA--
YES, AND I APPRECIATE THAT, PALMER, BUT SPIDER-MAN IS YESTERDAY'S NEWS.
HE'S THE DAILY BUGLE. THE DB! ON THE OTHER HAND--
THE DB?
--THE DB! ISN'T JUST NEWS...IT'S TOMORROW.
IT'S NOT ABOUT THE OLD QUESTION, "SPIDER-MAN: THREAT OR MENACE." WHO KNOWS? WHO CARES?
THE DB! IS ABOUT THIS NEW MENACE. THE MENACE RESPONSIBLE FOR THIS MORNING'S NEAR-DISASTER.
DAILY BUGL
EADLIER THAN EVE
AND THE FIRST PERSON TO GET ME A PHOTOGRAPH OF HIM GETS A TEN THOUSAND DOLLAR BONUS.
SO LET'S REVIEW...

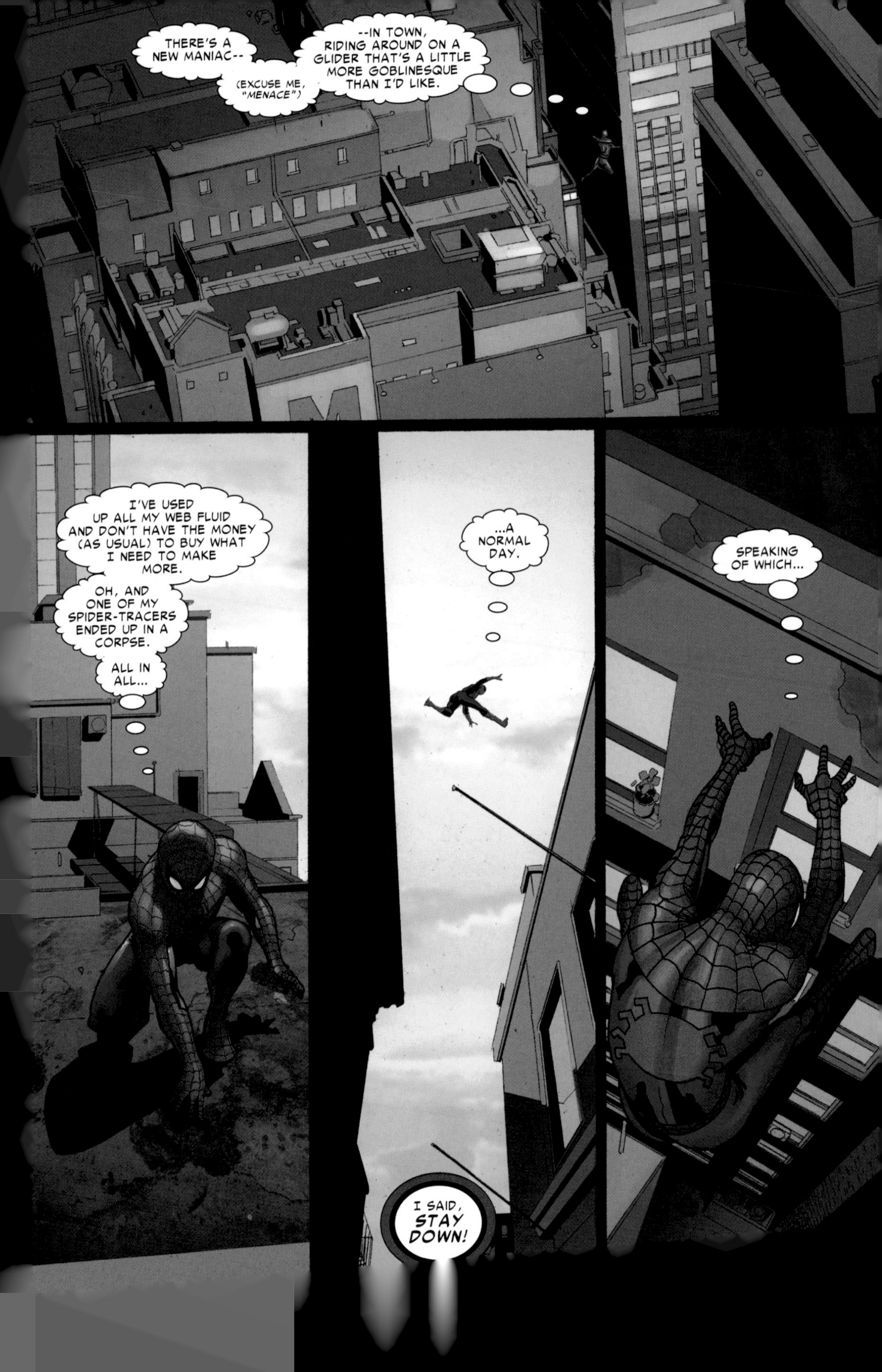
THERE'S A NEW MANIAC--
(EXCUSE ME, "MENACE")
--IN TOWN, RIDING AROUND ON A GLIDER THAT'S A LITTLE MORE GOBLINESQUE THAN I'D LIKE.
I'VE USED UP ALL MY WEB FLUID AND DON'T HAVE THE MONEY (AS USUAL) TO BUY WHAT I NEED TO MAKE MORE.
OH, AND ONE OF MY SPIDER-TRACERS ENDED UP IN A CORPSE.
ALL IN ALL...
...A NORMAL DAY.
SPEAKING OF WHICH...
I SAID, STAY DOWN!

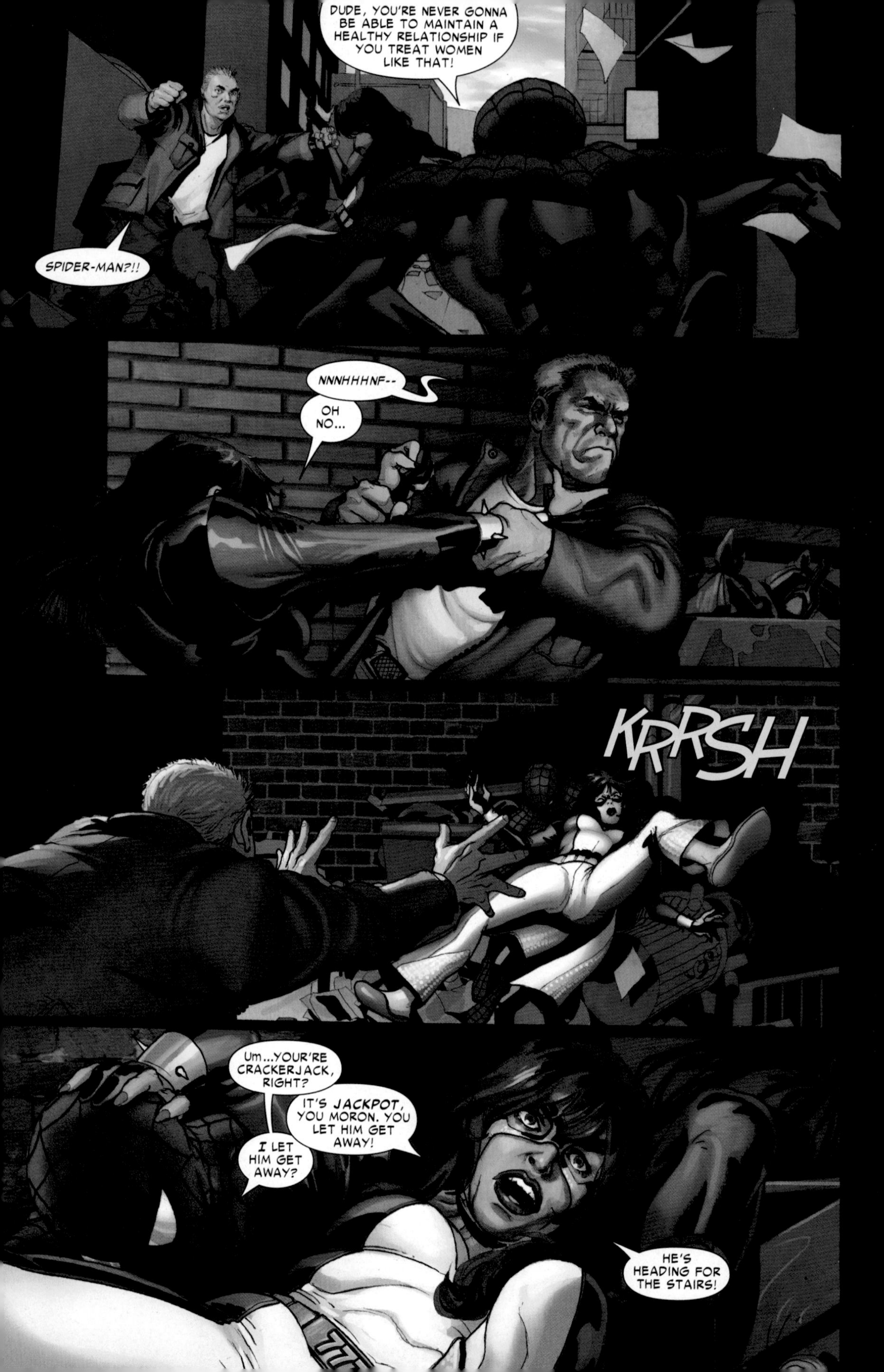
DUDE, YOU'RE NEVER GONNA BE ABLE TO MAINTAIN A HEALTHY RELATIONSHIP IF YOU TREAT WOMEN LIKE THAT!
SPIDER-MAN?!!
NNNHHHNF--
OH NO...
KRRSH
Um...YOUR'RE CRACKERJACK, RIGHT?
IT'S JACKPOT, YOU MORON. YOU LET HIM GET AWAY!
I LET HIM GET AWAY?
HE'S HEADING FOR THE STAIRS!

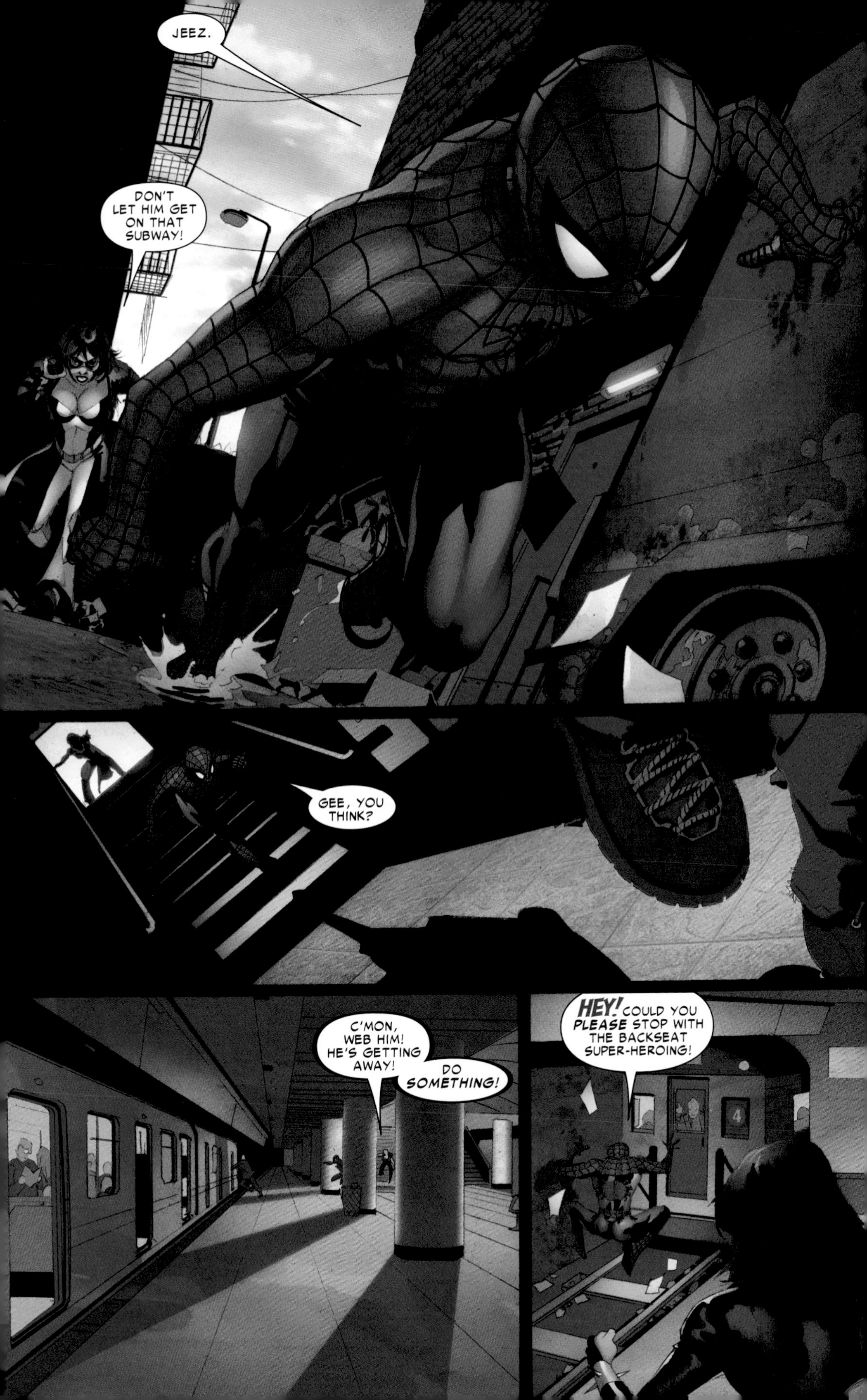
JEEZ.
DON'T LET HIM GET ON THAT SUBWAY!
GEE, YOU THINK?
C'MON, WEB HIM! HE'S GETTING AWAY!
DO SOMETHING!
HEY! COULD YOU PLEASE STOP WITH THE BACKSEAT SUPER-HEROING!
4

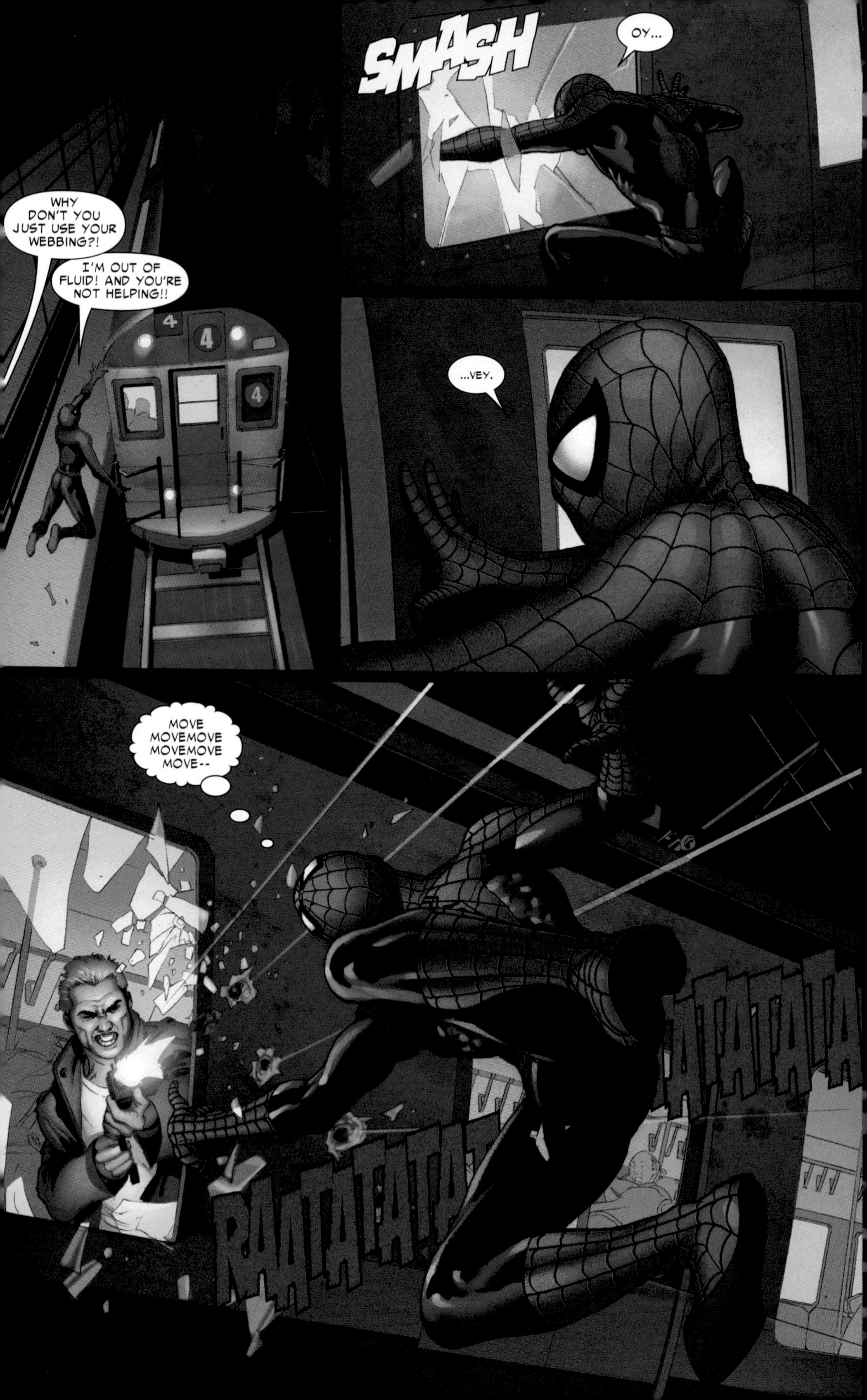
SMASH
OY...
WHY DON'T YOU JUST USE YOUR WEBBING?!
I'M OUT OF FLUID! AND YOU'RE NOT HELPING!!
...VEY.
MOVE MOVEMOVE MOVEMOVE MOVE--
RAATATATATA
TATATATA

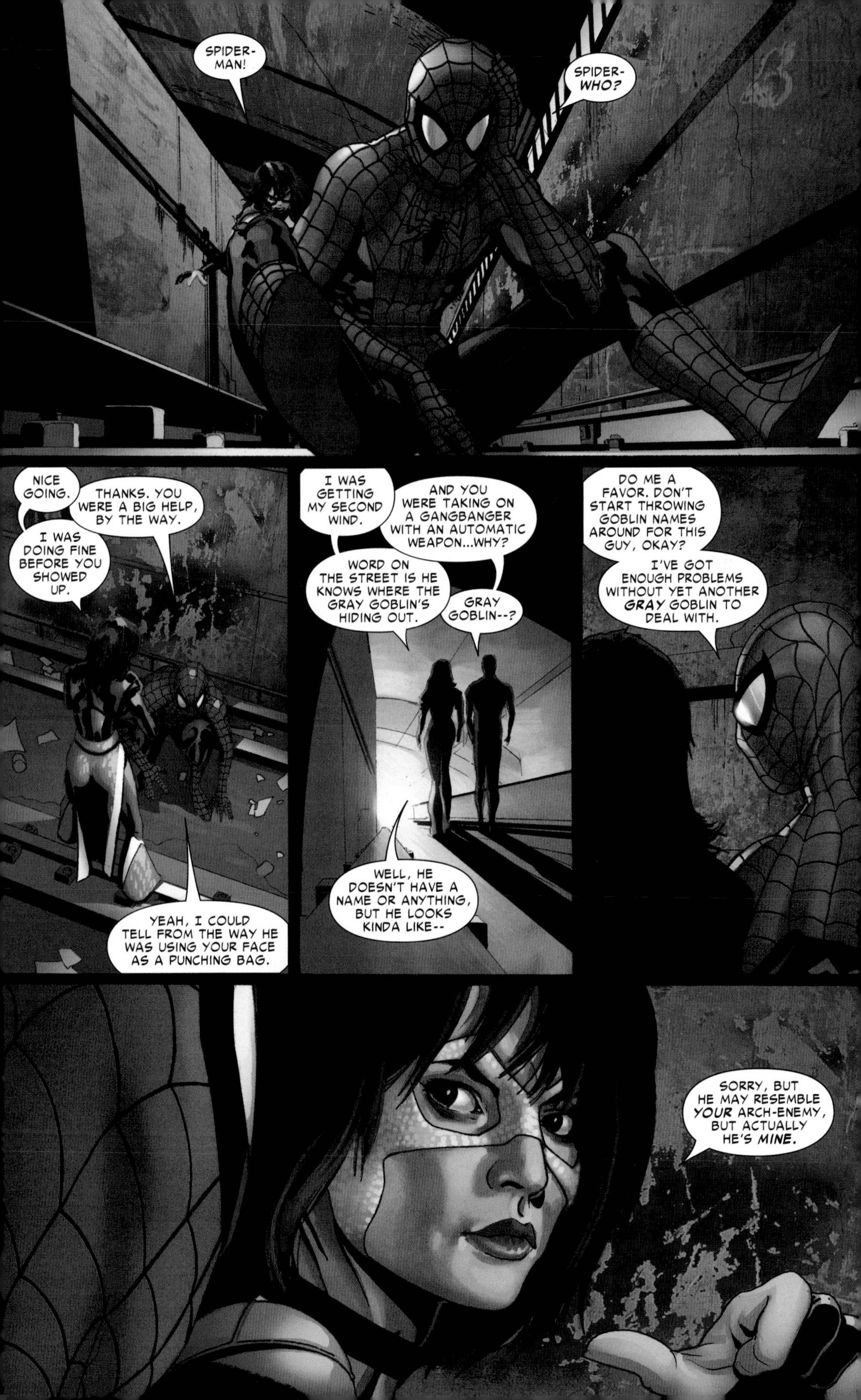
SPIDER-MAN!
SPIDER-WHO?
NICE GOING.
I WAS DOING FINE BEFORE YOU SHOWED UP.
THANKS. YOU WERE A BIG HELP, BY THE WAY.
YEAH, I COULD TELL FROM THE WAY HE WAS USING YOUR FACE AS A PUNCHING BAG.
I WAS GETTING MY SECOND WIND.
AND YOU WERE TAKING ON A GANGBANGER WITH AN AUTOMATIC WEAPON...WHY?
WORD ON THE STREET IS HE KNOWS WHERE THE GRAY GOBLIN'S HIDING OUT.
GRAY GOBLIN--?
WELL, HE DOESN'T HAVE A NAME OR ANYTHING, BUT HE LOOKS KINDA LIKE--
DO ME A FAVOR. DON'T START THROWING GOBLIN NAMES AROUND FOR THIS GUY, OKAY?
I'VE GOT ENOUGH PROBLEMS WITHOUT YET ANOTHER GRAY GOBLIN TO DEAL WITH.
SORRY, BUT HE MAY RESEMBLE YOUR ARCH-ENEMY, BUT ACTUALLY HE'S MINE.

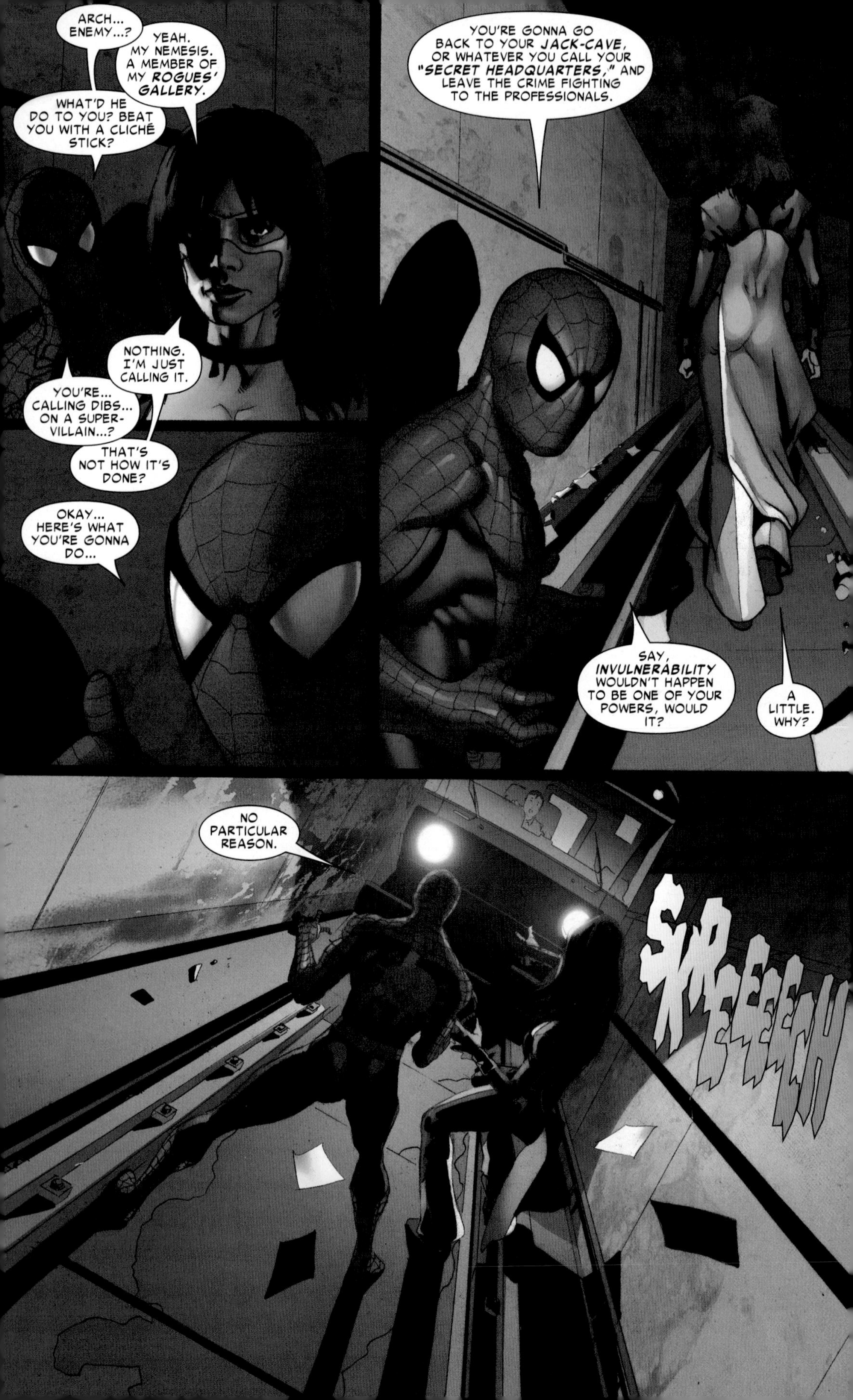
ARCH... ENEMY...?
YEAH. MY NEMESIS. A MEMBER OF MY ROGUES' GALLERY.
WHAT'D HE DO TO YOU? BEAT YOU WITH A CLICHÉ STICK?
NOTHING. I'M JUST CALLING IT.
YOU'RE... CALLING DIBS... ON A SUPER-VILLAIN...?
THAT'S NOT HOW IT'S DONE?
OKAY... HERE'S WHAT YOU'RE GONNA DO...
YOU'RE GONNA GO BACK TO YOUR JACK-CAVE, OR WHATEVER YOU CALL YOUR "SECRET HEADQUARTERS," AND LEAVE THE CRIME FIGHTING TO THE PROFESSIONALS.
SAY, INVULNERABILITY WOULDN'T HAPPEN TO BE ONE OF YOUR POWERS, WOULD IT?
A LITTLE. WHY?
NO PARTICULAR REASON.
SKREEEECH

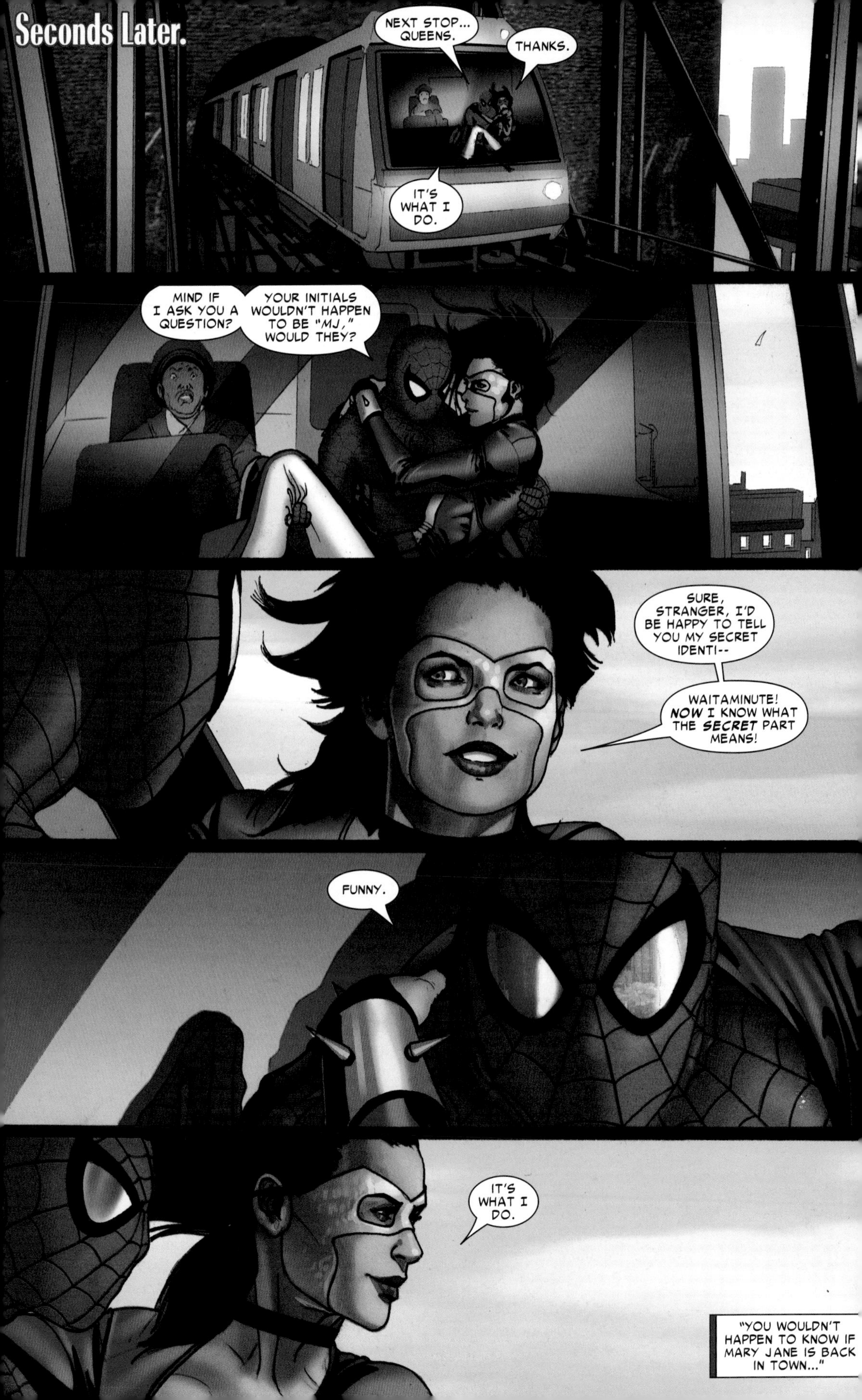
Seconds Later.
NEXT STOP... QUEENS.
THANKS.
IT'S WHAT I DO.
MIND IF I ASK YOU A QUESTION?
YOUR INITIALS WOULDN'T HAPPEN TO BE "MJ," WOULD THEY?
SURE, STRANGER, I'D BE HAPPY TO TELL YOU MY SECRET IDENTI--
WAITAMINUTE! NOW I KNOW WHAT THE SECRET PART MEANS!
FUNNY.
IT'S WHAT I DO.
"YOU WOULDN'T HAPPEN TO KNOW IF MARY JANE IS BACK IN TOWN..."

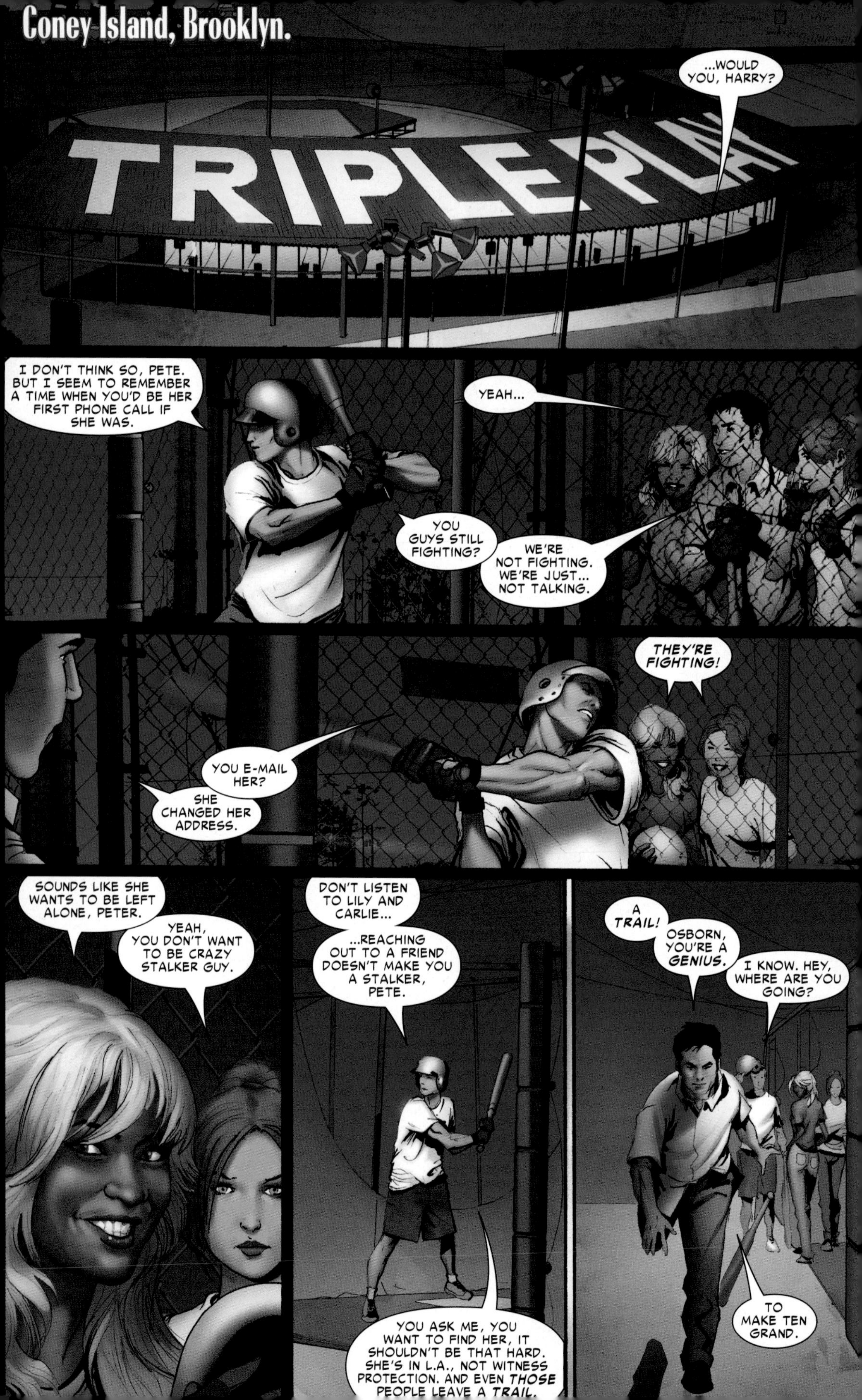
Coney Island, Brooklyn.
TRIPLE PLAY
...WOULD YOU, HARRY?
I DON'T THINK SO, PETE. BUT I SEEM TO REMEMBER A TIME WHEN YOU'D BE HER FIRST PHONE CALL IF SHE WAS.
YEAH...
YOU GUYS STILL FIGHTING?
WE'RE NOT FIGHTING. WE'RE JUST... NOT TALKING.
THEY'RE FIGHTING!
YOU E-MAIL HER?
SHE CHANGED HER ADDRESS.
SOUNDS LIKE SHE WANTS TO BE LEFT ALONE, PETER.
YEAH, YOU DON'T WANT TO BE CRAZY STALKER GUY.
DON'T LISTEN TO LILY AND CARLIE...
...REACHING OUT TO A FRIEND DOESN'T MAKE YOU A STALKER, PETE.
YOU ASK ME, YOU WANT TO FIND HER, IT SHOULDN'T BE THAT HARD. SHE'S IN L.A., NOT WITNESS PROTECTION. AND EVEN THOSE PEOPLE LEAVE A TRAIL.
A TRAIL!
OSBORN, YOU'RE A GENIUS.
I KNOW. HEY, WHERE ARE YOU GOING?
TO MAKE TEN GRAND.

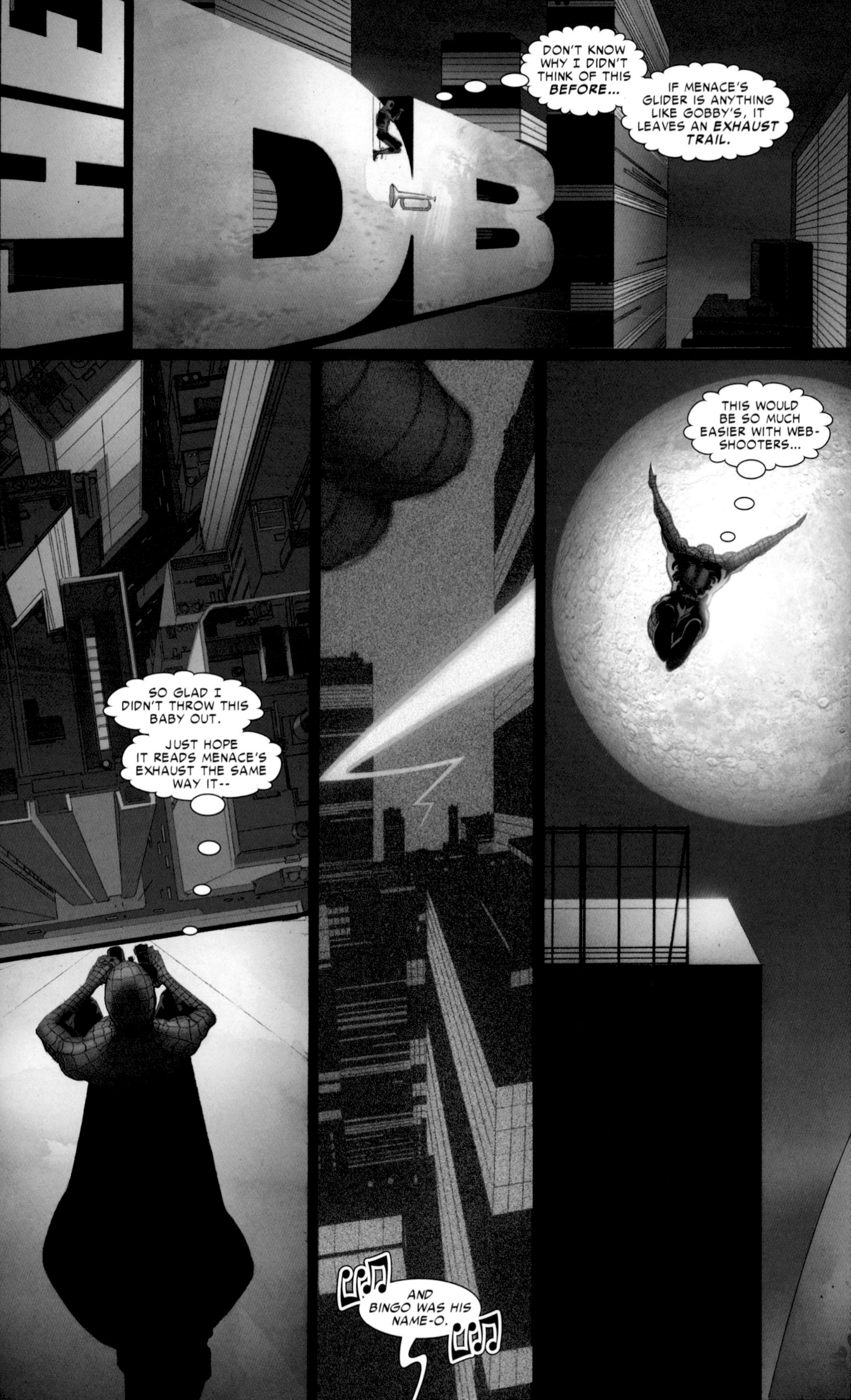
DON'T KNOW WHY I DIDN'T THINK OF THIS BEFORE...
IF MENACE'S GLIDER IS ANYTHING LIKE GOBBY'S, IT LEAVES AN EXHAUST TRAIL.
THIS WOULD BE SO MUCH EASIER WITH WEB-SHOOTERS...
SO GLAD I DIDN'T THROW THIS BABY OUT.
JUST HOPE IT READS MENACE'S EXHAUST THE SAME WAY IT--
AND BINGO WAS HIS NAME-O.

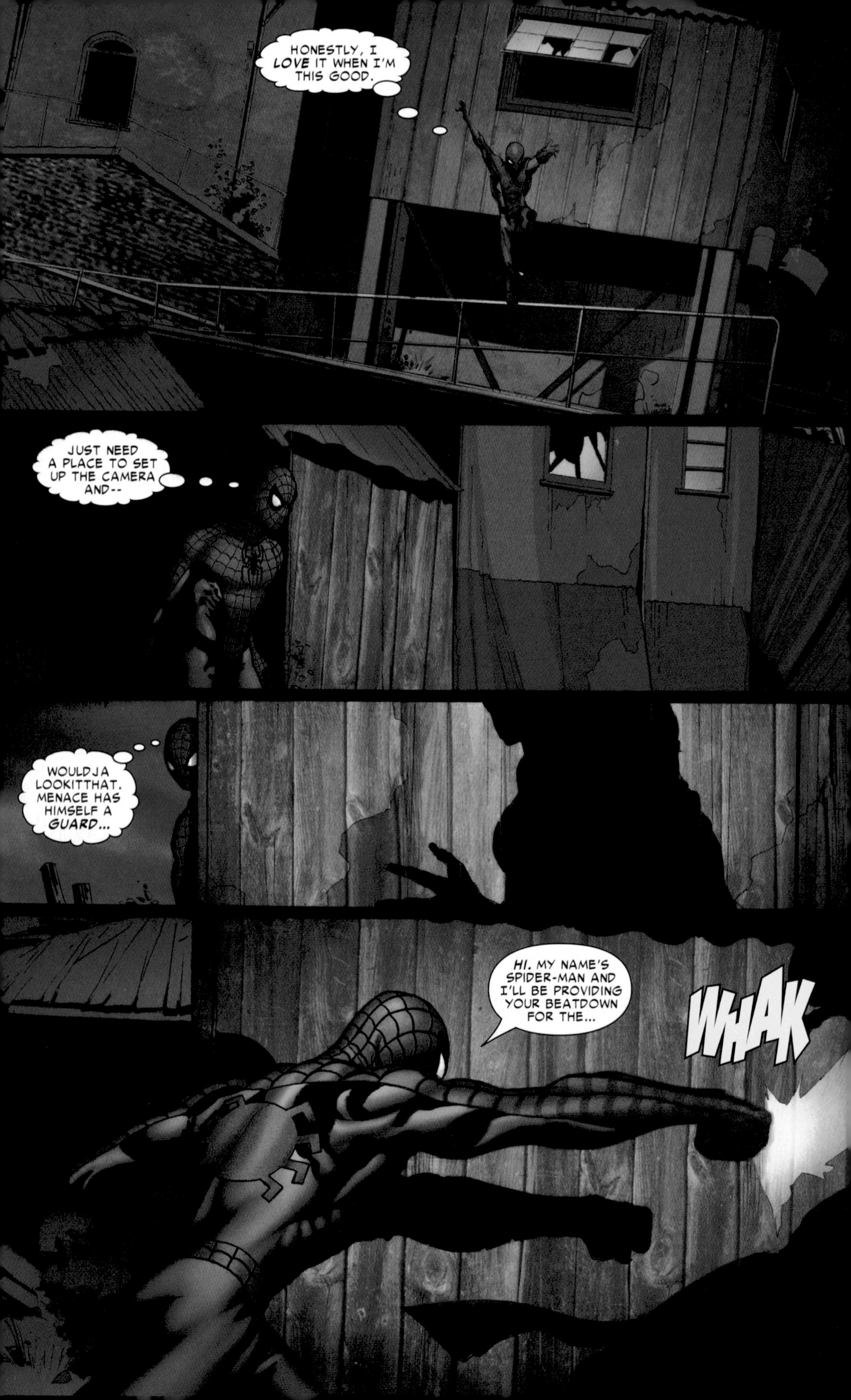
HONESTLY, I LOVE IT WHEN I'M THIS GOOD.
JUST NEED A PLACE TO SET UP THE CAMERA AND--
WOULDJA LOOKITTHAT. MENACE HAS HIMSELF A GUARD...
HI. MY NAME'S SPIDER-MAN AND I'LL BE PROVIDING YOUR BEATDOWN FOR THE...
WHAK

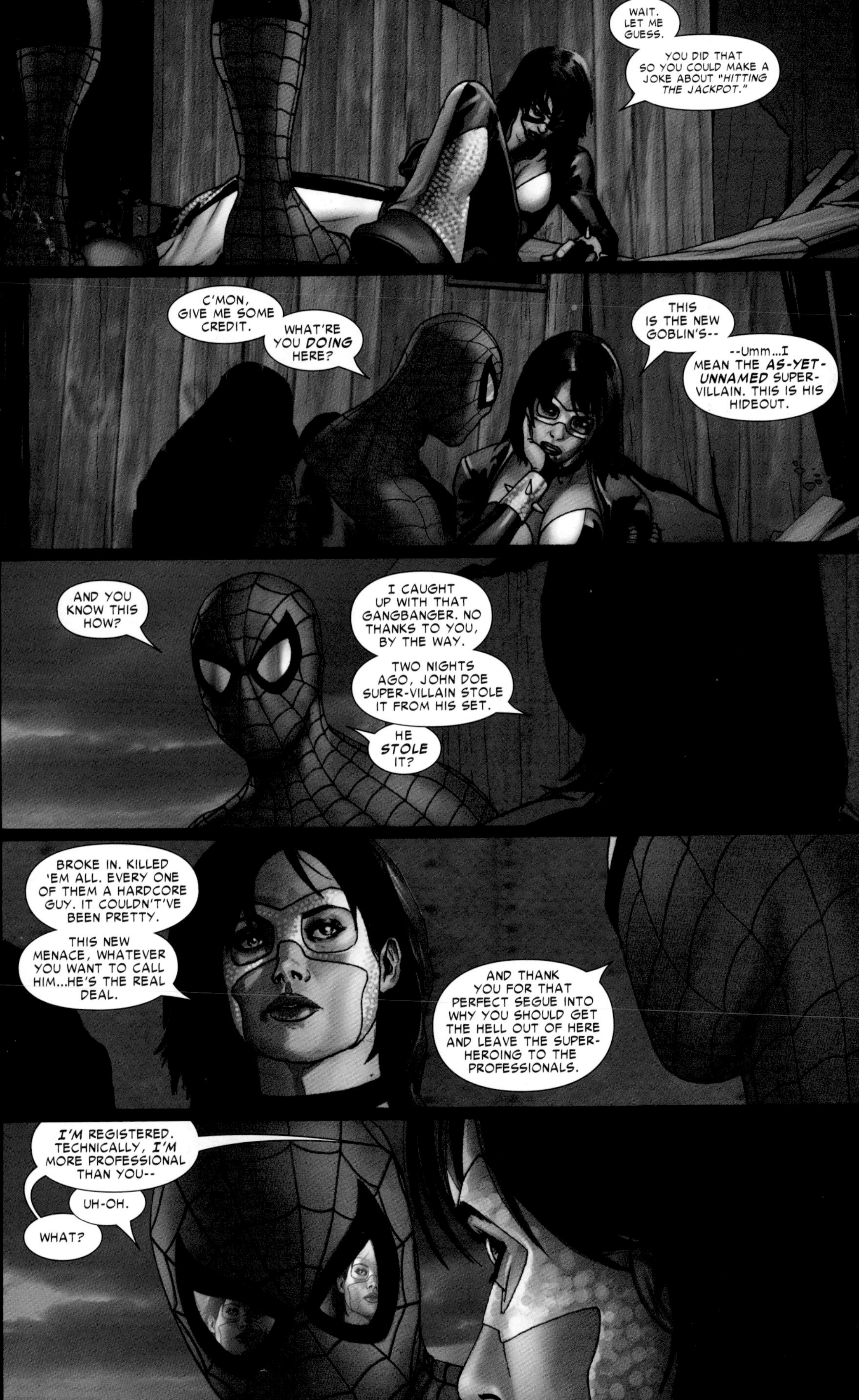
WAIT. LET ME GUESS.
YOU DID THAT SO YOU COULD MAKE A JOKE ABOUT "HITTING THE JACKPOT."
C'MON, GIVE ME SOME CREDIT.
WHAT'RE YOU DOING HERE?
THIS IS THE NEW GOBLIN'S--
--Umm...I MEAN THE AS-YET-UNNAMED SUPER-VILLAIN. THIS IS HIS HIDEOUT.
AND YOU KNOW THIS HOW?
I CAUGHT UP WITH THAT GANGBANGER. NO THANKS TO YOU, BY THE WAY.
TWO NIGHTS AGO, JOHN DOE SUPER-VILLAIN STOLE IT FROM HIS SET.
HE STOLE IT?
BROKE IN. KILLED 'EM ALL. EVERY ONE OF THEM A HARDCORE GUY. IT COULDN'T'VE BEEN PRETTY.
THIS NEW MENACE, WHATEVER YOU WANT TO CALL HIM...HE'S THE REAL DEAL.
AND THANK YOU FOR THAT PERFECT SEGUE INTO WHY YOU SHOULD GET THE HELL OUT OF HERE AND LEAVE THE SUPER-HEROING TO THE PROFESSIONALS.
I'M REGISTERED. TECHNICALLY, I'M MORE PROFESSIONAL THAN YOU--
UH-OH.
WHAT?

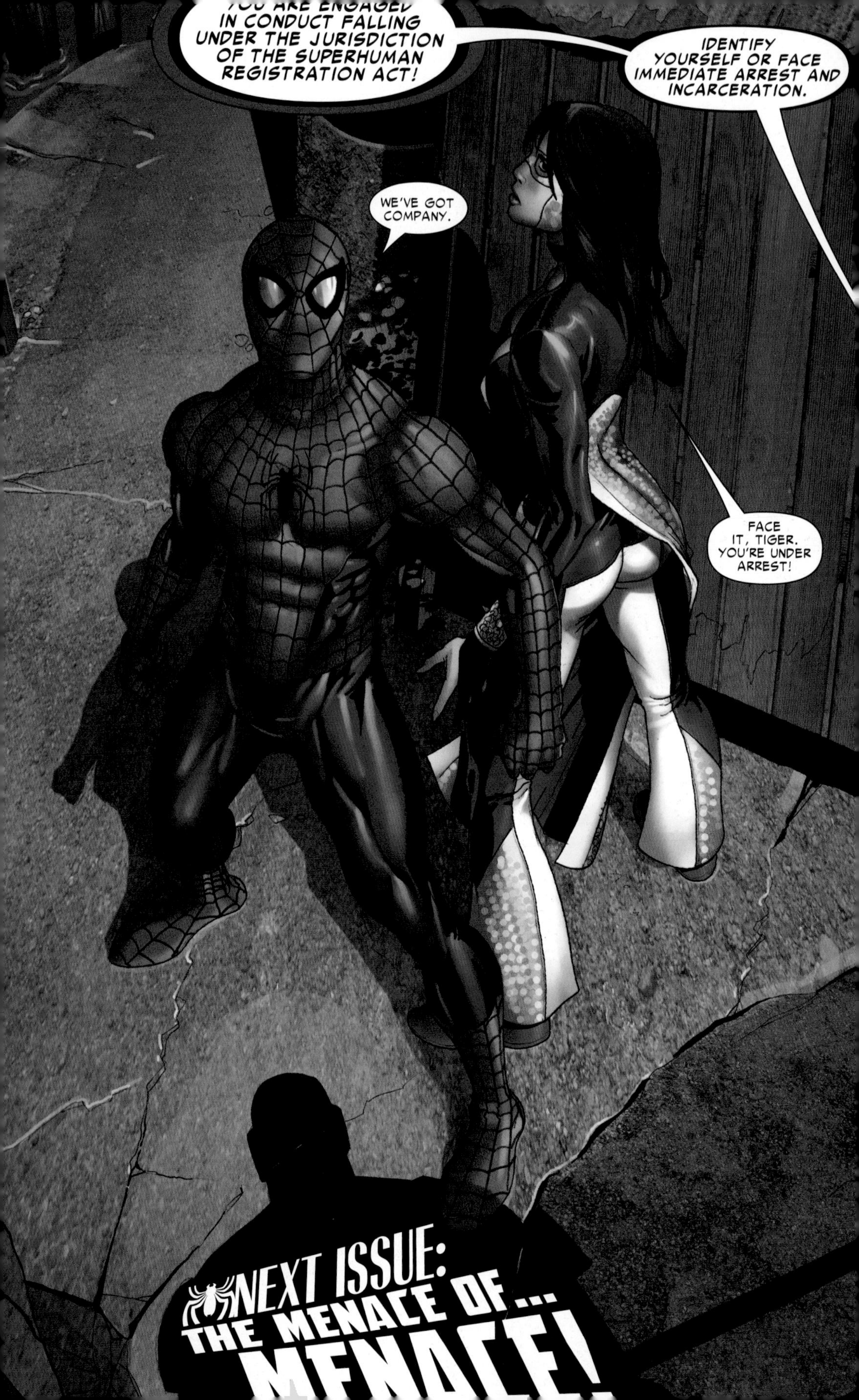
YOU ARE ENGAGED IN CONDUCT FALLING UNDER THE JURISDICTION OF THE SUPERHUMAN REGISTRATION ACT!
IDENTIFY YOURSELF OR FACE IMMEDIATE ARREST AND INCARCERATION.
WE'VE GOT COMPANY.
FACE IT, TIGER. YOU'RE UNDER ARREST!
NEXT ISSUE: THE MENACE OF...

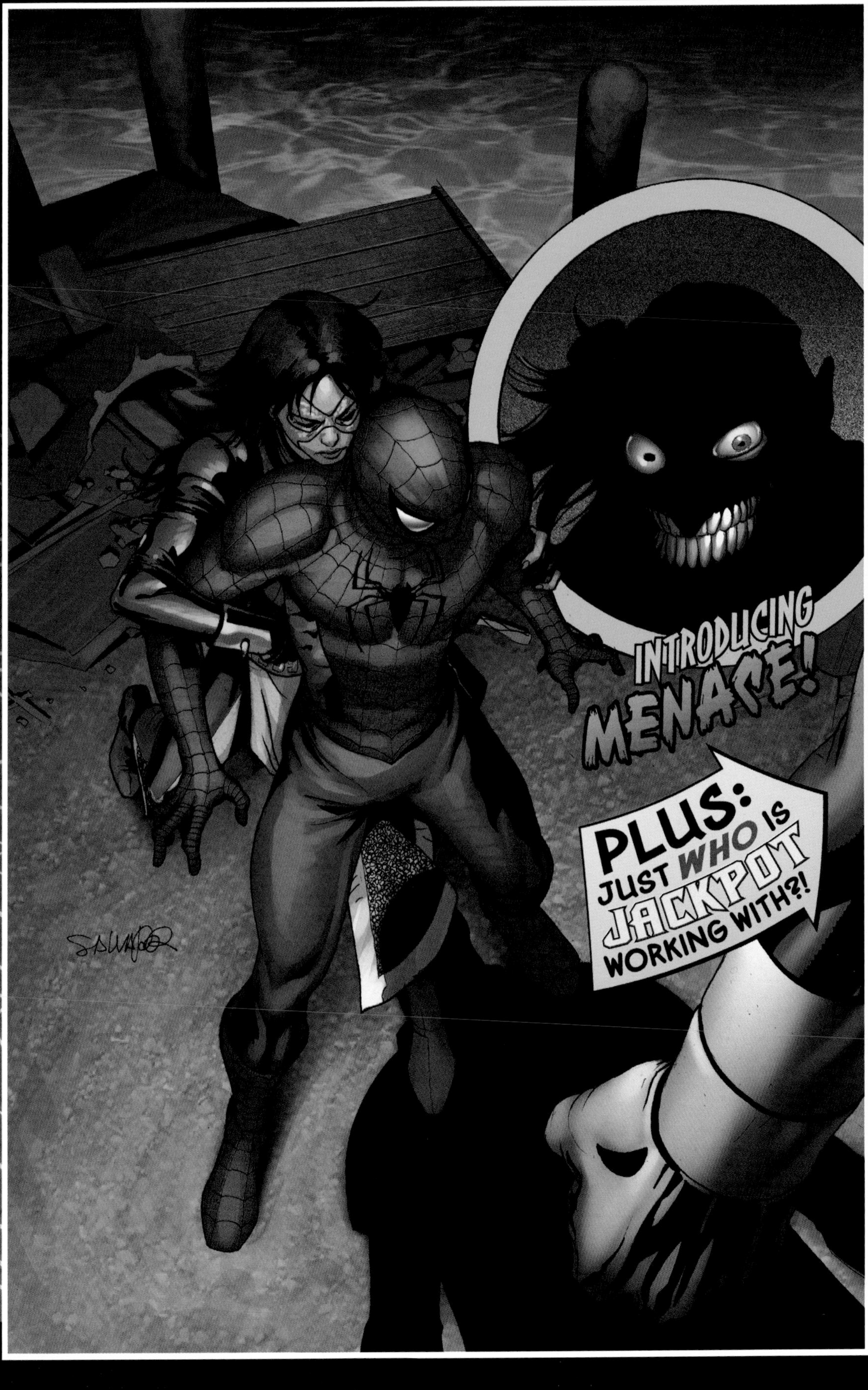
INTRODUCING MENACE!
PLUS: JUST WHO IS JACKPOT WORKING WITH?!

AMAZING SPIDER-MAN #550

WHILE ATTENDING A DEMONSTRATION IN RADIOLOGY, HIGH SCHOOL STUDENT **PETER PARKER** WAS BITTEN BY A SPIDER WHICH HAD ACCIDENTALLY BEEN EXPOSED TO **RADIOACTIVE RAYS.** THROUGH A MIRACLE OF SCIENCE, PETER SOON FOUND THAT HE HAD **GAINED** THE SPIDER'S POWERS…AND HAD, IN EFFECT, BECOME A HUMAN SPIDER! FROM THAT DAY ON HE WAS…

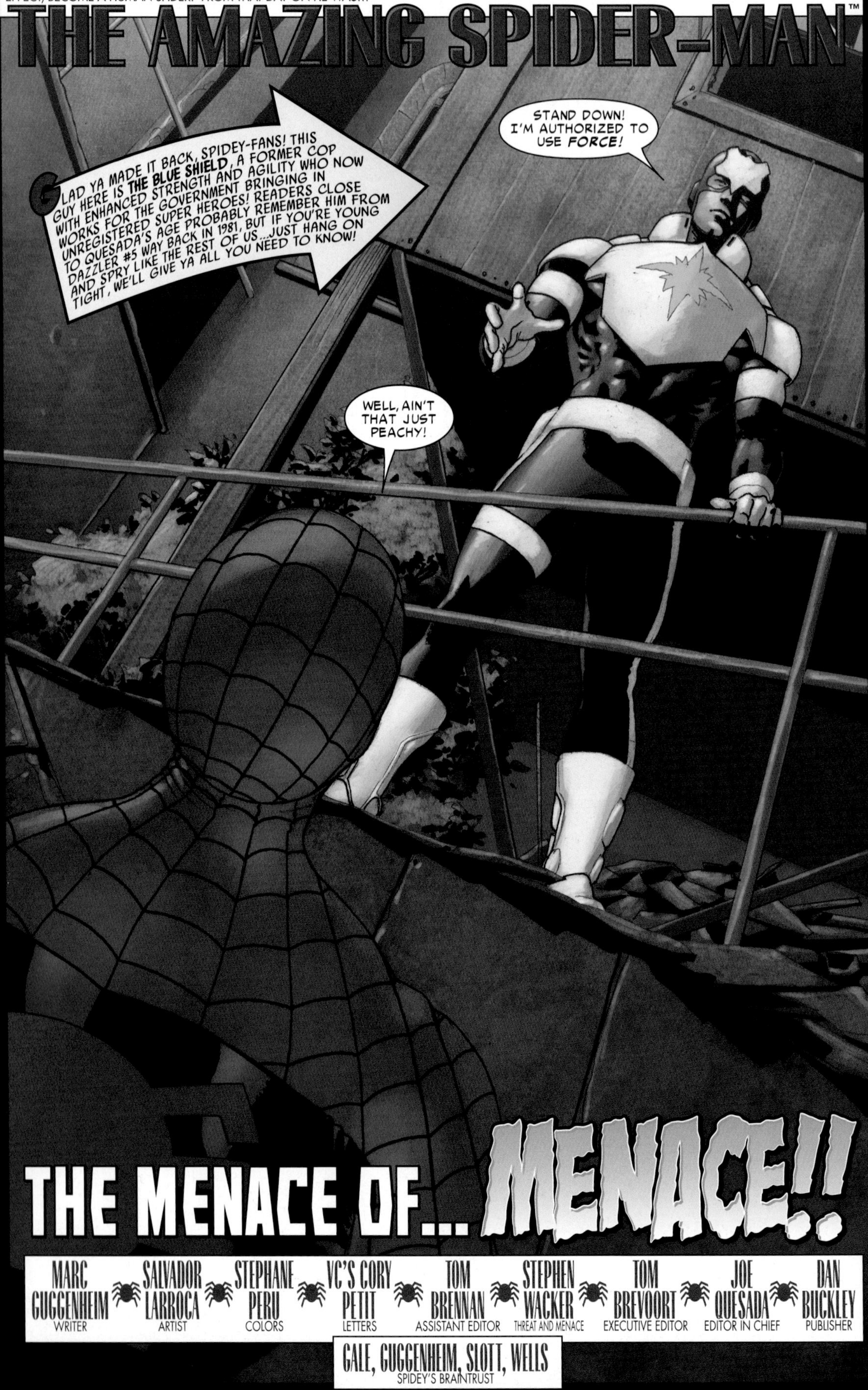

THE AMAZING SPIDER-MAN™
GLAD YA MADE IT BACK, SPIDEY-FANS! THIS GUY HERE IS THE BLUE SHIELD, A FORMER COP WITH ENHANCED STRENGTH AND AGILITY WHO NOW WORKS FOR THE GOVERNMENT BRINGING IN UNREGISTERED SUPER HEROES! READERS CLOSE TO QUESADA'S AGE PROBABLY REMEMBER HIM FROM DAZZLER #5 WAY BACK IN 1981, BUT IF YOU'RE YOUNG AND SPRY LIKE THE REST OF US...JUST HANG ON TIGHT, WE'LL GIVE YA ALL YOU NEED TO KNOW!
STAND DOWN! I'M AUTHORIZED TO USE FORCE!
WELL, AIN'T THAT JUST PEACHY!
THE MENACE OF... MENACE!!
MARC GUGGENHEIM WRITER
SALVADOR LARROCA ARTIST
STEPHANE PERU COLORS
VC'S CORY PETIT LETTERS
TOM BRENNAN ASSISTANT EDITOR
STEPHEN WACKER THREAT AND MENACE
TOM BREVOORT EXECUTIVE EDITOR
JOE QUESADA EDITOR IN CHIEF
DAN BUCKLEY PUBLISHER
GALE, GUGGENHEIM, SLOTT, WELLS
SPIDEY'S BRAINTRUST

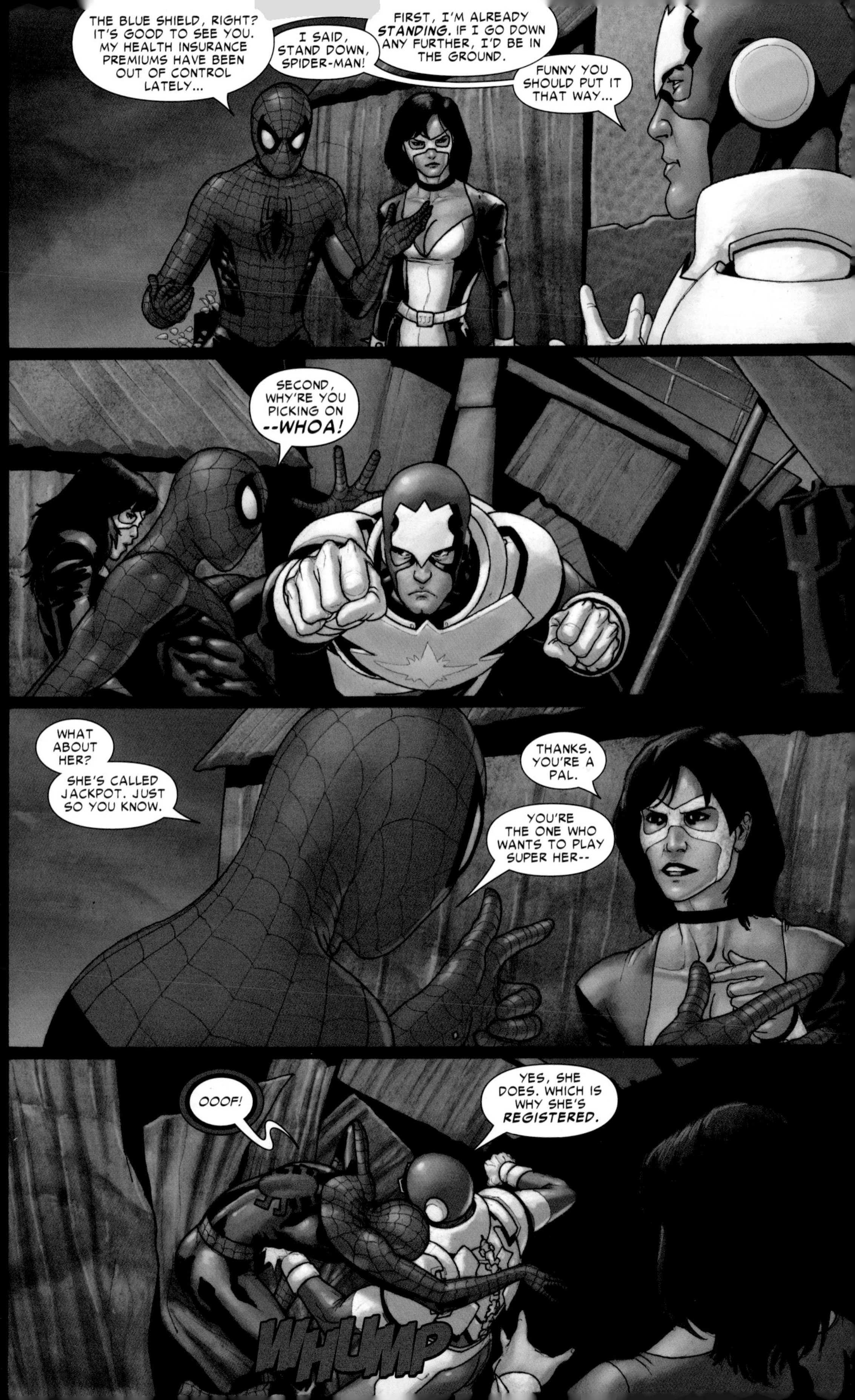
THE BLUE SHIELD, RIGHT? IT'S GOOD TO SEE YOU. MY HEALTH INSURANCE PREMIUMS HAVE BEEN OUT OF CONTROL LATELY...
I SAID, STAND DOWN, SPIDER-MAN!
FIRST, I'M ALREADY STANDING. IF I GO DOWN ANY FURTHER, I'D BE IN THE GROUND.
FUNNY YOU SHOULD PUT IT THAT WAY...
SECOND, WHY'RE YOU PICKING ON --WHOA!
WHAT ABOUT HER?
SHE'S CALLED JACKPOT. JUST SO YOU KNOW.
THANKS. YOU'RE A PAL.
YOU'RE THE ONE WHO WANTS TO PLAY SUPER HER--
OOOF!
YES, SHE DOES. WHICH IS WHY SHE'S REGISTERED.
WHUMP

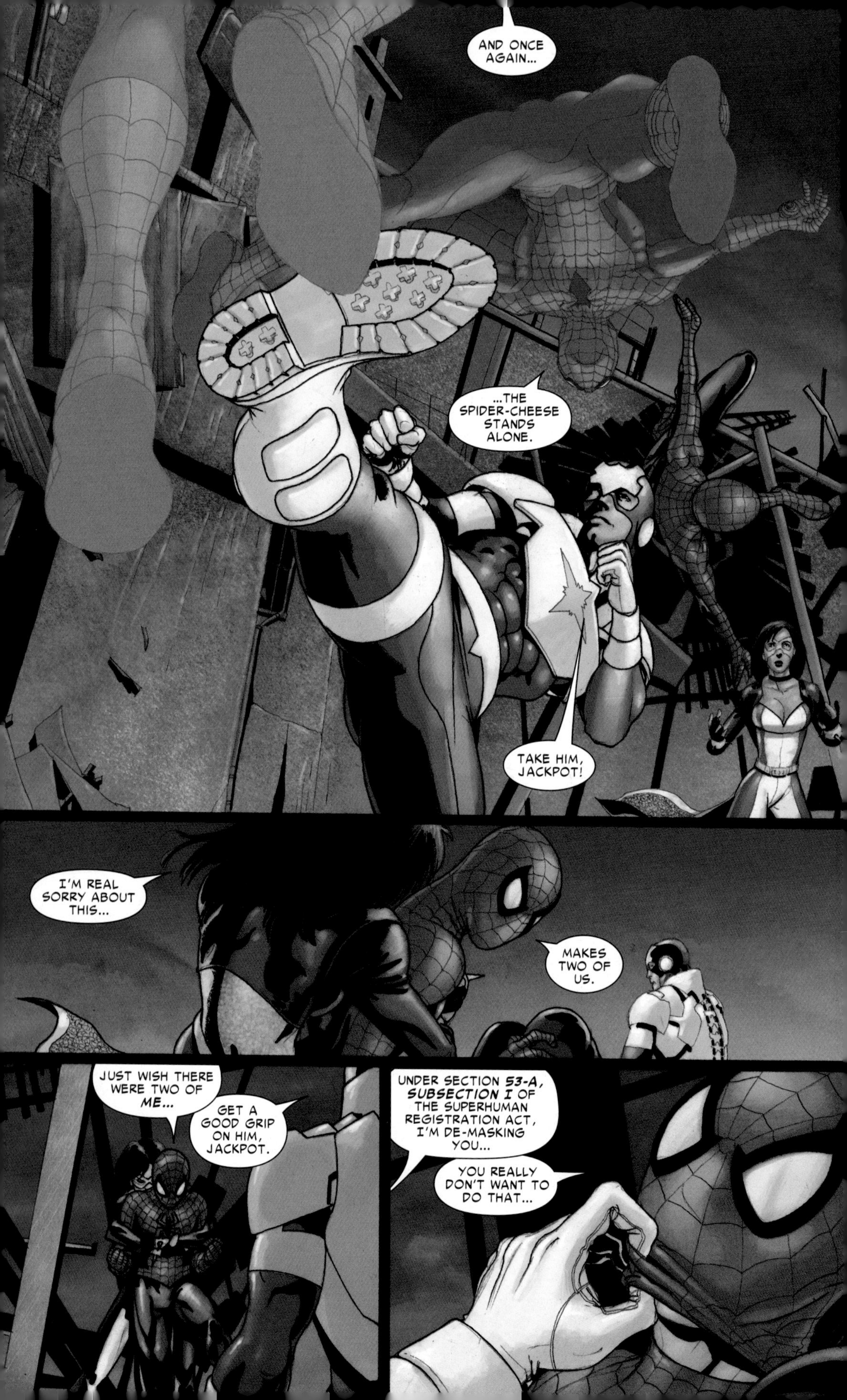
AND ONCE AGAIN...
...THE SPIDER-CHEESE STANDS ALONE.
TAKE HIM, JACKPOT!
I'M REAL SORRY ABOUT THIS...
MAKES TWO OF US.
JUST WISH THERE WERE TWO OF ME...
GET A GOOD GRIP ON HIM, JACKPOT.
UNDER SECTION 53-A, SUBSECTION I OF THE SUPERHUMAN REGISTRATION ACT, I'M DE-MASKING YOU...
YOU REALLY DON'T WANT TO DO THAT...

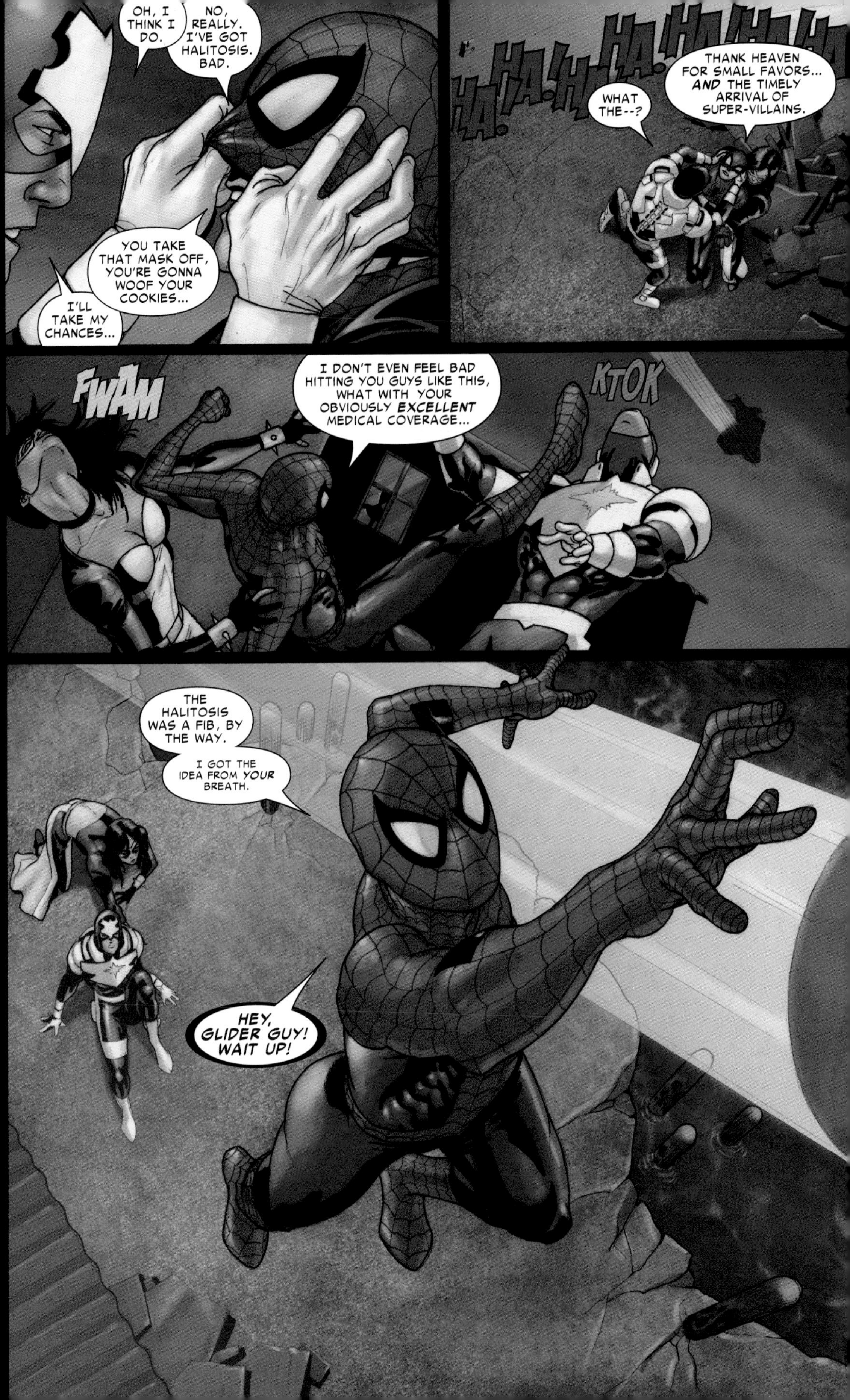

OH, I THINK I DO.
NO, REALLY. I'VE GOT HALITOSIS. BAD.
YOU TAKE THAT MASK OFF, YOU'RE GONNA WOOF YOUR COOKIES...
I'LL TAKE MY CHANCES...
HA! HA! HA! HA! HA! HA! HA!
WHAT THE--?
THANK HEAVEN FOR SMALL FAVORS... AND THE TIMELY ARRIVAL OF SUPER-VILLAINS.
FWAM
I DON'T EVEN FEEL BAD HITTING YOU GUYS LIKE THIS, WHAT WITH YOUR OBVIOUSLY EXCELLENT MEDICAL COVERAGE...
KTOK
THE HALITOSIS WAS A FIB, BY THE WAY.
I GOT THE IDEA FROM YOUR BREATH.
HEY, GLIDER GUY! WAIT UP!

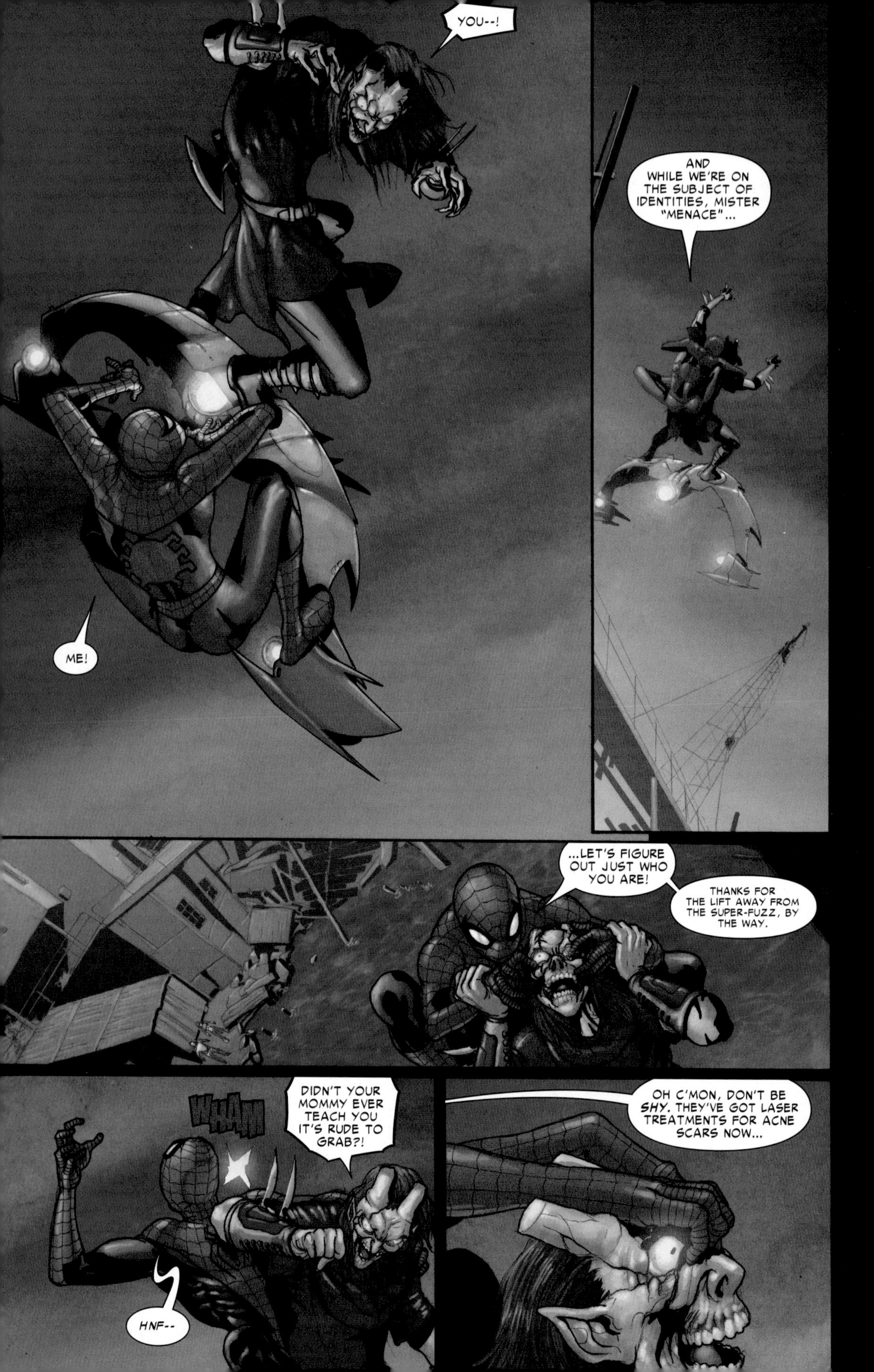
YOU--!
ME!
AND WHILE WE'RE ON THE SUBJECT OF IDENTITIES, MISTER "MENACE"...
...LET'S FIGURE OUT JUST WHO YOU ARE!
THANKS FOR THE LIFT AWAY FROM THE SUPER-FUZZ, BY THE WAY.
WHAM
DIDN'T YOUR MOMMY EVER TEACH YOU IT'S RUDE TO GRAB?!
HNF--
OH C'MON, DON'T BE *SHY*. THEY'VE GOT LASER TREATMENTS FOR ACNE SCARS NOW...

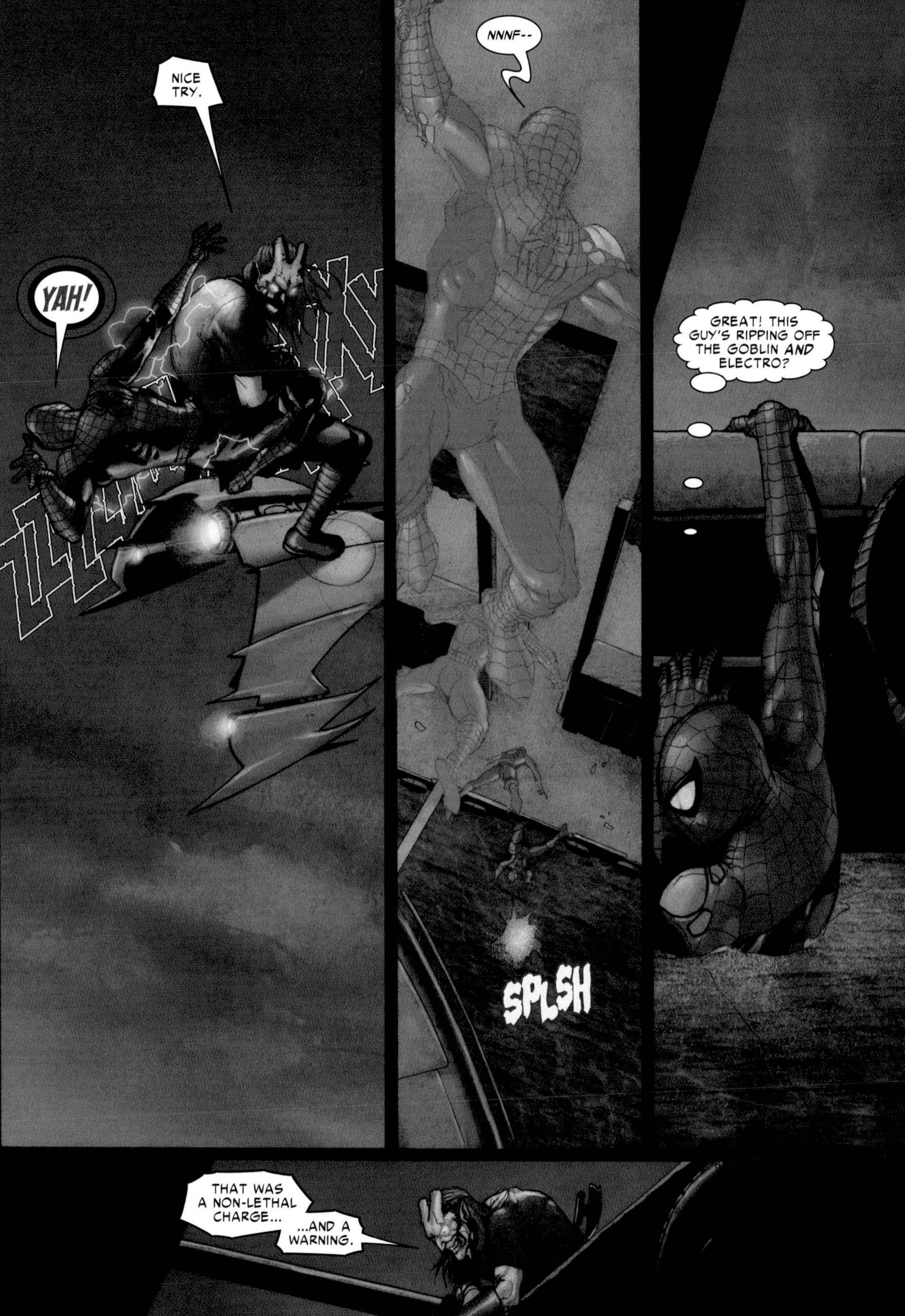
NICE TRY.
YAH!
NNNF--
SPLSH
GREAT! THIS GUY'S RIPPING OFF THE GOBLIN *AND* ELECTRO?
THAT WAS A NON-LETHAL CHARGE...
...AND A WARNING.

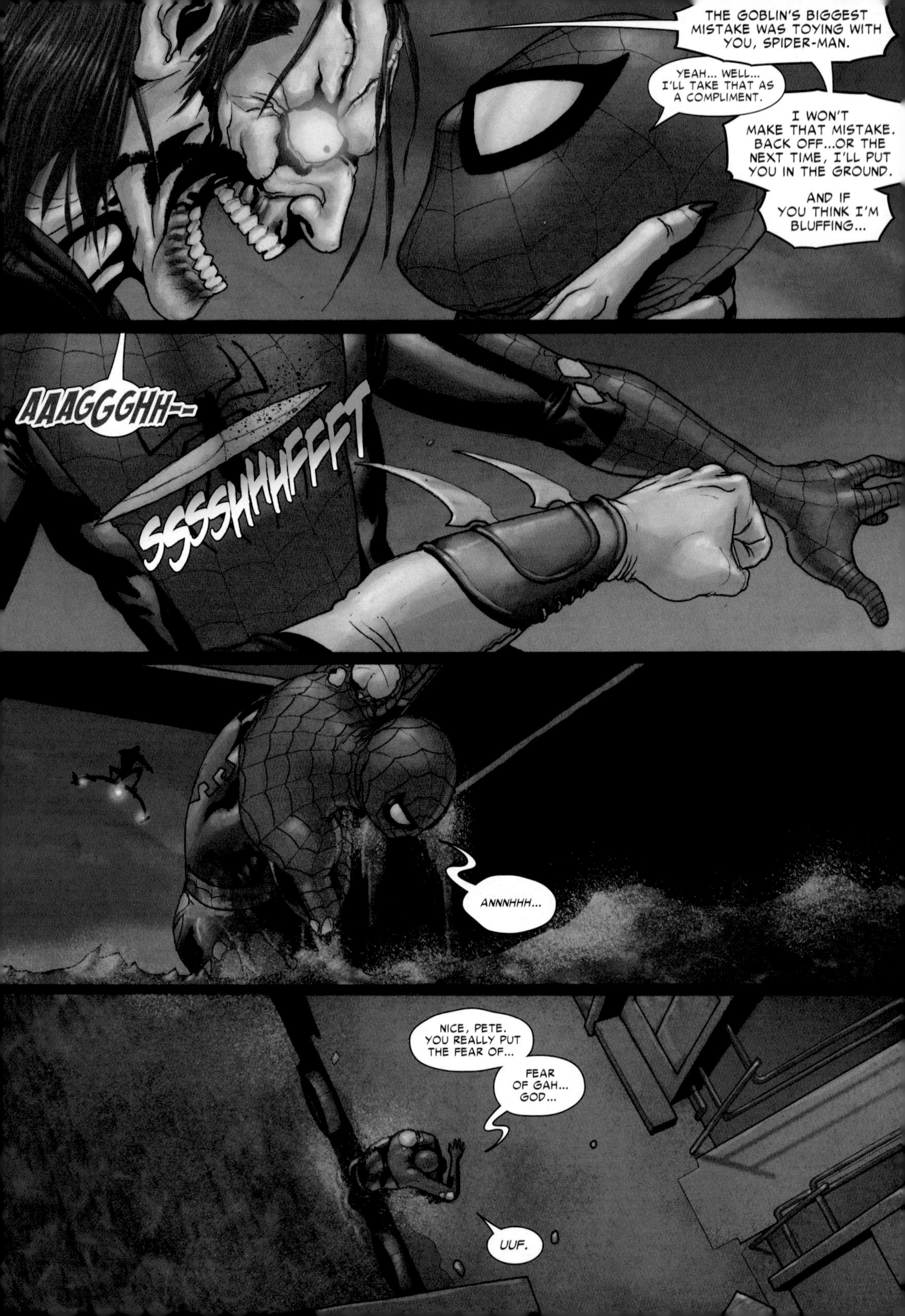
THE GOBLIN'S BIGGEST MISTAKE WAS TOYING WITH YOU, SPIDER-MAN.
YEAH... WELL... I'LL TAKE THAT AS A COMPLIMENT.
I WON'T MAKE THAT MISTAKE. BACK OFF...OR THE NEXT TIME, I'LL PUT YOU IN THE GROUND.
AND IF YOU THINK I'M BLUFFING...
AAAGGGHH--
SSSSHHHFFFT
ANNNHHH...
NICE, PETE. YOU REALLY PUT THE FEAR OF...
FEAR OF GAH... GOD...
UUF.

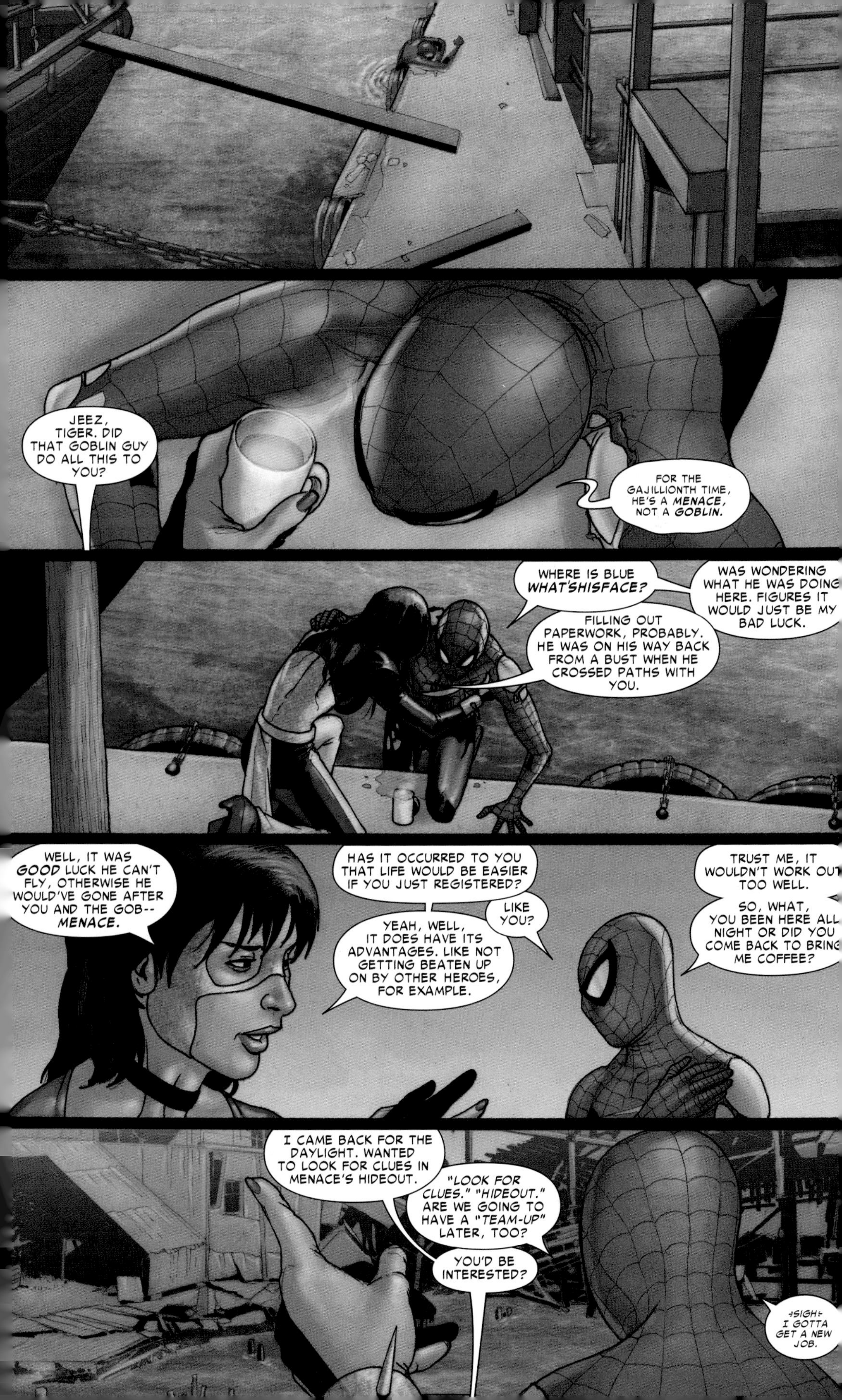

JEEZ, TIGER. DID THAT GOBLIN GUY DO ALL THIS TO YOU?
FOR THE GAJILLIONTH TIME, HE'S A *MENACE,* NOT A *GOBLIN.*
WHERE IS BLUE *WHAT'SHISFACE?*
FILLING OUT PAPERWORK, PROBABLY. HE WAS ON HIS WAY BACK FROM A BUST WHEN HE CROSSED PATHS WITH YOU.
WAS WONDERING WHAT HE WAS DOING HERE. FIGURES IT WOULD JUST BE MY BAD LUCK.
WELL, IT WAS *GOOD* LUCK HE CAN'T FLY, OTHERWISE HE WOULD'VE GONE AFTER YOU AND THE GOB-- *MENACE.*
HAS IT OCCURRED TO YOU THAT LIFE WOULD BE EASIER IF YOU JUST REGISTERED?
LIKE YOU?
YEAH, WELL, IT DOES HAVE ITS ADVANTAGES. LIKE NOT GETTING BEATEN UP ON BY OTHER HEROES, FOR EXAMPLE.
TRUST ME, IT WOULDN'T WORK OUT TOO WELL.
SO, WHAT, YOU BEEN HERE ALL NIGHT OR DID YOU COME BACK TO BRING ME COFFEE?
I CAME BACK FOR THE DAYLIGHT. WANTED TO LOOK FOR CLUES IN MENACE'S HIDEOUT.
"*LOOK FOR CLUES.*" "*HIDEOUT.*" ARE WE GOING TO HAVE A "*TEAM-UP*" LATER, TOO?
YOU'D BE INTERESTED?
SIGH I GOTTA GET A NEW JOB.

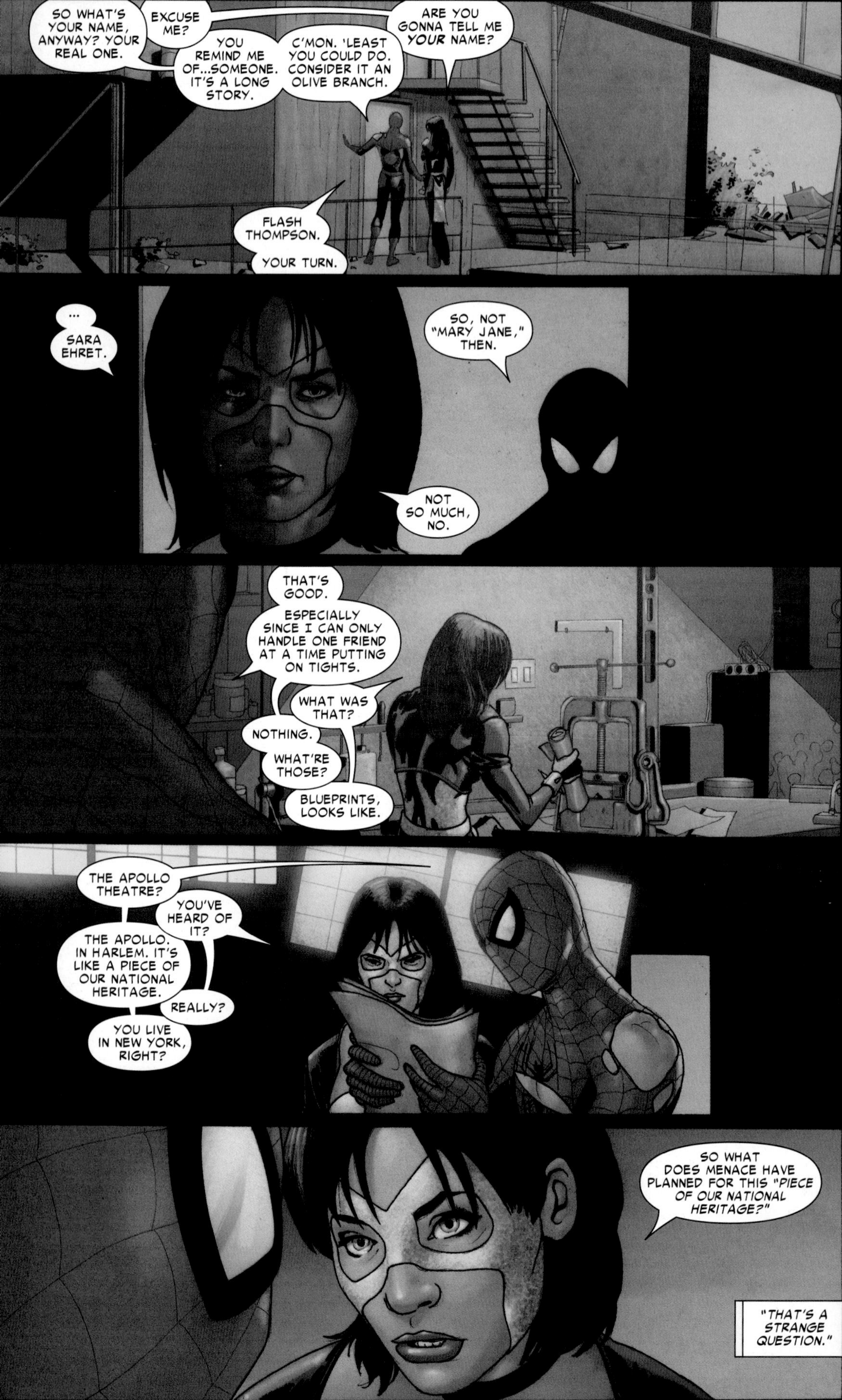
SO WHAT'S YOUR NAME, ANYWAY? YOUR REAL ONE.
EXCUSE ME?
YOU REMIND ME OF...SOMEONE. IT'S A LONG STORY.
C'MON. 'LEAST YOU COULD DO. CONSIDER IT AN OLIVE BRANCH.
ARE YOU GONNA TELL ME *YOUR* NAME?
FLASH THOMPSON.
YOUR TURN.
... SARA EHRET.
SO, NOT "MARY JANE," THEN.
NOT SO MUCH, NO.
THAT'S GOOD.
ESPECIALLY SINCE I CAN ONLY HANDLE ONE FRIEND AT A TIME PUTTING ON TIGHTS.
WHAT WAS THAT?
NOTHING.
WHAT'RE THOSE?
BLUEPRINTS, LOOKS LIKE.
THE APOLLO THEATRE?
YOU'VE HEARD OF IT?
THE APOLLO. IN HARLEM. IT'S LIKE A PIECE OF OUR NATIONAL HERITAGE.
REALLY?
YOU LIVE IN NEW YORK, RIGHT?
SO WHAT DOES MENACE HAVE PLANNED FOR THIS "*PIECE OF OUR NATIONAL HERITAGE?*"
"THAT'S A STRANGE QUESTION."

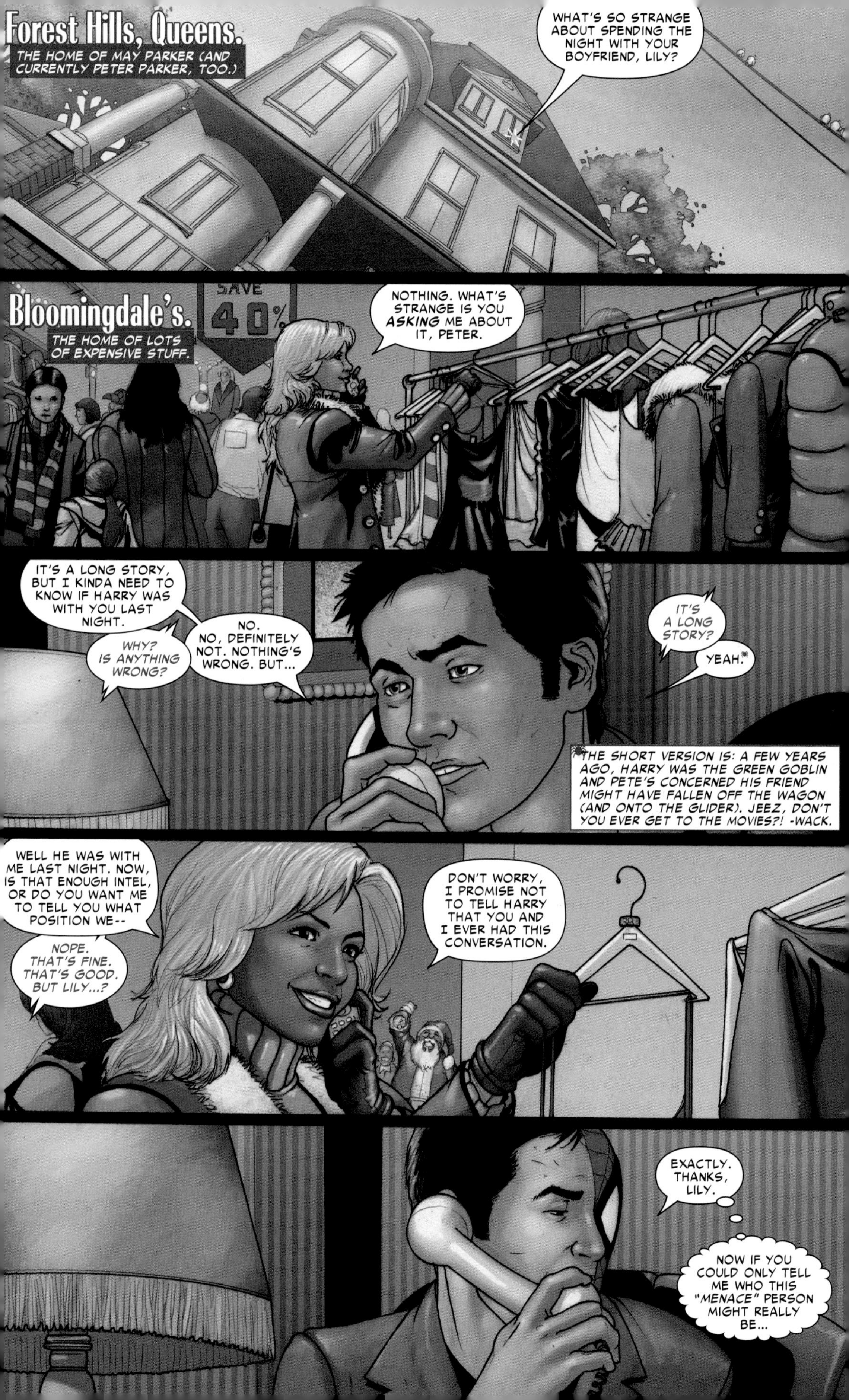
Forest Hills, Queens.
THE HOME OF MAY PARKER (AND CURRENTLY PETER PARKER, TOO.)
WHAT'S SO STRANGE ABOUT SPENDING THE NIGHT WITH YOUR BOYFRIEND, LILY?
Bloomingdale's.
THE HOME OF LOTS OF EXPENSIVE STUFF.
SAVE 40%
NOTHING. WHAT'S STRANGE IS YOU ASKING ME ABOUT IT, PETER.
IT'S A LONG STORY, BUT I KINDA NEED TO KNOW IF HARRY WAS WITH YOU LAST NIGHT.
WHY? IS ANYTHING WRONG?
NO. NO, DEFINITELY NOT. NOTHING'S WRONG. BUT...
IT'S A LONG STORY?
YEAH.*
*THE SHORT VERSION IS: A FEW YEARS AGO, HARRY WAS THE GREEN GOBLIN AND PETE'S CONCERNED HIS FRIEND MIGHT HAVE FALLEN OFF THE WAGON (AND ONTO THE GLIDER). JEEZ, DON'T YOU EVER GET TO THE MOVIES?! -WACK.
WELL HE WAS WITH ME LAST NIGHT. NOW, IS THAT ENOUGH INTEL, OR DO YOU WANT ME TO TELL YOU WHAT POSITION WE--
NOPE. THAT'S FINE. THAT'S GOOD. BUT LILY...?
DON'T WORRY, I PROMISE NOT TO TELL HARRY THAT YOU AND I EVER HAD THIS CONVERSATION.
EXACTLY. THANKS, LILY.
NOW IF YOU COULD ONLY TELL ME WHO THIS "MENACE" PERSON MIGHT REALLY BE...

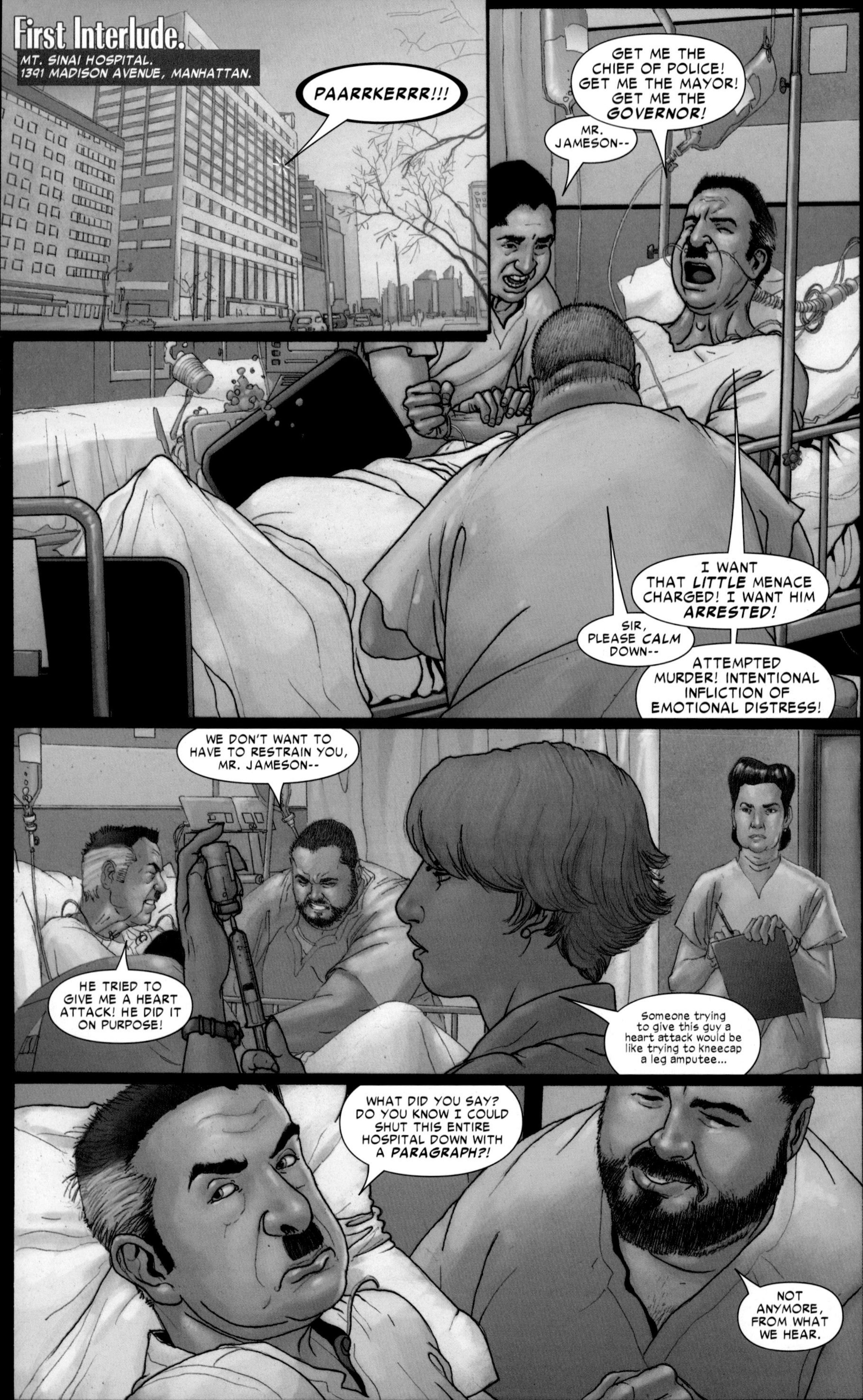
First Interlude.
MT. SINAI HOSPITAL.
1391 MADISON AVENUE, MANHATTAN.
PAARRKERRR!!!
GET ME THE CHIEF OF POLICE! GET ME THE MAYOR! GET ME THE GOVERNOR!
MR. JAMESON--
I WANT THAT LITTLE MENACE CHARGED! I WANT HIM ARRESTED!
SIR, PLEASE CALM DOWN--
ATTEMPTED MURDER! INTENTIONAL INFLICTION OF EMOTIONAL DISTRESS!
WE DON'T WANT TO HAVE TO RESTRAIN YOU, MR. JAMESON--
HE TRIED TO GIVE ME A HEART ATTACK! HE DID IT ON PURPOSE!
Someone trying to give this guy a heart attack would be like trying to kneecap a leg amputee...
WHAT DID YOU SAY? DO YOU KNOW I COULD SHUT THIS ENTIRE HOSPITAL DOWN WITH A PARAGRAPH?!
NOT ANYMORE, FROM WHAT WE HEAR.

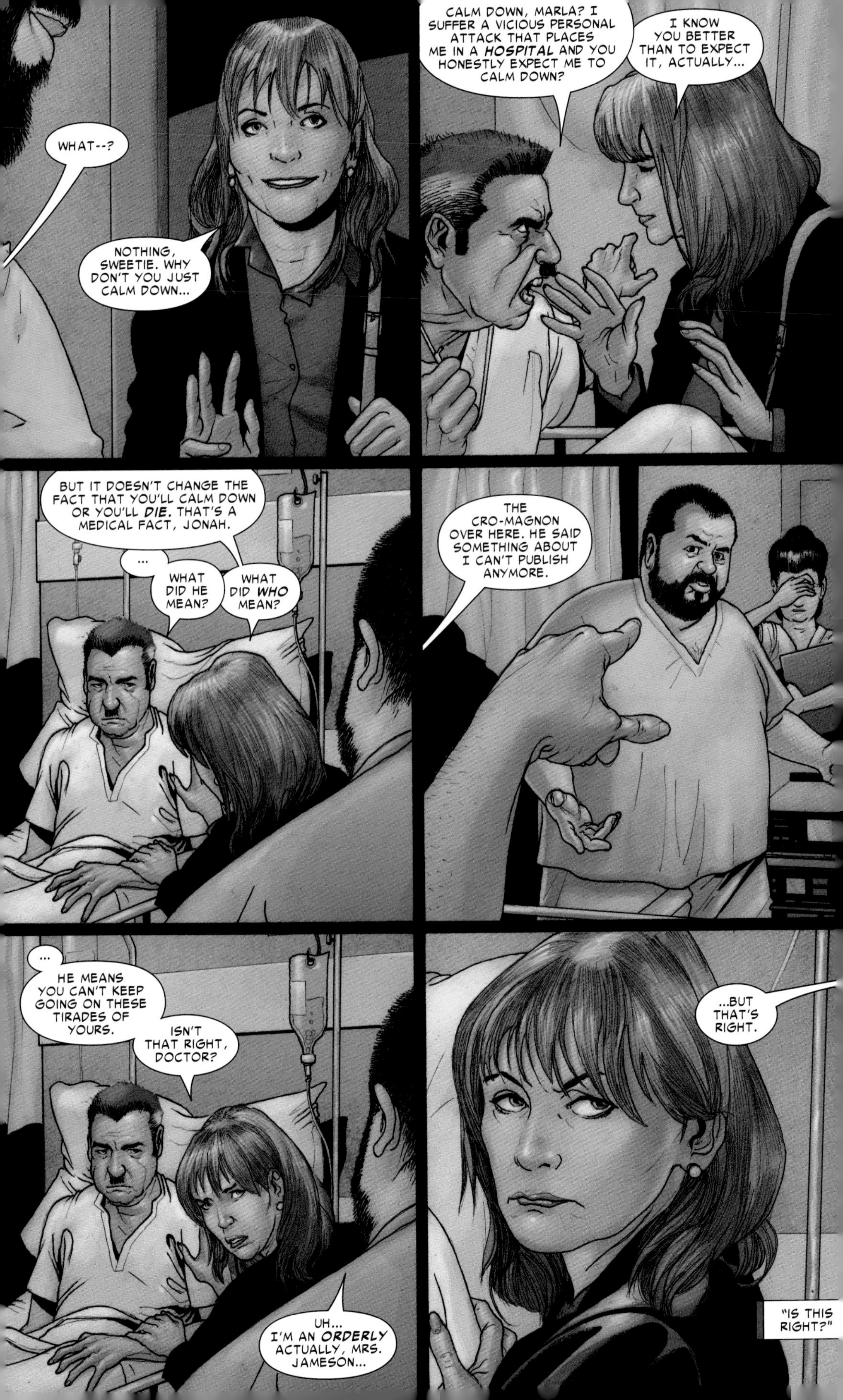
WHAT--?
NOTHING, SWEETIE. WHY DON'T YOU JUST CALM DOWN...
CALM DOWN, MARLA? I SUFFER A VICIOUS PERSONAL ATTACK THAT PLACES ME IN A *HOSPITAL* AND YOU HONESTLY EXPECT ME TO CALM DOWN?
I KNOW YOU BETTER THAN TO EXPECT IT, ACTUALLY...
BUT IT DOESN'T CHANGE THE FACT THAT YOU'LL CALM DOWN OR YOU'LL *DIE.* THAT'S A MEDICAL FACT, JONAH.
...
WHAT DID HE MEAN?
WHAT DID *WHO* MEAN?
THE CRO-MAGNON OVER HERE. HE SAID SOMETHING ABOUT I CAN'T PUBLISH ANYMORE.
...
HE MEANS YOU CAN'T KEEP GOING ON THESE TIRADES OF YOURS.
ISN'T THAT RIGHT, DOCTOR?
UH... I'M AN *ORDERLY* ACTUALLY, MRS. JAMESON...
...BUT THAT'S RIGHT.
"IS THIS RIGHT?"

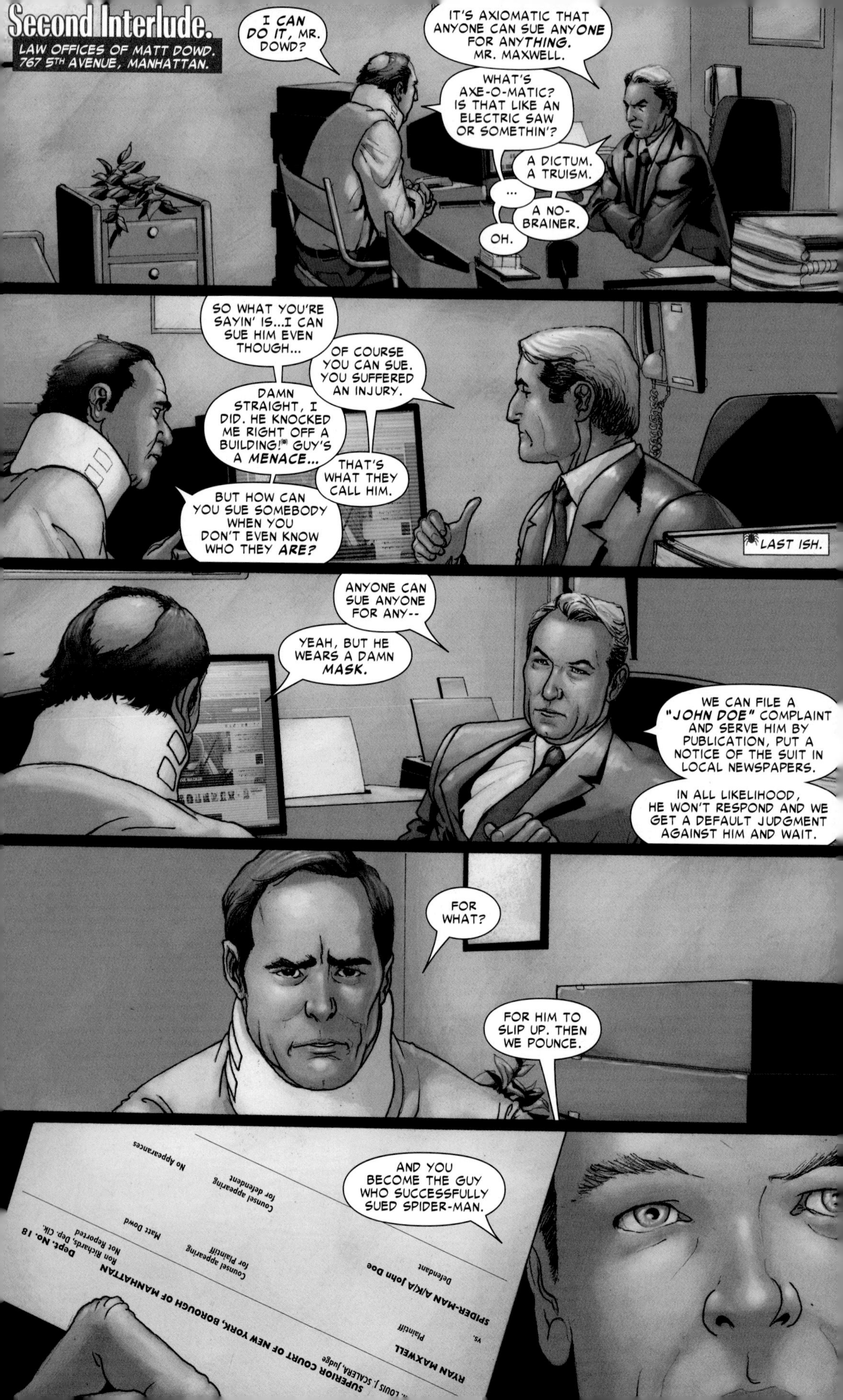

Second Interlude.
LAW OFFICES OF MATT DOWD. 767 5TH AVENUE, MANHATTAN.
I CAN DO IT, MR. DOWD?
IT'S AXIOMATIC THAT ANYONE CAN SUE ANYONE FOR ANYTHING. MR. MAXWELL.
WHAT'S AXE-O-MATIC? IS THAT LIKE AN ELECTRIC SAW OR SOMETHIN'?
A DICTUM. A TRUISM.
...
A NO-BRAINER.
OH.
SO WHAT YOU'RE SAYIN' IS...I CAN SUE HIM EVEN THOUGH...
OF COURSE YOU CAN SUE. YOU SUFFERED AN INJURY.
DAMN STRAIGHT, I DID. HE KNOCKED ME RIGHT OFF A BUILDING!* GUY'S A MENACE...
THAT'S WHAT THEY CALL HIM.
BUT HOW CAN YOU SUE SOMEBODY WHEN YOU DON'T EVEN KNOW WHO THEY ARE?
*LAST ISH.
ANYONE CAN SUE ANYONE FOR ANY--
YEAH, BUT HE WEARS A DAMN MASK.
WE CAN FILE A "JOHN DOE" COMPLAINT AND SERVE HIM BY PUBLICATION, PUT A NOTICE OF THE SUIT IN LOCAL NEWSPAPERS.
IN ALL LIKELIHOOD, HE WON'T RESPOND AND WE GET A DEFAULT JUDGMENT AGAINST HIM AND WAIT.
FOR WHAT?
FOR HIM TO SLIP UP. THEN WE POUNCE.
AND YOU BECOME THE GUY WHO SUCCESSFULLY SUED SPIDER-MAN.
SUPERIOR COURT OF NEW YORK, BOROUGH OF MANHATTAN
Dept. No. 18
LOUIS J. SCALERA, Judge
Ron Richards, Dep. Clk.
Not Reported
RYAN MAXWELL
Plaintiff
vs.
SPIDER-MAN A/K/A John Doe
Defendant
Counsel appearing for Plaintiff
Matt Dowd
Counsel appearing for defendant
No Appearances

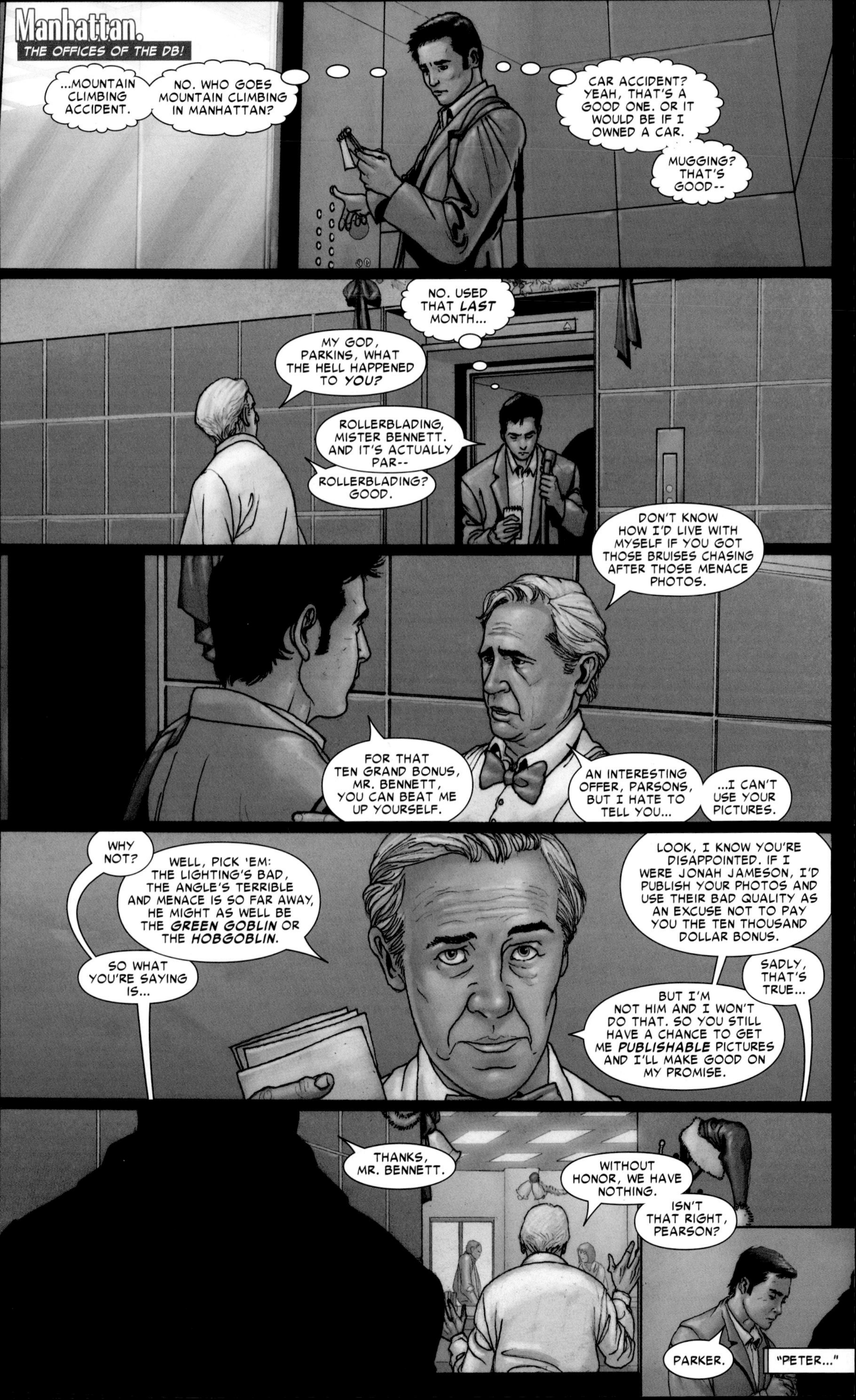
Manhattan.
THE OFFICES OF THE DB!
...MOUNTAIN CLIMBING ACCIDENT.
NO. WHO GOES MOUNTAIN CLIMBING IN MANHATTAN?
CAR ACCIDENT? YEAH, THAT'S A GOOD ONE. OR IT WOULD BE IF I OWNED A CAR.
MUGGING? THAT'S GOOD--
NO. USED THAT LAST MONTH...
MY GOD, PARKINS, WHAT THE HELL HAPPENED TO YOU?
ROLLERBLADING, MISTER BENNETT. AND IT'S ACTUALLY PAR--
ROLLERBLADING? GOOD.
DON'T KNOW HOW I'D LIVE WITH MYSELF IF YOU GOT THOSE BRUISES CHASING AFTER THOSE MENACE PHOTOS.
FOR THAT TEN GRAND BONUS, MR. BENNETT, YOU CAN BEAT ME UP YOURSELF.
AN INTERESTING OFFER, PARSONS, BUT I HATE TO TELL YOU...
...I CAN'T USE YOUR PICTURES.
WHY NOT?
WELL, PICK 'EM: THE LIGHTING'S BAD, THE ANGLE'S TERRIBLE AND MENACE IS SO FAR AWAY, HE MIGHT AS WELL BE THE GREEN GOBLIN OR THE HOBGOBLIN.
SO WHAT YOU'RE SAYING IS...
LOOK, I KNOW YOU'RE DISAPPOINTED. IF I WERE JONAH JAMESON, I'D PUBLISH YOUR PHOTOS AND USE THEIR BAD QUALITY AS AN EXCUSE NOT TO PAY YOU THE TEN THOUSAND DOLLAR BONUS.
SADLY, THAT'S TRUE...
BUT I'M NOT HIM AND I WON'T DO THAT. SO YOU STILL HAVE A CHANCE TO GET ME PUBLISHABLE PICTURES AND I'LL MAKE GOOD ON MY PROMISE.
THANKS, MR. BENNETT.
WITHOUT HONOR, WE HAVE NOTHING.
ISN'T THAT RIGHT, PEARSON?
PARKER.
"PETER..."

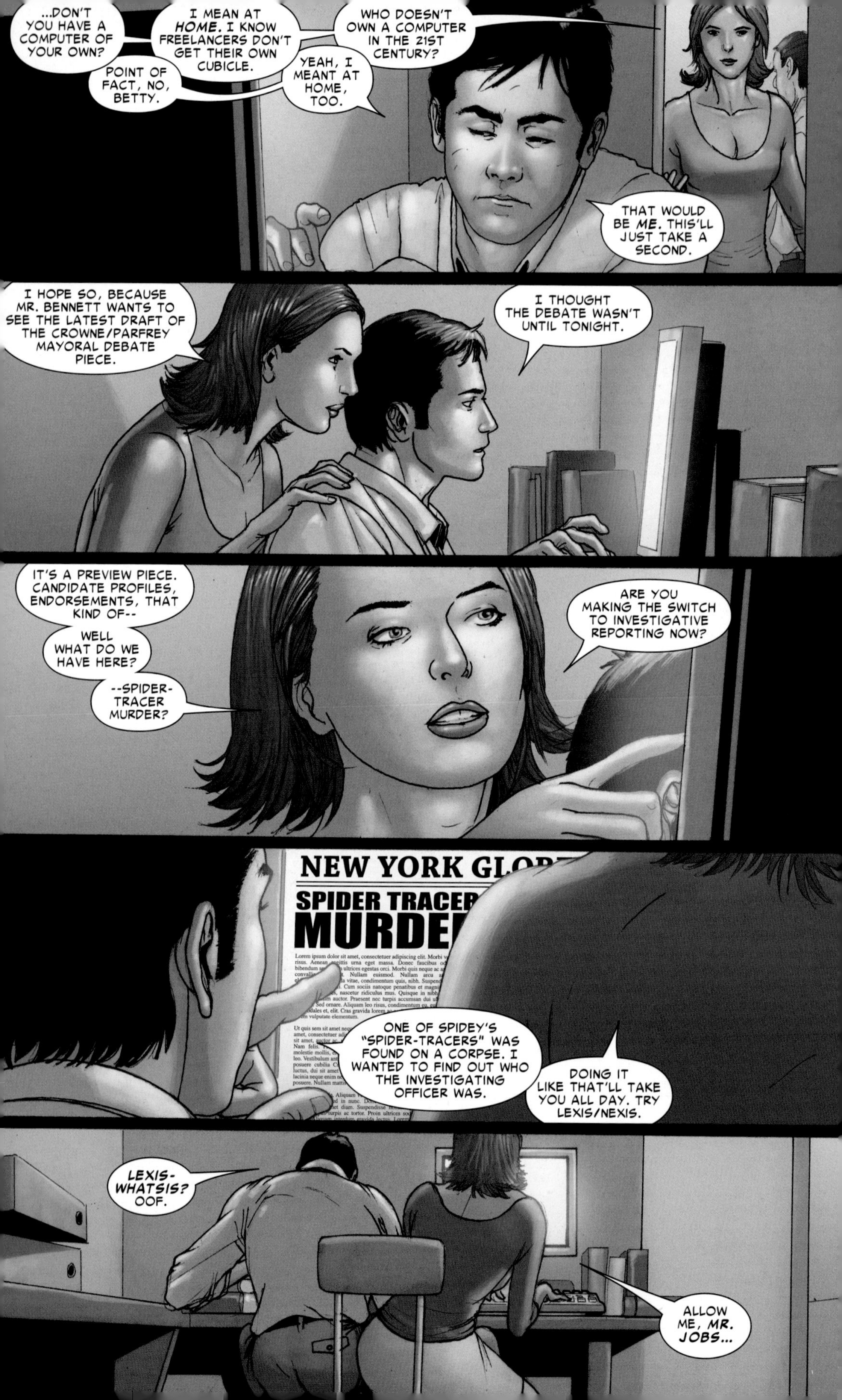

...DON'T YOU HAVE A COMPUTER OF YOUR OWN?
I MEAN AT HOME. I KNOW FREELANCERS DON'T GET THEIR OWN CUBICLE.
WHO DOESN'T OWN A COMPUTER IN THE 21ST CENTURY?
POINT OF FACT, NO, BETTY.
YEAH, I MEANT AT HOME, TOO.
THAT WOULD BE ME. THIS'LL JUST TAKE A SECOND.
I HOPE SO, BECAUSE MR. BENNETT WANTS TO SEE THE LATEST DRAFT OF THE CROWNE/PARFREY MAYORAL DEBATE PIECE.
I THOUGHT THE DEBATE WASN'T UNTIL TONIGHT.
IT'S A PREVIEW PIECE. CANDIDATE PROFILES, ENDORSEMENTS, THAT KIND OF--
WELL WHAT DO WE HAVE HERE?
--SPIDER-TRACER MURDER?
ARE YOU MAKING THE SWITCH TO INVESTIGATIVE REPORTING NOW?
NEW YORK GLO
SPIDER TRACER
MURDE
ONE OF SPIDEY'S "SPIDER-TRACERS" WAS FOUND ON A CORPSE. I WANTED TO FIND OUT WHO THE INVESTIGATING OFFICER WAS.
DOING IT LIKE THAT'LL TAKE YOU ALL DAY. TRY LEXIS/NEXIS.
LEXIS-WHATSIS? OOF.
ALLOW ME, MR. JOBS...

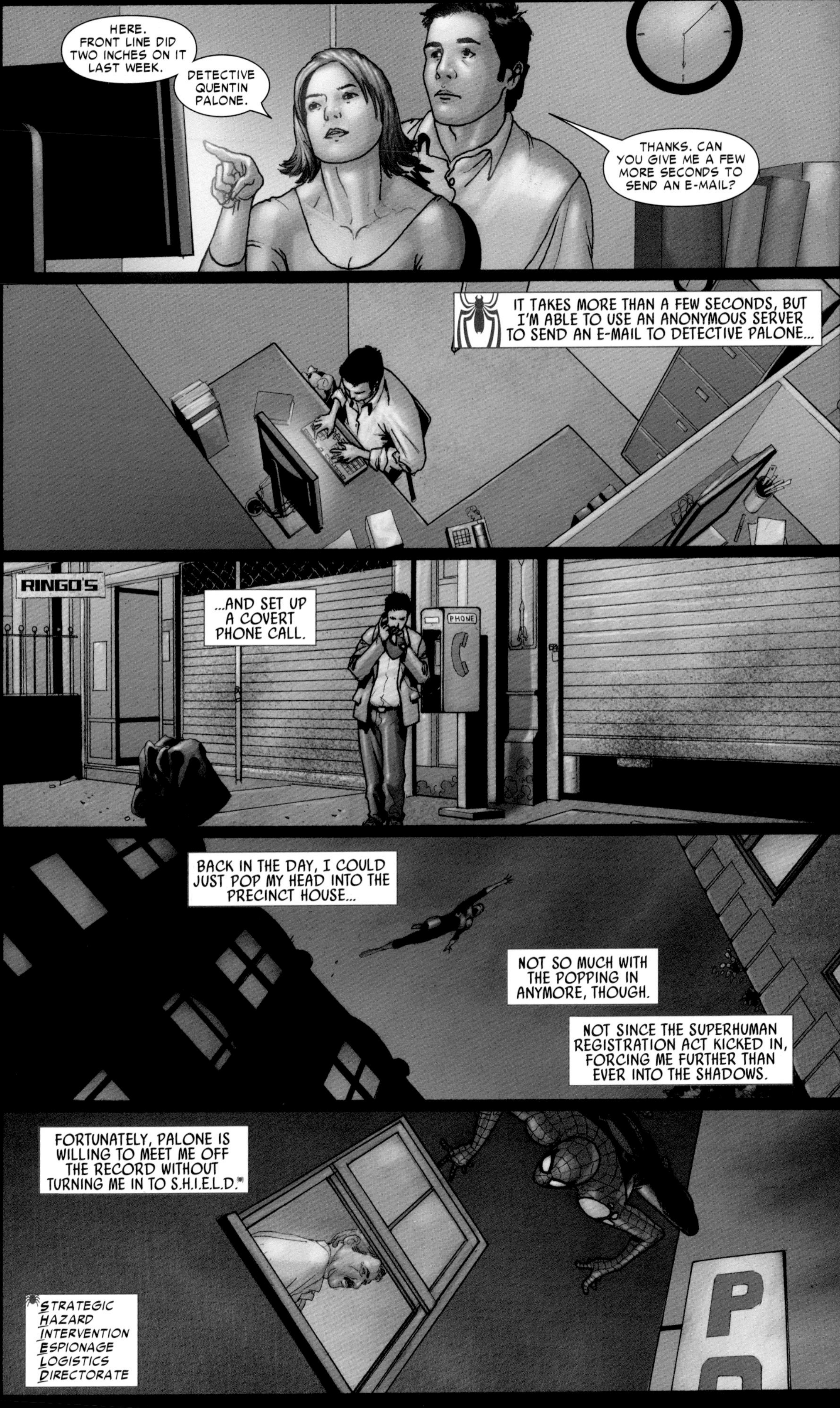
HERE. FRONT LINE DID TWO INCHES ON IT LAST WEEK.
DETECTIVE QUENTIN PALONE.
THANKS. CAN YOU GIVE ME A FEW MORE SECONDS TO SEND AN E-MAIL?
IT TAKES MORE THAN A FEW SECONDS, BUT I'M ABLE TO USE AN ANONYMOUS SERVER TO SEND AN E-MAIL TO DETECTIVE PALONE...
RINGO'S
...AND SET UP A COVERT PHONE CALL.
PHONE
BACK IN THE DAY, I COULD JUST POP MY HEAD INTO THE PRECINCT HOUSE...
NOT SO MUCH WITH THE POPPING IN ANYMORE, THOUGH.
NOT SINCE THE SUPERHUMAN REGISTRATION ACT KICKED IN, FORCING ME FURTHER THAN EVER INTO THE SHADOWS.
FORTUNATELY, PALONE IS WILLING TO MEET ME OFF THE RECORD WITHOUT TURNING ME IN TO S.H.I.E.L.D.*
*STRATEGIC HAZARD INTERVENTION ESPIONAGE LOGISTICS DIRECTORATE
P

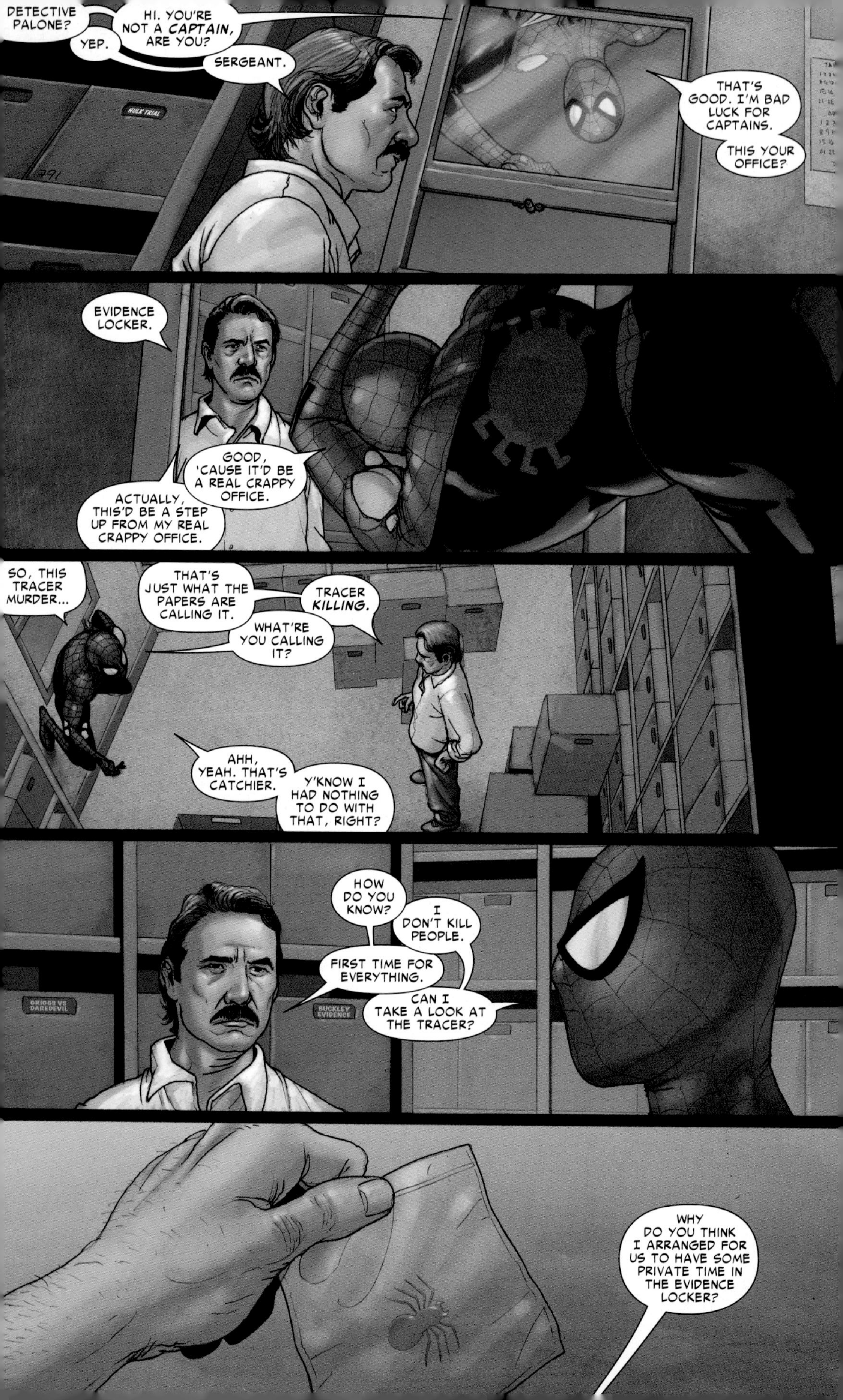
DETECTIVE PALONE?
HI. YOU'RE NOT A *CAPTAIN*, ARE YOU?
YEP.
SERGEANT.
THAT'S GOOD. I'M BAD LUCK FOR CAPTAINS.
THIS YOUR OFFICE?
HULK TRIAL
EVIDENCE LOCKER.
GOOD, 'CAUSE IT'D BE A REAL CRAPPY OFFICE.
ACTUALLY, THIS'D BE A STEP UP FROM MY REAL CRAPPY OFFICE.
SO, THIS TRACER MURDER...
THAT'S JUST WHAT THE PAPERS ARE CALLING IT.
TRACER *KILLING.*
WHAT'RE YOU CALLING IT?
AHH, YEAH. THAT'S CATCHIER.
Y'KNOW I HAD NOTHING TO DO WITH THAT, RIGHT?
HOW DO YOU KNOW?
I DON'T KILL PEOPLE.
FIRST TIME FOR EVERYTHING.
CAN I TAKE A LOOK AT THE TRACER?
GRIGGS VS DAREDEVIL
BUCKLEY EVIDENCE
WHY DO YOU THINK I ARRANGED FOR US TO HAVE SOME PRIVATE TIME IN THE EVIDENCE LOCKER?

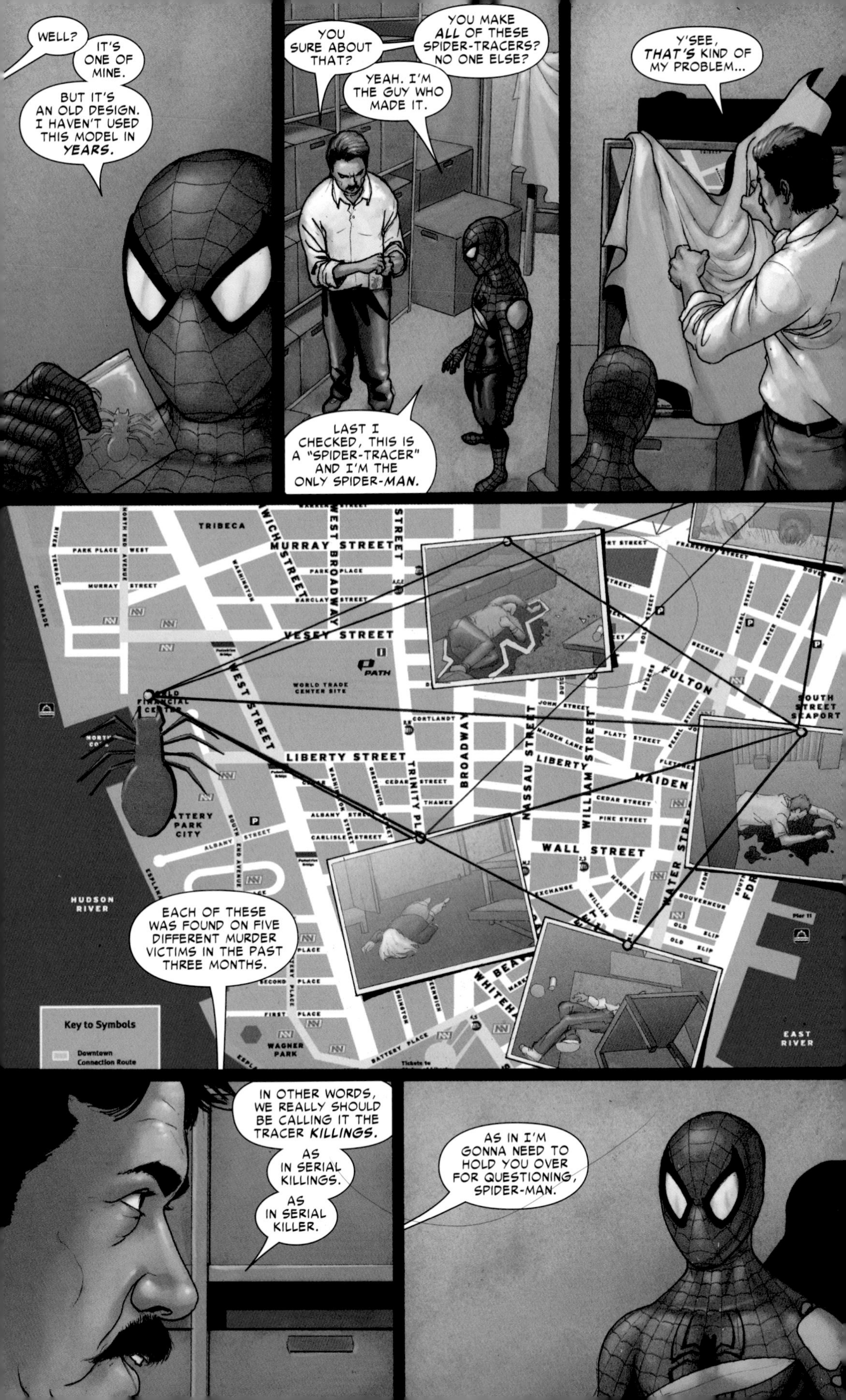
WELL?
IT'S ONE OF MINE.
BUT IT'S AN OLD DESIGN. I HAVEN'T USED THIS MODEL IN *YEARS.*
YOU SURE ABOUT THAT?
YOU MAKE *ALL* OF THESE SPIDER-TRACERS? NO ONE ELSE?
YEAH. I'M THE GUY WHO MADE IT.
LAST I CHECKED, THIS IS A "SPIDER-TRACER" AND I'M THE ONLY SPIDER-*MAN.*
Y'SEE, *THAT'S* KIND OF MY PROBLEM...
TRIBECA
MURRAY STREET
WEST BROADWAY
VESEY STREET
WEST STREET
WORLD TRADE CENTER SITE
PATH
LIBERTY STREET
TRINITY PL
BROADWAY
NASSAU STREET
WILLIAM STREET
MAIDEN LANE
FULTON
MAIDEN
WALL STREET
WATER STREET
SOUTH STREET SEAPORT
FDR
BATTERY PARK CITY
HUDSON RIVER
WAGNER PARK
EAST RIVER
Key to Symbols
Downtown Connection Route
EACH OF THESE WAS FOUND ON FIVE DIFFERENT MURDER VICTIMS IN THE PAST THREE MONTHS.
IN OTHER WORDS, WE REALLY SHOULD BE CALLING IT THE TRACER *KILLINGS.*
AS IN SERIAL KILLINGS.
AS IN SERIAL KILLER.
AS IN I'M GONNA NEED TO HOLD YOU OVER FOR QUESTIONING, SPIDER-MAN.

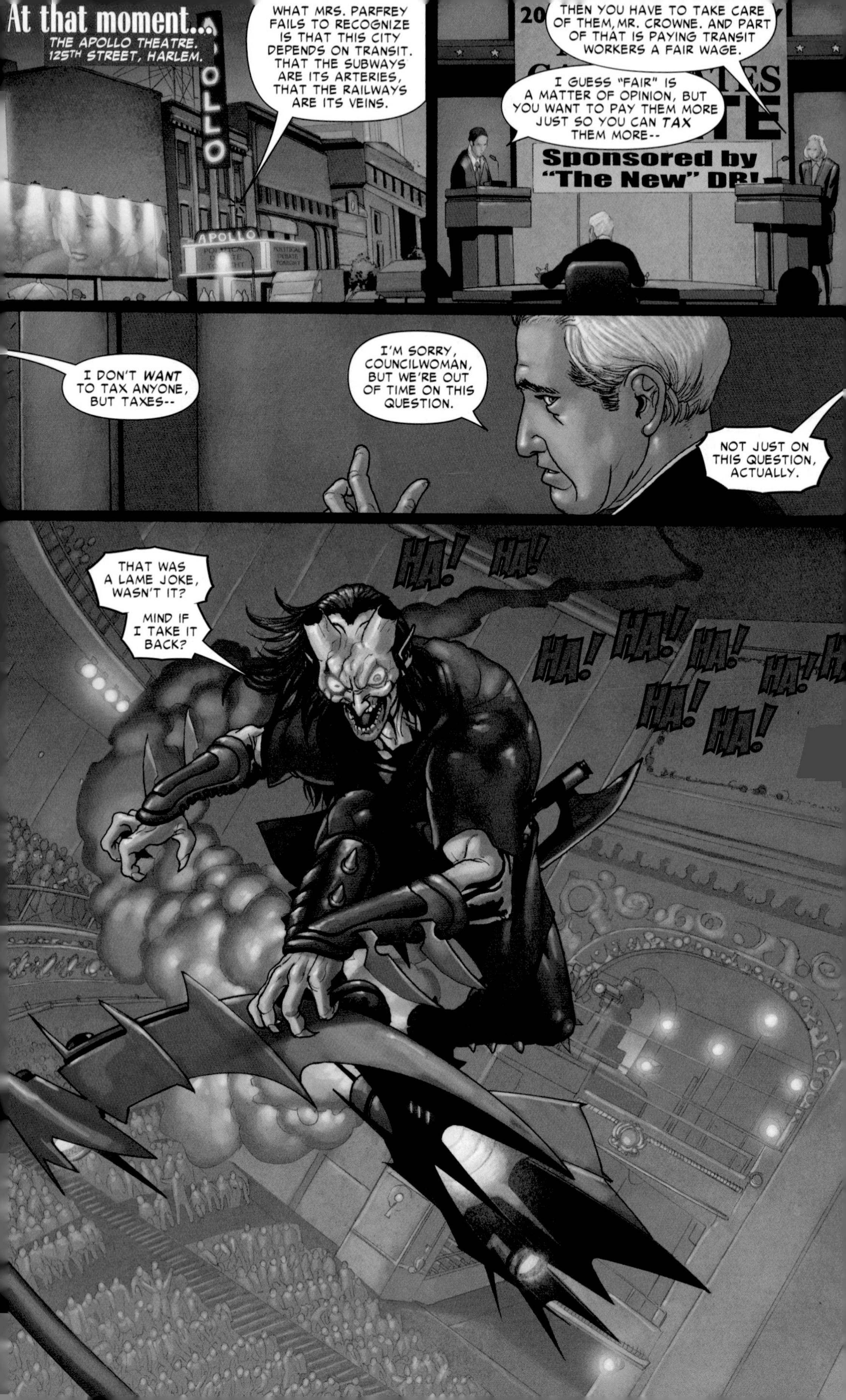

At that moment...
THE APOLLO THEATRE. 125TH STREET, HARLEM.
WHAT MRS. PARFREY FAILS TO RECOGNIZE IS THAT THIS CITY DEPENDS ON TRANSIT. THAT THE SUBWAYS ARE ITS ARTERIES, THAT THE RAILWAYS ARE ITS VEINS.
APOLLO
THEN YOU HAVE TO TAKE CARE OF THEM, MR. CROWNE. AND PART OF THAT IS PAYING TRANSIT WORKERS A FAIR WAGE.
I GUESS "FAIR" IS A MATTER OF OPINION, BUT YOU WANT TO PAY THEM MORE JUST SO YOU CAN TAX THEM MORE--
Sponsored by "The New" DB!
I DON'T WANT TO TAX ANYONE, BUT TAXES--
I'M SORRY, COUNCILWOMAN, BUT WE'RE OUT OF TIME ON THIS QUESTION.
NOT JUST ON THIS QUESTION, ACTUALLY.
THAT WAS A LAME JOKE, WASN'T IT?
MIND IF I TAKE IT BACK?
HA! HA!
HA! HA! HA! HA! HA! HA! HA!

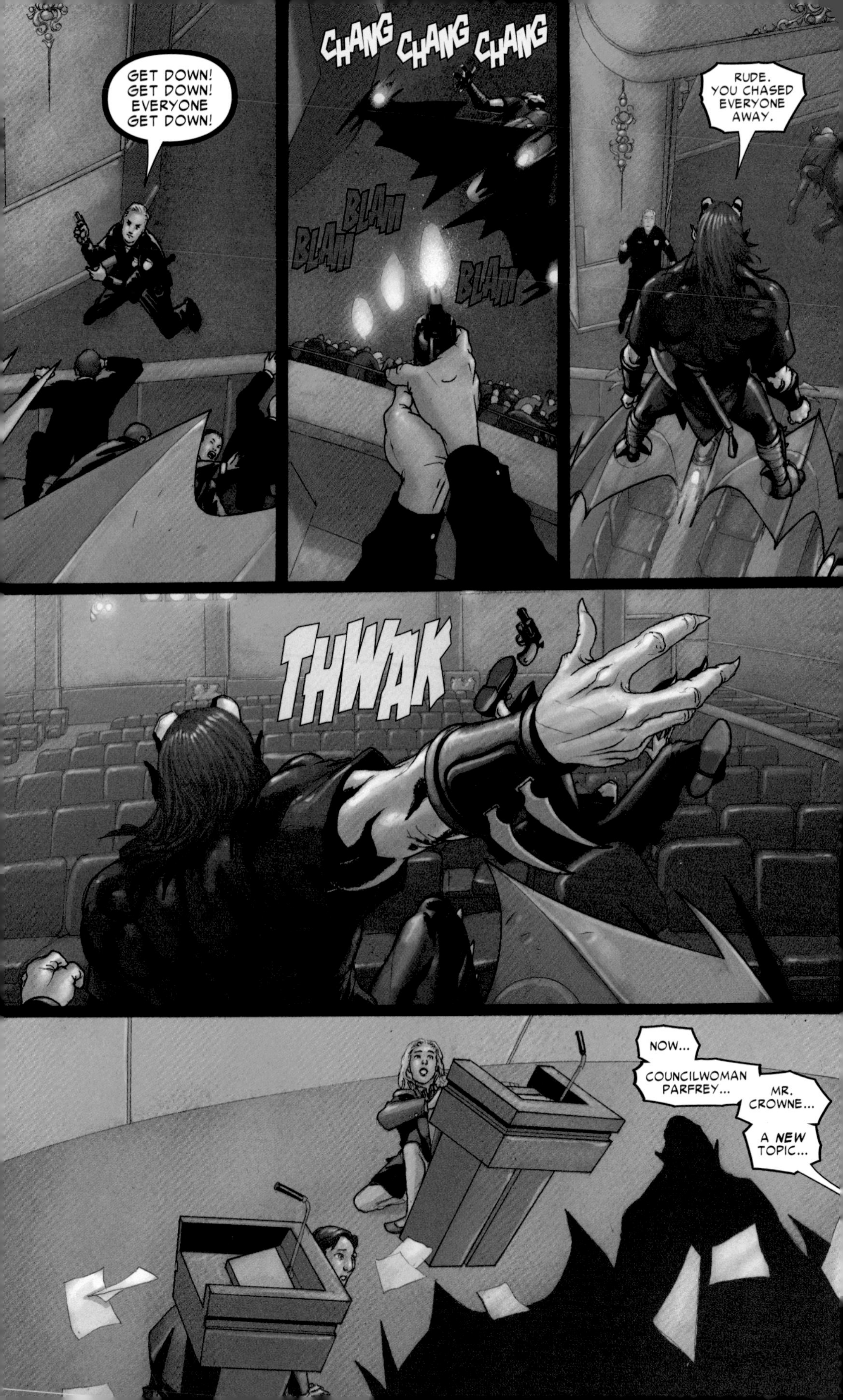
GET DOWN! GET DOWN! EVERYONE GET DOWN!
CHANG CHANG CHANG
BLAM BLAM
BLAM
RUDE. YOU CHASED EVERYONE AWAY.
THWAK
NOW...
COUNCILWOMAN PARFREY...
MR. CROWNE...
A NEW TOPIC...

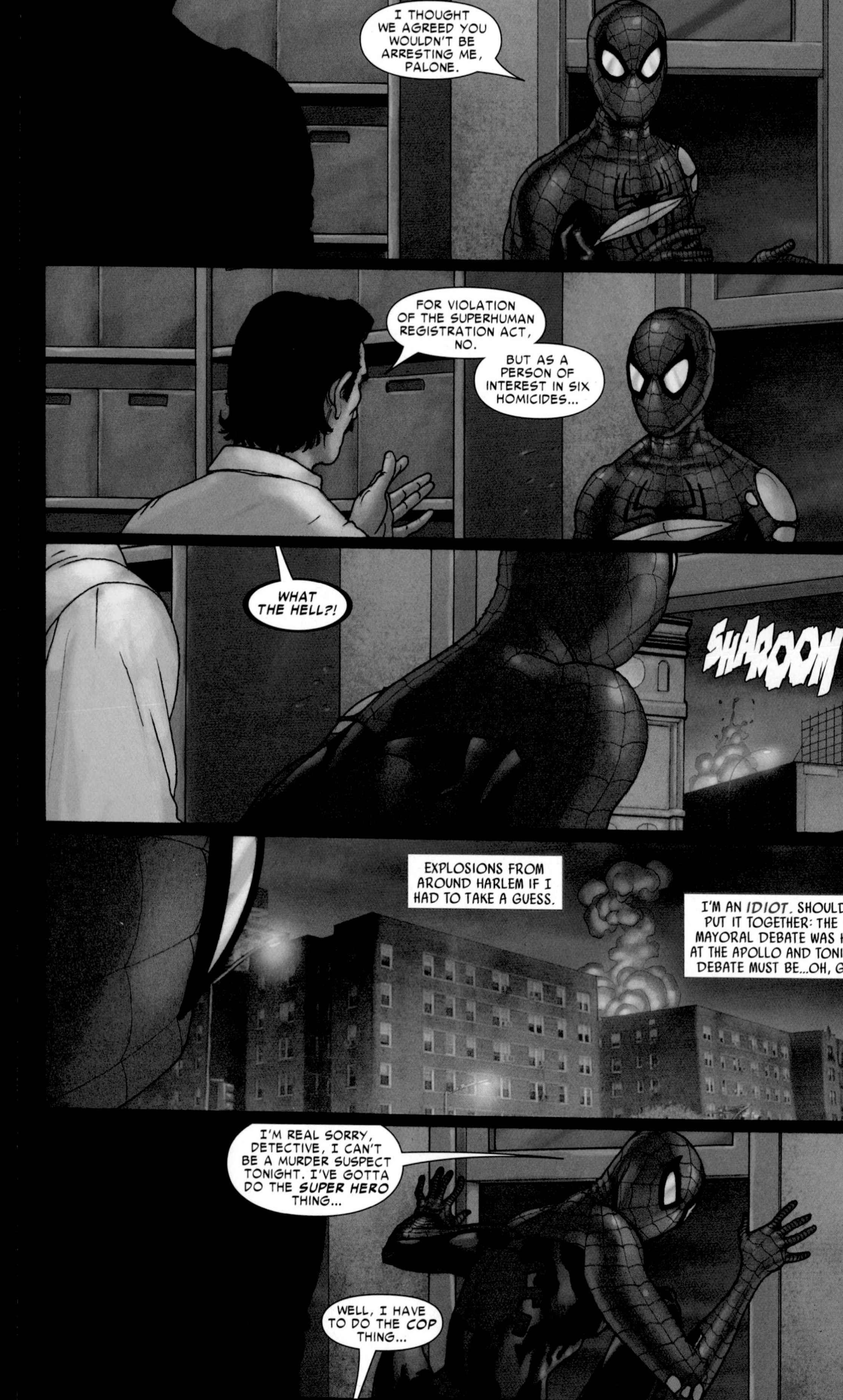
I THOUGHT WE AGREED YOU WOULDN'T BE ARRESTING ME, PALONE.
FOR VIOLATION OF THE SUPERHUMAN REGISTRATION ACT, NO.
BUT AS A PERSON OF INTEREST IN SIX HOMICIDES...
WHAT THE HELL?!
SHAROOM
EXPLOSIONS FROM AROUND HARLEM IF I HAD TO TAKE A GUESS.
I'M AN IDIOT. SHOULD PUT IT TOGETHER: THE MAYORAL DEBATE WAS AT THE APOLLO AND TON DEBATE MUST BE...OH,
I'M REAL SORRY, DETECTIVE, I CAN'T BE A MURDER SUSPECT TONIGHT. I'VE GOTTA DO THE SUPER HERO THING...
WELL, I HAVE TO DO THE COP THING...

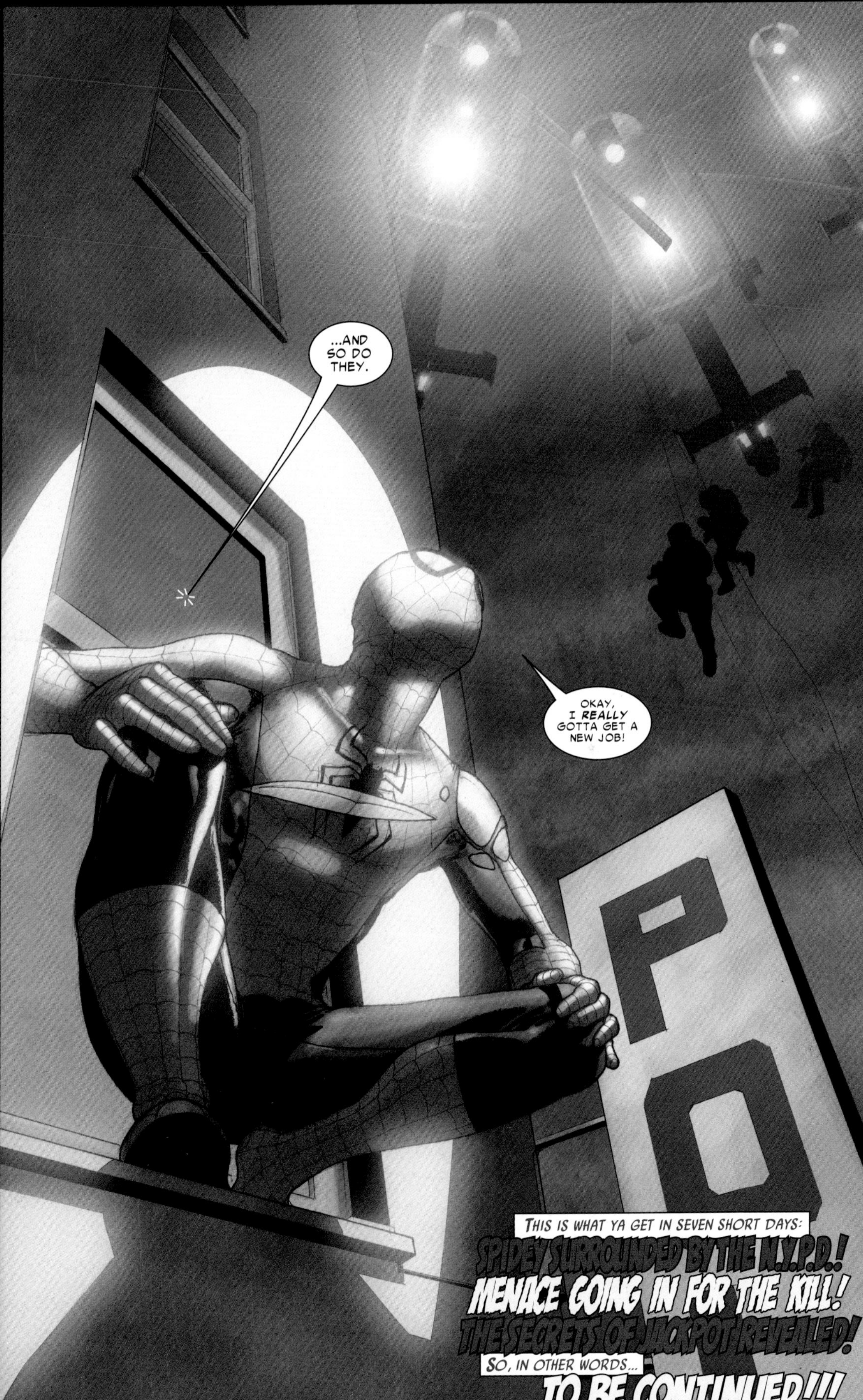
...AND SO DO THEY.
OKAY, I REALLY GOTTA GET A NEW JOB!
THIS IS WHAT YA GET IN SEVEN SHORT DAYS:
SPIDEY SURROUNDED BY THE N.Y.P.D.!
MENACE GOING IN FOR THE KILL!
THE SECRETS OF JACKPOT REVEALED!
SO, IN OTHER WORDS...
TO BE CONTINUED!!!

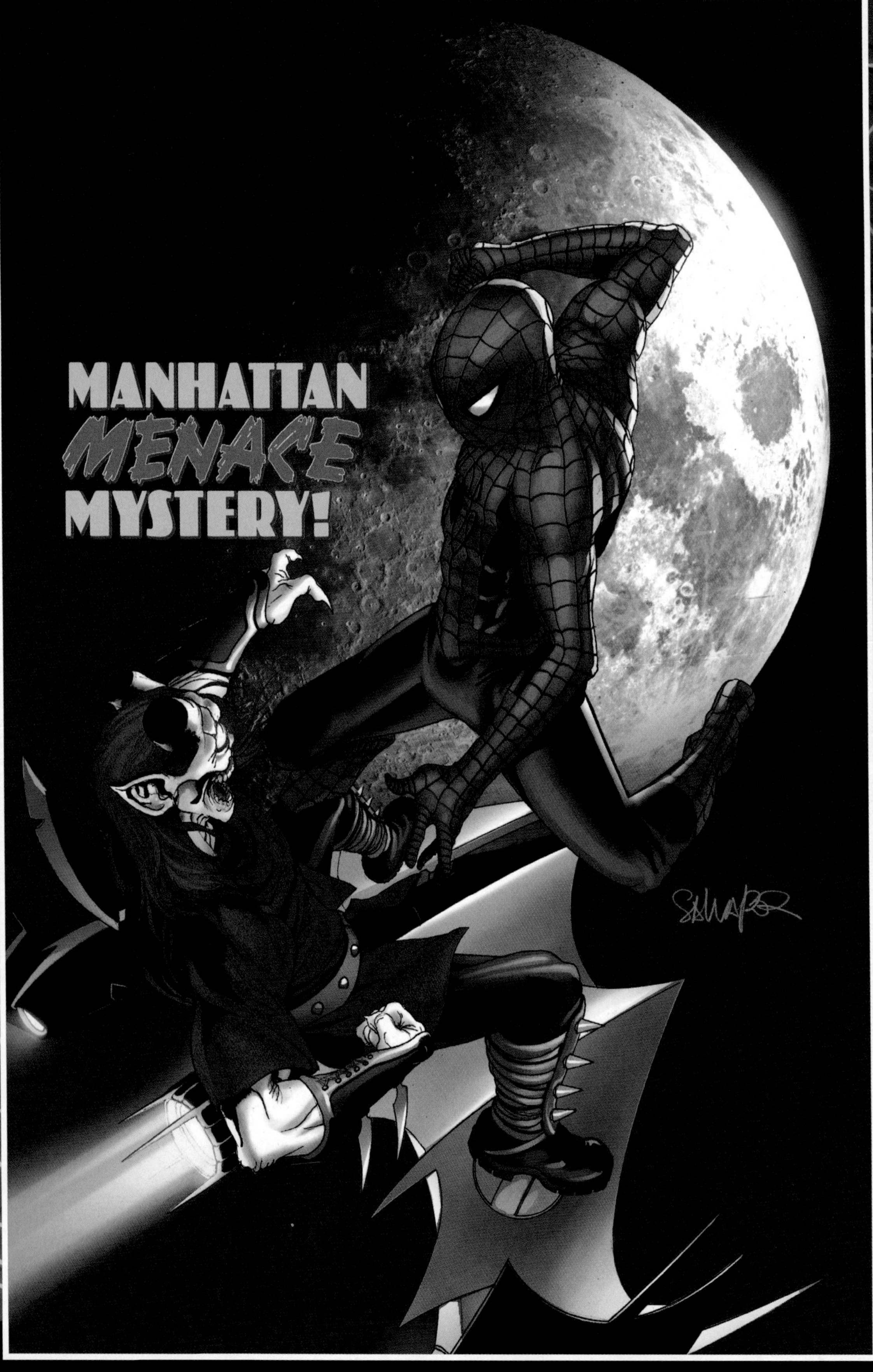
MANHATTAN
MENACE
MYSTERY!

AMAZING SPIDER-MAN #551

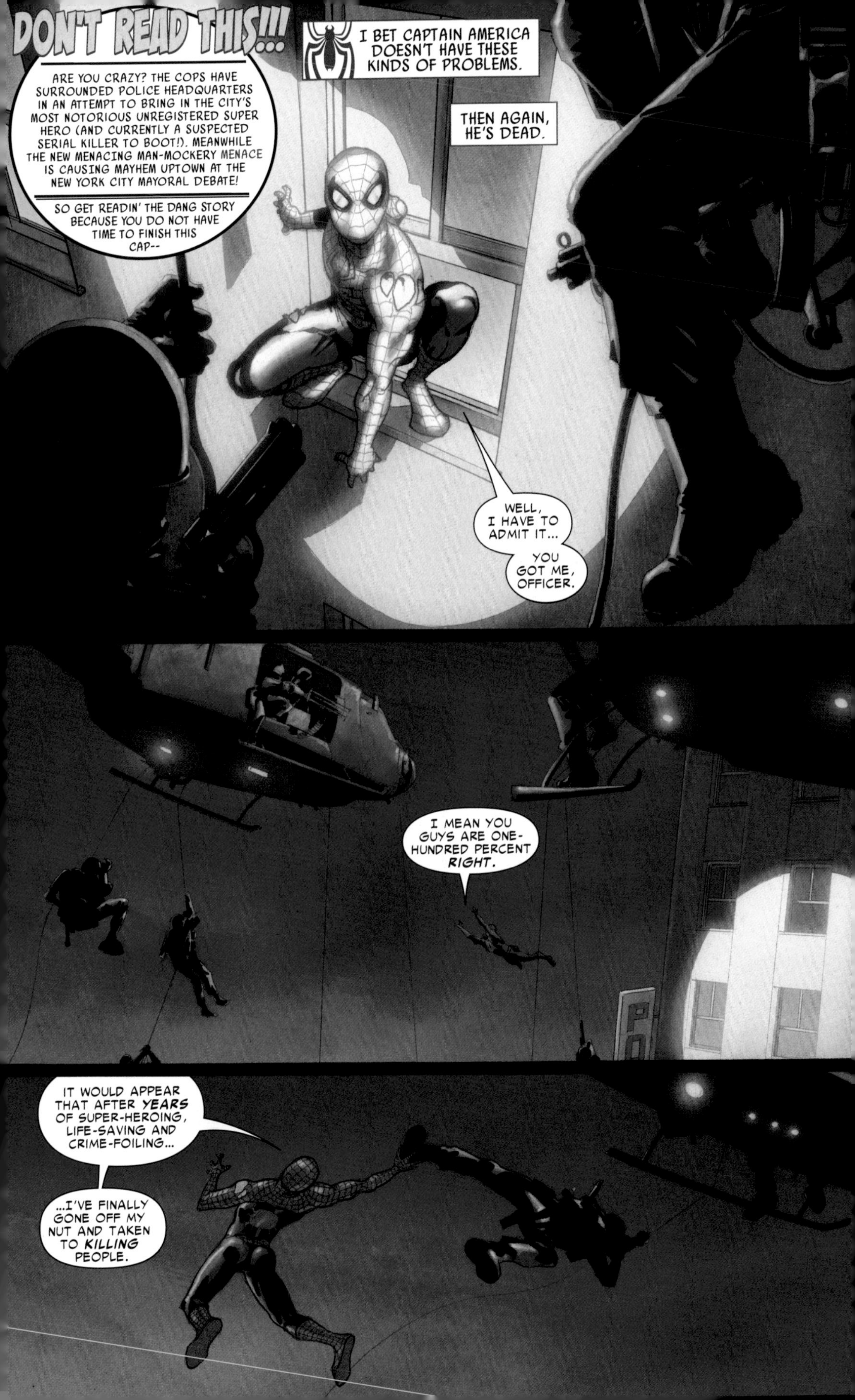
DON'T READ THIS!!!
ARE YOU CRAZY? THE COPS HAVE SURROUNDED POLICE HEADQUARTERS IN AN ATTEMPT TO BRING IN THE CITY'S MOST NOTORIOUS UNREGISTERED SUPER HERO (AND CURRENTLY A SUSPECTED SERIAL KILLER TO BOOT!). MEANWHILE THE NEW MENACING MAN-MOCKERY MENACE IS CAUSING MAYHEM UPTOWN AT THE NEW YORK CITY MAYORAL DEBATE!
SO GET READIN' THE DANG STORY BECAUSE YOU DO NOT HAVE TIME TO FINISH THIS CAP--
I BET CAPTAIN AMERICA DOESN'T HAVE THESE KINDS OF PROBLEMS.
THEN AGAIN, HE'S DEAD.
WELL, I HAVE TO ADMIT IT...
YOU GOT ME, OFFICER.
I MEAN YOU GUYS ARE ONE-HUNDRED PERCENT *RIGHT*.
IT WOULD APPEAR THAT AFTER *YEARS* OF SUPER-HEROING, LIFE-SAVING AND CRIME-FOILING...
...I'VE FINALLY GONE OFF MY NUT AND TAKEN TO *KILLING* PEOPLE.

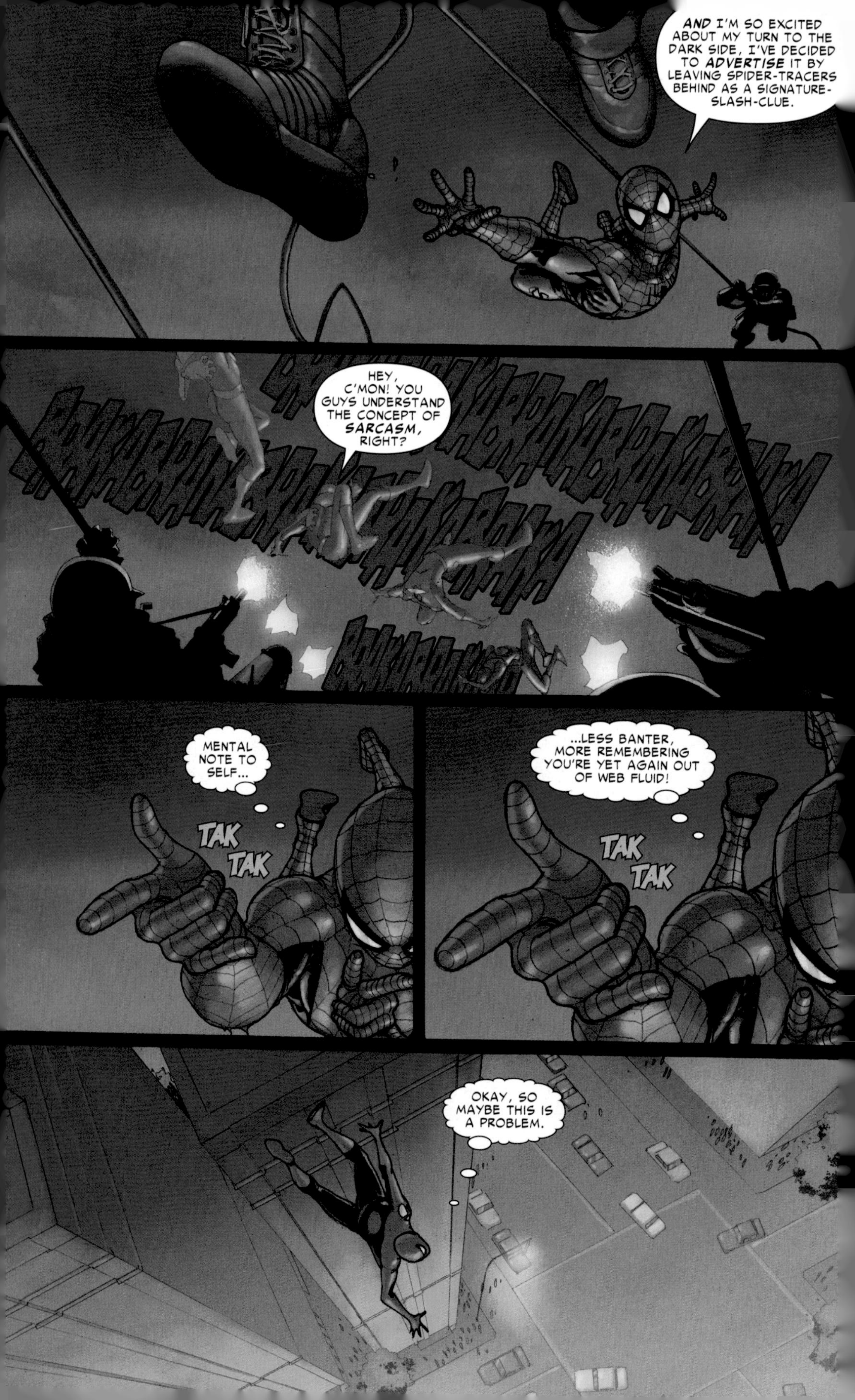
AND I'M SO EXCITED ABOUT MY TURN TO THE DARK SIDE, I'VE DECIDED TO ADVERTISE IT BY LEAVING SPIDER-TRACERS BEHIND AS A SIGNATURE-SLASH-CLUE.
HEY, C'MON! YOU GUYS UNDERSTAND THE CONCEPT OF SARCASM, RIGHT?
MENTAL NOTE TO SELF...
TAK
TAK
...LESS BANTER, MORE REMEMBERING YOU'RE YET AGAIN OUT OF WEB FLUID!
TAK
TAK
OKAY, SO MAYBE THIS IS A PROBLEM.

HEY TIGER...

IT'S JACKPOT! MISS ME?

LO, THERE SHALL COME A MENACE!!

MARC GUGGENHEIM
WRITER

SALVADOR LARROCA
ART AND COVER

STEPHANE PERU COLORS	VC'S CORY PETIT LETTERS	JASON KEITH COVER COLORS
TOM BRENNAN ASSISTANT EDITOR	STEPHEN WACKER "EDITOR"	TOM BREVOORT EXECUTIVE EDITOR
JOE QUESADA EDITOR IN CHIEF	GALE, GUGGENHEIM, SLOTT & WELLS SPIDEY'S BRAINTRUST	DAN BUCKLEY PUBLISHER

WHILE ATTENDING A DEMONSTRATION IN RADIOLOGY, HIGH SCHOOL STUDENT **PETER PARKER** WAS BITTEN BY A SPIDER WHICH HAD ACCIDENTALLY BEEN EXPOSED TO **RADIOACTIVE RAYS.** THROUGH A MIRACLE OF SCIENCE, PETER SOON FOUND THAT HE HAD **GAINED** THE SPIDER'S POWERS...AND HAD, IN EFFECT, BECOME A HUMAN SPIDER! FROM THAT DAY ON HE WAS...

THE AMAZING SPIDER-MAN™

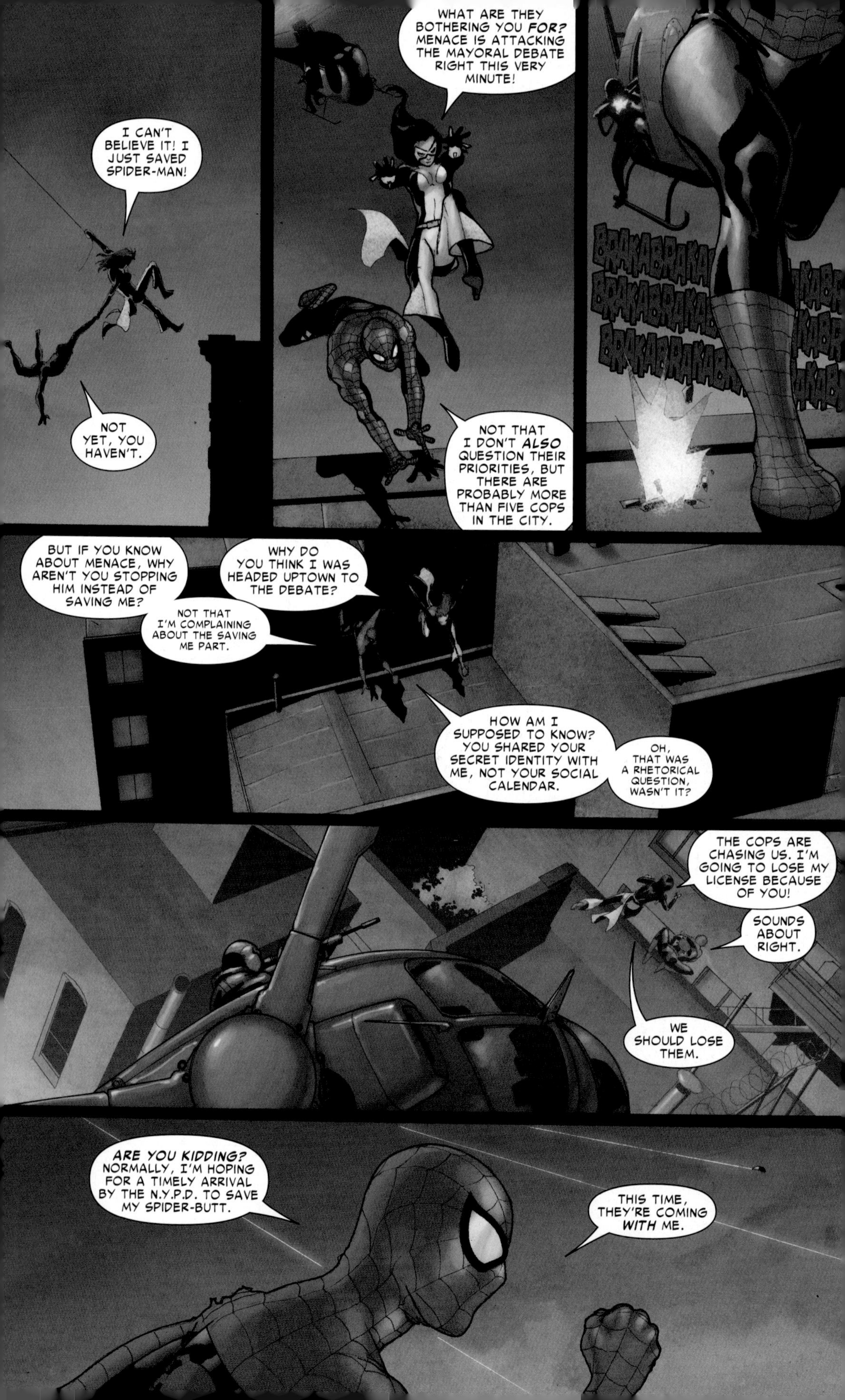
I CAN'T BELIEVE IT! I JUST SAVED SPIDER-MAN!
NOT YET, YOU HAVEN'T.
WHAT ARE THEY BOTHERING YOU FOR? MENACE IS ATTACKING THE MAYORAL DEBATE RIGHT THIS VERY MINUTE!
NOT THAT I DON'T ALSO QUESTION THEIR PRIORITIES, BUT THERE ARE PROBABLY MORE THAN FIVE COPS IN THE CITY.
BRAKABRAKABRAKA
BUT IF YOU KNOW ABOUT MENACE, WHY AREN'T YOU STOPPING HIM INSTEAD OF SAVING ME?
NOT THAT I'M COMPLAINING ABOUT THE SAVING ME PART.
WHY DO YOU THINK I WAS HEADED UPTOWN TO THE DEBATE?
HOW AM I SUPPOSED TO KNOW? YOU SHARED YOUR SECRET IDENTITY WITH ME, NOT YOUR SOCIAL CALENDAR.
OH, THAT WAS A RHETORICAL QUESTION, WASN'T IT?
THE COPS ARE CHASING US. I'M GOING TO LOSE MY LICENSE BECAUSE OF YOU!
SOUNDS ABOUT RIGHT.
WE SHOULD LOSE THEM.
ARE YOU KIDDING? NORMALLY, I'M HOPING FOR A TIMELY ARRIVAL BY THE N.Y.P.D. TO SAVE MY SPIDER-BUTT.
THIS TIME, THEY'RE COMING WITH ME.

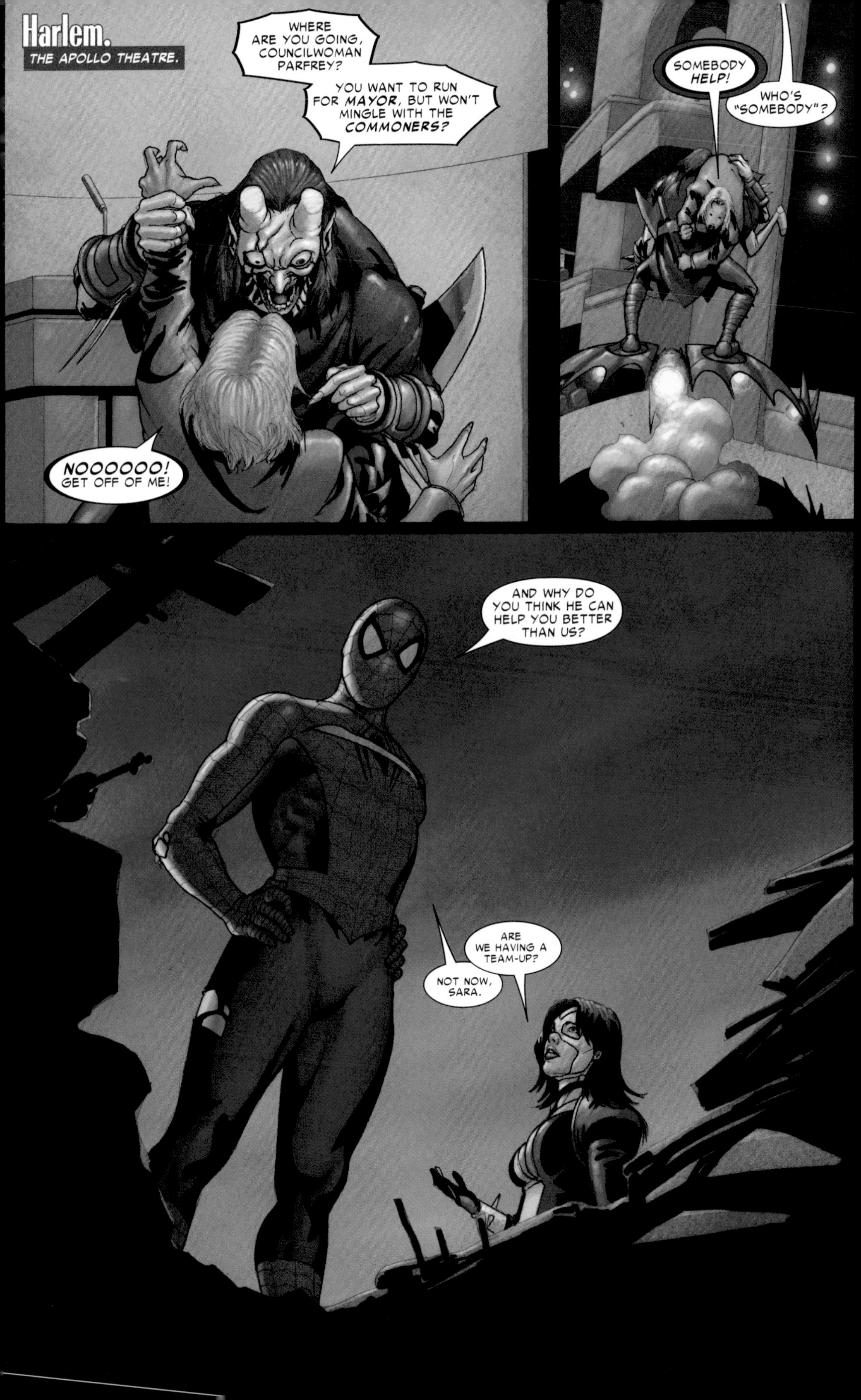
Harlem.
THE APOLLO THEATRE.
WHERE ARE YOU GOING, COUNCILWOMAN PARFREY?
YOU WANT TO RUN FOR MAYOR, BUT WON'T MINGLE WITH THE COMMONERS?
NOOOOOO! GET OFF OF ME!
SOMEBODY HELP!
WHO'S "SOMEBODY"?
AND WHY DO YOU THINK HE CAN HELP YOU BETTER THAN US?
ARE WE HAVING A TEAM-UP?
NOT NOW, SARA.

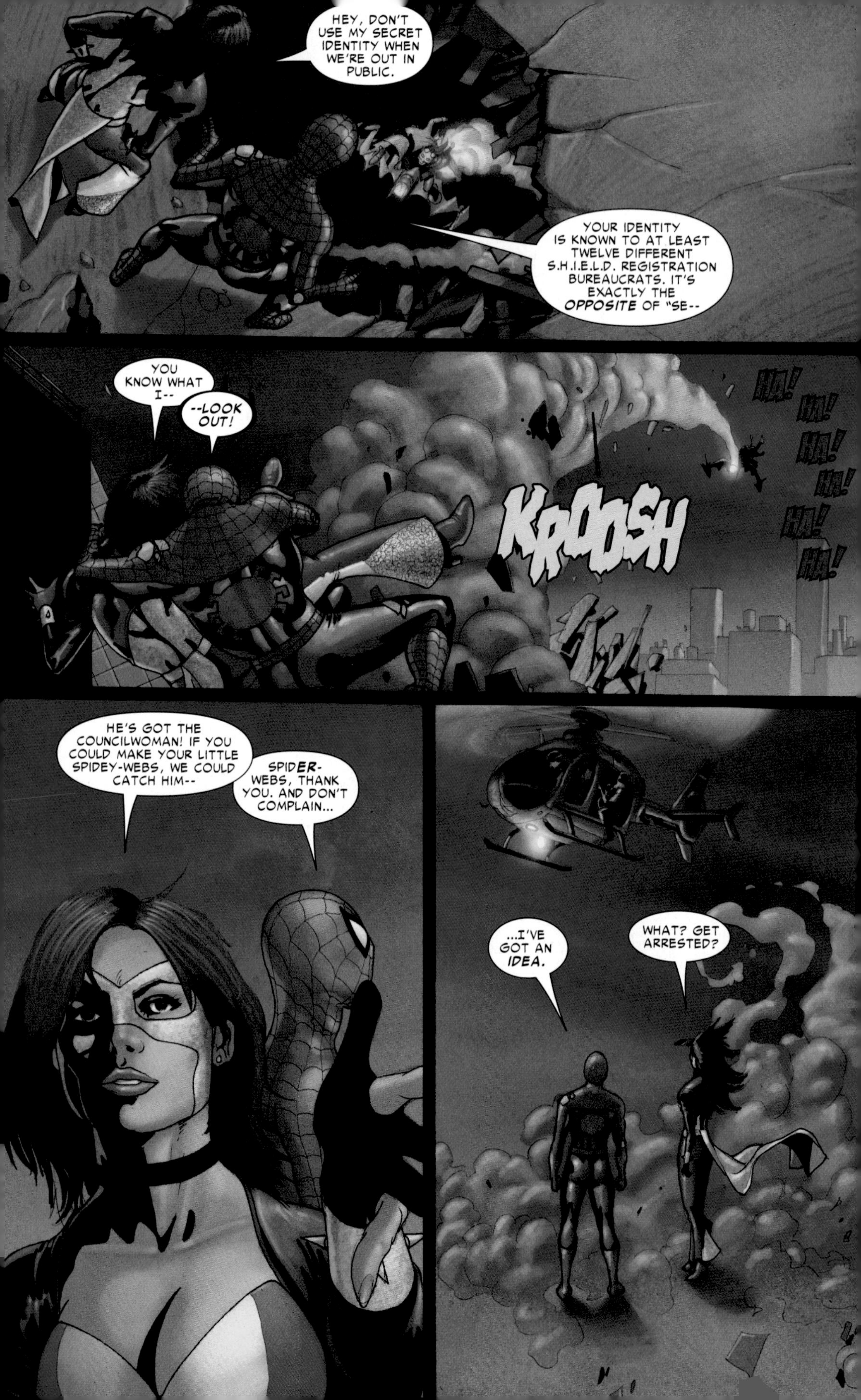
HEY, DON'T USE MY SECRET IDENTITY WHEN WE'RE OUT IN PUBLIC.
YOUR IDENTITY IS KNOWN TO AT LEAST TWELVE DIFFERENT S.H.I.E.L.D. REGISTRATION BUREAUCRATS. IT'S EXACTLY THE *OPPOSITE* OF "SE--
YOU KNOW WHAT I--
--LOOK OUT!
KROOSH
HA! HA! HA! HA! HA! HA!
HE'S GOT THE COUNCILWOMAN! IF YOU COULD MAKE YOUR LITTLE SPIDEY-WEBS, WE COULD CATCH HIM--
SPID*ER*-WEBS, THANK YOU. AND DON'T COMPLAIN...
...I'VE GOT AN *IDEA.*
WHAT? GET ARRESTED?

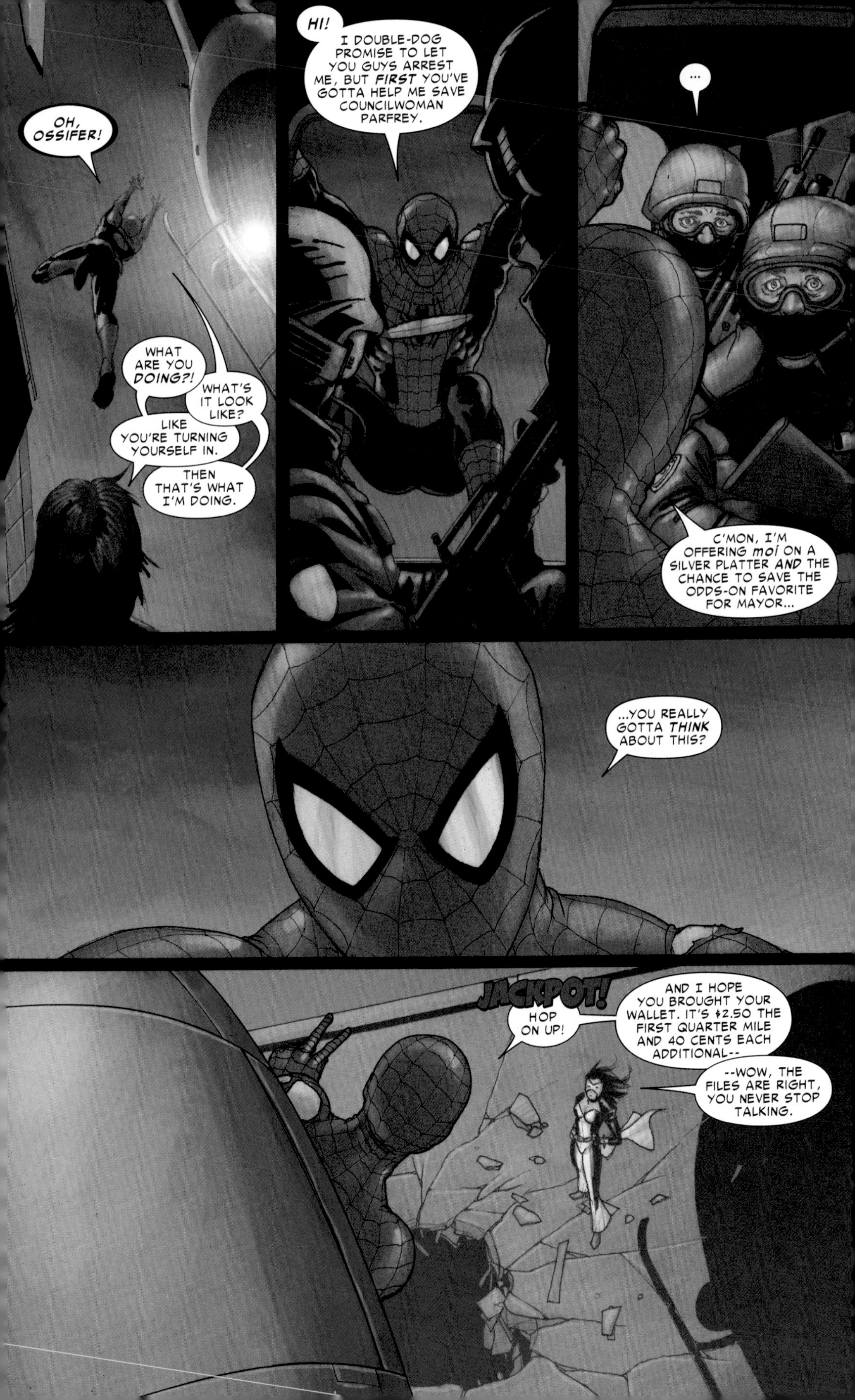
OH, OSSIFER!
WHAT ARE YOU DOING?!
WHAT'S IT LOOK LIKE?
LIKE YOU'RE TURNING YOURSELF IN.
THEN THAT'S WHAT I'M DOING.
HI!
I DOUBLE-DOG PROMISE TO LET YOU GUYS ARREST ME, BUT FIRST YOU'VE GOTTA HELP ME SAVE COUNCILWOMAN PARFREY.
...
C'MON, I'M OFFERING moi ON A SILVER PLATTER AND THE CHANCE TO SAVE THE ODDS-ON FAVORITE FOR MAYOR...
...YOU REALLY GOTTA THINK ABOUT THIS?
JACKPOT!
HOP ON UP!
AND I HOPE YOU BROUGHT YOUR WALLET. IT'S $2.50 THE FIRST QUARTER MILE AND 40 CENTS EACH ADDITIONAL--
--WOW, THE FILES ARE RIGHT, YOU NEVER STOP TALKING.

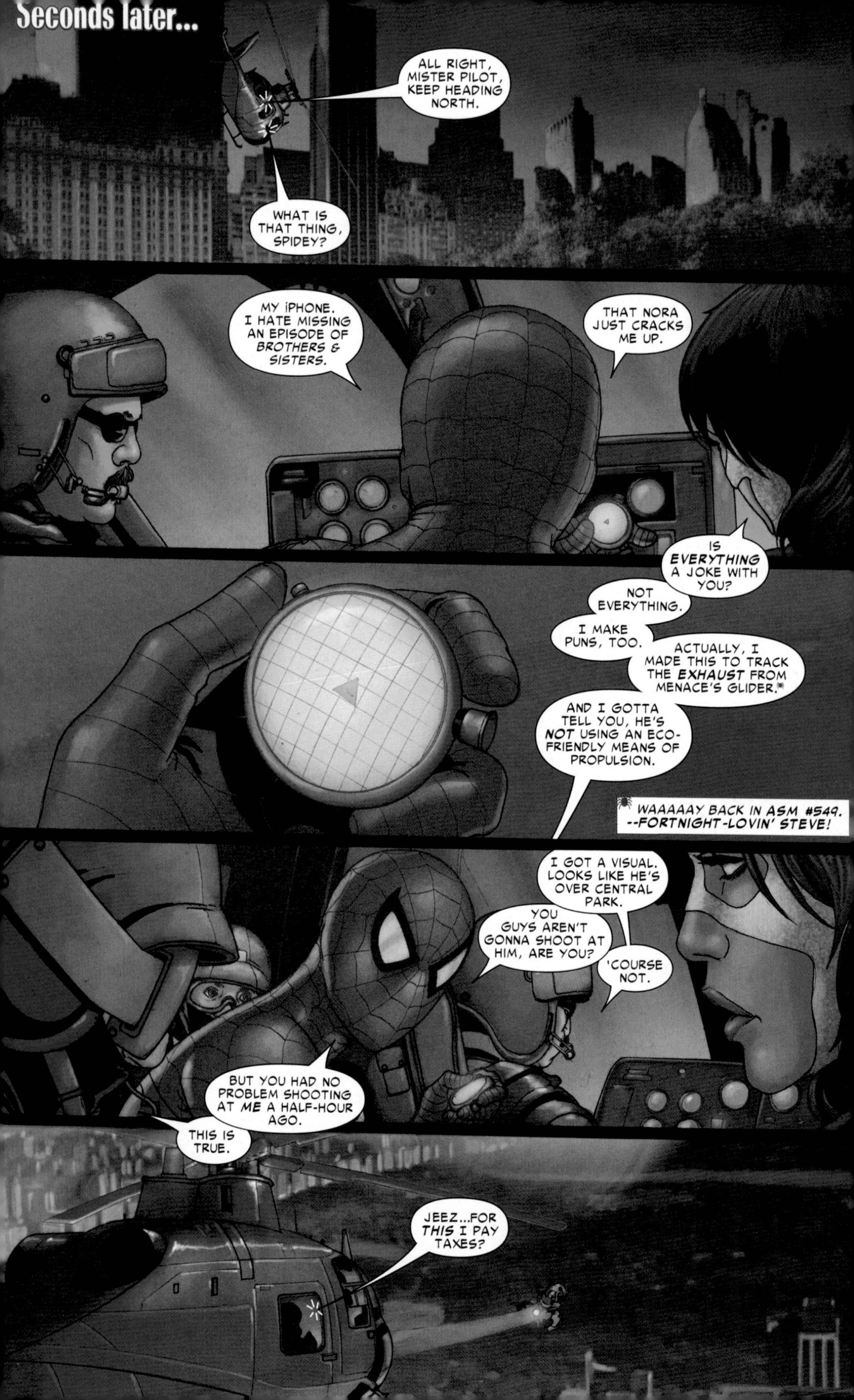
Seconds later...
ALL RIGHT, MISTER PILOT, KEEP HEADING NORTH.
WHAT IS THAT THING, SPIDEY?
MY iPHONE. I HATE MISSING AN EPISODE OF BROTHERS & SISTERS.
THAT NORA JUST CRACKS ME UP.
IS EVERYTHING A JOKE WITH YOU?
NOT EVERYTHING.
I MAKE PUNS, TOO.
ACTUALLY, I MADE THIS TO TRACK THE EXHAUST FROM MENACE'S GLIDER.*
AND I GOTTA TELL YOU, HE'S NOT USING AN ECO-FRIENDLY MEANS OF PROPULSION.
WAAAAAY BACK IN ASM #549. --FORTNIGHT-LOVIN' STEVE!
I GOT A VISUAL. LOOKS LIKE HE'S OVER CENTRAL PARK.
YOU GUYS AREN'T GONNA SHOOT AT HIM, ARE YOU?
'COURSE NOT.
BUT YOU HAD NO PROBLEM SHOOTING AT ME A HALF-HOUR AGO.
THIS IS TRUE.
JEEZ...FOR THIS I PAY TAXES?

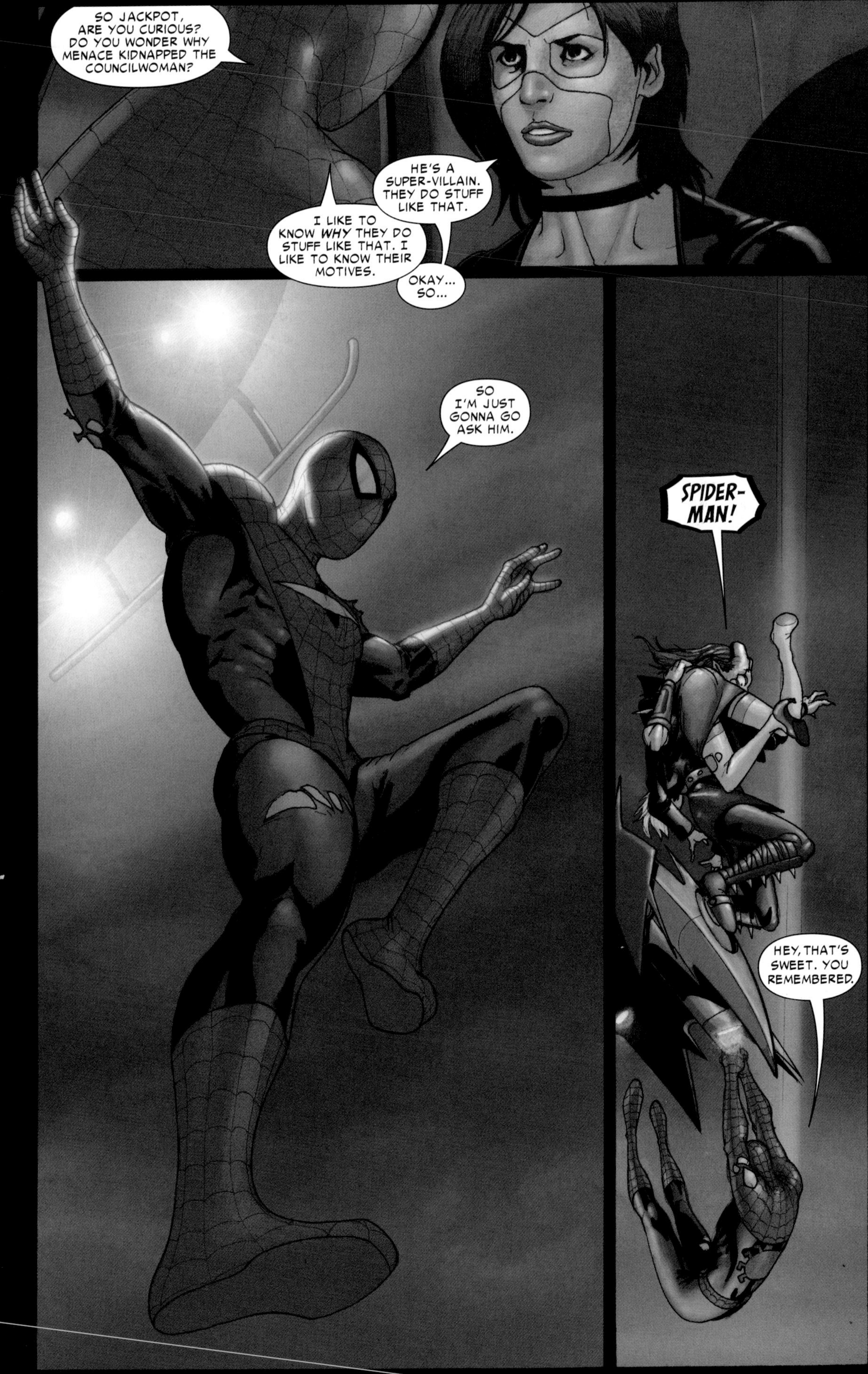
SO JACKPOT, ARE YOU CURIOUS? DO YOU WONDER WHY MENACE KIDNAPPED THE COUNCILWOMAN?
HE'S A SUPER-VILLAIN. THEY DO STUFF LIKE THAT.
I LIKE TO KNOW WHY THEY DO STUFF LIKE THAT. I LIKE TO KNOW THEIR MOTIVES.
OKAY... SO...
SO I'M JUST GONNA GO ASK HIM.
SPIDER-MAN!
HEY, THAT'S SWEET. YOU REMEMBERED.

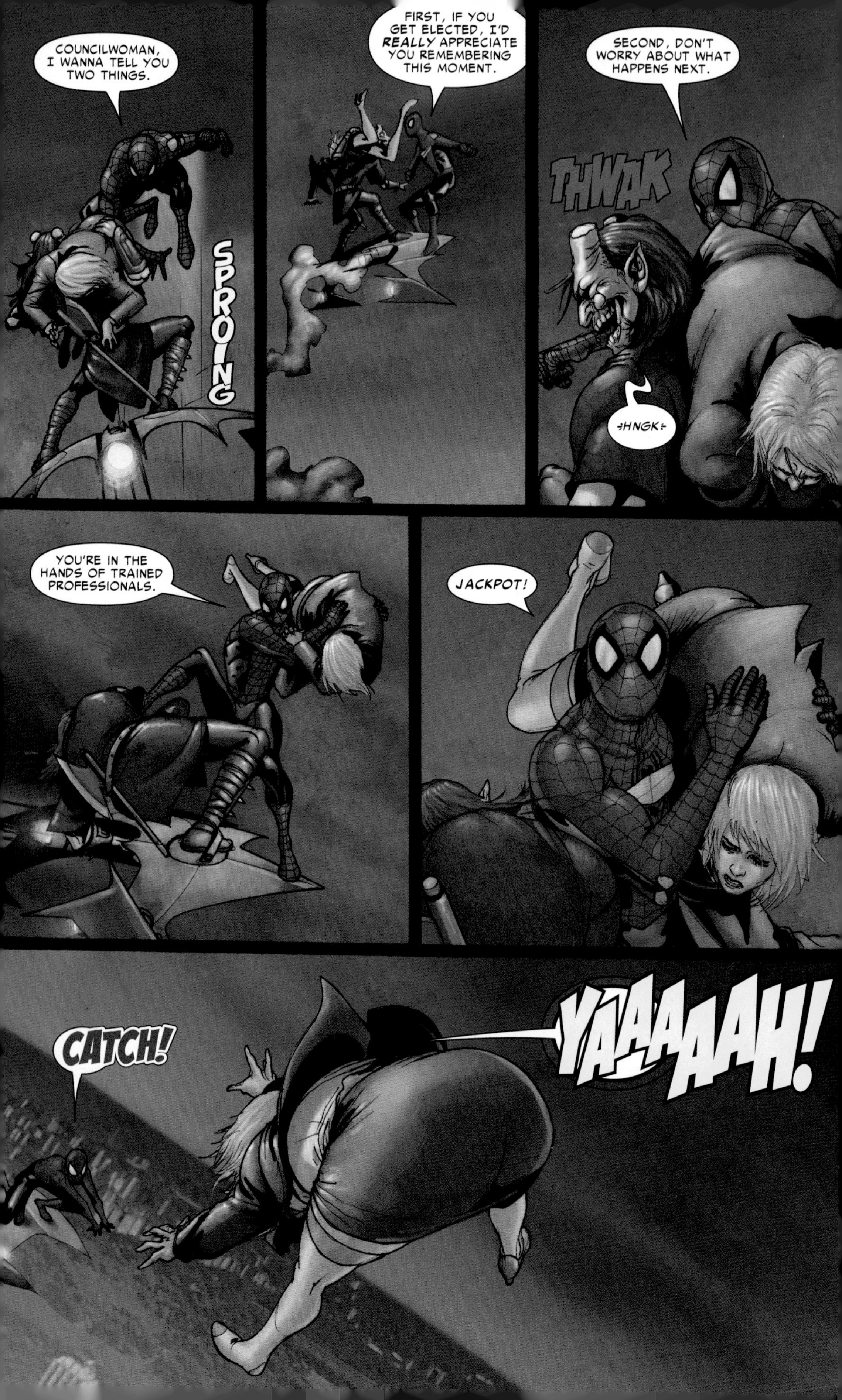
COUNCILWOMAN, I WANNA TELL YOU TWO THINGS.
SPROING
FIRST, IF YOU GET ELECTED, I'D *REALLY* APPRECIATE YOU REMEMBERING THIS MOMENT.
SECOND, DON'T WORRY ABOUT WHAT HAPPENS NEXT.
THWAK
HNGK
YOU'RE IN THE HANDS OF TRAINED PROFESSIONALS.
JACKPOT!
CATCH!
YAAAAAH!

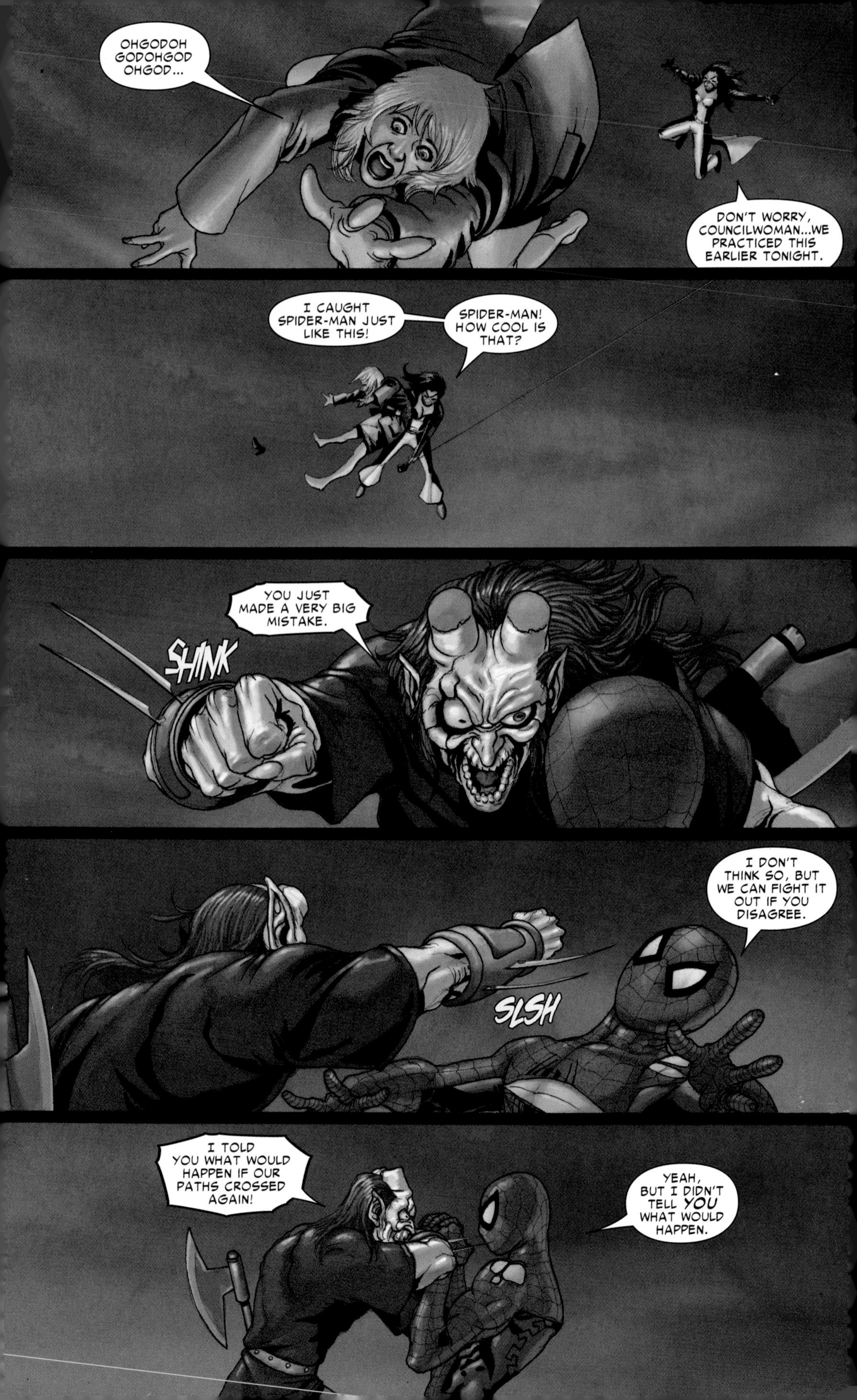
OHGODOH GODOHGOD OHGOD...
DON'T WORRY, COUNCILWOMAN...WE PRACTICED THIS EARLIER TONIGHT.
I CAUGHT SPIDER-MAN JUST LIKE THIS!
SPIDER-MAN! HOW COOL IS THAT?
YOU JUST MADE A VERY BIG MISTAKE.
SHINK
I DON'T THINK SO, BUT WE CAN FIGHT IT OUT IF YOU DISAGREE.
SLSH
I TOLD YOU WHAT WOULD HAPPEN IF OUR PATHS CROSSED AGAIN!
YEAH, BUT I DIDN'T TELL YOU WHAT WOULD HAPPEN.

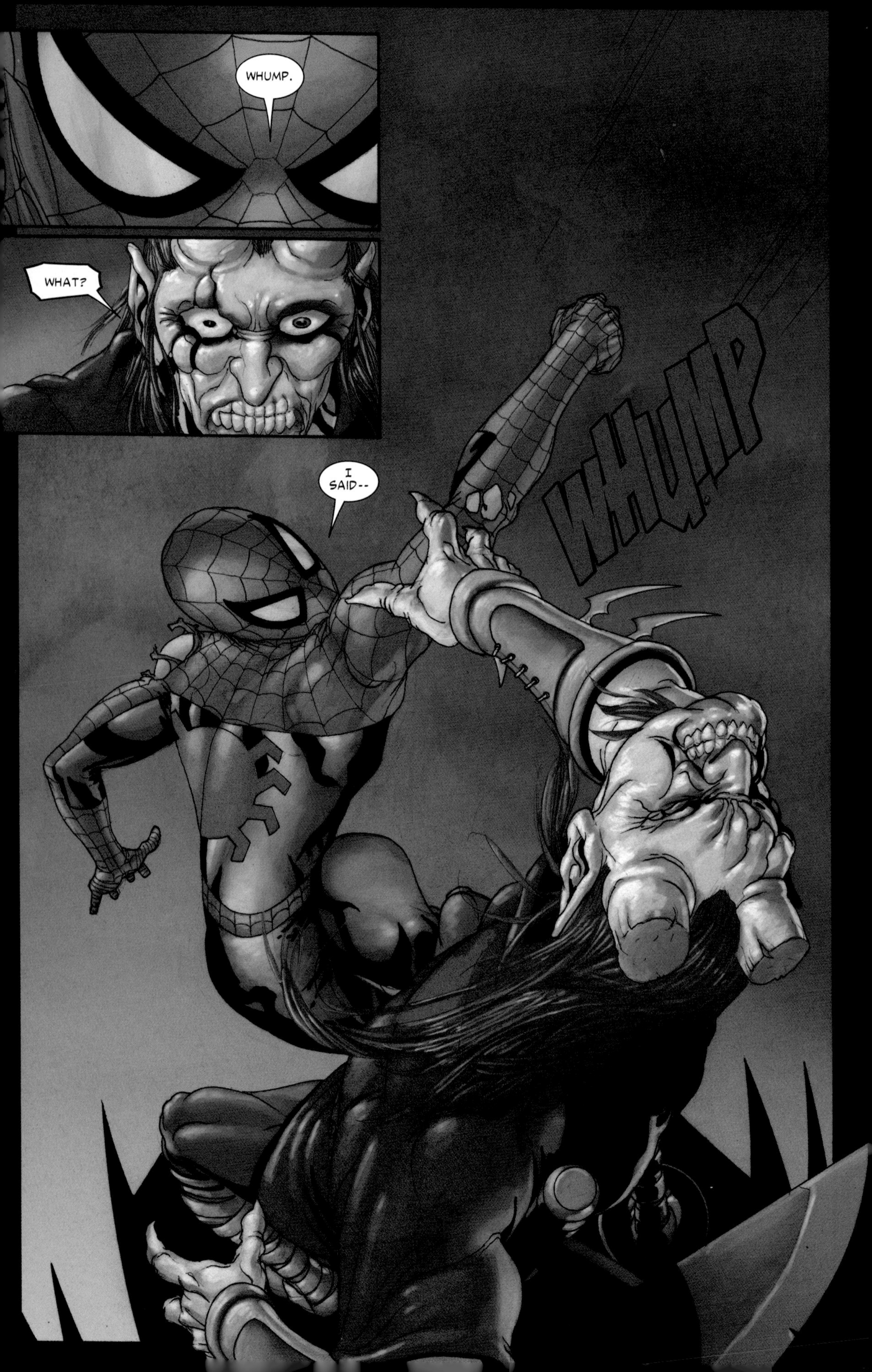
WHUMP.
WHAT?
I SAID--
WHUMP

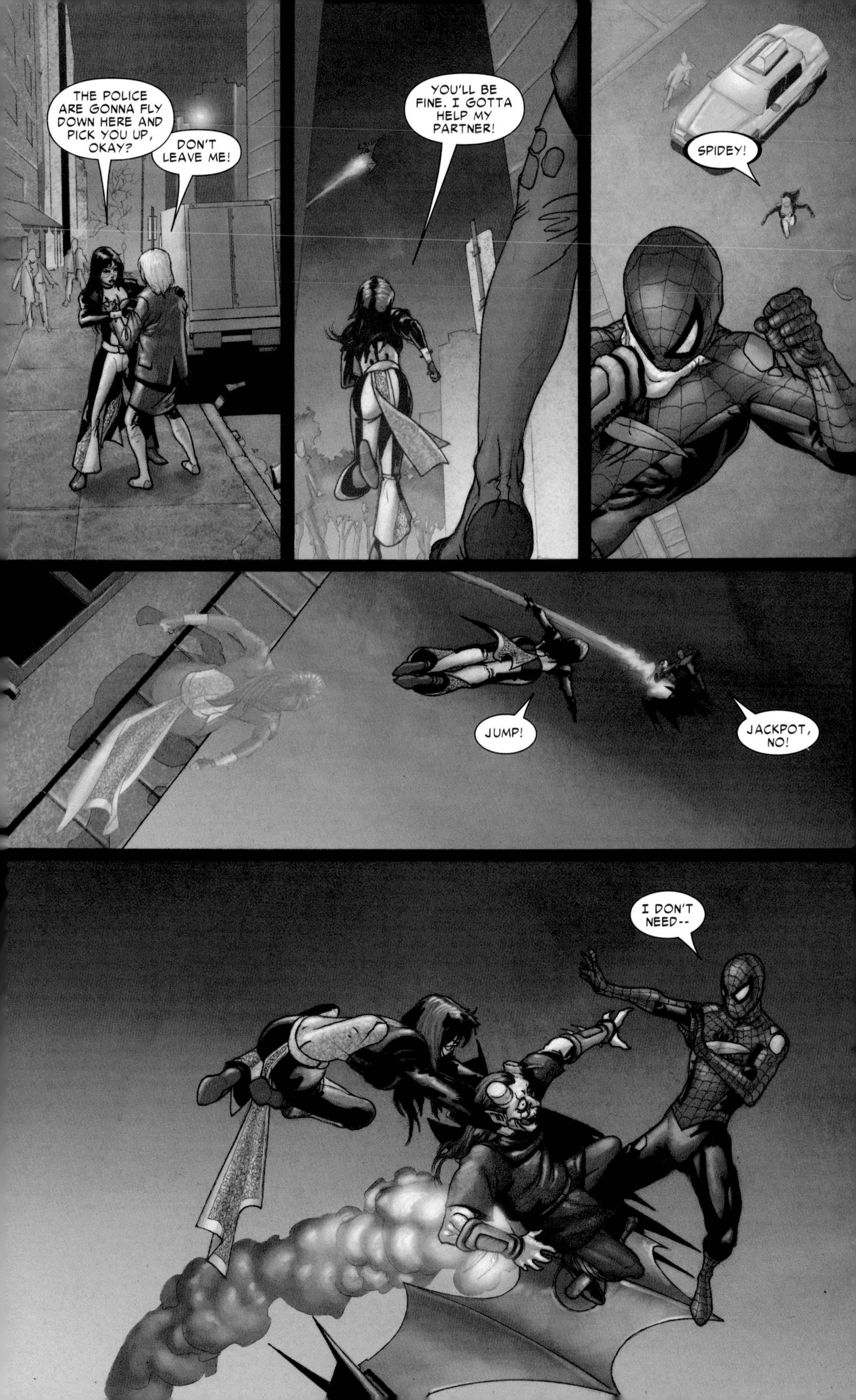
THE POLICE ARE GONNA FLY DOWN HERE AND PICK YOU UP, OKAY?
DON'T LEAVE ME!
YOU'LL BE FINE. I GOTTA HELP MY PARTNER!
SPIDEY!
JUMP!
JACKPOT, NO!
I DON'T NEED--

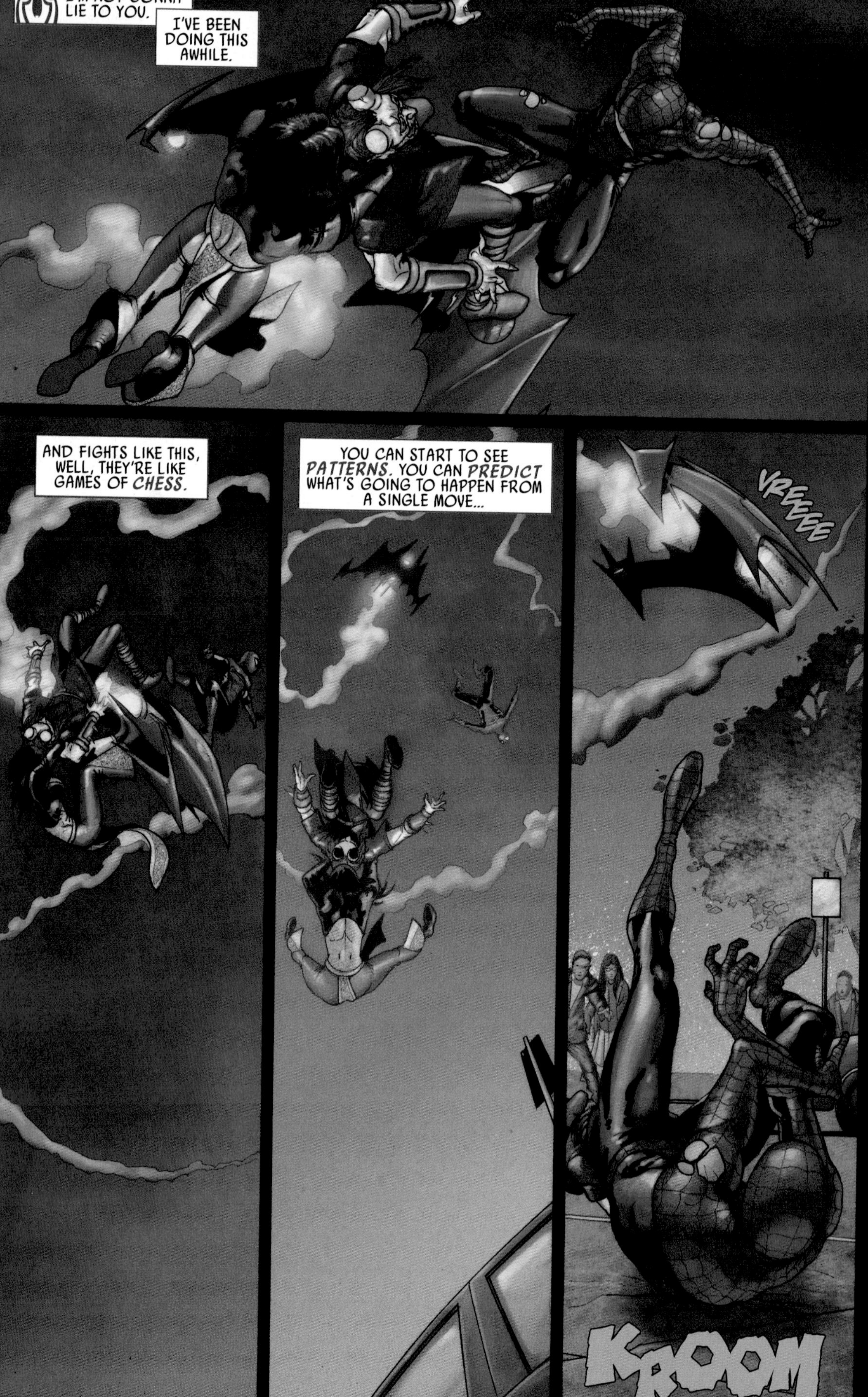

LIE TO YOU.
I'VE BEEN DOING THIS AWHILE.
AND FIGHTS LIKE THIS, WELL, THEY'RE LIKE GAMES OF *CHESS*.
YOU CAN START TO SEE *PATTERNS*. YOU CAN *PREDICT* WHAT'S GOING TO HAPPEN FROM A SINGLE MOVE...
VREEEE
KROOM

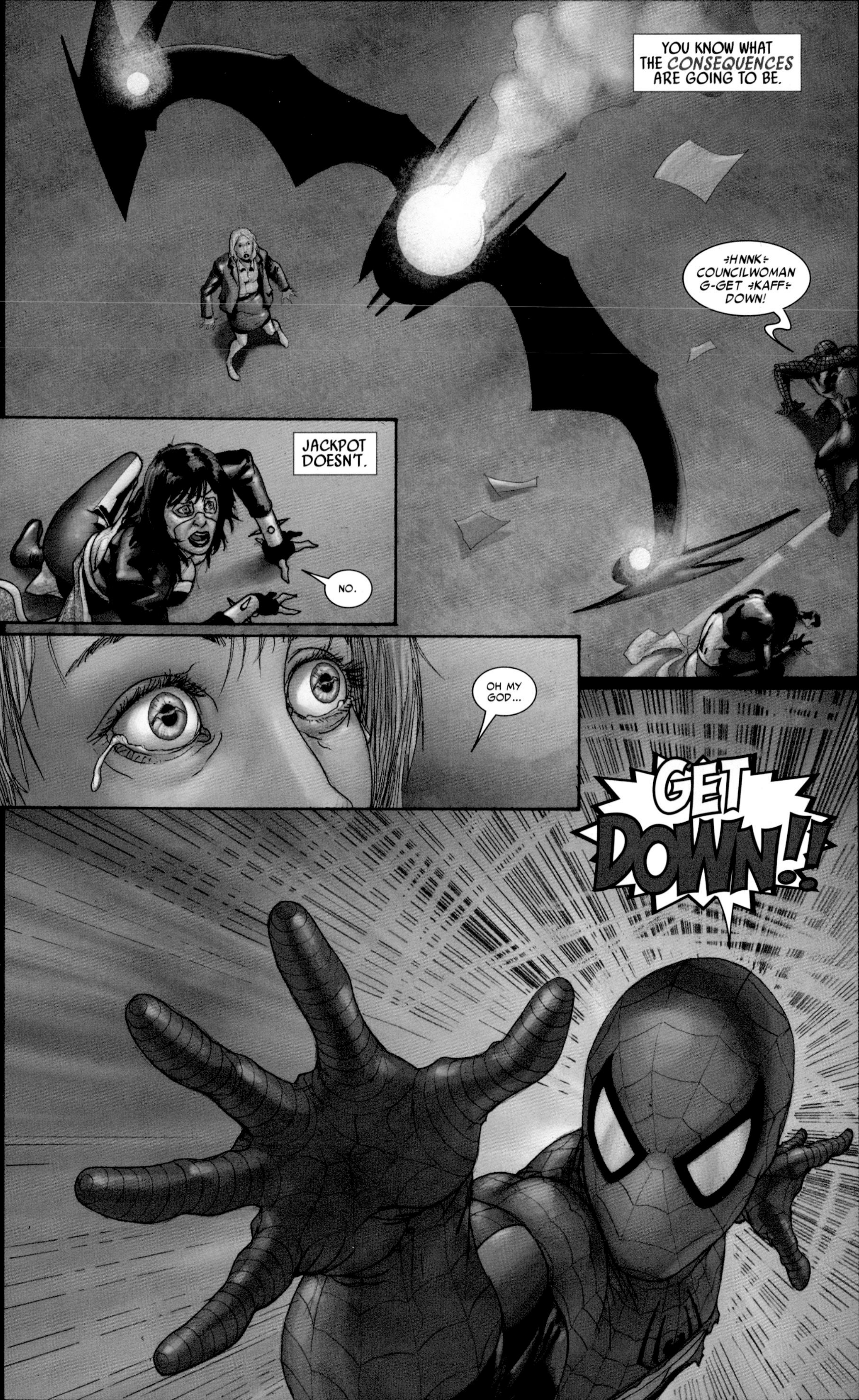
YOU KNOW WHAT THE CONSEQUENCES ARE GOING TO BE.
=HNNK= COUNCILWOMAN G-GET =KAFF= DOWN!
JACKPOT DOESN'T.
NO.
OH MY GOD...
GET DOWN!!

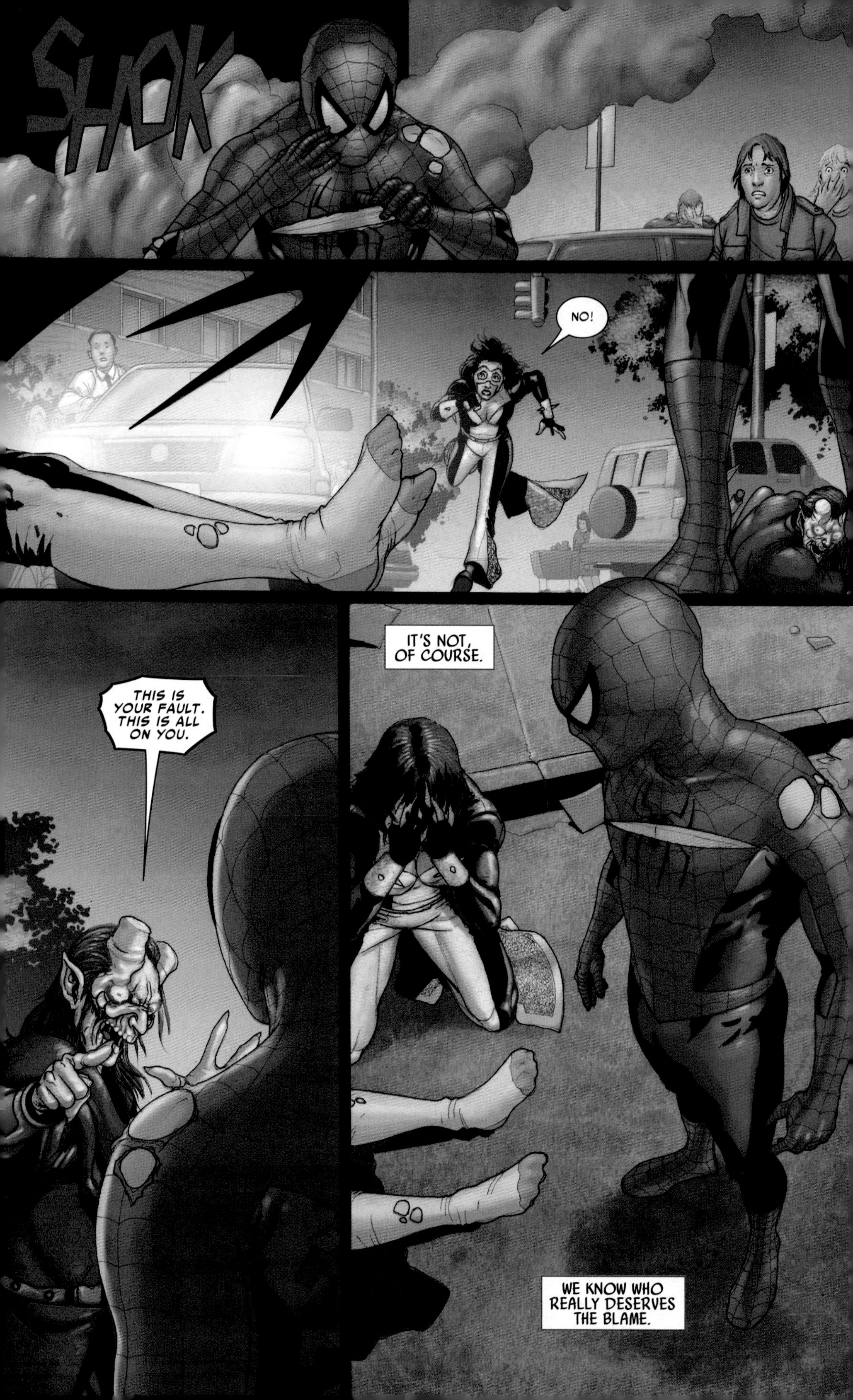
SHOK
NO!
THIS IS YOUR FAULT. THIS IS ALL ON YOU.
IT'S NOT, OF COURSE.
WE KNOW WHO REALLY DESERVES THE BLAME.

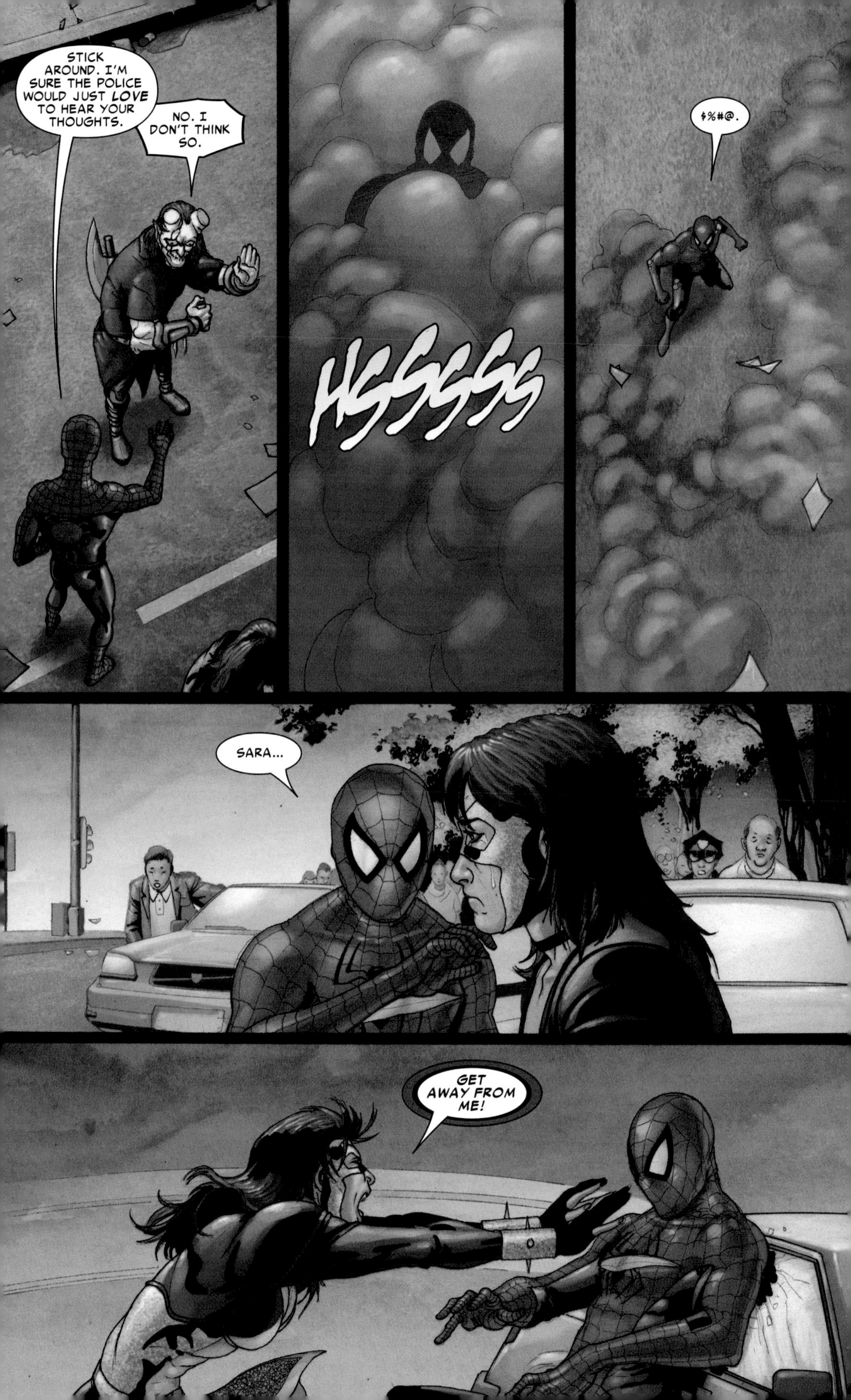
STICK AROUND. I'M SURE THE POLICE WOULD JUST LOVE TO HEAR YOUR THOUGHTS.
NO. I DON'T THINK SO.
HSSSSS
$%#@.
SARA...
GET AWAY FROM ME!

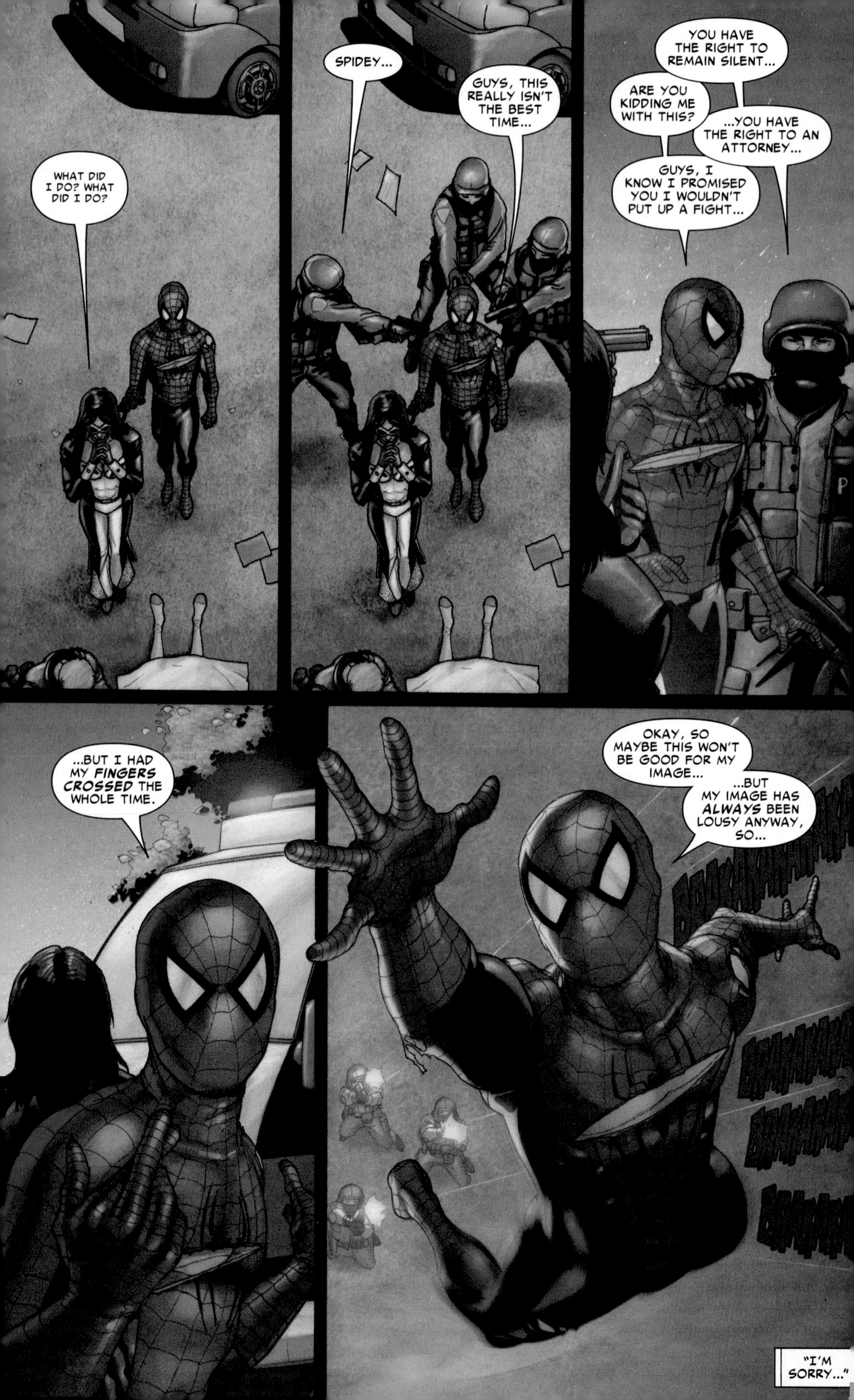
WHAT DID I DO? WHAT DID I DO?
SPIDEY...
GUYS, THIS REALLY ISN'T THE BEST TIME...
YOU HAVE THE RIGHT TO REMAIN SILENT...
ARE YOU KIDDING ME WITH THIS?
...YOU HAVE THE RIGHT TO AN ATTORNEY...
GUYS, I KNOW I PROMISED YOU I WOULDN'T PUT UP A FIGHT...
...BUT I HAD MY ***FINGERS CROSSED*** THE WHOLE TIME.
OKAY, SO MAYBE THIS WON'T BE GOOD FOR MY IMAGE...
...BUT MY IMAGE HAS ***ALWAYS*** BEEN LOUSY ANYWAY, SO...
"I'M SORRY..."

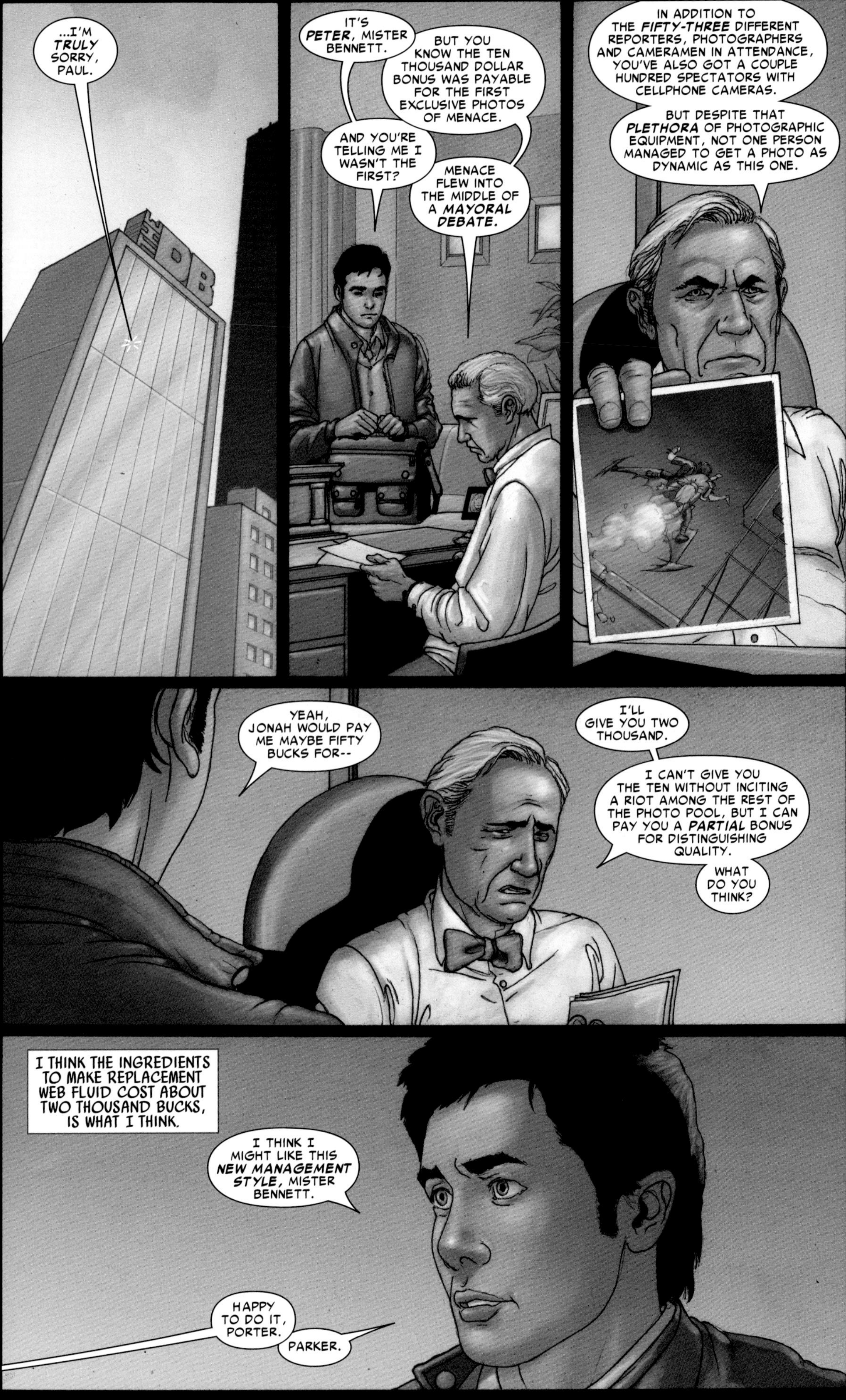
...I'M *TRULY* SORRY, PAUL.
IT'S *PETER*, MISTER BENNETT.
BUT YOU KNOW THE TEN THOUSAND DOLLAR BONUS WAS PAYABLE FOR THE FIRST EXCLUSIVE PHOTOS OF MENACE.
AND YOU'RE TELLING ME I WASN'T THE FIRST?
MENACE FLEW INTO THE MIDDLE OF A *MAYORAL DEBATE.*
IN ADDITION TO THE *FIFTY-THREE* DIFFERENT REPORTERS, PHOTOGRAPHERS AND CAMERAMEN IN ATTENDANCE, YOU'VE ALSO GOT A COUPLE HUNDRED SPECTATORS WITH CELLPHONE CAMERAS.
BUT DESPITE THAT *PLETHORA* OF PHOTOGRAPHIC EQUIPMENT, NOT ONE PERSON MANAGED TO GET A PHOTO AS DYNAMIC AS THIS ONE.
YEAH, JONAH WOULD PAY ME MAYBE FIFTY BUCKS FOR--
I'LL GIVE YOU TWO THOUSAND.
I CAN'T GIVE YOU THE TEN WITHOUT INCITING A RIOT AMONG THE REST OF THE PHOTO POOL, BUT I CAN PAY YOU A *PARTIAL* BONUS FOR DISTINGUISHING QUALITY.
WHAT DO YOU THINK?
I THINK THE INGREDIENTS TO MAKE REPLACEMENT WEB FLUID COST ABOUT TWO THOUSAND BUCKS, IS WHAT I THINK.
I THINK I MIGHT LIKE THIS *NEW MANAGEMENT STYLE,* MISTER BENNETT.
HAPPY TO DO IT, PORTER.
PARKER.

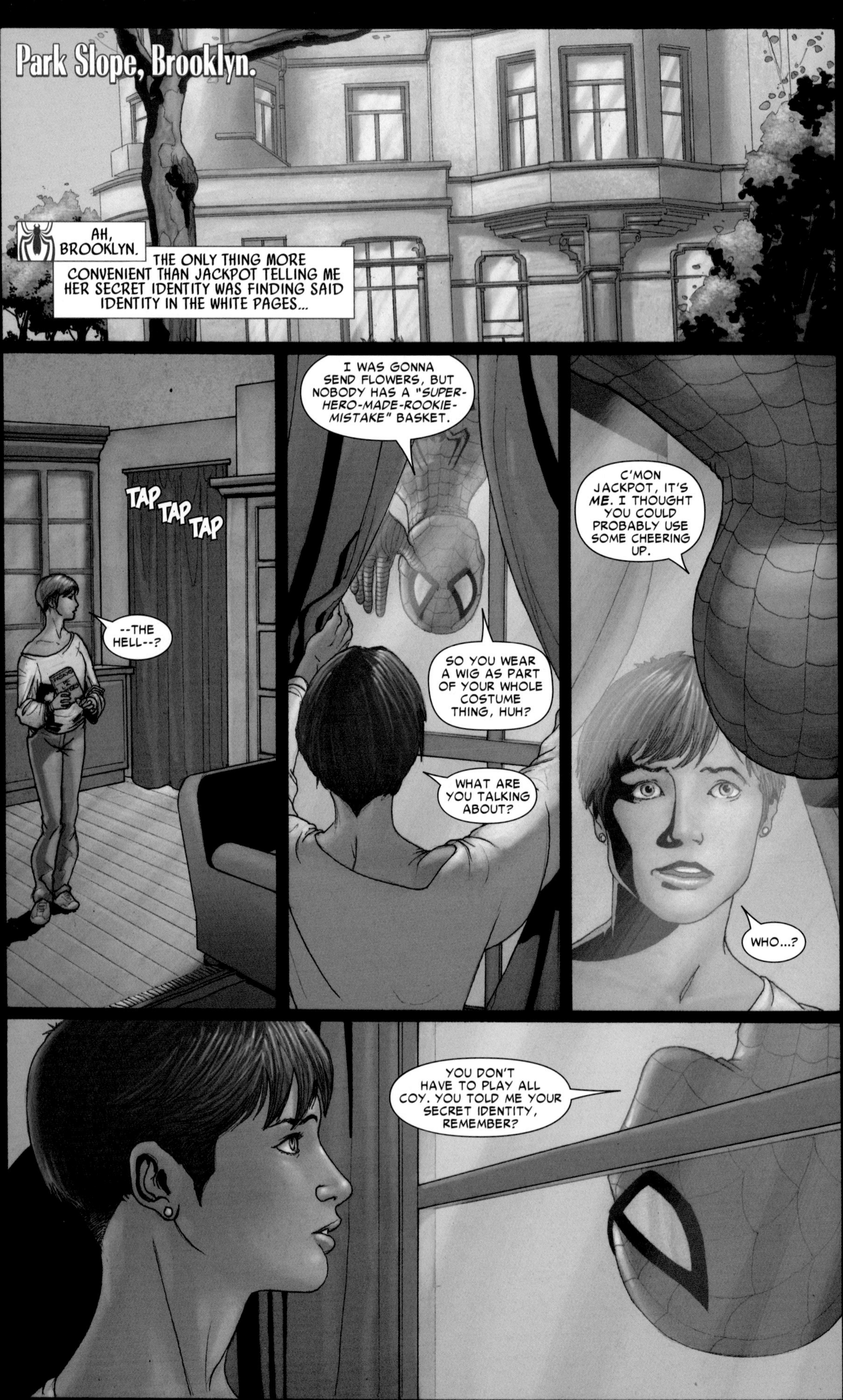
Park Slope, Brooklyn.
AH, BROOKLYN.
THE ONLY THING MORE CONVENIENT THAN JACKPOT TELLING ME HER SECRET IDENTITY WAS FINDING SAID IDENTITY IN THE WHITE PAGES...
TAP TAP TAP
--THE HELL--?
I WAS GONNA SEND FLOWERS, BUT NOBODY HAS A "SUPER-HERO-MADE-ROOKIE-MISTAKE" BASKET.
SO YOU WEAR A WIG AS PART OF YOUR WHOLE COSTUME THING, HUH?
WHAT ARE YOU TALKING ABOUT?
C'MON JACKPOT, IT'S ME. I THOUGHT YOU COULD PROBABLY USE SOME CHEERING UP.
WHO...?
YOU DON'T HAVE TO PLAY ALL COY. YOU TOLD ME YOUR SECRET IDENTITY, REMEMBER?

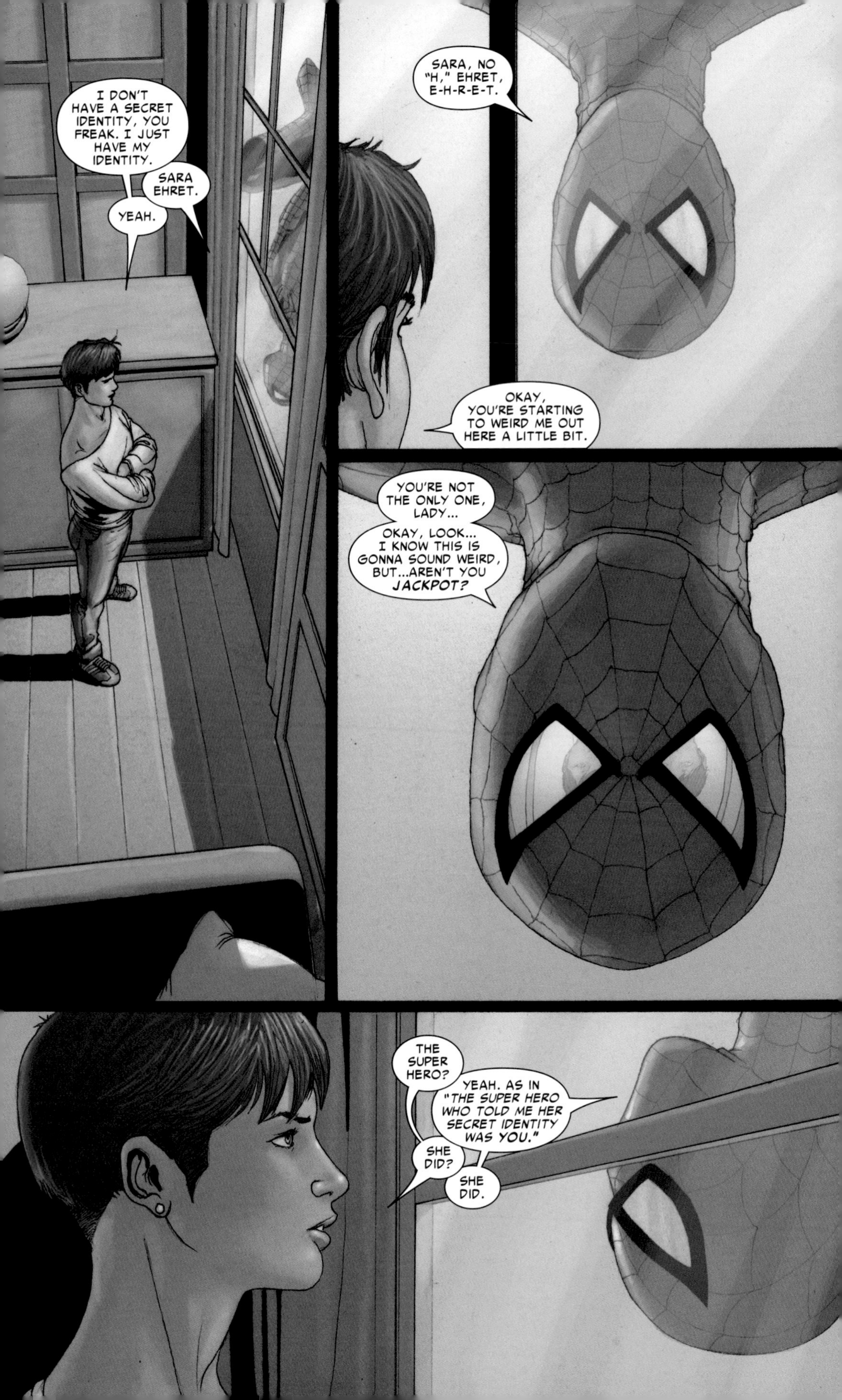
I DON'T HAVE A SECRET IDENTITY, YOU FREAK. I JUST HAVE MY IDENTITY.
SARA EHRET.
YEAH.
SARA, NO "H," EHRET, E-H-R-E-T.
OKAY, YOU'RE STARTING TO WEIRD ME OUT HERE A LITTLE BIT.
YOU'RE NOT THE ONLY ONE, LADY...
OKAY, LOOK... I KNOW THIS IS GONNA SOUND WEIRD, BUT...AREN'T YOU JACKPOT?
THE SUPER HERO?
YEAH. AS IN "THE SUPER HERO WHO TOLD ME HER SECRET IDENTITY WAS YOU."
SHE DID?
SHE DID.

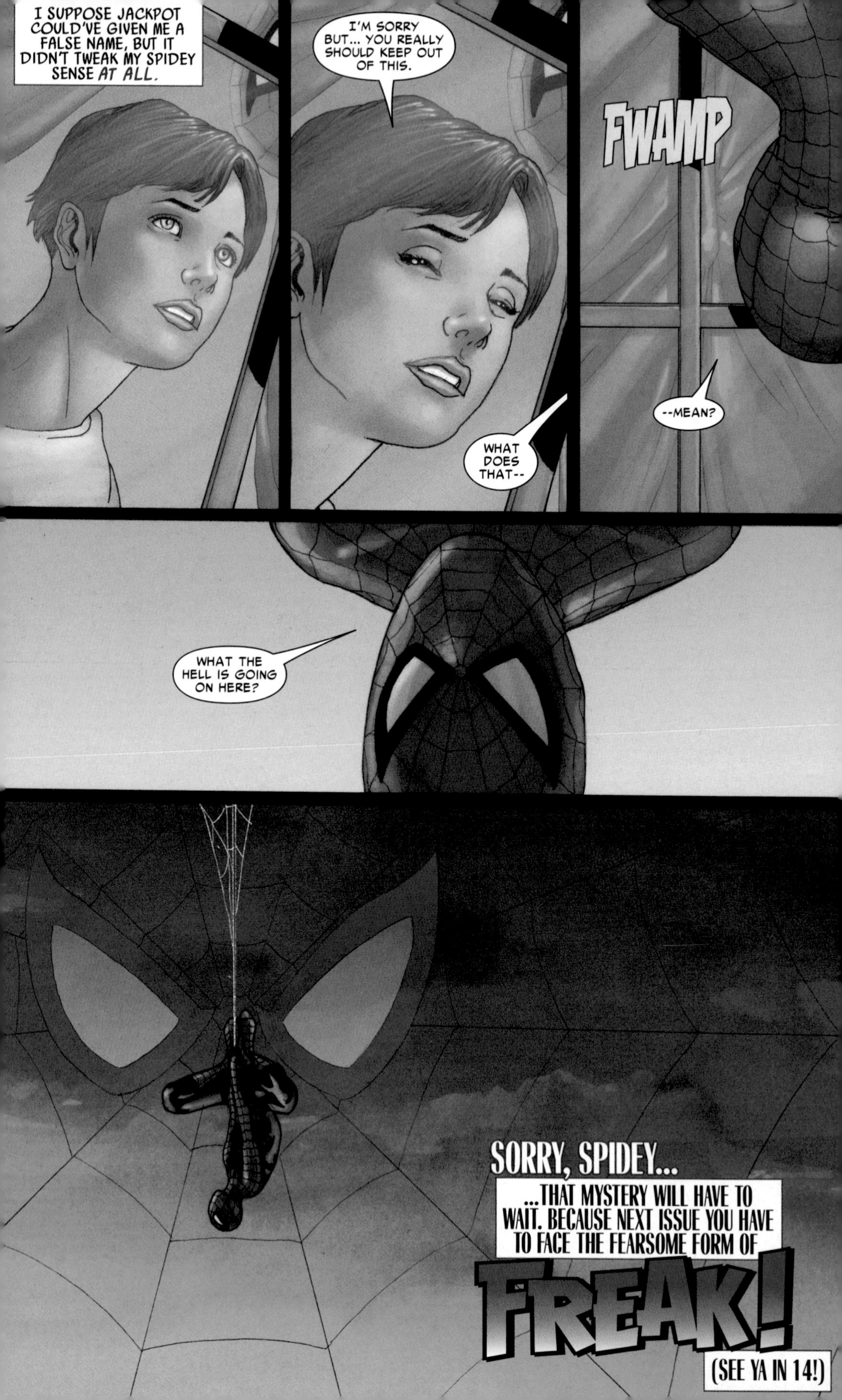

I SUPPOSE JACKPOT COULD'VE GIVEN ME A FALSE NAME, BUT IT DIDN'T TWEAK MY SPIDEY SENSE AT ALL.
I'M SORRY BUT... YOU REALLY SHOULD KEEP OUT OF THIS.
FWAMP
WHAT DOES THAT--
--MEAN?
WHAT THE HELL IS GOING ON HERE?
SORRY, SPIDEY...
...THAT MYSTERY WILL HAVE TO WAIT. BECAUSE NEXT ISSUE YOU HAVE TO FACE THE FEARSOME FORM OF
FREAK!
(SEE YA IN 14!)

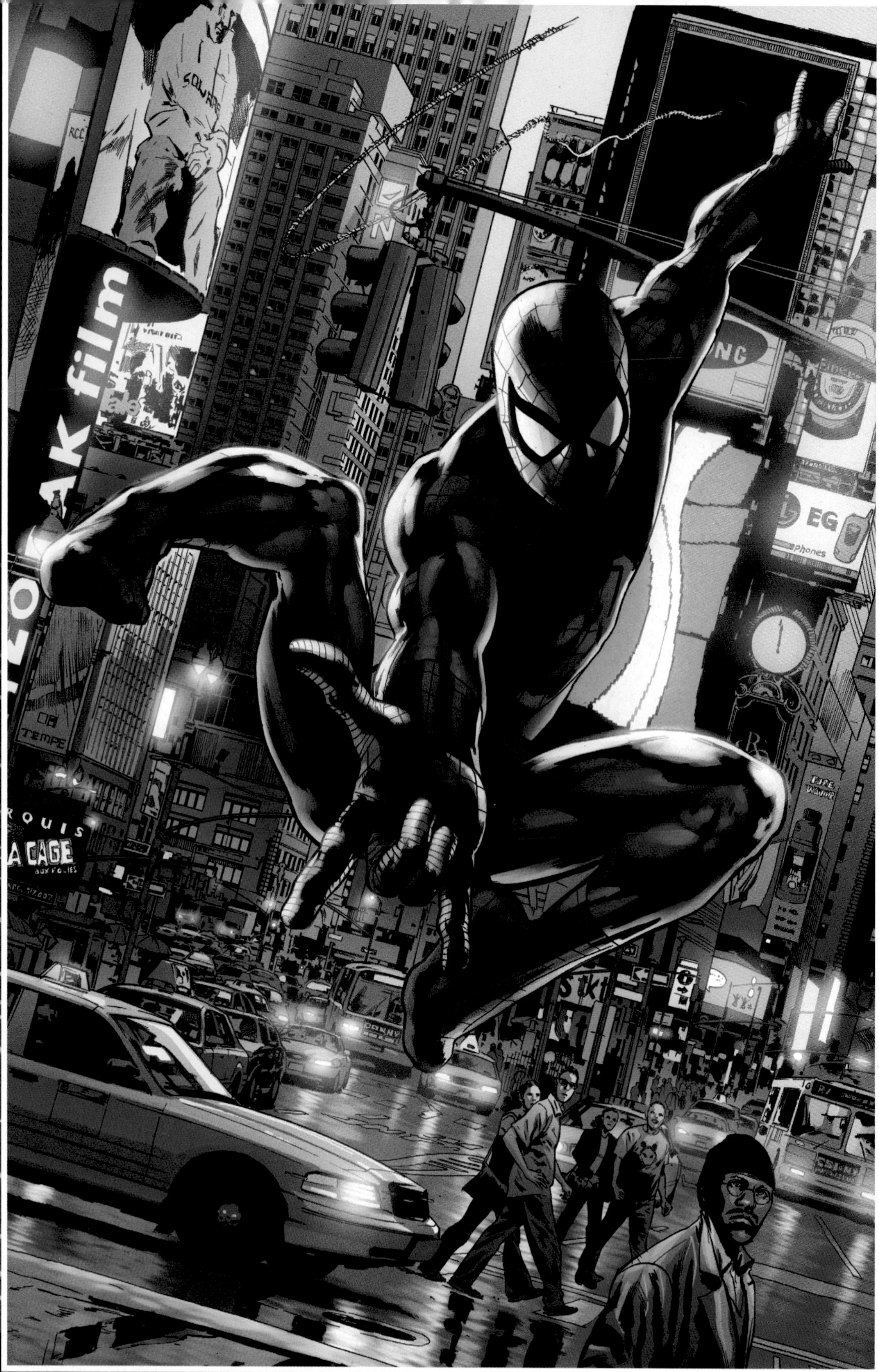
film
TEMPE
A CAGE
AUX FOLIES
EG
Phones

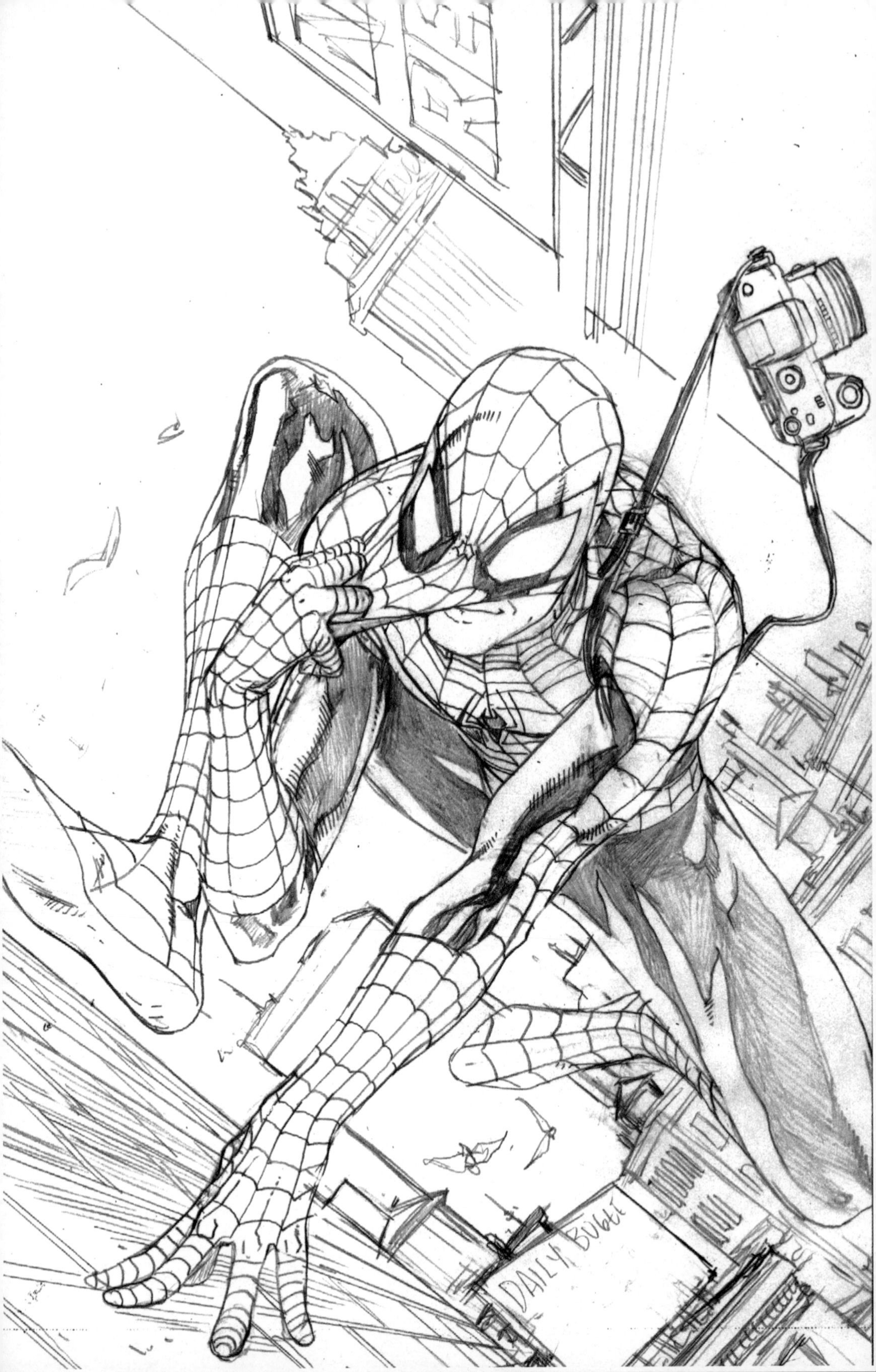
DAILY BUGLE

AMAZING SPIDER-MAN #546 SKETCH VARIANT BY STEVE McNIVEN

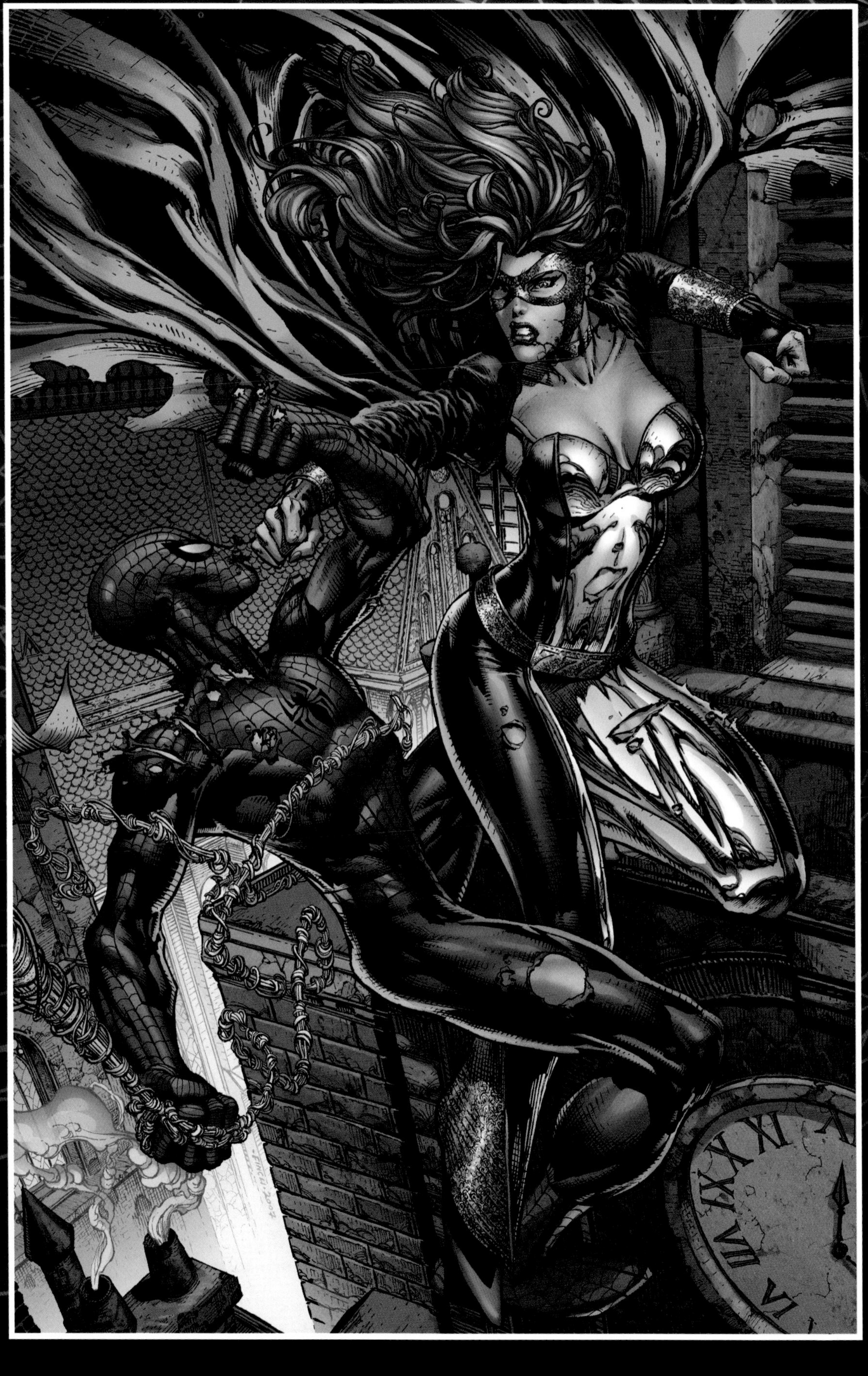

AMAZING SPIDER-MAN #549 VARIANT BY DAVID FINCH

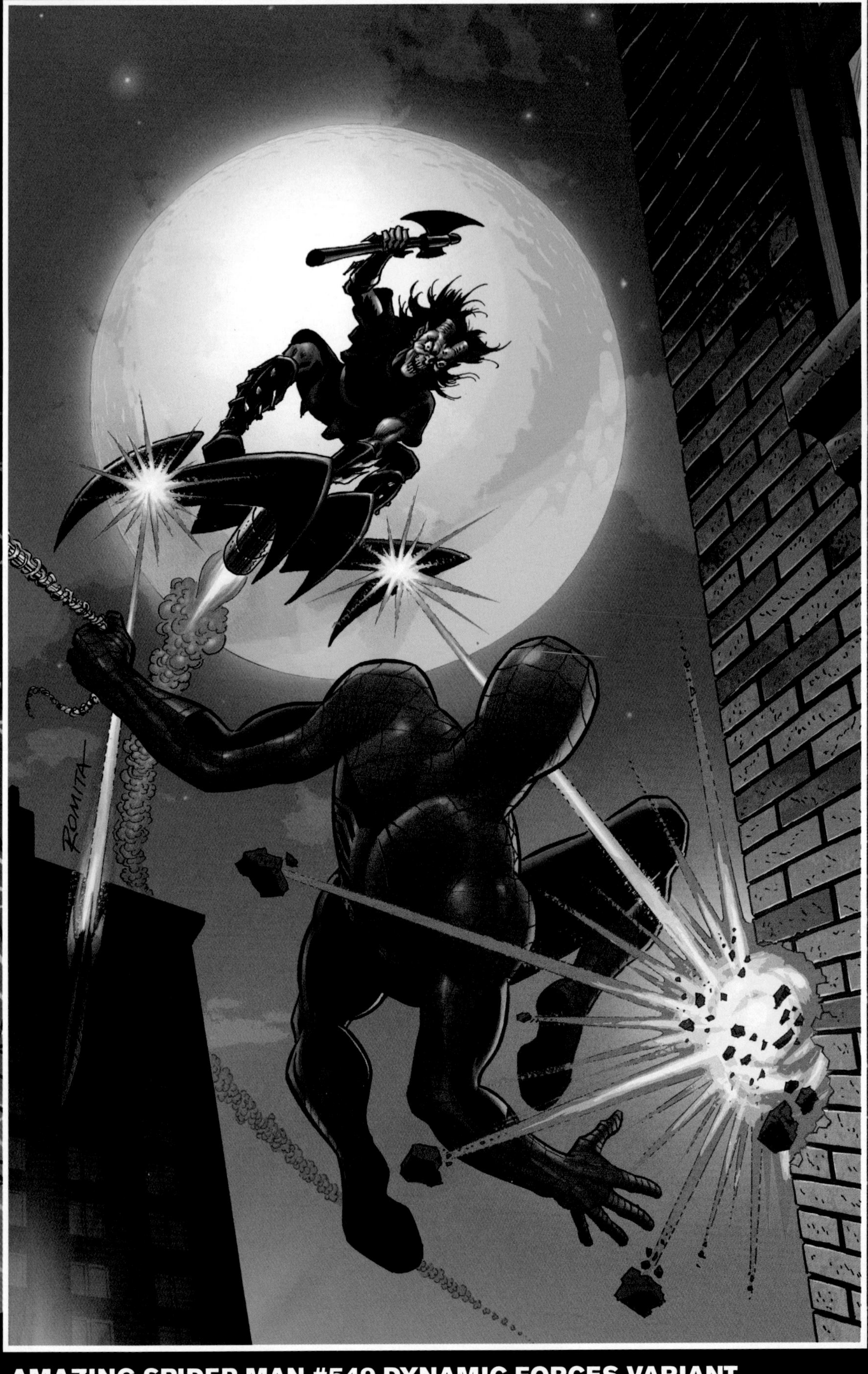
ROMITA

AMAZING SPIDER-MAN #549 DYNAMIC FORCES VARIANT
BY JOHN ROMITA SR.

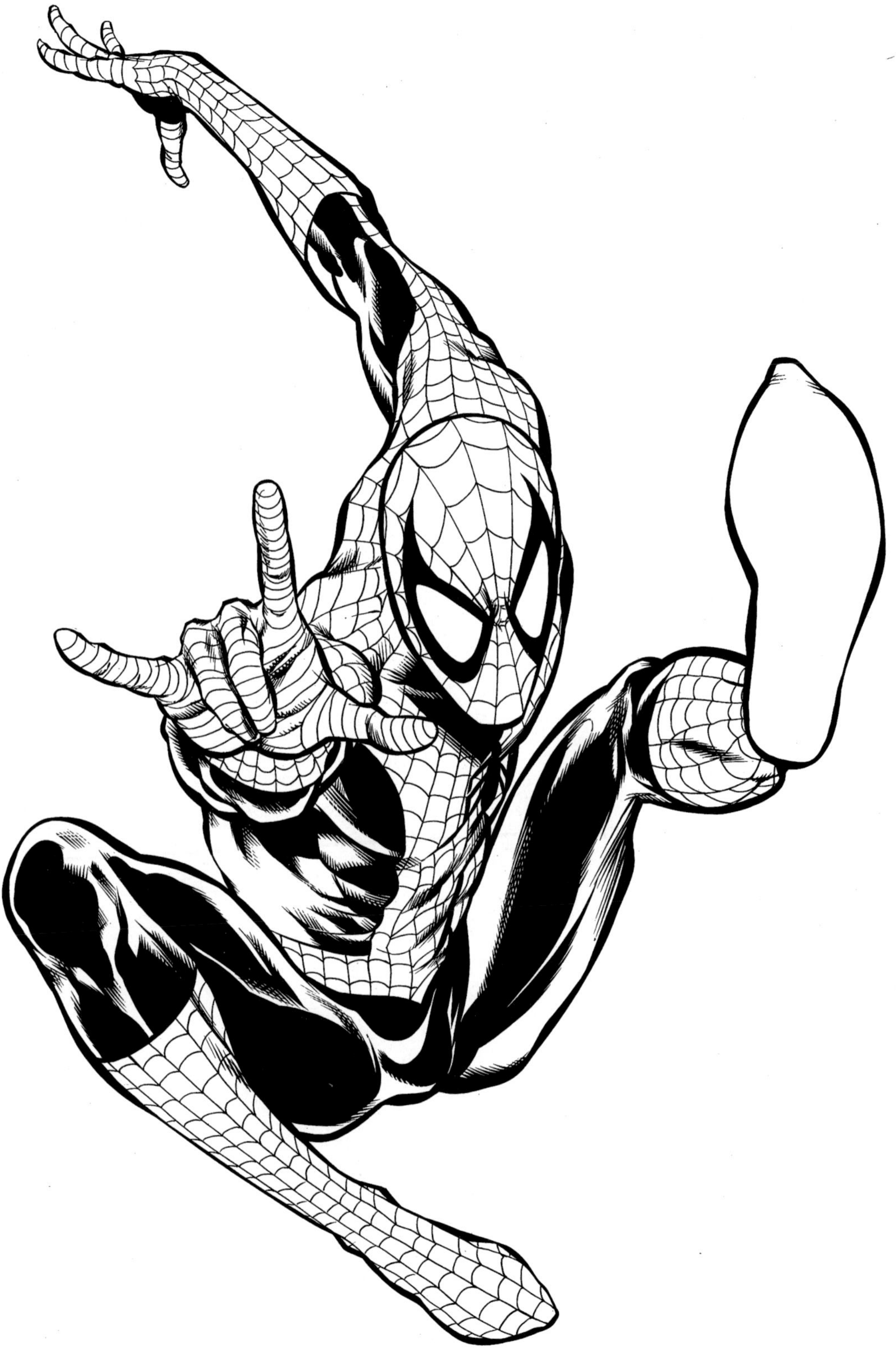

SPIDER-MAN: FREE COMIC BOOK DAY 2007 COVER INKS
BY PHIL JIMENEZ

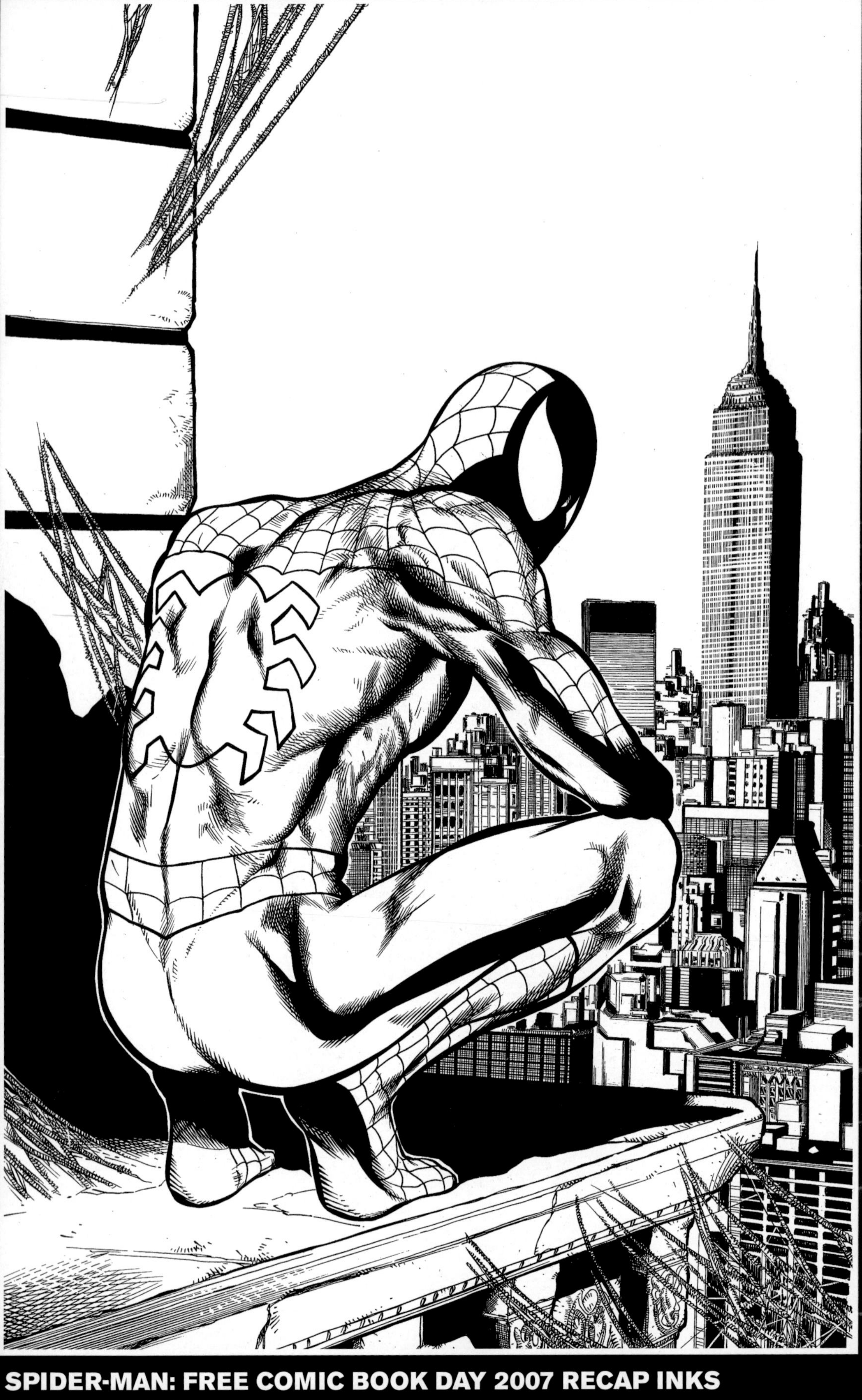

SPIDER-MAN: FREE COMIC BOOK DAY 2007 RECAP INKS
BY PHIL JIMENEZ

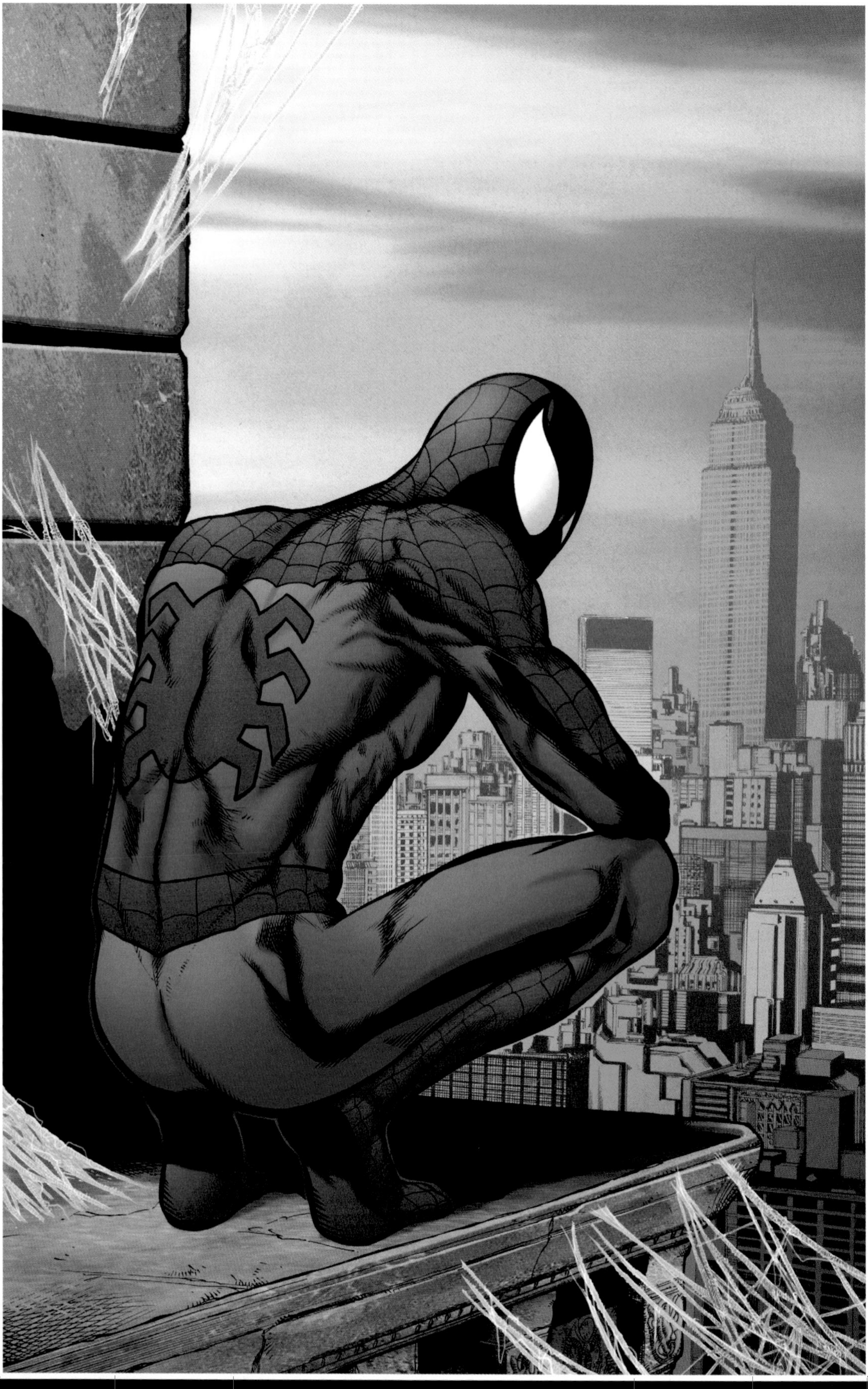

SPIDE[illegible] 2007 RECAP ART
BY PHIL JIMENEZ

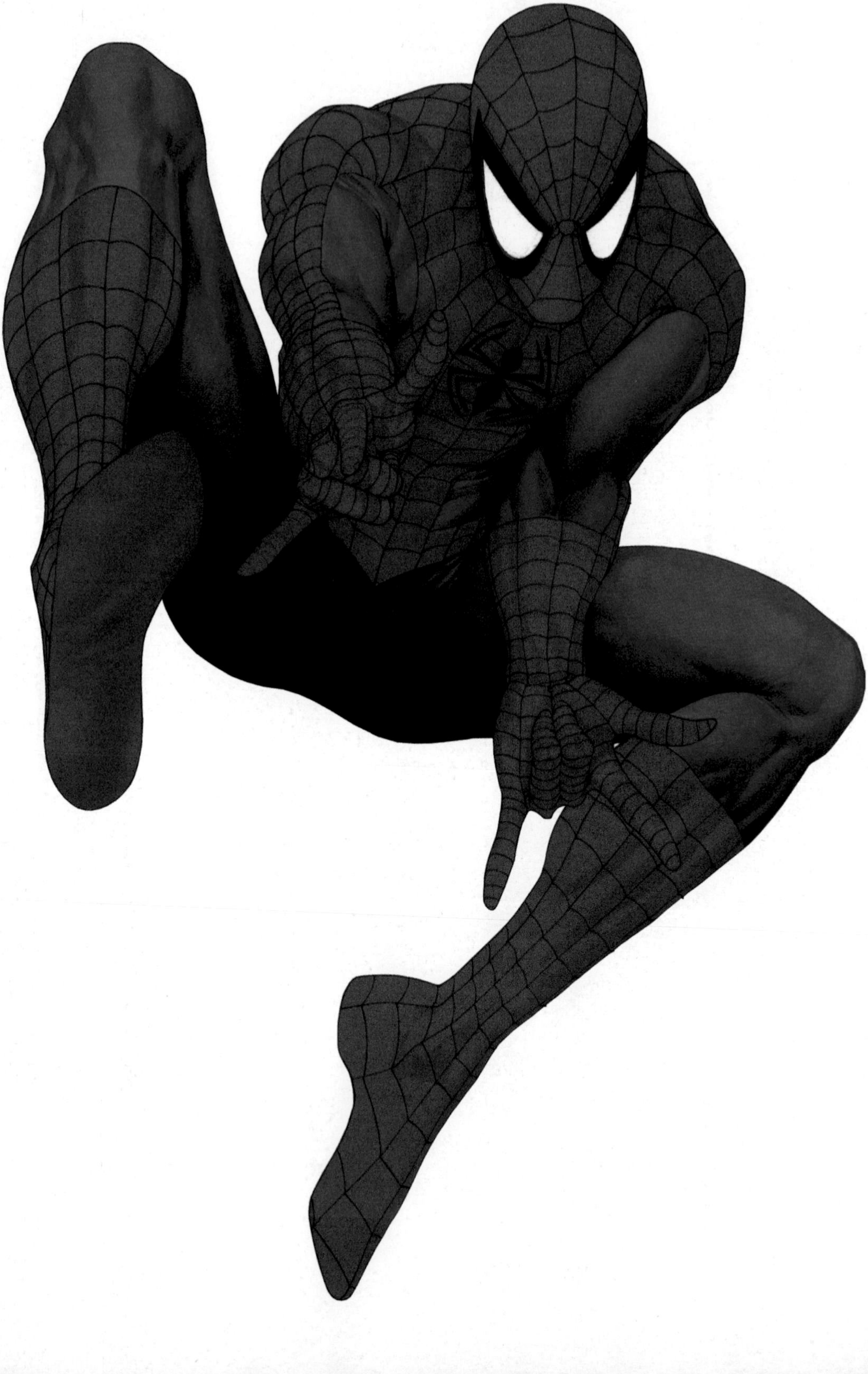

As plans began to develop for the Spider-Man: Brand New Day relaunch, new Executive Editor of Amazing Spider-Man Tom Brevoort wrote the following document. It outlines for his creative and editorial teams his thoughts on what makes Spider-Man so appealing and enduring as a character along with the types of Spider-Man stories Marvel should be telling in a post-"One More Day" universe.

SPIDER-MAN MANIFESTO
by Tom Brevoort — 9/18/06

This'll be my vague attempt to sum up what I think we need to get the SPIDER-MAN books back to, what I think has been missing from the character and his world, and a general set of guidelines for how I'd like to proceed. None of this is intended to be looked upon as hard-and-fast rules, as there can always be exceptions. But this is where my mind is at right now.

SPIDER-MAN IS ABOUT PETER PARKER

This is the biggest and most basic concept that's kind of escaped us in the Spidey titles for the last decade or two. Peter Parker is Spider-Man, Spider-Man is not Peter Parker. By that I mean that it's Peter and his life and tribulations that's the through-line of the SPIDER-MAN titles, or should be, and Peter being Spider-Man is just one component part of the overall whole. But in the last few years, it's seemed like Pete is Spider-Man, first and foremost, and he kinda half-squeezes in a life around being Spidey — and that's wrong.

What made SPIDER-MAN the flagship of the Marvel line was the soap opera aspect of Peter's life, the fact that he was a young character, a character who could screw up, a character that life seemed to occasionally dump on in humorous ways, and yet would keep on striving to do right by everybody. An everyman, a schlemiel. Grounded in the real world. Grounded in Manhattan, Queens, Brooklyn.

One of the big advantages that ULTIMATE SPIDER-MAN has, beyond the fact of starting again at ground zero, is that there's only the one book, with the one writer. So the soap opera aspect of Peter's life is clearly the backbone of that series, and the engine that drives it. Even when a particular adventure isn't extraordinarily compelling, readers want to know what's going to happen with Peter and Mary and Gwen and Kitty and Flash and so forth and so on.

SPIDER-MAN 2 GETS IT RIGHT

The second SPIDER-MAN movie hits all of the right essential notes: Pete is a struggling young guy, has a tough time making ends meet, and his romantic life is complicated by the pull he feels to go out and take action as Spidey. Being Spider-Man is a release, but it's also a sacrifice. If you're not always putting Peter in a situation where he has to choose between his everyday responsibilities and those of being a super hero, then you're doing something wrong.

In my head, my ideal structure for the first issue of SPIDER-MAN that we do after the cosmic reset of the "One More Day" storyline spends the first 17 pages or so on Peter Parker: This is who he is, this is where his life is right now. This is his crummy apartment, he's 25 and trying to figure out what he wants from his life. This is his circle of friends, these are his personal conflicts, this is his Aunt May, etc. And in the background, some menace or threat is beginning to bubble up — so that, by page 18 or so, we bring Spidey on camera with a big, dramatic, Marvel-style splash and a quip, and then we rocket to a cliff-hanger or a story-twist at the end of the book. But you plant the stake in the ground right away: This is Peter Parker's comic book, not Spider-Man's.

SPIDER-MAN IS THE HARD-LUCK HERO

Somewhere along the line, we started to become afraid to humiliate our heroes for a laugh. But this sort of thing — life dumping on Peter — was such a hallmark in the Stan days. Nothing Spider-Man did ever turned out right. Even the simple things — he'd wash his costume, and it'd shrink, and he'd have to go out to fight the Green Goblin with it all bunching up. Or he'd hide his civilian clothes in a convenient smokestack, and when he'd get back to them, they'd smell like fish. And so forth. And the reverse was also true — Peter would spend issue after issue after issue ducking Aunt May's attempts to fix him up with Anna Watson's niece, figuring that she was a dog, and then he finally got to meet Mary Jane for the punchline.

Spider-Man was also always the hero who had to fight with a disadvantage. He'd sprain his arm, or have the flu, or develop an ulcer, and still have to go out and fight the villain of the day. This sort of thing tended to humanize him and make him relatable to the readers.

SPIDER-MAN MAKES MISTAKES AND BAD CHOICES

As a young guy, and a put-upon guy, Spidey was given the freedom by his writers to occasionally make the wrong move. One of my favorite classic panels is from an early Spidey story, in which Flash Thompson, masquerading in a Spider-Man costume, has been captured by Doctor Doom, who believes he's the real Spider-Man. Peter and Aunt May see a bulletin about this on the news, and there's this one evil-looking shot of Peter, with this big %&$*-eating grin on his face, as he thinks to himself that all he has to do is stay on the sidelines, and his nemesis Flash Thompson will never bother him again. A panel later, of course, he finds that he cannot bring himself to do this, but that one moment is so honest and so relatable. Similarly, Spidey would occasionally try to cash in on his powers, or think about using them to steal a present for Gwen's birthday or whatnot. Spider-Man isn't a square-jawed paragon of virtue. Spider-Man is heroic because he finds it within himself to be heroic.

Spider-Man also works best when he's an outsider hero. By and large, Spidey is distrusted by the authorities and the common man on the street. And no wonder — he's got an entire media outlet campaigning against him. And he's kind of creepy, and wears a mask, and so on. Spidey's intentions are often misunderstood, which is another way he's relatable to the audience — events tend to backfire on him, and trying to do the right thing often gets him in even more hot water.

SPIDER-MAN IS FUNNY

If you don't have at least one funny line or exchange or situation from Spidey in your issue (assuming he's in costume in the thing), then you've done something wrong. Spider-Man is the Groucho Marx and Bugs Bunny of super heroes.

WHERE WE START

Just to set the stage, so that everybody knows where we'll be after the JMS run on AMAZING wraps up in July, here are the Cliffs Notes: In order to save the life of Aunt May, who was struck down by a bullet intended for Mary Jane, Peter and Mary Jane make a deal with Mephisto. But the cost is their marriage. Using his demonic abilities, Mephisto "uncreates" the marriage, and all of the events associated with it — so all of those Spider-Man adventures of the last twenty years still happened, but they happened somewhat differently. So not only are Peter and MJ not married, they have never been married. Spider-Man's secret identity is a secret once again. And formerly dead characters such as Harry Osborn and possibly Gwen Stacy are alive again and back on the canvas. Some of the particulars are still open to change (and are discussed in more detail later), but this is the landscape when we set up shop.

GO FORWARD

Part of not looking backward is finding new wrinkles on the old, classic tropes. So if we've got Harry Osborn back in the picture, let's find something new to do with him, some way to put him into a new position in Peter's life, rather than just rehashing the past. The worst thing that can happen is for the aftermath of the "unmarrying" to feel like it's 1968 again. We want the familiar comfort food of the old characters, but we need to do something modern and interesting with them. We need to put them into new, interesting configurations.

For example, I think Betty Brant should be one of Peter's closest friends. They dated when Pete was in high school, and now they're friends, they hang out together in a non-involved way — she's the person who sets Peter up

with dates, gives him the woman's perspective, and who ultimately "approves" of the women he gets involved with. This gives him a good touch-point at the Daily Bugle (where Betty is still working as a reporter), and gives Pete a non-involved female friend that goes back to the classic days. (And as a complication down the line, perhaps there could be a moment where they got involved for a second, in response to problems or difficulties in each of their lives at that moment. And then they'd spend the next few months trying to deal with it, and repair their friendship — or not.)

Mary Jane, on the other hand, should be off-the-canvas when we start our first issue. Some indeterminate amount of time will have passed since the end of "One More Day," and Mary Jane is simply not around. We probably don't even mention her at first. And then, we play with the notion of a reunion all through the year — maybe Aunt May gets a postcard from her at around the third month. Maybe she's in town in the sixth month, but because of bad timing, she and Peter never meet face-to-face. And then, in the ninth month, we get Peter and MJ together in the same place — and she introduces Peter to her fiancé. (Perhaps this is the point where Peter hooks up with Betty, if we go that route.)

Also, part of going forward is to cease the unending homages to the same three great Spidey stories of the past. So please, no girl-falling-from-the-bridge, and no lift-the-big-heavy-thing-off-his-back-to-save-Aunt-May. Let's stop repeating the story iconography of the past and come up with some new images to stick in the readers' minds.

CIRCLE OF FRIENDS

The biggest detriment to Peter Parker being at the core of the Spidey books right now is that he no longer has a circle of friends to function as a supporting cast. Time was, Spider-Man had the best supporting cast in comics, but one by one, over the years, they've either fallen away, been turned into villains, been killed off, or have become completely irrelevant. And most latter-day attempts to bring new people into Peter's circle have only lasted as long as the particular writer who invented them (much like most of the Spidey villains created in the last ten years). So, this is something we're going to need to fix.

I think we need to come at this from both directions at once. Even though we've more or less got all of the classic characters back and available, I want to be careful that the book doesn't feel retro. There's something creepy about a guy who's still hanging out with the same six guys he went to high school with. I'm not saying that we dump the classic cast members, though — only that we look at where they are on the canvas and what role they play, and make sure that it makes sense in 2006. Flash Thompson, for example, was traditionally the foil — yet he hasn't really had a structure in which to play that role since Peter left school. As a result, he's kind of been in Peter's orbit whenever there's been a need for Spidey to have a friend who's abducted by the villain or injured in a battle. But he hasn't really fulfilled a function that's made sense in a long time.

At the same time, I do think we need to bring some new people into Peter's circle. I think the trick is to do this incrementally, rather than trying to shove half-a-dozen new characters down the readers' throats at once. But this should be easy enough to do organically, especially if all of the Spidey writers are working in a coordinated effort.

PETER LIVES & BEHAVES LIKE A 25-YEAR-OLD

Spider-Man doesn't grow up. He doesn't get a 9-to-5 job (and couldn't hold it if he did get one). The idea that JMS set up, with him teaching in his old school, had its merits, but they never really got fleshed out and explored enough — and making Peter a teacher definitely made him seem older.

The classic Stan Lee setup of Peter making his scratch by taking photos for the Daily Bugle is such a perfect structure that I'd like to get back to that. It also gave the book the Bugle regulars as another pool from which to draw the cast — J. Jonah Jameson and company have felt out of place since Peter stopped taking pictures for the newspaper regularly.

There's something lovely about the fact that, in order to support himself, Peter has to perpetuate the media machine that makes his life more difficult as a super hero. And at the same time, there's that secret satisfaction of knowing that he's putting one over on the guy who hates him the most. Additionally, the need to put food on the table always propelled Spider-Man into action, and gave writers a way to get him involved in stories that wouldn't otherwise immediately concern him — he'd hear about something going on, swing over to get some pictures, his spider-sense would go off, and he'd get embroiled in the conflict. With this structure taken away, we've been forced to have Spidey going "on patrol," which just seems wrong to me—being Spider-Man isn't a job, it's both a responsibility and a release. But Peter has an actual life to deal with, and so he's not really looking for excuses to be Spider-Man (unless he simply needs to blow off some steam by swinging around the rooftops — it is cool, after all).

Peter can try to do other things — one of the driving motivations for his character in the next year, I would think, is a general feeling that his life has gone off-track. Like so many young twentysomethings, he hasn't quite worked out what he wants to do with his life long-term, and he's been too busy trying to stay on the treadmill to really be able to ponder it. (Plus, he's subconsciously reeling from the loss of his marriage, not that we ever say this — it's simply a subtext.) But unless somebody comes up with something brilliant, these are probably all short-term solutions, and won't work out over the long haul (typically because Peter's life as Spider-Man will get in the way).

I also think there's something to the uncertainty of a freelancer's life that helps drive Peter onward to explore other options and possibilities in life — whether he makes any long-term progress or not.

WOULD PETE BE SHOOTING VIDEO FOOTAGE THESE DAYS?

It's worth examining the specifics of the classic setups, though, rather than simply defaulting to them, to make sure that they still hold water in 2006. For example, in the '60s it made sense for Peter to take still photos of himself in action and sell them in order to make his rent. But given the proliferation of technology today, and the needs of 24-hour news channels and the like, wouldn't it make more sense for him to have a small digital video camera and to shoot video of himself in action as Spider-Man? The payday would have to be better, especially if he could produce such footage on a regular basis. Is there some other drawback to doing this? And is this something that Peter should perhaps try, as an alternative to providing pictures to the Bugle, only to have it backfire in some way?

THE VILLAINS

Spider-Man has probably got just about the best rogues' gallery in comics. However, these classic villains have become somewhat tarnished due to years of overuse or misuse. And there really hasn't been a new Spidey villain created in the last ten years who's really stuck beyond his originator's tenure on the series. So this, too, is something we need to address.

NEW VILLAINS

We can't continue to coast on the laurels of the past, so we need to get some new blood into the Spider-Man universe when it comes to exciting new foes for the web-slinger to face. Again, much like with the supporting cast, this needs to be done selectively and deliberately, in that the readers aren't going to care if we just throw a bunch of costumes at them randomly.

The best Spider-Man foes tend to be "ground-level" villains — criminals, street thugs, crimelords, mercenaries and the like. As Spidey is more grounded in the real world, so too should be the opponents he goes up against. It's not a hard and fast rule, but in general Spider-Man should probably not often be dealing with aliens from space or magical creatures from another dimension.

One of the (probably unconscious) common traits of most of the classic Spidey villains when they were introduced is the fact that they're more or less all older men, which gave Spidey's battles a subtext of generational conflict. This doesn't mean that any new creations need to follow the same pattern — but it's helpful to be aware of these subtexts, as they can add another almost unconscious layer to the surface action conflicts between Spidey and his foes.

REVAMP OLD VILLAINS AND STICK TO THE REVAMPS

Everybody loves the classic Spider-Man villains, but they've become so overused in the past couple of years (and not just in the Spider-Man titles) that their impact has been largely blunted. Characters who once had very specific motives and M.O.'s have been ground down to generic criminals. So as we consider each character in turn, I think we need to delve into finding the defining characteristics of each, and then making those the centerpiece of whatever story we use them in, so that a Vulture story doesn't have the same tone or style as an Electro story. And, once we redefine these characters, we need to stick to that redefinition, at least for awhile. On some of these villains, they were turning up every two months with a completely different outlook, depending on the needs of that writer and series. That weakens the characters tremendously, and it's got to stop. So for any classic villain that we choose to use again, we need to give careful consideration as to how we use them to maximize their impact and longevity, and then we need to hold to it.

These villains need to be defined sharply, their personas and actions made dangerous and interesting again.

MYSTERY

One of the hallmarks of the Spider-Man books has always been the "mystery villain" — the crimelord whose true identity and motives are unknown to the readers, and whose true face, when it is finally revealed, comes as a shock. This worked with the Green Goblin, it worked with the Hobgoblin years later, and it can work again. Doing this sort of a mystery character in the Internet age creates a whole new level of problem, however, in that, in the pre-computer days, if one guy in Idaho tumbled to your reveal, the information didn't really travel much farther than that. Whereas now, it only takes one perceptive reader anywhere in the world to undercut the payoff for everybody.

Still, this is a very effective element, especially within the sort of yearlong uber-arc storytelling we're talking about, so it's worth giving some thought to. (And no, Uncle Ben cannot be the man behind the mystery villain's mask.)

ISSUES TO RESOLVE:

With the structure of the end of "One More Day" and the undoing of the Spider-Man marriage, there are a number of elements in play whose resolution we're going to want to lock down so that we can go forward smoothly. These include:

1) WHO WILL KNOW PETER'S SECRET NOW?

The world at large will have forgotten that Peter Parker is Spider-Man — but how far does this extend? Does Aunt May know any longer? Does Mary Jane know? (In continuity, she discovered that Peter was Spider-Man on the night he gained his powers — a retcon that did more damage than good.) What about folks like Norman Osborn or Eddie Brock?

This is crucial information to know, in that the conflict in Peter's life should always in some way be between his responsibilities as Spidey and his responsibilities as Peter. But if his closest friends and family know his true identity, and accept his mission, then there's no conflict — heck,

they'll aid him in covering his exit and making excuses for his sudden departures.

There was always a nice paranoid edge to Peter's desperation towards keeping his costumed life a secret — one that any reader with a secret of his own could relate to: "My friends and family wouldn't accept me, wouldn't love me, if they knew what I really was." Whether this took the form of fearing that Aunt May would drop dead of a heart attack, or that the Green Goblin would throw another girlfriend off another bridge, this was always a powerful subtext, and a powerful motivator for the character.

2) DO WE WANT THE WEB-SHOOTERS BACK?

This restart gives us the opportunity to revert to the traditional mechanical web-shooters, as opposed to the latter-day movie-inspired organic ones. I think there's something to the added complications the mechanical ones allow (running out of webbing, breaking down, needing to purchase the chemicals necessary to mix up new batches of webbing — not to mention finding the time to do so, etc.).

3) GWEN?

For a while now, there's been talk about resurrecting Gwen as a component of the end of "One More Day." I think the problem with doing this is twofold: A) it robs the character of one of the essential tragedies that defines his character, and B) it locks you onto the treadmill of 1968 — if Peter's not going to go back to dating Gwen, then what's the point of bringing her back? And if he is going to go back to dating Gwen, doesn't that bring us back to 1968 again?

The only thing I can think of to do with Gwen that's different and yet makes sense with the setup (since it's the deal with Mephisto that's bringing her back to life) would be to have her be a spoiler—have her be a character whose sole purpose in life was to screw Peter's life up. She'd be his personal demon, in a sense. The problem is that this only really works if you understand that she's been resurrected by Mephisto, and supernatural elements like this are an awkward fit in the Spidey milieu, at least on a consistent basis.

Speaking for myself, I think it's probably a mistake to bring her back; good for the shock of the moment, but detrimental in the long run.

THE NEW METHODOLOGY

One of the factors that's sidelined the soap opera aspect of the SPIDER-MAN series from a logistical standpoint has been the fact that he's headlined in more than one ongoing title since the mid-'70s. The way this tended to play out, especially as more and more books were added, is that the core book, AMAZING, would be perceived as the "real deal," and the other titles would be looked upon as lesser adjuncts — and would sell at a lower level, to boot. And with different creative teams on each title, it's become harder and harder to coordinate the message, and to provide a consistent vision of the character. The line's identity became fractured because of the diverse hands and diverse directions across the different books. While there are some advantages to this approach, the one thing it really kiboshed, in an almost subliminal way, is the feeling that SPIDER-MAN is the linear story of Peter Parker's life.

So what I propose to do is not only to take us back down to only a single title, but to have that title come out as frequently as the many books do now. In essence, we'd bring SENSATIONAL SPIDER-MAN and FRIENDLY NEIGHBORHOOD SPIDER-MAN to an end, and instead we'd release AMAZING SPIDER-MAN three times a month.

HOW TO RUN THE THRICE-AMAZING:

The logistical difficulties with making all of the Spidey titles one series are pretty obvious: If one thing goes wrong, you potentially have books falling like dominos. But I think this is just a matter of clever planning, and of taking a cue from creator-driven television shows that practice arc-storytelling. In other words, you'd need to "block out" the major character beats, reversals, developing conflicts and story concepts for pretty much an entire year of the thrice-AMAZING at one time. This would also take the form of making the entire year one large 36-part Spider-Man novel.

From a manpower standpoint, you'd also need to adopt a system similar to that of a television series. I think you'd need a team of about five writers, with one functioning as the Head Writer. The Head Writer would take point in blocking out the overall year-beats (in consultation with everybody else on the team, of course), would probably write perhaps a quarter of the overall output if possible, and would function as a script doctor and overseer on everybody else's stories, making sure that the voice and the style was somewhat consistent.

Then, within the structure, the remaining writers would come on to the book to do stories ranging between one and six parts in length, largely devised by themselves within the larger structure (so that they would have an appropriate emotional investment in the material, and we'd avoid the problem the connected SUPERMAN titles faced years ago, in which a given writer would wind up writing only Part Two of another writer's idea). We'd need to get all of these writers working simultaneously, and we'd need to have them all supported by a similar team of artists, working as far ahead as possible to avoid deadline problems. This way, you could keep a consistent artist on each individual story as well, and these artists would rotate in and out, much as the writers do.

As a safeguard, we'd also want to commission three or four single-issue evergreen-style stories, which could be folded into the run at whatever point the schedule started to slip.

Also, each main story would probably be produced as 20-page installments, which would give us room to insert modular subplot pages in order to properly set up future developments. So, for example, if Writer A has a Doctor Octopus storyline coming up in a few months, and there's a need to seed Doc's status quo or to foreshadow him ahead of time, then Writer A would write the subplot pages that do this, and they'd be inserted into earlier issues as necessary — even if those earlier stories were otherwise written by Writer B. This is where the Head Writer would be of help, as a backup in making sure that these drop-ins felt somewhat seamless. (And, ideally, the artist who was drawing Writer B's story would also draw the subplot pages written by Writer A — though we could break this guideline if we had to.)

Additionally, the five-man Spidey squad would be a good resource to have at our disposal when it comes to producing separate side Spidey limited series, either to tie into larger events in the Marvel U, or because of a budgetary need. Because these writers would be so enmeshed in the world and the tone of the core Spidey books, this should enable us to make such ancillary Spidey product feel more connected to the larger super-story running throughout the year, and thus of greater import to the readers.

Of greatest import in this plan: We shouldn't allow the fact that we'll be working with a team of writers to make us timid about trying interesting things with the way that stories are told within the Spider-Man books. For example, some of the strongest issues of ULTIMATE SPIDER-MAN have been the ones that focused on Mary Jane or Aunt May, and told a complete story from their point of view. Multiple writers needn't mean generic styling: In the same way that a series like Buffy can find a way to do "special" episodes based around either a narrative technique (the silent episode, the musical episode) or an offbeat approach to the story (the Death of Buffy's Mom episode), so too should we find a way to have that same latitude. We need to be careful not to become so locked into the process of production that we stifle creativity — nobody's ever quite run a regular ongoing title like this before, so we need to be cautious not to throw the baby out with the bathwater.

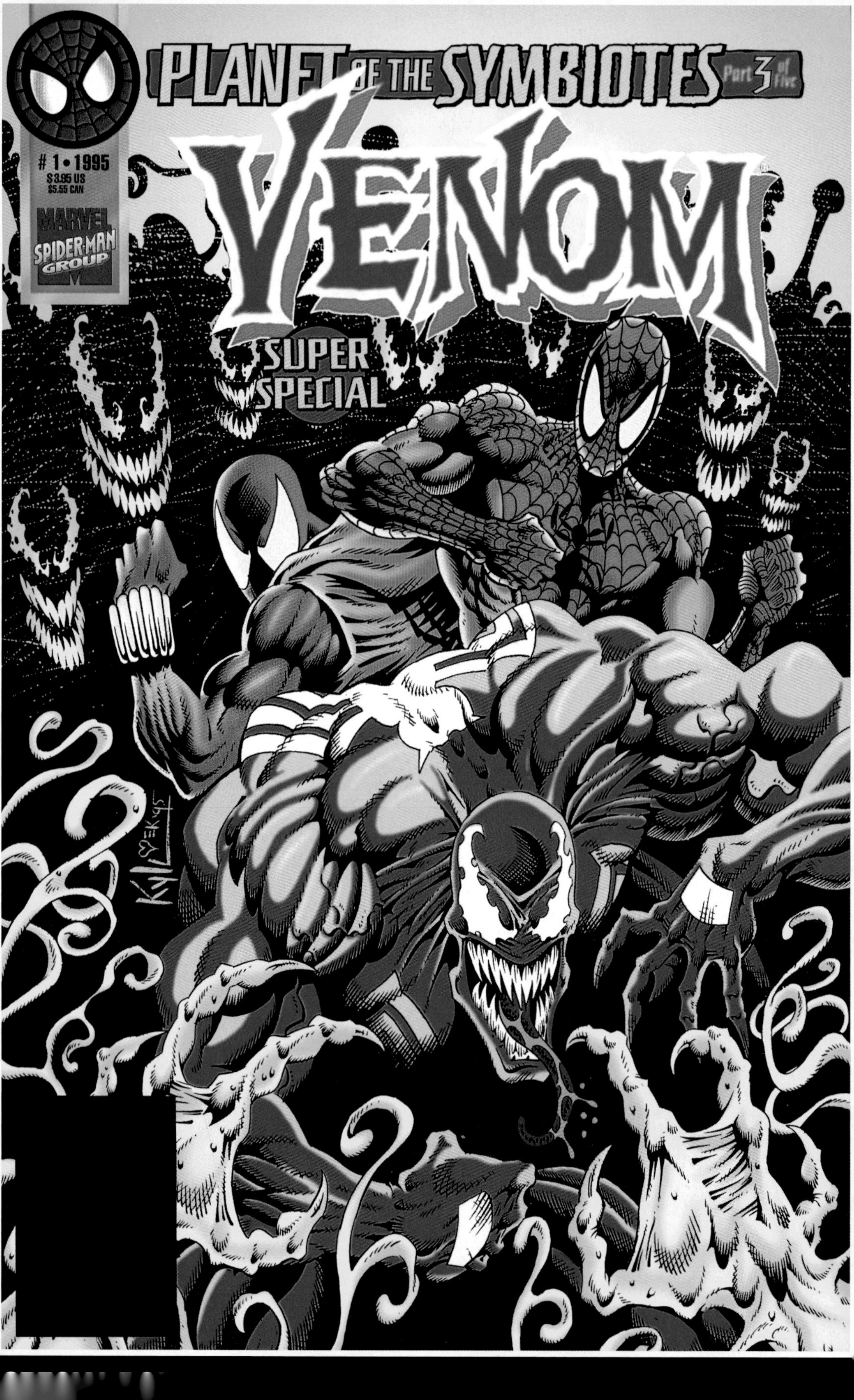
PLANET OF THE SYMBIOTES
Part 3 of Five
1 • 1995
$3.95 US
$5.55 CAN
MARVEL
SPIDER-MAN GROUP
VENOM
SUPER SPECIAL

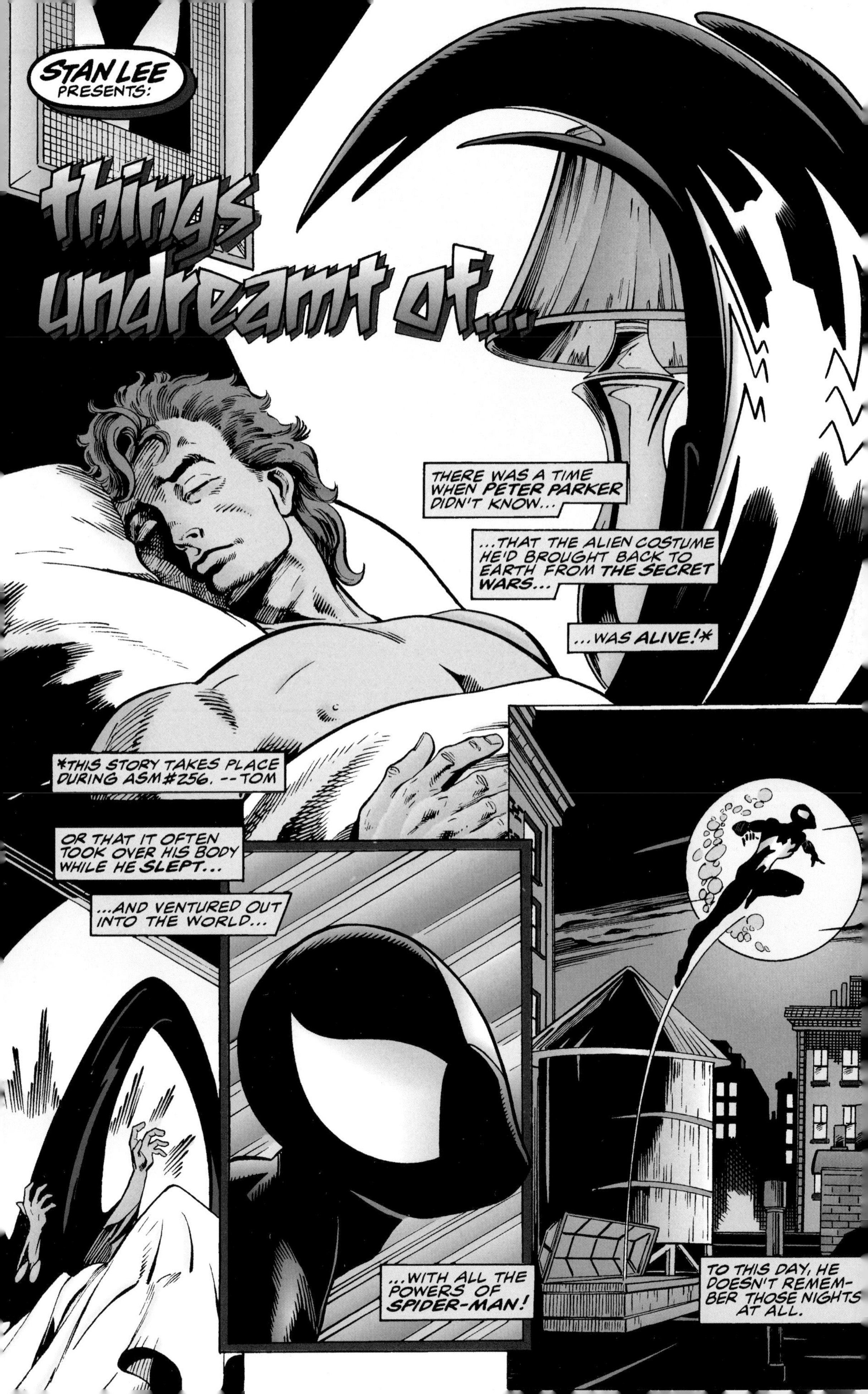
STAN LEE PRESENTS:
things undreamt of...
THERE WAS A TIME WHEN PETER PARKER DIDN'T KNOW...
...THAT THE ALIEN COSTUME HE'D BROUGHT BACK TO EARTH FROM THE SECRET WARS...
...WAS ALIVE!*
*THIS STORY TAKES PLACE DURING ASM #256. --TOM
OR THAT IT OFTEN TOOK OVER HIS BODY WHILE HE SLEPT...
...AND VENTURED OUT INTO THE WORLD...
...WITH ALL THE POWERS OF SPIDER-MAN!
TO THIS DAY, HE DOESN'T REMEMBER THOSE NIGHTS AT ALL.

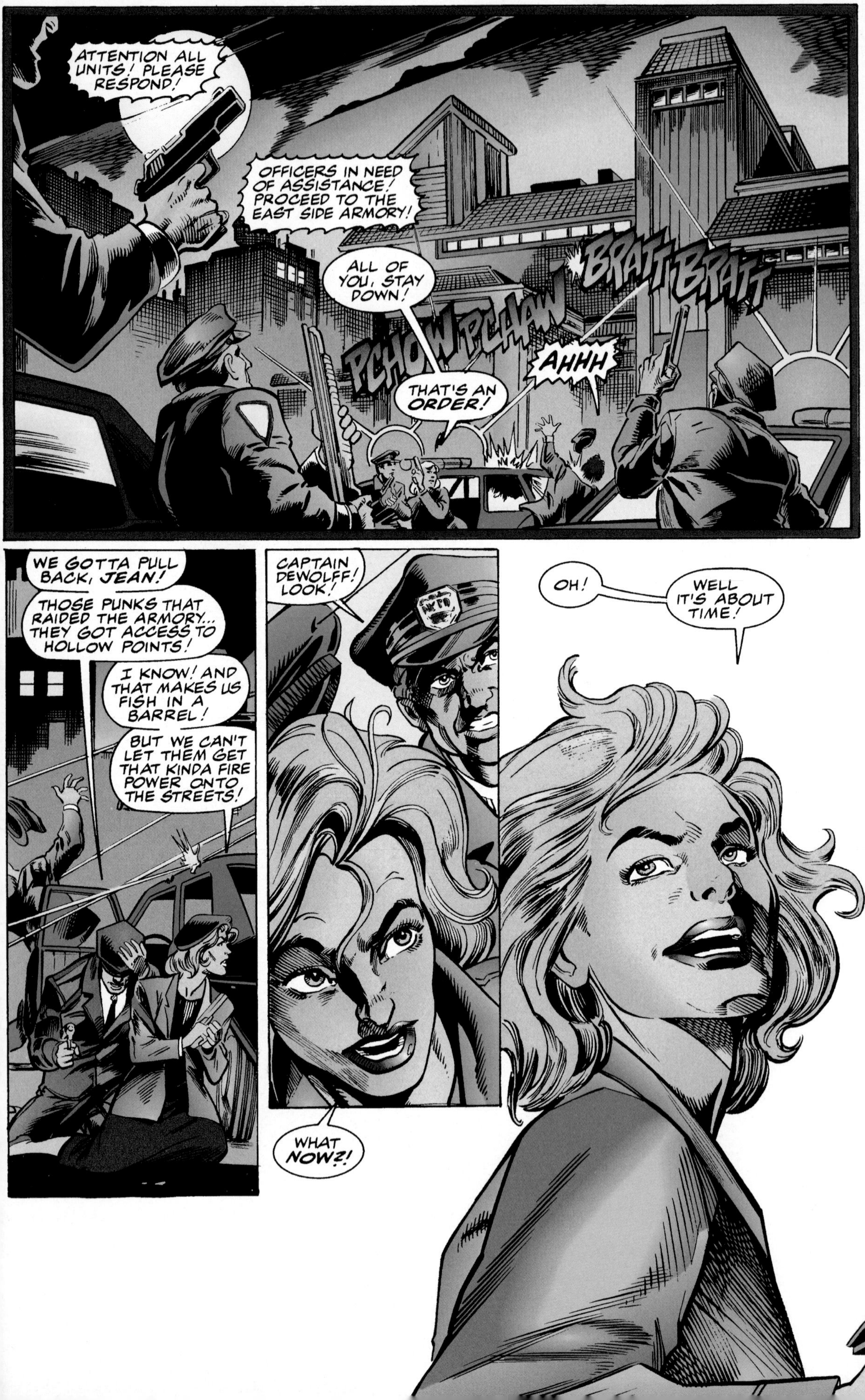
ATTENTION ALL UNITS! PLEASE RESPOND!
OFFICERS IN NEED OF ASSISTANCE! PROCEED TO THE EAST SIDE ARMORY!
ALL OF YOU, STAY DOWN!
PCHOW PLAAW
BRATT BRATT
AHHH
THAT'S AN ORDER!
WE GOTTA PULL BACK, JEAN!
THOSE PUNKS THAT RAIDED THE ARMORY... THEY GOT ACCESS TO HOLLOW POINTS!
I KNOW! AND THAT MAKES US FISH IN A BARREL!
BUT WE CAN'T LET THEM GET THAT KINDA FIRE POWER ONTO THE STREETS!
CAPTAIN DEWOLFF! LOOK!
WHAT NOW?!
OH!
WELL IT'S ABOUT TIME!

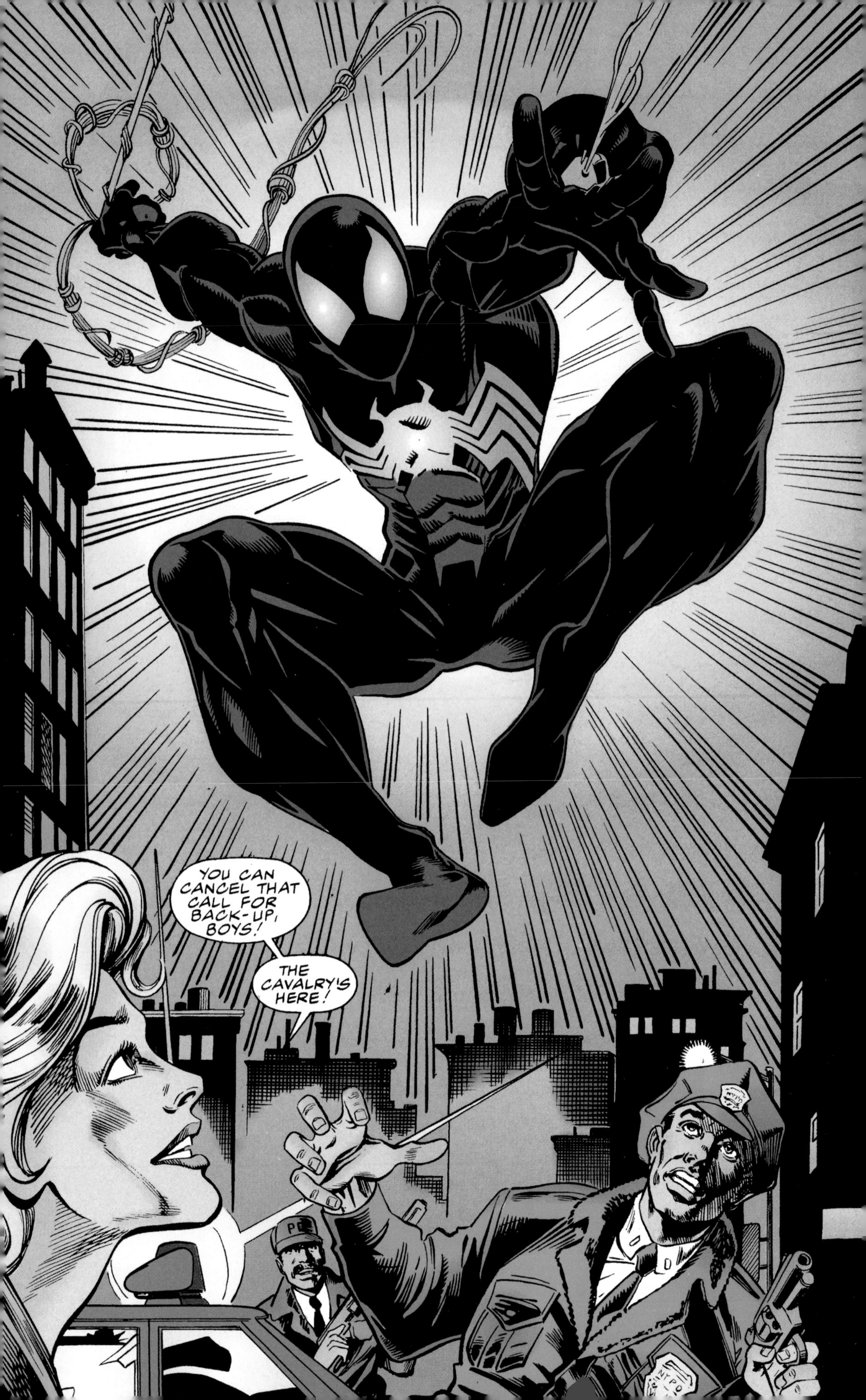
YOU CAN CANCEL THAT CALL FOR BACK-UP, BOYS!
THE CAVALRY'S HERE!

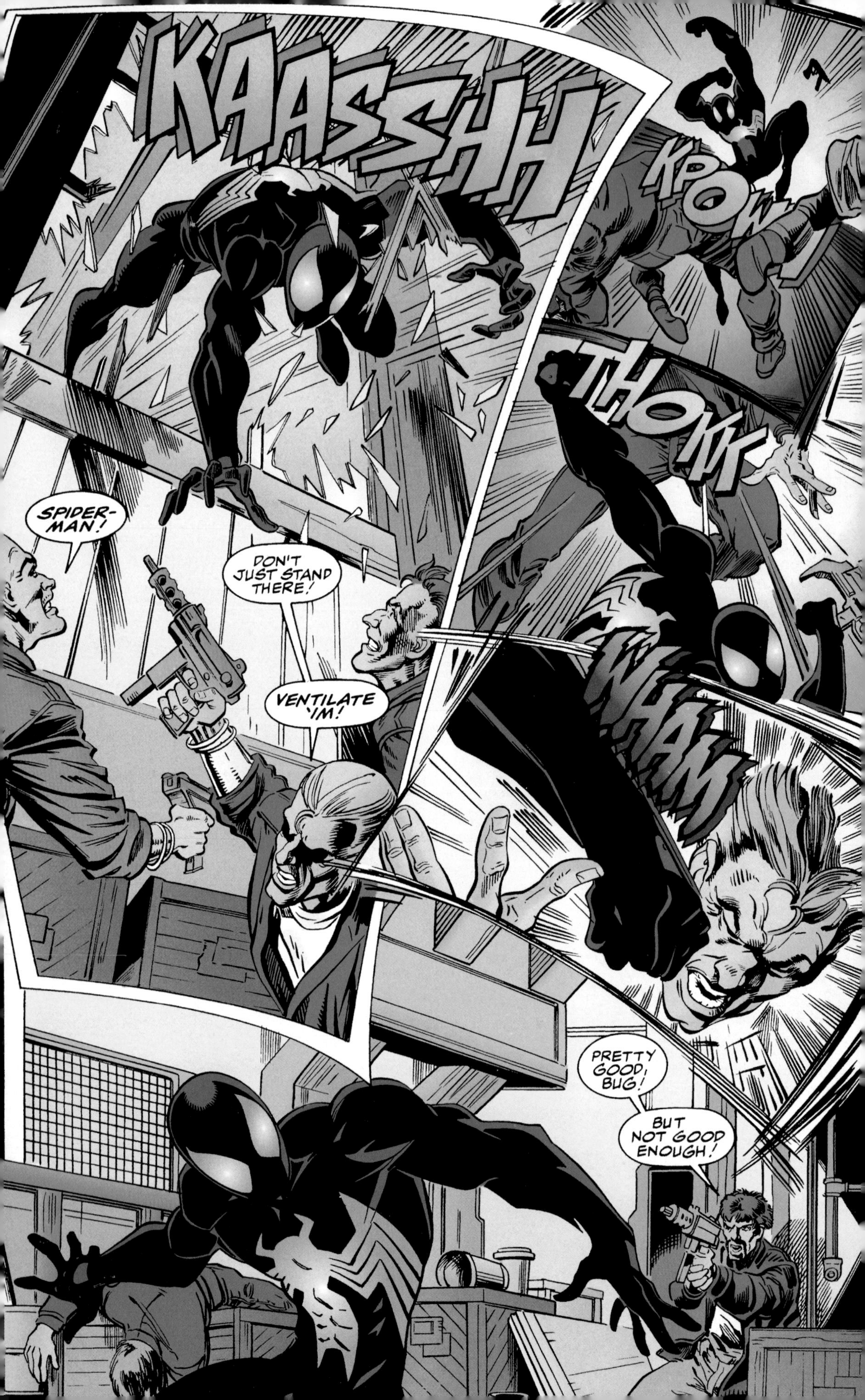
KAASSHH
KPOW
THONK
SPIDER-MAN!
DON'T JUST STAND THERE!
VENTILATE 'IM!
WHAM
PRETTY GOOD, BUG!
BUT NOT GOOD ENOUGH!

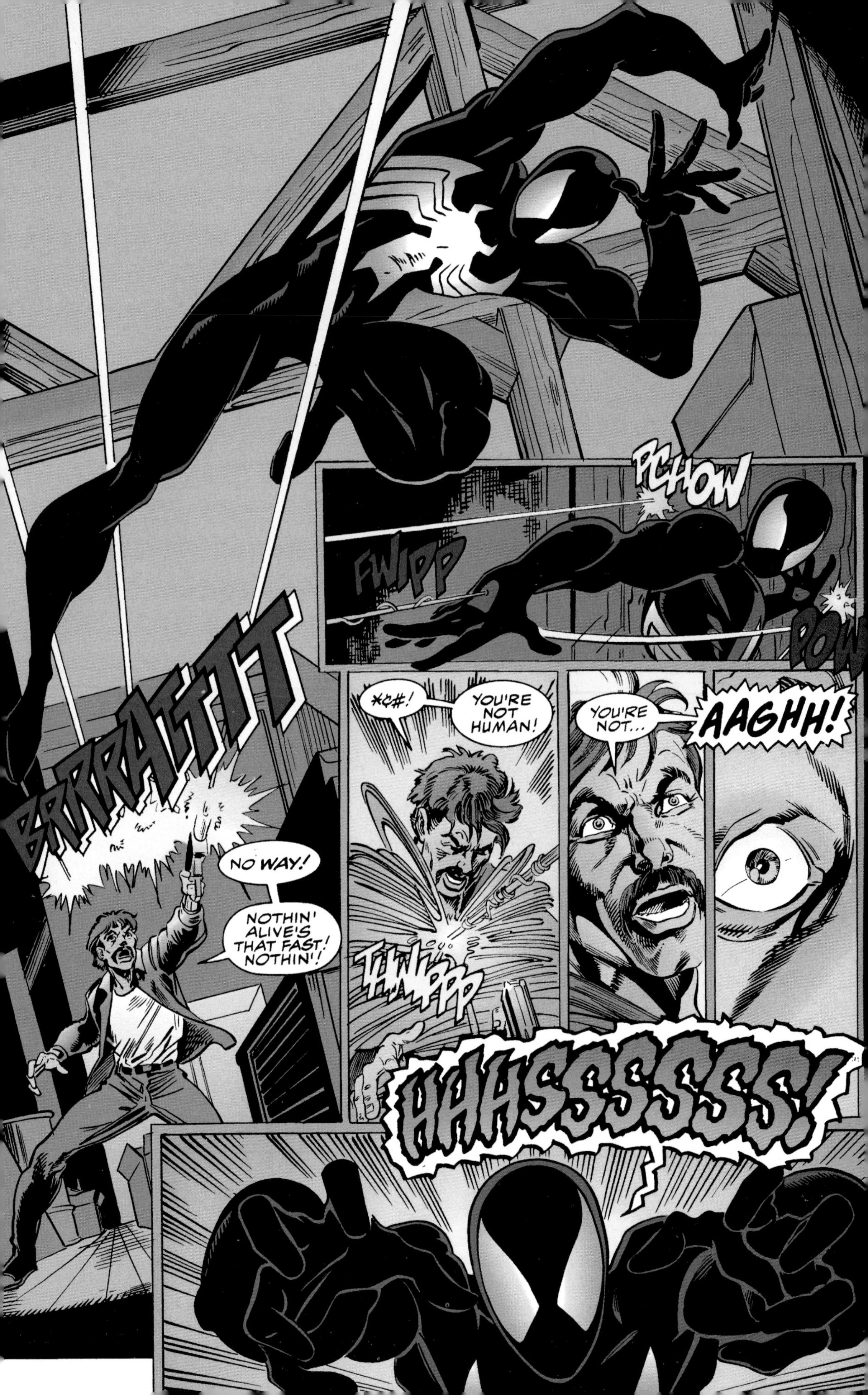

BRRRATTTT
NO WAY!
NOTHIN' ALIVE'S THAT FAST! NOTHIN'!
PCHOW
FWIPP
POW
*¢#!
YOU'RE NOT HUMAN!
THWIPP
YOU'RE NOT...
AAGHH!
HHASSSSSS!

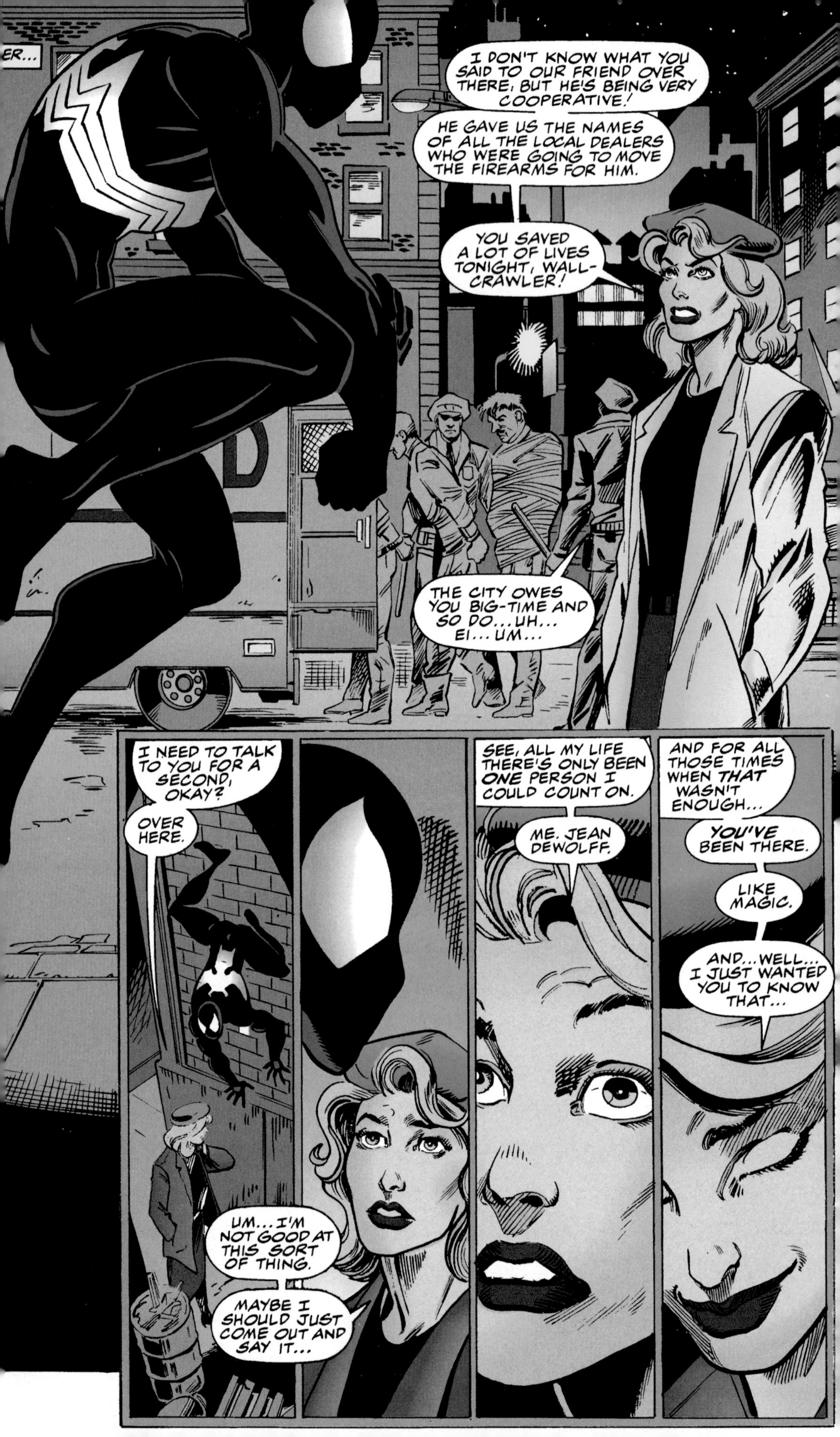

ER...
I DON'T KNOW WHAT YOU SAID TO OUR FRIEND OVER THERE, BUT HE'S BEING VERY COOPERATIVE!
HE GAVE US THE NAMES OF ALL THE LOCAL DEALERS WHO WERE GOING TO MOVE THE FIREARMS FOR HIM.
YOU SAVED A LOT OF LIVES TONIGHT, WALL-CRAWLER!
THE CITY OWES YOU BIG-TIME AND SO DO...UH... EI...UM...
I NEED TO TALK TO YOU FOR A SECOND, OKAY?
OVER HERE.
UM...I'M NOT GOOD AT THIS SORT OF THING.
MAYBE I SHOULD JUST COME OUT AND SAY IT...
SEE, ALL MY LIFE THERE'S ONLY BEEN ONE PERSON I COULD COUNT ON.
ME. JEAN DEWOLFF.
AND FOR ALL THOSE TIMES WHEN THAT WASN'T ENOUGH...
YOU'VE BEEN THERE.
LIKE MAGIC.
AND...WELL... I JUST WANTED YOU TO KNOW THAT...

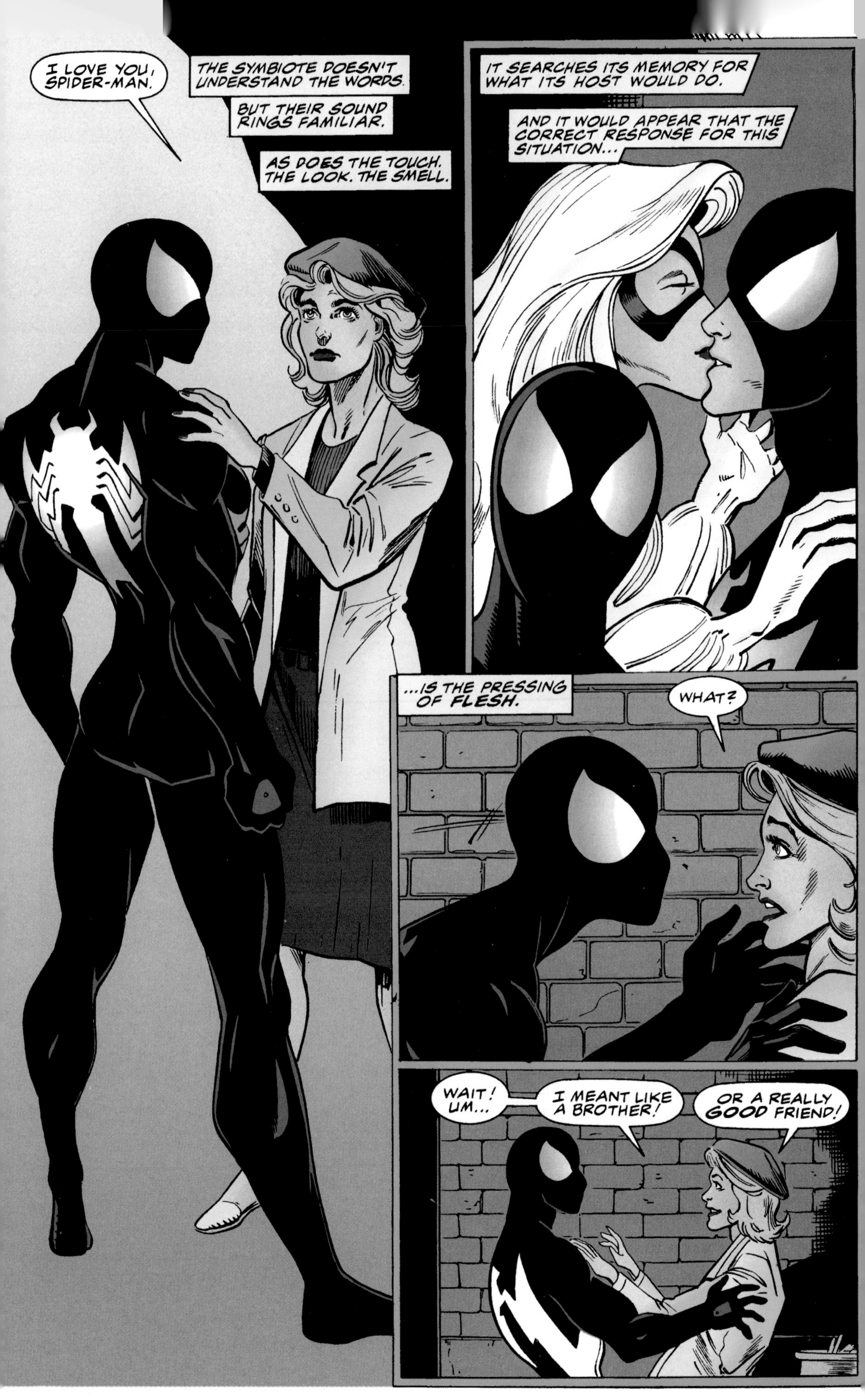
I LOVE YOU, SPIDER-MAN.
THE SYMBIOTE DOESN'T UNDERSTAND THE WORDS.
BUT THEIR SOUND RINGS FAMILIAR.
AS DOES THE TOUCH. THE LOOK. THE SMELL.
IT SEARCHES ITS MEMORY FOR WHAT ITS HOST WOULD DO.
AND IT WOULD APPEAR THAT THE CORRECT RESPONSE FOR THIS SITUATION...
...IS THE PRESSING OF FLESH.
WHAT?
WAIT! UM...
I MEANT LIKE A BROTHER!
OR A REALLY GOOD FRIEND!

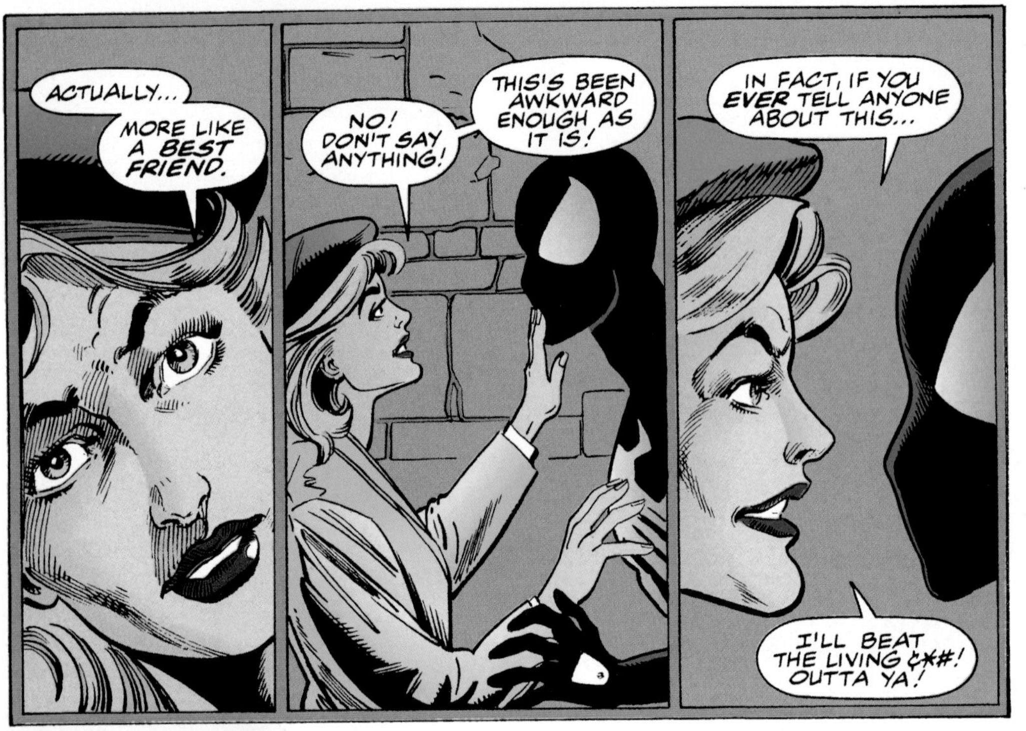
ACTUALLY...
MORE LIKE A BEST FRIEND.
NO! DON'T SAY ANYTHING!
THIS'S BEEN AWKWARD ENOUGH AS IT IS!
IN FACT, IF YOU EVER TELL ANYONE ABOUT THIS...
I'LL BEAT THE LIVING ¢*#! OUTTA YA!

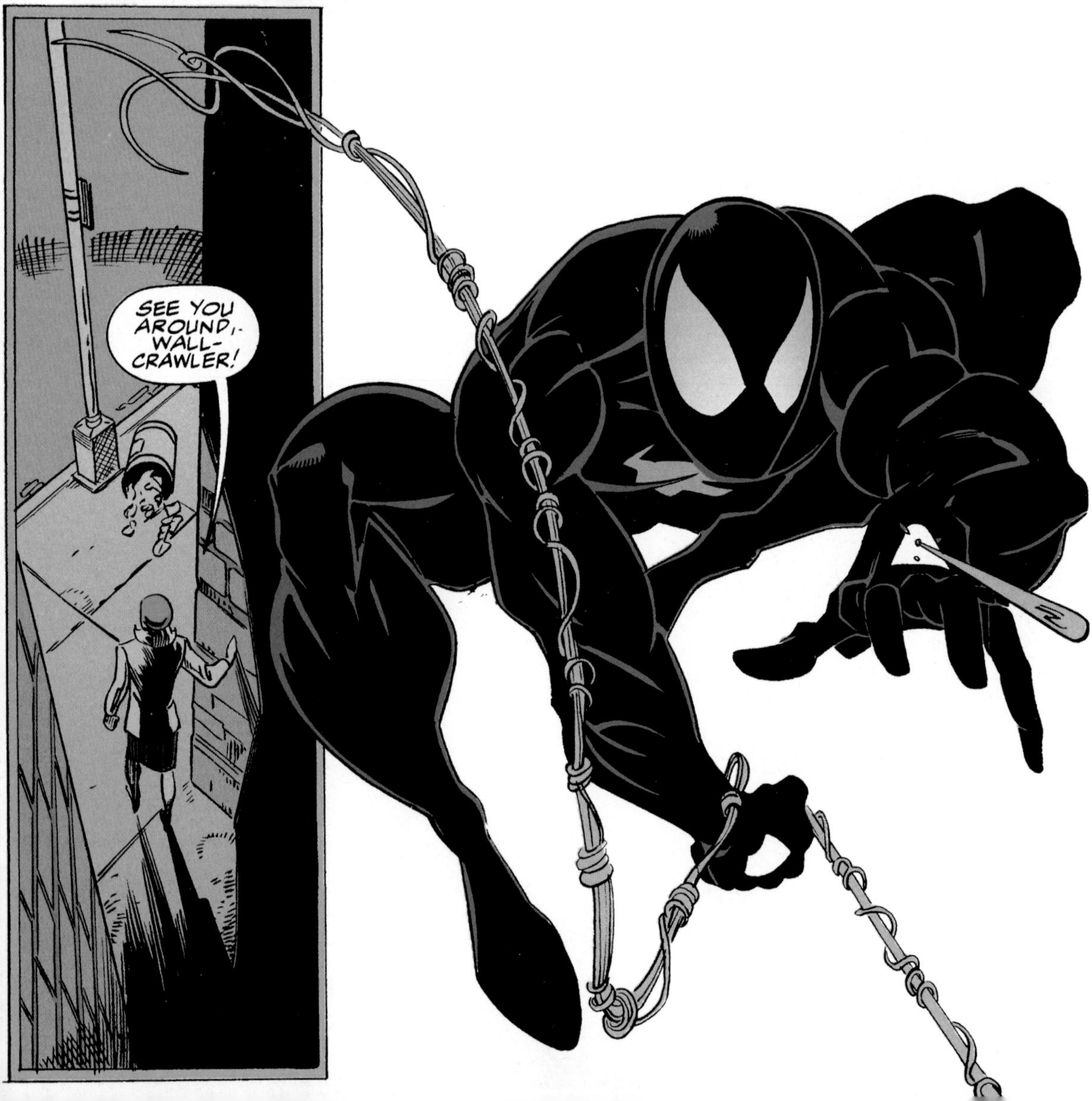
SEE YOU AROUND, WALL-CRAWLER!

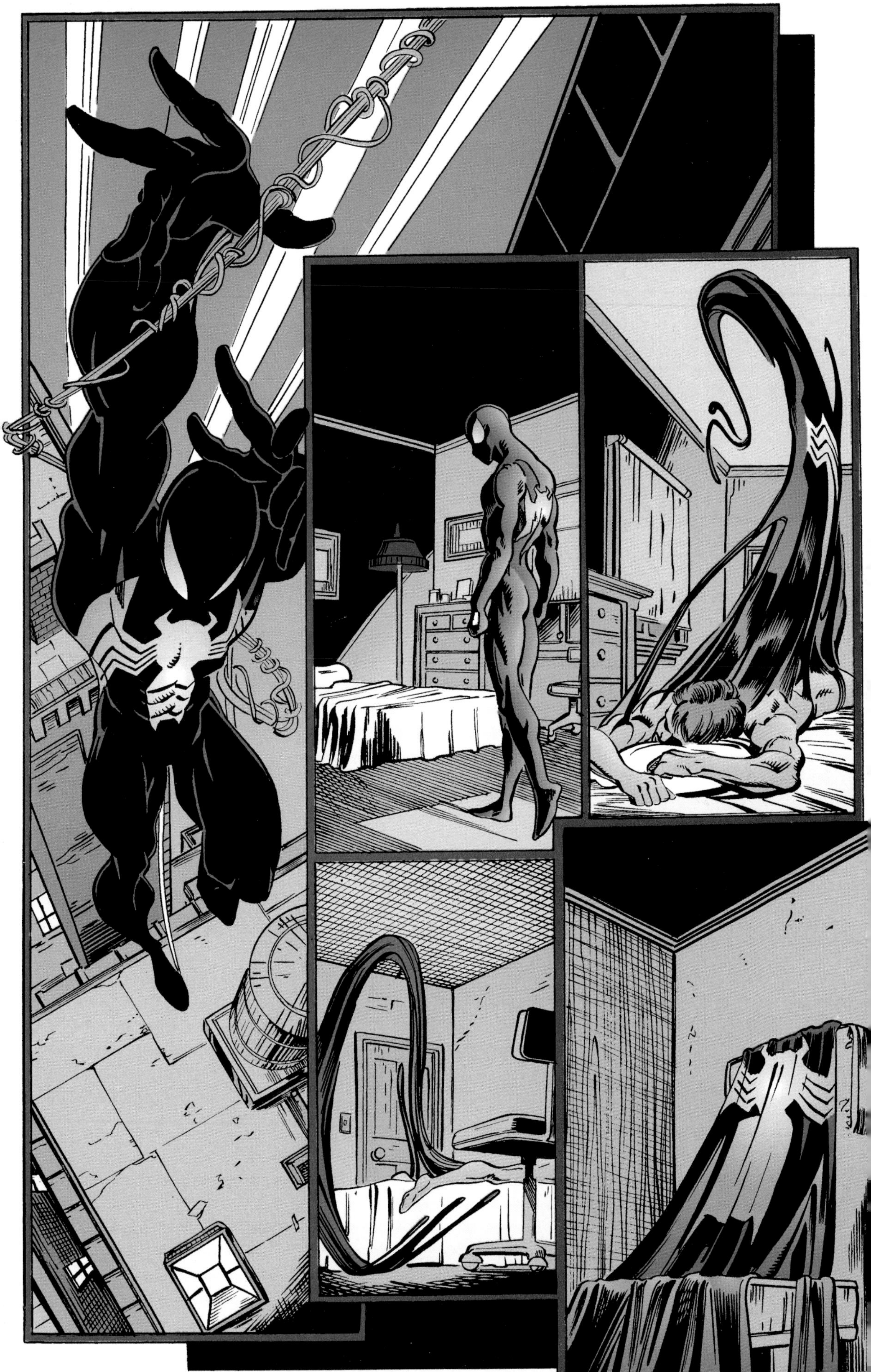